DIPLOMATICALLY
SPEAKING

Lloyd C. Griscom.

DIPLOMATICALLY SPEAKING

BY LLOYD C. GRISCOM

BOSTON

LITTLE, BROWN AND COMPANY

1940

TO AUDREY, MY WIFE

CONTENTS

DIPLOMATICALLY
SPEAKING

THE GOLDEN AGE

The *Belgenland's* gangplank slid aboard with a rattle and bump, hawsers were flung free, bells clanged, the whistle boomed.

"Come on, Roddy," I shouted above the clamor, "I'll race thee to the bridge."

Simultaneously we dived for the ladder but Rodman, who was ten, two years older than I, pushed ahead and was first aloft, waving and calling good-by to Father across the widening sliver of water between us and the Philadelphia pier.

Already the peaceful streets of the familiar city, the trim green slopes and hollows of the Main Line, and the restraining influence of our Quaker relatives and upbringing seemed very far away; for the moment we had also forgotten we were bound for the Haccius School near Geneva. We were looking forward to the voyage as a great adventure. Mother would be busy taking care of our two-year-old sister Pansy, we knew we could take care of our grandfather, Dr. John Denn Griscom, and, being sons of the President of the line, we would have the run of the ship. For dinner we ordered all the dishes on the menu, and at bedtime retired to our own cabin, well pleased with our independence.

Towards dawn we awoke to find the three-thousand-ton *Belgenland* dancing about like a cork. With every lurch our baggage skidded over the floor, stopped with a thud, and skidded back. We braced ourselves in our bunks and waited for morning, then gazed sadly at each other and decided we preferred to stay where we were. The steward appeared with breakfast but we were not interested. As the hours dragged along, nobody else came near us; Mother was always seasick and Grandfather apparently did not miss us.

That day passed, and another and another, and still the gray-green waves banged on the porthole. When darkness closed down, our only light was a dim glow from a candle behind a piece of ground glass in the wall. The atmosphere in our tiny cabin grew thick and foul. Rod groaned, "I wish I were at Dolobran," and I agreed with him heartily. A half-hour at our new home in Haverford now seemed to us worth ten Atlantic crossings as they were in the winter of 1881.

It was seven days before the sea began to subside and we were recovered enough to stagger on deck. A few breaths of fresh air made us feel ourselves again, and, delighted to discover the ship coated with sleet, we patted some of it into balls with which we stormed the bridge. Bushy-bearded Captain Randall put up only a slight resistance. We pursued him all the way to his cabin, messed his papers, fingered excitedly the revolver which he told us he kept to quell mutinies.

After we had once investigated the ship from stem to stern, we were impatient for the end of the voyage. Our ice was soon exhausted, and sour milk, rancid butter, strong meat, added to the choking fumes of kerosene from the swinging lamps in the dining room, almost made us ill. Worse still our coal supply was low. One day during the gale we had slipped backward thirty knots while steaming full speed forward. Even though we used our sails, it was nip and tuck whether the fuel would last. When we finally docked at Flushing at the mouth of the Scheldt, we had no more than a few tons left in the bunkers. We had to take the train to Antwerp because the river was frozen for the first time in years.

We were overjoyed to be ashore, except that now the ordeal of the new school was close at hand. Hitherto we had attended the quiet orderly Friends' School at Fifteenth and Race Streets. There at every Wednesday morning meeting the other students had looked at us envyingly on account of our relationship to Grandfather William Biddle, who sat on the elders' bench in front, his head moving jerkily from right to left, from left to right. More than a grandfather with St. Vitus' dance would be needed to give us a standing at the *Pensionnat Haccius*. Helen and Clement, our older sister and brother, had already been students in Switzerland — Clem had preceded us at the Haccius — and from their descriptions we knew it was going to be a rough life.

One bright Sunday we drove through the tall iron gates of the Château de Lancy, an ancient structure of gray stone, five miles out of

Geneva on the highway to Aix-les-Bains. Mother delivered us to M. Haccius, who eyed us searchingly from under tufts of grizzled hair and hustled us into the dining room. Dinner was a sketchy affair. I watched the master in charge of my section of the huge U-shaped table carve up a withered old fowl, wondering how he would make it do for his dozen boys. My minute portion was supplemented by a soggy potato and tasteless spinach — the masters were served first and before it reached us all the egg on top was gone.

The seventy-odd students seemed predominantly English and American, but in addition there were representatives of many other nationalities — Greek, Bulgarian, Rumanian, Egyptian, German, Danish, Spanish-American. Being newcomers, we were scrutinized with much curiosity and even hostility. As we streamed out to the terrace, I found myself beside a big Texan of twenty-two who was evidently getting his education late. "You stay with me," he said, and I was glad to tag along at his heels. Under his wing nobody bothered me, but I saw poor Rod being forced to walk an inch-wide railing while a crowd of boys stuck pen points in his legs — one jab to go ahead, two to go faster, three to stop, and four to go backwards. When he was finally across, his calves were spotted with drops of blood.

The Haccius School provided the minimum of comfort. The latrines were a disgrace, we never could wash properly because the single bathroom was reserved exclusively for the Haccius family, our unheated rooms were like refrigerators, and we were forever conscious of hunger. Our first meal was a feast compared with the ordinary fare — one roll, a pat of butter, and chicory for breakfast, stringy horseflesh the mainstay for lunch. At morning recess a servant appeared with an enormous basket of *petits pains,* one for each of us. I used to keep an end of bread from supper, poke a hole in it, hide a bit of butter inside, and secrete it in my pocket so that the dry hard roll would slip down more easily.

Every centime we had went for food, and the whole week we waited open-mouthed for the moment when M. Haccius would step on the gymnasium stage to distribute coins from a tin box. Rod and I cast covetous glances at Daoud Pasha, a nephew of the Khedive of Egypt, who collected five francs; we received only two apiece. Much of our forty cents was exchanged for chocolate which we procured in the village and melted in a pannikin over an alcohol lamp to make a filling hot drink.

We always tried to save something for the monthly five-mile tramp to the Turkish baths in Geneva — long in advance the study hall was odorous beyond belief from the unwashed boys. After being scrubbed so thoroughly that rolls of skin peeled off, we were set free and dashed for a *pâtisserie,* where we ate all the pastries we could afford; it was a terrible test of a boy's honesty to give the true number to the cashier. The road back was mostly uphill, and, by the time we had covered it at a brisk walk, we were already in need of another bath and another meal as well.

At the arrival of spring no two boys were ever more eager to get home. The boat crawled, the train crept, and it seemed the last few miles would never pass. Before we came to a halt at Haverford Station, we were on the platform shouting "Hello" to Augustus Archfield, our Irish coachman, an imposing figure with his side whiskers, great weight, and splendid livery. Since we could remember, he had been our model and hero; he had taught us to swim, to ride, to box, and entertained us with stories of the South of Ireland where he had been brought up. All the way to Dolobran we asked questions about the horses, the dogs, the tennis court, the swimming pond, everything that had happened in our absence.

Our vacation flew by, and in the fall Mother took us off again, this time to Paris to be enrolled in a day school. While she went in search of an apartment, we were left in our room at the Grand Hôtel du Louvre, with a bag of cherries to keep us from mischief. Glancing about for a good place in which to deposit our pits, we caught sight of the open window, and were hanging over the sill just as an enormous horse-drawn bus rumbled into view. The temptation was irresistible. Suddenly the passengers on top were startled by a shower of pits raining around their heads.

We were laughing at our success when to our alarm the driver pulled his bus to a stop, the irate riders tumbled out, a crowd sprang from nowhere, gesticulating and pointing at different windows along the side of the hotel. Funny gendarmes in baggy trousers, pleated and tucked in at the bottoms, marched into the building. Hastily we bobbed back, locked ourselves in, hid the evidence, and trembled at every footfall in the hall. Our hearts fairly jumped into our mouths at a knock on the door, but to our boundless relief it was only Mother.

Although we were never detected, the feeling of guilt did not leave us until we moved into our apartment on the corner of the Rue Washington and the Champs Elysées. In spite of the fact that we now had plenty to eat, life at the day school was almost as Spartan as at the Château de Lancy. We were obliged to arrive about six in the morning for an hour of lessons before breakfast.

Our apartment was tiny and we would have wrecked everything in it if Mother had not hired a *gouvernante* to take us out Saturday and Sunday afternoons. In succession she led us through the Tuileries gardens, walked us through the Bois de Boulogne, and introduced us to the animals in the zoo at the Jardin des Plantes. One day we demanded something more lively. *Mademoiselle* must have been as bored as we, because without urging she said, "Come along," and set off purposefully.

"Where are we going?" we asked, but all she would answer was "Wait and see. You'll love it."

She piloted us through a door. The next thing Rod and I knew our noses were plastered against a plate-glass partition, and our eyes were confronted by a whole row of corpses laid on marble slabs with water dripping on them to keep them nice and fresh. We were in the Morgue. After one good look we bolted, screaming at the top of our lungs. For nights we started awake with visions of corpses floating about, but it never occurred to us to mention our scare to Mother.

One more year was spent at the Haccius School before Father, who liked to have his family around him, decided we should complete our education in Philadelphia. We then lived at 1018 Spruce Street, in one of the red brick, white-marble–trimmed houses typical of the city, and attended the school on Delancy Street established by Henry Brown. He had brought with him from England the idea that boys should be advanced as rapidly as possible, a progressive theory of education which suited us exactly. Not only had we acquired a better than average knowledge of languages, but being dragged here and there and left to stand on our own feet had sharpened our wits, toughened our bodies, and broadened our minds.

Philadelphia seemed even more quaint and old-fashioned than I remembered it. As we trudged to school along the worn, irregular brick sidewalks, our eyes would be attracted upwards by a moving gleam of light; some elderly lady was adjusting her "busybody," a mirror fastened on the outside of the house so that sitting in her chair she could see everything that went on below. In bad weather we were allowed to take one of the horsecars which rattled up and down the cobbled streets, traveling so slowly that if one passed the corner just ahead of us we could always run after it; hoisting ourselves aboard, we would scuff our feet in the crisp hay strewn on the floor for warmth.

Many of the older people we met still wore the Quaker gray — the men in broad-brimmed hats, the women in poke bonnets. On both sides of the family we traced our descent from the original Quaker settlers of Pennsylvania. Andrew Griscom had come over from Wales two years before William Penn; I was named for Father's ancestor Thomas Lloyd, who had served as the Proprietor's deputy during his long absences.

Our grandparents had all joined the liberal branch of the Quakers, known as "Hicksites" after Elias Hicks of Long Island; in the early Nineteenth Century he had split the Society of Friends into two factions which had as little as possible to do with each other. When Helen married one of Father's clerks, Samuel Bettle from Camden, his orthodox relatives arrived in a body for the wedding, faces stern, set, and disapproving. They made it apparent they regarded themselves as going among the heathen; nevertheless, they ate heartily of the baked meats. Then they trooped back to Camden, solemnly held a meeting, and expelled Sam.

Hicksites though they were, my grandparents had never been inside a theater, and had never permitted a pack of cards or even a piano in the house. In our case these restrictions had been lifted, and we were the first of our line to be seen at parties. On the whole, however, our upbringing was strict, particularly in the matter of an allowance.

In an emergency I often had a better chance of obtaining an extra dollar by going directly to Father's office at 307 Walnut Street. Joseph, the dignified, side-whiskered, mulatto doorman, showed me in promptly with a bow and a flourish. If Father were in conference I might have to wait an hour, meanwhile getting in the way

of secretaries, bothering people generally, perhaps stopping to talk
to Uncle Frank L. Neal, one of Father's partners. He was fully
aware of the reason for my presence, and chaffed me amiably about
my monetary mission.

When I was finally admitted to Father's sanctum he would keep
on working at the papers piled on his desk while I stood as
quietly as I could, gazing at the charts on the wall behind him.
Abruptly he would demand, "Well what the devil does thee want?"

"Father, I've been under quite a financial strain. Thee knows
Christmas is coming, Freddy borrowed fifty cents from me and
didn't pay it back, Augustus asked me for ten cents for the Clan-
na-Gael, and . . ." I began stammering around to list other calls
on my pocketbook.

Father looked at me severely. "Thee must learn, Lloyd, never
to give three poor reasons. Give one good one and stick to it."

After some such remark he usually relented, opened his wallet
bulging with bills, and fished out a dollar.

It was not easy for the head of a great shipping business to remain
even-tempered under the weight of never-ending responsibility for
the lives and property of others. Our household peace was always
being disrupted by the arrival of messages and telegrams — engines
broken, boilers burst, rudders or propellers off, fires in cotton cargoes, ammonia leaks in cold-storage plants, ships aground. The
most disturbing news was that a vessel was overdue and unreported.
Father would pace up and down with a worried face; if a wire came
that all was well, he would brighten up immediately; but the loss
of a ship meant weeks of gloom.

One evening we were startled to see our living room invaded
by a committee of elders of the Race Street Meeting; although
Father had become "worldly" he had continued a member in good
standing. The leader gravely addressed him: "We have been reliably
informed thee is operating sixteen saloons where alcoholic beverages are sold."

"What's that? What's that?" Father indignantly protested his
innocence.

"Has thee not sixteen ships?" the spokesman persisted.

"Quite true; what has that to do with it?"

"Does not each ship carry a bar?"

"Oh, that's it, is it? Well, sit down." And Father began explaining to his practical-minded visitors that the sale of liquor was essential to his business. However, he was not satisfied with convincing them by argument. An hour later, hearing a clink, I peered around the door. The elders had drawn up to the table, each with a glass in his hand, judiciously sniffing and tasting. No further objections were ever raised by the Meeting.

Father had made his way in the world because he always did more than was required of him. At fifteen he had gone to work as an office boy in the old firm of Peter Wright and Sons, importers and exporters of china, and in a few years had dominated the firm. When he saw much of his profits being eaten up by freight rates, he chartered his own ships and filled extra space with the goods of others. Following the Civil War the directors of the Pennsylvania Railroad were anxious to have an outlet to Europe for the quantities of grain, pig iron, and oil that were pouring into Philadelphia. With their backing, and that of the Standard Oil trust, Father formed the American Line; soon the *Pennsylvania, Ohio, Illinois,* and *Indiana* were carrying freight and a few passengers to and from Liverpool.

Seamen on ships flying the American flag had to be paid such high wages that costs of operation made competition with European companies difficult. A few weeks after I was born in 1872, Father and Edgar Thompson, the president of the Pennsylvania Railroad, decided to start a line under some foreign flag from Philadelphia to some port on the continent. Father, hurrying to his office, called for the largest available map of Europe to be hung on the wall. With a red pencil he dotted the principal manufacturing towns of England, Belgium, France, and Germany. From the far side of the room he aimed a pointer at the center of the red spots and strode forward. The tip struck exactly on the ancient city of Antwerp, formerly a busy port, but then so isolated by the silting of the Scheldt that no steamer of any size could reach it.

When Father arrived home that night he announced he had to sail for Belgium at once. "And thee must come with me," he said to Mother. She would not go without me, and consequently the three of us departed the next day.

At Antwerp Father conferred with the burgomaster and his council; they were willing to dredge the channel, build docks, do anything, but said a venture of such magnitude must have the sanction of the Government. Leaving Mother and me behind, Father took the short train ride to Brussels, where he explained what he wanted to our Minister, John Sanford.

"The person for you to see is King Leopold," said Mr. Sanford, and sent a messenger to the palace who returned with word the King would receive them immediately.

"Your Majesty," began Sanford, "here's a young American with a scheme which should boom Belgium's foreign trade."

The King, reputed the shrewdest businessman in Europe, listened intently to Father and nodded approbation. "Your plan seems sound, Mr. Griscom. However, since it's so late I'd like you to dine with the Queen and me. Afterwards we can discuss it further."

Father, who was unused to royal etiquette, replied bluntly, "Sorry, Your Majesty, it's impossible."

Sanford's expression registered consternation, but the King, somewhat amused, inquired: "It's seldom we have our invitations refused. Won't you tell me your reason?"

"Well, Sir, my wife and young baby are back at the hotel in Antwerp. Before I left this morning she made me promise to return for dinner."

The King shook Father's hand. "You could not have a better reason. Another time you must bring Mrs. Griscom. And don't worry about a charter or a postal subsidy. I'll see that Parliament grants you everything you need."

King Leopold was as good as his word, and the Red Star Line was a success from the start. Father told me once that in three decades no one of its ships had, on any voyage or in any year, lost money.

Although Father's manner was often brusque and he stormed at subordinates when anything went wrong, he had a gift for adjusting differences of opinion. No strikes ever occurred among the thousands of men in his companies. The same feeling prevailed in the household. Augustus trembled in his boots every time he submitted his stable accounts, but he would go to any lengths to win Father's approval. During the visit of the Russian Grand Duke Alexander Mikhailovitch one winter, Mr. Frank Thomson, then president of the Pennsylvania Railroad, gave a banquet in his honor. Augustus, resplendent in breeches and claret jacket with primrose facings and pipings, yellow and black striped waistcoat, shiny leather boots, and curved top hat, brought to the door our fastest team of trotters so that Father might put on a show.

Father took the reins, the Grand Duke mounted beside him, the rest of us filled the sleigh and, leaving Augustus standing at attention, we skimmed out of the yard. A crack of the whip and we darted down Gray's Lane so swiftly that the Grand Duke was breathless. In less than half an hour we shot through the Thomson entrance, steam rising from the horses' backs. There on the steps, standing at attention exactly as we had left him at Dolobran, was Augustus.

The Grand Duke blinked. "Why, isn't that your coachman? How could he be here?"

"Oh," replied Father, who himself had no idea, "I told him to meet us and I expect my servants to follow my instructions."

I dropped behind to ask Augustus how he had managed it. With a chuckle he explained that the instant we were out of sight, he had jumped into another sleigh, driven furiously to the Haverford Station, and arrived barely in time to haul himself aboard a train for Philadelphia. At Merion he had got off and then, as nimbly as his size and bunions would permit, had lumbered the few hundred yards to the porte-cochère, reaching it a split second before us.

Father's friends had all made their mark in some business or profession. Alexander J. Cassatt's fortune came from financing an unknown young man named Westinghouse who had invented an air brake for freight cars; George B. Roberts and Frank Thomson had helped to build up the Pennsylvania Railroad; H. H. Houston was a leader in the oil industry; William Elkins and P. A. B. Widener bought up old horsecar lines and combined them into modern street-railway systems; Thomas A. Dolan was president of the United Gas Improvement Company, a pioneer public utility; Rudolph Ellis and Effingham Morris were bankers, and DeWitt Cuyler was a promising young lawyer.

These men were always cordial to each others' children, treated us as equals, and asked us to their dinners and parties. Having plenty of money to spend, they had developed entertaining to a fine art and were great *bons vivants*. Philadelphia was noted for good food; it was the last place north to which Negro servants came, and the cooking had a Southern flavor — sweet potatoes, fried chicken, terrapin, deviled crabs. Philadelphians also prided themselves on their cellars. Guests of Dr. S. Weir Mitchell were served rare Napoleon brandies and Madeiras sent round the world. Father purchased annually the entire vintage of Carle Frères champagne, which contained a minimum of sugar and therefore of gout. He took his pint a day without fail and followed up dinner with a black cigar. However, Clem and Rod and I were each promised a thousand dollars for not smoking or drinking until we were twenty-one.

Practically everyone with wealth then collected art, a fashion set in Philadelphia by John G. Johnson, one of the prominent members of the bar, who had accumulated priceless Italian primitives before anybody else had suspected their value. The walls of his house on South Broad Street were lined with them from molding to baseboard. You could not even go into a bathroom without making five or six masterpieces rattle back and forth.

Mr. Widener forged ahead of everybody as soon as he started in, laying the foundation for what became one of the most perfect private art collections in the world, unmarred by inferior or spurious examples. Father began with the Barbizon School — Corot and his group — but later grew more sophisticated, buying Lawrence and Romney and finally a Rembrandt which was his prize. After his death his pictures were sold for more than he paid for them, an unusual experience for any collector.

The era of great fortunes which permitted individuals to own whatever they desired was also the era of unparalleled privilege. Because I was my father's son, I could walk into any telegraph office, compose as long a message as I wished, sign his name to it, and walk out; I could express anything I wanted anywhere free of all charge; I could step on any steamship and be transported to any point in the Seven Seas; I could board any train and ride from Portland, Maine, to Portland, Oregon, without paying a cent. I can still remember my humiliation when, obeying an Interstate Commerce Commission ruling, for the first time I had to stand at the window and buy a ticket like everybody else.

As a director of the Pennsylvania Railroad, Father wore a little gold medal on his watch chain. If he were suddenly called to Chicago, he did not have to go into Philadelphia; the station agent at Haverford flagged the limited for him. Once I was accompanying Mr. Frank Thomson along a platform of the Broad Street Station. On both sides a train was waiting; we turned into one and sat down. The conductor bustled up: "Mr. Thomson, this is an express which doesn't stop at Merion."

"Well, stop it," commanded Mr. Thomson.

It stopped.

These captains of industry had no idea that the order of things which they had created was impermanent; Father to the end of his life did not realize the Golden Age would not last. None of them dreamed that the United States would be left with a large population which business could not employ. There were still vast forests to cut, rich mines to open, unexplored natural resources to exploit.

I have never been able to determine whether the opportunities developed the men or the men the opportunities. It seemed as though money were there, to be made by anyone of energy and brains; the pioneers of those days had the Midas touch.

Unconscious of the kernel of truth in it, we all laughed at the story frequently told of Mr. Dolan. His four sons had been going through his money at such a rate that finally he called them into conference. "Boys," he said, "I must speak to you very seriously. I've worked hard and accumulated a fortune of sorts, but you're spending it faster than I can make it. Something must be done. I want you to talk the matter over and then come back and tell me what you think."

They were gone almost an hour and when they returned Brook, the eldest, rendered their decision. "Father, we've considered your predicament from every angle, and it's quite true something must be done. As far as we can see there's only one solution — you'll have to work at night."

CHAPTER II

WILLINGLY TO SCHOOL

I put on my first long trousers for my first lecture at the University of Pennsylvania as a member of the Class of 1891; even in those days fourteen was young to enter college. Few of us took our Freshman year very seriously. Every morning we poured into the single ugly building of gray-green stone, plumped ourselves on hard seats in a bare unventilated classroom, and devoted our surplus energy to devising methods of annoying our instructors.

Our German teacher found the going particularly difficult. The whole front row sat with right knees crossed over left until someone whispered "one, two, three"; at this signal down with a stamp came a line of right legs, and up with a rustle went a line of left. We had him at our mercy. If he objected, we merely answered politely that it was very uncomfortable to remain for an hour without shifting position.

We really liked Felix Schelling, who taught us English literature in a cultivated English voice, then a rarity in Philadelphia, yet he did not escape our attentions. One day we bribed the Negroes of the restaurant in the basement to deliver a quarter of a pie to his classroom at ten-minute intervals. The lecture started. Promptly on the dot of ten minutes past, the door opened, a white-aproned waiter shuffled up to the desk, and with a grin offered Mr. Schelling a section of blueberry.

"What's this?"

"You ordered it, Suh."

"I'm afraid you've made a mistake. Take it away, please."

Ten minutes later a slice of apple pie appeared. By the time a piece of pumpkin was proffered him, Mr. Schelling caught on. Accepting the plate he remarked, "Apparently some of my friends are worried about my weight. I'm obliged to them for their thoughtfulness."

We all laughed and after that we left him alone.

I did not begin to benefit much from college until my third year, when, like Clem and Rod before me, I enrolled in the Wharton School of Finance and Economy, a special branch of the university intended to provide practical training for business life. Juniors and seniors together numbered only some forty.

Students in Political Science were given periodic leaves to go to Washington to visit Congress. I used to stay with the Donald Camerons; Pennsylvania's senior Senator was Father's stanch ally in his fight for a ship subsidy bill. The beauty and charm of his young wife brought to the house on Lafayette Square many of the coterie who made Washington of the Nineties a place to be remembered with nostalgia.

If you dropped in at the Camerons' at teatime, you were sure to find in one corner of the room a Senator or Representative repeating the chatter of Congress, and, near by, a group exchanging the latest gossip, perhaps some new malapropism of Mrs. Leiter of Chicago. She announced her son Joe was attending a masquerade "in the garbage of a monk," and her daughter Mary, whose dress had been copied from that in the familiar picture of St. Cecilia at the organ, was going "en sainte."

The Camerons traveled widely, and the atmosphere of the salon had an international leaven. Among the foreigners who came there was Cecil Spring Rice, then a secretary at the British Legation. He was always ready to entertain an audience with humorous anecdotes of his adventures. Once, after carrying dispatch bags to Paris, he had sent in an expense sheet to the Foreign Office which included one shilling each for cab and porter. The latter item had been disallowed by the auditor on the ground that Her Majesty's servants while on duty were not permitted to include charges for alcoholic beverages. Spring Rice had written to explain that "porter" did not refer to malt liquor but to the individual who conveyed his bags from the train to the cab. He would be glad to revise the entry if the auditor would inform him of the correct term. In due course a reply arrived advising him the word should be "porterage."

Spring Rice thereupon amended his statement,

To porterage	one shilling	
To cabbage	"	"

The account was approved.

Hardly an afternoon at the Camerons' went by without the appearance of a small man with a small gray beard and an intellectual face. It was Henry Adams. He would sit down, glance around sardonically, and in a tired manner begin to hold forth. Apparently he enjoyed making what seemed the most preposterous assertions yet he could invariably back them up with facts.

Although Mr. Adams' memory was phenomenal, one of his many poses was to complain of it. He told me that what he remembered best of English history came from Scott's novels and of French from those of Dumas, a strange remark from one who had been for seven years Professor of History at Harvard University. Teaching he had found a very discouraging business. "Actually, during those years, I encountered only three students who, from the point of view of scholarship, I considered worth troubling about."

Senator Henry Cabot Lodge of Massachusetts, who had been one of his pupils, was listening and obviously was preening himself for the forthcoming compliment. Mr. Adams winked at me. "And not one of the three was Cabot Lodge. The first lost his mind and had to be confined in an insane asylum, the second's health failed and he had to give up his scholastic career, the third died young. Such was the net and entire result of my teaching at Harvard, that institution for turning out mediocrity."

As usual he was underestimating himself.

Henry Adams had a collection of nephews and nieces, some real, but most adopted. As one of this group, I frequently went to his breakfasts, served at twelve-thirty according to the French custom. When his colored major-domo answered your ring, you never inquired, "Is Mr. Adams in?" He was always in, and the right number of seats were ready.

Uncle Henry presided and discoursed in his dry ironical manner on everything under the sun, from the daily movement of gold to the evolution of furniture at the French court. For generations its chairs had been designed in accordance with the rule of etiquette by which each lady must hold herself bolt upright and never let her spinal column sag against the back. Once upon a time a certain king's mistress, a daughter of the plain people, was installed in the royal suite. She eyed disdainfully the gilded array, and as soon as the

King appeared she demanded, "Sire, where in God's name are we going to sit? We can't stay in bed all day long."

"But, my love, what do you want? You shall have anything, anything."

"Have somebody find me some armchairs in which I can be comfortable."

The cabinetmakers were summoned and from her description designed the *bergère*.

Going to Washington, listening to debates in Congress, meeting leading political figures, gave courses at Wharton much more meaning. Our class in Government, under Edmond J. James, was organized into a miniature Congress; we juniors were "Representatives" and the seniors were "Senators." We went through all the formalities of legislative procedure, and as "Chairman of the Ways and Means Committee" I learned more about how the Government was run than I ever would have absorbed from a textbook.

Progressive as Wharton was, it still required examinations; we did not like them, but neither did our Professor of History, John Bach McMaster, an emaciated skeleton of a man with a domelike head, totally bald except for a few reddish remnants of hair. At the end of my junior year he entered the room where we were all assembled in readiness, and announced: "Your question, gentlemen, is to write the history of the United States from 1800 to 1814." Then he looked at us owlishly and went home, leaving us entirely to ourselves.

Professor McMaster returned at noon to find us working like beavers, our copies of his *History of the United States* propped before us. Without comment he collected our papers. During the luncheon intermission we concluded that he never intended to open them and equipped ourselves for the afternoon session with bits of sealing wax. After another four hours of summarizing his book, we rolled up our abstracts, tied them with the prescribed red ribbon, and unobtrusively dropped a gob of wax on the knot.

Professor McMaster gathered in the scrolls, his face still expressionless. As he put them in his briefcase, he remarked in his precise fashion, "Gentlemen, I have a feeling that at least this examination may have accomplished something in the way of teaching you a little American history."

The whole class was marked excellent; the highest grade attainable. When my paper came back, I inspected it curiously; the seal was intact.

I had been pursuing my education without devoting much thought to a career, and suddenly in the spring of my senior year it dawned upon me that I was on the point of graduating and as yet had no plans for the future. I was offered a fellowship to study for a Ph.D., but this would have meant a scholar's life, for which I decided I was not well fitted.

According to Father's theory, the businessman, as the creator of wealth, was the most important factor in society. Clem, Rod, and Sam Bettle had all gone into the firm, but that prospect did not attract me. I was aware that in Father's eyes the professions were parasitic; nevertheless I suggested to him that admiralty law was essential to shipping. After some discussion, he agreed that if I were serious in wanting a legal career, I might enter Pennsylvania Law School in the fall. To round out my education he presented me with five hundred dollars for a grand tour of Europe that summer.

During my four years I had formed a friendship with a quiet, reserved Japanese boy named Hisaya Iwasaki; I used to visit him in his down-at-the-heels boarding house, and he frequently was at Dolobran for Sunday dinner. I was describing my plans to him one day when — to my surprise, because he had always been aloof and undemonstrative — he asked, "If you are going alone would you mind if I crossed the ocean with you?"

"Nothing I'd like better," I assured him.

Iwasaki had engaged a stuffy little cabin way below the water line, and I proposed he share my suite. Even in this close association he never mentioned his family or his life in Japan, but we found we wanted to see the same things in Europe, and decided to continue on together after leaving England.

As soon as I reached London, I set out to deliver a letter of introduction given me by Senator Lodge to our Minister, Robert Todd Lincoln, the son of Abraham Lincoln; the United States then had no Ambassadors. Because Congress persisted in cutting appropriations for the foreign service to the lowest possible point, a Minister had to fend for himself at his own expense, and American diplomatic affairs were conducted from a few rooms located in some quarter where rents were cheap.

Looking for Number 123, I walked down Victoria Street — a bustling, business thoroughfare. The Chancery proved to be on the ground floor of a grimy, gloomy building, and the Minister's office was directly off the street in a small, dark, noisy room. Mr. Lincoln, rather stout, red-bearded, sprucely dressed, received me cordially, and as I was departing he said, "I suppose you'd like to see something of diplomatic life in London. Would you care to go to the Foreign Office Reception?"

I jumped at the chance; and two evenings later, about ten o'clock, I climbed into the Legation brougham — coachman on the box and footmen behind with red, white, and blue cockades on their high hats. From every street carriages were converging on St. James's Park. The approaches were packed solid, but at sight of our official insignia policemen opened a way for us straight to the door.

The reception hall was at the head of a magnificent marble staircase, which we mounted between lines of liveried footmen in powdered wigs, colored coats, and satin breeches. At the top we took our appointed positions — first the Ambassadors according to their length of service in England, and then the Ministers in the same order. The United States delegation stood nowhere near the Great Powers; in fact, when Mr. Lincoln had arrived in London, he had ranked below the envoys from Siam and Haiti.

The Guards Band struck up "God Save the Queen," the signal that the Prince and Princess of Wales were ascending the stairway. I watched them coming down the line, a tall regal couple, the Prince heavy and florid, with close-trimmed beard touched with gray. We bowed as they passed, and after the *défilé* the line dissolved.

Through suites and suites of drawing rooms I followed Mr. Lincoln. The light from the great chandeliers flashed on the diamond tiaras of the women. Enormous jewels winked from the turbans of Indian princes clad in red, blue, and yellow silks, and draped in ropes of pearls. I had never seen such dazzling attire — Austro-Hungarians in fabulous fur capes; Russians of the Imperial Guard in snowy white, military attachés in their regimentals, a Negro from Santo Domingo swathed in gold lace, white shirt bosoms slashed with ribbons — emerald, claret, burgundy, and occasionally the azure of the Garter.

I went back to the Bath Hotel that night so wrought up that for hours I could not sleep. No matter how successful I might be at the law, I was certain I could not possibly find it so exciting as diplomacy.

According to plan, Iwasaki and I once more joined forces. At Christiania we engaged two carioles — giglike conveyances with a little platform in the rear on which our baggage was tied. The narrow road to Trondhjem, three hundred miles away, led through lovely forests of pine and spruce, past waterfalls glinting in the sun, now and then skirting the tip of a fjord that cut far inland from the sea.

Our vehicles rattled and jolted up and down precipitous hills and around sharp turns with sheer drops hundreds of feet below. The danger was slight as long as we had gentle horses. However, every ten miles or so we stopped to change at post houses, and occasionally we were supplied with animals too high-spirited for our peace of mind. On one stretch my cariole was drawn by a roan, obviously out to make trouble if he could. We were barely under way when something startled him; he tossed his head, a shower of pebbles flew from under his hooves, he took the bit in his teeth and bolted.

We began lurching perilously from side to side; each time we hit a stone I bounced off my seat and was sure we would upset. On we tore, shooting over bridges, grazing the edges of precipices, slewing around curves on one wheel. Finally the road bent abruptly upgrade. The panting horse charged the hill, but it was so steep that he had to slacken speed, and before he could reach the top he came to a halt, sweating and trembling. I slumped back exhausted; two miles was a long distance to be frightened.

Thanking my lucky stars for my escape, I turned to see how my baggage had fared. All that remained of it was the handle of my Gladstone bag, trailing at the end of a rope. By retracing our route I retrieved a few things, but they were so ripped and torn that I realized I should have to buy a new outfit.

A little train carried us the last lap into Trondhjem, every few hundred yards or so crawling on trestles over cavernous rock-bottomed gorges. Fascinated we gazed down, and as we crossed a particularly deep one, the temptation was too much for me: I tossed out an empty bottle from the débris of our picnic lunch, and we both watched it crash far below. At the next bridge Iwasaki hurled a bottle. And so we continued at every ravine until sardine tins, boxes, eggshells, all our rubbish, had disappeared except one bottle. Although it belonged to Iwasaki, I jokingly snatched it and dangled it from the window. With unexpected feeling he exclaimed, "That's mine. You mustn't touch it."

Heedlessly I flung the bottle. Instantly Iwasaki's face grew suffused and red with anger. I thought he was about to hit me or at least break into a storm of abuse. Instead he silently picked up his favorite pipe, to which he was more attached than to any other of his possessions, and dropped it overboard. Then, while I looked on with increasing dismay, he continued to pitch out his tobacco pouch, hat, mackintosh, overcoat, steamer rug. He dragged from the rack his two heavy bags and heaved them over the sill. When he had disposed of everything but the clothes he was wearing, he took his seat again without a word and stared straight ahead of him.

I was humiliated and miserable, especially since I knew how poor Iwasaki was. I was certain my act of stupidity had ended our joint travels, but on our arrival at Trondhjem, as though nothing had happened, he remarked pleasantly: "The stores are still open. We both need some things. Why not come with me and we'll buy them together?"

Having in his Oriental manner made me atone for my lack of consideration, Iwasaki had apparently forgotten his annoyance entirely. Neither of us ever mentioned the matter again.

After visiting Stockholm and Helsingfors, we reached St. Petersburg, the fur center of the world, where I wanted to get a sealskin cap. We inquired for the best shop, and there were installed on a raised dais, while below us on the parquet floor were spread dozens of hats of every sort of fur. I finally selected one and Iwasaki asked politely, "Have you finished?"

Nodding, I rose to go, but Iwasaki motioned to the display, "I'll take those."

"Which ones?" asked the astonished clerk.

"All of them, and I'd like to see some ladies' coats, capes, and muffs."

The clerk rushed for assistance, and soon the floor was literally heaped with bear, wolf, fox, sealskin, astrakhan, and beaver. Iwasaki regarded them approvingly and without further inspection said, "Yes, I'll take those also. Have you shown me everything?"

Remembering the wretched boarding house where Iwasaki had lived four years, the cheap little cabin he had chosen on the ship, and his frugal habits, I could hardly believe my ears. The manager and the whole staff of the store were now gathered around. They cleared the floor again, and this time laid carefully at our feet the rarest specimens they had — the softest mink, the darkest sables, the whitest ermine.

In the most matter-of-fact tone Iwasaki remarked, "I'll take those too," and he gave the Japanese Legation as reference. Then he said to me, "You know Japanese women love furs. My family is very large, and this is my chance to buy presents for them." I was dying to ask him how he expected to settle the bill, which must have amounted to thousands of dollars, but he offered no explanation.

By coincidence I was able to satisfy my curiosity that very evening. We ran into a Japanese at the hotel who had dinner with us. I talked and joked with Iwasaki as usual; our new companion treated him with the utmost respect and when we were alone, inquired whether I realized with whom I was traveling. "Well, I thought I did until this afternoon. Now I'm not so sure."

It turned out that Iwasaki was sole heir of the great business house of the Mitsubishi and some day would become one of the richest men in the world, occupying in Japan a position like that of Carnegie and Rockefeller combined; he had been paying the expenses of a dozen or so of his countrymen at the University of Pennsylvania on condition they would not let it be known.

At Vienna I suddenly discovered I had made a mistake in my accounts so that I had barely enough money to take me to London. Knowing Father would not send me more, I told Iwasaki I could not continue with him to Italy and Spain. He was terribly upset, saying he might never again be free and footloose. Would I not go on as his guest? I did not feel I could incur this obligation, and we returned by the shortest route to London — where he sailed East and I sailed West. He promised to write, but no word ever came from him.

Once more back in Philadelphia, I found that the study of law left me little free time. Mornings I listened to lectures; Charles C. Townshend and George Wharton Pepper were just starting their brilliant careers. Afternoons I pored over Blackstone and ran errands in the large offices of Biddle and Ward, who handled Father's business. I joined a law club, and certain evenings we held mock trials for which we prepared briefs and presented cases. As though that were not sufficient, Saturday nights I put on a white uniform — blouse open at the collar, trousers tucked into leggings, jaunty naval cap — and reported for drill at the armory on South Broad Street. New York had just formed a battalion of naval reserves to support the Navy in case of war, and a group in Philadelphia had decided to do the same.

When we considered our drilling would pass muster and had received our new dark blue peajackets, we gave the city an opportunity to see us. Everything was going off splendidly until we heard a feminine voice from the sidewalk, "Oh, look at them walking in their drawers." We had to get used to this sort of chaff.

In the spring I spent a short vacation in Florida, and soon after reaching home began to have severe headaches and fever. Dr. George Gerhard, the family doctor of the Main Line, diagnosed my illness as a bad case of typhoid; I had drunk polluted water at a hotel.

I went completely out of my head and had to have two nurses in constant attendance. My violent dislike was roused by one of them, probably because she had forced on me some especially vile-tasting medicine. Once while their backs were turned I made a dash for the window. As I was disappearing over the sill, they caught me by the ankles and there I hung with my nightgown about my neck, struggling so that they were unable to pull me in.

At that moment Mother stepped out the front door, ready to get into the carriage which Augustus was bringing up the drive. A glance showed her there was no time to lose. Without betraying the least alarm, she asked quietly, "Lloyd, what is thee doing?"

"Mother, these women are trying to poison me. I'm escaping."

"Stay where thee is. I'll send help."

Meanwhile Augustus was puffing upstairs. Just as I was almost unconscious from the blood in my head, he grabbed me and hauled me back. After that bars were put across the window, and he slept outside in the hall to be on call in case of need. For three weeks nobody knew whether I would live. Dr. Gerhard said I would not have recovered except that my system, never having become accustomed to alcohol, reacted remarkably to teaspoonfuls of brandy every half-hour.

I kept having the most vivid dream. When you are delirious you are in another world, which is nevertheless very real to you. I was again in London at the Foreign Office Reception. I could see plainly the great marble stairway. At the top stood the Prince and Princess of Wales and behind them in the candlelight Ambassadors and Ministers and royalty in all their regalia. I too tried to go up, but my head buzzed, and I reeled. I realized I was very drunk and was overcome by the disgrace I was bringing upon my country.

Although I was still far from well in the fall, I started once more at the law. The first time I went to the office my fellow students were sitting around glumly. Courteously they said they were glad to see I was restored to health, and then the spokesman remarked I had hardly behaved fairly. On hearing that my family had been assembled by my bedside waiting for the end, they had consulted together to find some farewell tribute in which they could all join.

"He had a wonderful sense of humor," began one.

"Yes, but he was too easily taken in," objected another.

"He was a good tennis player," volunteered a third.

"But he had no backhand," amended a fourth.

Finally one of them, in default of anything better, contributed, "He was the best-dressed man I knew."

"Yes," they had shouted in chorus, delighted to be in agreement, "he was the best-dressed man we knew."

The winter dragged on and I dragged about, invariably exhausted, barely able to stay awake through classes, afterwards plodding home to sleep until dinnertime. Nevertheless, I kept up my naval reserve activities and, having advanced from boatswain's mate to ensign and exchanged the whistle for the sword, I insisted on going to Washington to lead my platoon in the parade at President Cleveland's inauguration.

It was bitter cold. We sloshed through several inches of half-melted snow to our assembling point to the east of the Capitol, and there stood for two solid hours, shivering in the wind, our wet feet aching. Once we were under way, the lift of the music and the enthusiasm of the crowds dispelled any fatigue. The Navy, as always, was popular, and our battalion received a great ovation as it passed the presidential stand.

Fortunately I did not contract pneumonia, but my health was definitely made worse, and Dr. Gerhard ordered me to give up law school. I was at loose ends when Mrs. Cameron came to the rescue, "Maybe there's something in that dream of Lloyd's. Why don't you get him into the diplomatic service? Thomas Bayard's packing to go to London and I hear he wants a private secretary. There's no salary but it would be a marvelous opportunity for Lloyd. I'll see whether Don can arrange it."

The Bayards held a position in Delaware much like that of the Camerons, who had owned Pennsylvania politically for generations. Mr. Bayard's uncle and father had both been senators, he himself had been in the Senate from 1869 to 1885, and Secretary of State during Cleveland's earlier administration. Now in the second term he had been made our first Ambassador to the Court of St. James's.

Father, who included diplomats among the parasites of society, under pressure reluctantly gave me permission to go to Wilmington to be looked over. Mr. Bayard was a large-boned, tall, broad-shouldered man; his shock of gray hair was just beginning to grow white, but his figure and clean-shaven face were those of a young man. As he welcomed me, his gray eyes, under heavy brows, had a twinkle of friendliness. He was deaf enough so that I had to shout the answers to his questions, but after only a brief examination he said, "Yes, young man, I think you'll do. I'll have your name put on the diplomatic list."

Jubilant I returned to Dolobran — I was leaving in a week as private secretary of the first ambassador the United States had ever sent to any country.

CHAPTER III

A DREAM COME TRUE

Mr. Bayard was given a royal reception in England. On the pier at Southampton stood the Corporation, led by the Lord Mayor in his robes of office — flat velvet cap, furred gown of scarlet, and an enormous chain almost to his waist. Representatives of the Foreign Office in top hats and frock coats came forward: "Welcome to England, Your Excellency." Two tall, dark, handsome Americans shook hands with us — Henry White and Larz Anderson, the first and second secretaries of our Embassy. At Waterloo Station more English officials in top hats were waiting to conduct Mr. and Mrs. Bayard along the red streak of carpet laid on the dingy platform. The liveried coachman of the Embassy carriage flourished his whip, the liveried footmen jumped up behind, and off we clattered.

On arriving at our small hotel across from Buckingham Palace, Mr. Bayard told White he wished to start business at the Embassy as soon as possible. Accordingly, early the next morning White called for us, and we drove down Victoria Street, noisy with the roar of horse buses and wagons on wooden paving-blocks, until we reached the unprepossessing entrance of Number 123. To greet us at the door was the chief clerk, Charles Hodson, a big, burly Englishman with gray hair and red cheeks; at his elbow was his son Frank, the Chancery handy boy. I was assigned a desk with Anderson in a dark little hole looking into a forlorn yard. Although the sun shone brightly outside, the yellow gaslight flared and flickered; often we could not see to work unless it were lit.

I reported for duty in the front office to find Mr. Bayard and White busy going through a heap of invitations. Some were for special events in honor of the Ambassador; more had to do with festivities centering around the approaching marriage of the heir presumptive, George, Duke of York, to Princess Mary of Teck — the diplomatic corps, being a part of the Court, was naturally present at all Court functions. White was advising which to accept when Mr. Bayard interrupted, "By the way, will you have Griscom's name added to the diplomatic list?"

"It isn't customary, sir," White protested. "In fact, it's absolutely forbidden. If you really want this, I'd better talk to the Foreign Office myself."

In an hour or so he returned with a long face. "It can't be done, sir. Too many ambassadors in the past have abused the privilege. One Spanish envoy brought fourteen private secretaries, who occupied so much room at Court that the Foreign Office put down its foot and barred them all."

For a moment my expectations of seeing diplomatic life seemed to be vanishing; if my name were not on the list I would not be included in any of the official invitations. Mr. Bayard, however, was annoyed that his first request should be thus rejected, and he drew himself up: "I've given this young gentleman my word."

White shook his head in perplexity, and rather than be a source of trouble I offered to resign. Mr. Bayard would not hear of it. Theoretically he did not exist until he had presented his credentials to the Queen, but, while White watched incredulously, he then and there drafted his first communication to Lord Rosebery, the Foreign Secretary. White's eyes opened even wider at the favorable reply. In deference to the new Ambassador, the sacred Foreign Office tradition would be broken. Since that time every envoy has been entitled to one private secretary with diplomatic status.

Actually I was never a personal secretary. Mr. Bayard kept his own papers, wrote his own letters, and liked to do things for himself. The Embassy was so short-handed that the work was months behind, and as soon as White and Anderson found I was not going to have much to do, they grabbed me. In the rear of the Chancery were stored piles and piles of dispatches, all waiting to be transferred in longhand to the Embassy archives. I was set down in front of a huge volume and told to start copying; the last entry had been made the year before.

Meanwhile, the formal launching of the Ambassador began with his call on Lord Rosebery, who arranged for the presentation of his credentials to Queen Victoria at Windsor. A day or two later came an invitation from Lord Rosebery to dine at Berkeley Square, with a postscript penned by the Minister himself to "bring along that Griscom."

Mr. Bayard showed me the note, remarking, "You didn't expect that from our teapot tempest, did you?"

I certainly had not expected to attend the dinner at which the Ambassador was to be introduced to the Cabinet and high Government officials. On the appointed night, when Mr. Bayard and I entered the reception room, as far as I could see it was filled entirely with gray beards. Lord Rosebery, clean-shaven and scholarly-looking, spoke to the Ambassador and then held out his hand to me, "So you're that Griscom who's caused us all the trouble."

At dinner I felt more conspicuous than ever. In England the host sits in the middle of the table; I was alone at one end, the Marquess of Breadalbane on my right and on my left James Bryce, Chancellor of the Duchy of Lancaster. Mr. Bryce, whose *American Commonwealth* had already become the leading text on our Government, asked me conversationally how Tammany Hall was getting on. I tried to think of something intelligent about Boss Richard Croker. He listened to me quite as though he valued my comments, but his replies indicated he was much more familiar with current events in New York than I.

Lord Breadalbane then inquired my opinion of Home Rule. Like many Americans I had deep sympathy for the Irish, and this had been intensified by Augustus' tales. Before dinner was over he said he hoped our paths would soon cross again. By the close of the evening I had forgotten that I was the only one of my generation present. More than any other people in the world the English know how to put the young at their ease.

The next afternoon I was working at the Chancery when White rushed in. "Come out! Come out! Lady Breadalbane's waiting in her carriage and she wants to meet you. Hurry up!"

The name meant little to me, but I dropped my pen and followed him. Lady Breadalbane said her husband had instructed her to invite me to dinner. Would next Tuesday suit me?

Naturally I accepted and, as she drove away, I asked White, "Who are the Breadalbanes?"

"Oh, they do a good deal of the entertaining for the Liberals. Most of the other owners of great houses are Conservatives."

On being shown into the Breadalbanes' drawing room I was immediately lost in the midst of at least fifty people, all complete strangers. As though the fate of the nation depended on it, they were discussing Gladstone's chances of getting his Home Rule Bill passed. The bitterness against the opposition was not confined to Parliament; the Breadalbanes apparently would not receive a Conservative in their house, and some of their friends would not speak to one on the street.

The instant dinner was over Lady Breadalbane took my arm. "Lady Battersea wants to meet you," and she marched me up to a gray-haired, heavily handsome dowager, who began: "I noticed you did not drink anything at dinner. Would you mind telling me why?"

"My father's giving me a thousand dollars if I don't touch alcohol until my twenty-first birthday."

"Sit down. I want to talk to you."

In a few minutes Home Rule was forgotten and we were deep in the subject of temperance. Lady Battersea traveled over the country making speeches which advocated not prohibition, but closing laws for public houses so that liquor could not be sold except with meals. Nothing would help improve the slums more than limiting the supply of gin, and she was always on the alert for examples to prove her point. I explained to her that, according to Dr. Gerhard, my life had been saved by a few half-teaspoonfuls of cognac, simply because my system had not been used to alcohol.

"That's the best story I've heard in a long time. I'm going to tour England with it. You must come to lunch tomorrow."

The next day before I left she asked me for a week end at her country house, Aston Clinton in Buckinghamshire.

My first sight of the Court was at Mr. Bayard's presentation at the levee of the Prince of Wales, who had assumed virtually all the royal social duties. Since the United States would not let its representatives have diplomatic uniforms, the Court had prescribed carefully what we should wear. When I had given myself the last touches, and was ready to depart for St. James's Palace, I looked in the mirror. Down as far as the waist I was quite presentable — a full dress coat with tails, and white waistcoat with special buttons and pearl studs. Below the waist, however, I suddenly tapered off most absurdly — silk knee breeches with small bows at the side, plain black silk stockings which drew attention to my almost calf-less legs, and pumps with jet buckles.

At a quarter to three St. James's Street was crowded with Londoners watching the line going to pay their respects — new admirals and governors and peers in uniform, as well as reluctant fathers who had daughters about to make their debuts in society. In a reception room the diplomatic corps assembled behind the Russian Ambassador who, as the oldest in residence, was the dean. Though our little group came at the end of the ambassadors, just ahead of the ministers, nobody could miss us. We were all over six feet, and a much more conspicuous black blot on the surrounding rainbow than our fellow democrats, the French. We seemed to be dressed identically with the Court Newsman who got up the Court Calendar, and at a quick glance might have been mistaken for any of the other servants. I was once offered half a crown to show a lady the way to the ballroom at Buckingham Palace.

The doors were thrown open, a hush descended, the column advanced slowly towards the Prince of Wales, a portly figure in the uniform of his own regiment, the Tenth Hussars. He conversed with Mr. Bayard an unusually long time, obviously putting himself out to be friendly. Then the Prince shook hands with me, and I followed the others in a curve into the center of the room where we remained while the ceremonies went on. If we tried to talk, a chamberlain bustled up immediately and requested silence; it was against the rules to cough or sneeze, and a disgrace to blow the nose. The elder diplomats found being on their feet for two hours very trying. Since my new pumps were too tight, I had to keep shifting my weight, and could hardly hobble when at last the Prince bowed formally and we, thus dismissed, bowed even more deeply and filed out.

Having learned my lesson, I made sure my pumps were as comfortable as slippers by the time Mr. and Mrs. Bayard and the staff were to go to the drawing room at Buckingham Palace. The Queen was still a dictator of moral behavior and had by no means surrendered her interest in politics; we used to hear constantly, "The Queen has intervened and stopped this," or "The Queen has just given the Prime Minister a wigging."

As the diplomats entered the throneroom the Queen, in black dress and lace cap, was standing on a raised dais in front of the throne. She had a most alarming dignity, which made one forget how small she really was; it was rumored she had her skirt draped around a little stool she stood on to make herself four inches taller. The first of a line of chamberlains picked up Mrs. Bayard's train, and it was passed on until she reached the Queen. We followed and Her Majesty's lips seemed to move as each of us bent over her hand, but if she said anything I did not hear it.

Once in position behind the chamberlains, we relieved the monotony by watching the women in their elaborate court costumes and three-feathered headdresses, all doing their best to carry out instructions. A particularly nervous young girl, attempting the deep royal curtsey, lost her balance and sat down on the floor; instantly two well-trained gentlemen-in-waiting took her by the arms and hoisted her to her feet.

At one point there was a pause, and then a stir near the door. We craned our necks to see a panic-stricken feminine figure come galloping towards the throne, her feathers waving and two bewildered chamberlains clinging desperately to her train. Rather than race by the Queen they finally dropped it. She, however, never slackened her pace, but continued her preposterous gallop around the room and out the door. The Queen smiled, the ladies-in-waiting tittered, and the diplomats exploded in a most undiplomatic roar of laughter.

Mr. Bayard had been presented to the statesmen and the Court; it remained for him to be presented to the British public, and we all went to the first banquet where he was to speak. He began in the manner that had never failed to captivate an American audience, his glorious voice rolling forth in a mellifluous rush of words. The English do not care for emotional oratory. After an hour we were distinctly conscious of hems, coughs, and a shuffling of feet, but the Ambassador was too rapt in his own eloquence to discern, and too deaf to hear, that anything was wrong.

Another quarter of an hour, and some of the audience started to leave while the remainder shuffled their feet even more noisily. I glanced at Mrs. Bayard, who was sitting on the edge of her chair in agonized suspense. Sporadic applause broke out; the Ambassador went blissfully on. It was an hour and forty minutes before he finished, and by that time the hall was almost empty. In the carriage on the way home Mrs. Bayard explained what had happened, and he was so overcome that he burst into tears.

The next morning he had me on the carpet, saying again and again, "You ought to have done something! You ought to have done something!" All I could reply was that I was very sorry; I still did not see how I could have walked up in front of the assembly and tugged at his coat tails.

Mr. Bayard was an unhappy man for a few days; however, he never repeated the mistake, and eventually became one of the most sought-after speakers in England.

I was looking forward particularly to the Reception at the Foreign Office. The minute I stepped inside the door everything was startlingly like my dream — both sides of the staircase were lined with guests; I was late, and they were waiting for the arrival of the Prince and Princess of Wales. Halfway to the top I was horrified to hear the opening bars of *God Save the Queen,* and I shrank against the rails, barely avoiding a collision with a dignified lady who was hurrying behind me. While I was admiring her necklace, I saw a huge emerald pendant, fully the size of my finger joint, drop to the floor. The Prince and Princess were only a few yards away; nevertheless, I darted out, scooped it up, and squeezed myself back.

Mrs. White recognized the jewel as an heirloom of the Abercorns, and conducted me to the Duchess. She had not even realized her loss, but seemed very grateful.

Some weeks later a friend in New York sent me a clipping from *Town Topics* — a fairy tale in the modern style. Lloyd Griscom at his first great party had found a priceless ruby. He had restored it to its owner, a Dowager Princess (on whose neck the writer said it hung like a red lantern on a wreck), and now she was introducing him to everyone.

As a matter of fact I met the Duchess face to face several nights afterwards and she had not the slightest idea who I was.

The principal affair of the season was the Court Ball in honor of the Tsarevitch Nicholas of Russia, who was in London for his cousin's wedding. Full of curiosity, I made a place for myself among the crowd in front of the stand occupied by the ladies of the diplomatic corps. The section reserved for the Court was marked by a red cord across the middle of the long room. At the far end to my left the gallery was bright with the scarlet uniforms of the enormous Guards Band. Another splash of red blazed from the carpet on the royal dais beside me to the right. Opposite sparkled the jeweled tiaras of the duchesses and their daughters.

The music blared out, and everyone wheeled towards the door to watch the royal procession. First came the Lord High Chamberlain, and following him the other officers of the Household — the Keeper of the Privy Purse, the Master of the Horse, the Master of the Buckhounds, the Gentlemen of the Bedchamber, equerries of all kinds. Many of them carried gold or silver staffs six or seven feet in length.

The Tsarevitch, stocky, unsmiling, and bearded, entered with the Princess of Wales on his arm. Some of the rest of the party I could identify — the Prince of Wales, the Princesses Victoria and Maud, the Tecks, the Duke of Connaught, and Princess Alix of Hesse-Darmstadt, whose beauty had caused a sensation that season. They ascended the dais, bowed to the assemblage, and sat down in their gilded chairs.

At the first measure of the quadrille the royal party rose and arranged themselves in hollow squares. The Prince had an eagle eye for anyone who made a mistake, and several times he spoke sharply to an offender. In the middle of one of the most complicated figures his partner, the tall, blond Princess Daisy of Pless, dropped her bouquet of roses. As the Prince gallantly leaned over to retrieve them, his skin-tight breeches brought him up in a round turn six inches from the floor. He bent down again and again, but his fingers brushed the petals only. No one dared to laugh, although occasionally I thought I saw a grin. Finally, with an apology, the Princess rescued them herself.

The figures of the quadrille appeared to me much like those of the lancers, which we did at home, except that here the dancers walked in measured step. Somehow the leisurely pace seemed to suit the stately, regular-featured women then considered most handsome. Public admiration for them was open and unabashed; their photographs were on sale everywhere, and at parties the guests would stand on tiptoe for a glimpse of the Duchesses of Sutherland, Portland, and Rutland, or of Lady Londonderry, Lady Helen Vincent, Lady Mar and Kellie, or the American-born Lady Randolph Churchill and Lady Paget. The great beauties were part of the sights of London.

The order of dances was always quadrille, waltz, and polka, with an intermission between, in which the Princesses could send out the chamberlains to bring them partners; no one less than their cousins could ask them to dance. The music started once more, and the room began to spin like a multicolored wheel. In America we used to pride ourselves on reversing in the waltz, but here the direction never changed.

Suddenly a Gold Stick chamberlain banged his staff in front of me. "His Royal Highness wishes you to dance." Evidently royalty did not consider it was a ball unless the floor was filled. Luckily on the far side of the cord I had noticed someone I knew — Miss Alida Chanler, Winthrop Chanler's sister from New York. I found her still without a partner and gingerly we slipped into the moving circle.

Just as we were breathing more easily, I looked up to see the Tsarevitch bearing down on us. Before I could brace myself we collided violently. "Ouch!" exclaimed Miss Chanler, and I could feel her wince as he trod heavily on her foot. However, since we had been commanded to dance, she limped gamely on.

We rounded the circle once more and again the Tsarevitch came into view, whirling more madly than ever. I squared my shoulder for the shock. We crashed. Unfortunately he slipped and went sprawling in the middle of the floor. Not daring to wait to discover what degree of lèse-majesté I had committed, I made for the further side of the room to get as many people as I could between us as quickly as possible.

A few seconds later a Gold Stick tapped me on the arm. "His Royal Highness wishes you to stop dancing." I was sure the Russian Bear had tracked me down until I observed the chamberlains were interrupting others. Apparently they were only thinning the crowded floor.

After taking Miss Chanler back to her party I was wondering what to do next when Colonel Cuthbert Larking, equerry of the Duke of Connaught, who had visited us at Dolobran, approached as solemn as an owl. Laying an arm over my shoulder he said, "You want to watch out. You're in danger of arrest."

Thinking to myself, "Good heavens, somebody must have seen me upset the Tsarevitch," I asked, "What for? What for?"

"For having no visible means of support," and he walked on, roaring with laughter.

I was very sensitive about my thin legs and at that moment would have given anything to be in America where I could always wear long trousers to parties.

Shortly Gold Stick stamped his staff again in front of me. "His Royal Highness wishes you to dance." White introduced me to the sprightly Lady Galway, and we hopped away in a polka. Everybody else had inquired how I liked England, but she wanted to hear about America. We enjoyed ourselves thoroughly, and she invited me to lunch the next day.

At midnight the royal party marched from the platform and trooped into the supper room. A buffet table was roped off for them at one side, and nobody could enter their enclosure unless summoned by a chamberlain. I could not even get near the rope where middle-aged, gray-haired men and women were crowding and elbowing in the endeavor to press a few inches closer.

I went to secure a plate of salad for Mrs. Bayard and encountered another pack of wolves, this time hungry ones. The guests were pushing and shoving and overturning dishes in the confusion. Then and there I concluded that humanity collectively was more unattractive than humanity individually. It was a relief to be back in the ballroom and on the other side of the cord where I could have more fun.

Because it was the height of an unusually gay season Americans were pouring into London. Every day our waiting room at the Embassy was filled with my fellow countrymen. White and Anderson would say to me, "Oh, you're the Ambassador's private secretary; you go out and see them." Receiving them was one of the delicate problems for any Embassy. How was I to tell whether a man who gave his name as Mr. Jones from Rochester might not be a cousin of a cabinet officer, or a state politician, or a power of some kind? If he did not obtain what he wanted he might go home and complain to his Senator or Representative that he had been treated badly.

Then the Congressman would pay a call at the State Department. Fortunately the older officials realized they must protect their representatives abroad. "Before we worry about Senator So-and-so's charges we had better listen to the Ambassador's story."

Among the most difficult visitors with whom we had to deal were the women who demanded to be presented at a Court drawing room. We had at least a dozen petitions for each one of the ten tickets allowed us and, no matter how carefully we explained, virtually every disappointed applicant seemed to regard a refusal as a personal injury. Sometimes we would be confronted by a wholesale request. Perhaps a schoolteacher would bring over from six to twenty American girls on an educational tour of Europe. As an inducement she had promised them a presentation at Buckingham Palace and often the girls had purchased their entire wardrobe in anticipation. I did not envy her when she had to make her excuses to them.

All I could offer in compensation were passes to the Royal Mews in Buckingham Palace, for which the supply was unlimited. Many people seemed to take extraordinary pleasure in viewing the cream-colored horses and the ancient historic chariots. The fact that the Mews were inside the Palace gates gave them a sense of having been near the throne.

I never knew who was going to walk through the Embassy door. One day appeared the flawlessly attired Richard Harding Davis, famous as the author of *Gallegher*. While I was at college I used to admire him at football games, striding up and down with the linesmen, reporting the match for his paper. His first question to me was, "Do you know the Princess Alix?"

Before I could answer he described how one moonlit evening in Athens during his recent tour of the Mediterranean he had climbed to the Acropolis, where he had chanced upon the loveliest girl he had ever laid eyes on. Though they were alone he had not dared address her, but had followed her back to her hotel. There he learned she was the Princess Alix.

Davis said her beauty had driven all other thoughts from his mind. He was green with envy when I told him I had spoken to her at Court, where she was always the cynosure. He never met the bride-to-be of the ill-fated Tsarevitch, but later he made her the heroine of his novel *Princess Aline*.

One July afternoon I looked up from my desk to find Henry Adams peering quizzically down at me. He wanted to ascertain how I was getting along in his former job (he had been private secretary to his father, Charles Francis Adams, during the Civil War). That evening Mrs. Cameron was lending him her box at Covent Garden. Would I not keep him company to hear Melba sing?

From the horseshoe we glanced around at the other boxes, bright with jewels; the Englishwomen put on everything they owned for such occasions. Philosophically Uncle Henry made a gesture towards the stalls below, "Do you see all those bald-headed men?"

"Yes."

"Nobody realizes what the years do to himself, but he does notice age in others. Those doddering old boys were dashing young blades about town when I was here first."

He went on to describe incidents which had happened to him — personal details of his father, Palmerston, the Prince Consort, the Queen. "It was a golden time for me and altered my whole life," he ended.

Then for a moment he lapsed from his usual cynical manner to give me a piece of advice which I never forgot: "You're in a remarkable position now. You've every opportunity to make friends that will influence your entire career. Be sure you keep your head and get the most you can out of it."

CHAPTER IV

EVERYTHING IN SEASON

Nobody less than a head of mission was invited to Westminster Abbey for the royal wedding, July 6th, 1893. White told me I would be lucky if I even caught a glimpse of the procession, because all points of vantage along the line of march had been taken up weeks before. Having seen so many pageants in a few weeks, I was not particularly disappointed. However, the marriage of the heir to the throne was bound to be a historic event, and, when every Englishman was clamoring for a place, it seemed very friendly of Colonel Larking to ask me to his rooms in Walsingham House.

I made my way down Piccadilly, hung with garlands, and on entering Colonel Larking's flat found him in the middle of a group of guests. He piloted me from one to the other: "My brother-in-law, Lord Listowel, Lady Listowel, my niece Lady Margaret Hare, Sir Francis and Lady Winnington, Colonel Charles Crichton, Miss Leila Crichton."

Knowing by now the formality which surrounded anything to do with the Court, I expected the usual stiff conversation while we waited. Rather to my surprise everybody was laughing and talking and having a good time. The Winningtons, he enormously tall and she hardly five feet, but obviously mistress of all she surveyed, had just returned from their annual trip to Monte Carlo, where they had been trying out their "infallible" system for breaking the bank. As a joke on themselves they were handing around two clippings, the first from a Monte Carlo paper announcing the arrival of Sir Francis and Lady Winnington at the Grand Hotel, the other from the London *World*, dated some weeks later, which reported, "Sir Francis and Lady Losington have left Monte Carlo."

To pass the time Lord Listowel entertained us with the story of the visit he had made with his bride to a great house in the North of England. Only twenty-four hours after their arrival the hostess had been dismayed by the disappearance of her butler. A search was instituted for him high and low, the local police were notified, finally a substitute had to be rushed from London so that the party could continue. Two weeks afterward, on the day it was to break up, the body of the missing butler was discovered in the water tank of the castle. "We always refer to our honeymoon," he concluded, "as the time we drank the butler."

Jolly and full of fun, these were not at all like most English I had met hitherto. Crichton and I, in spite of the difference in age, were particularly congenial. He had gone to Canada as a young Guards officer, and described his expeditions with Whyte-Melville, the writer of sporting classics, and his adventures at General Grant's headquarters as an observer of the Wilderness Campaign. His parting remark to me was, "Come to Mullaboden when the hunting starts and we Irish will show you a thing or two."

White placed prime importance on the social side of diplomacy. "Make friends everywhere. Know someone in every department of government" was his motto. As a matter of course, I had joined the St. James's Club, of which all the diplomats were members, but White suggested I ought also to belong to a new and rather dashing club called the Bachelors'. The season still had several weeks to run — teas, dinners, balls each day. As a result of being admitted to this club I frequently had ten invitations for one night, because whoever gave a party consulted the Club list of young and eligible males.

Seeing London as a boy with my father, I had always thought of it as a dull mercantile city, whose citizens spent all their lives going back and forth to business. Now it seemed gayer than anything I had ever imagined. On leaving the Embassy, I used to drop in at the Club, and there I would find a group discussing plans for the evening. Basil Blackwood, Alexander Thynne, Lord Kerry, and Geoffrey Brown-Guthrie became my special companions. Where we went depended to a certain extent on which host they expected to furnish the best champagne.

Cabs were very expensive. We all had bicycles, and often through the deepening twilight we would pedal to Kensington, carefully keeping our coat tails out of range of the spokes, calling merrily to each other. We would park our bicycles in racks outside the front door and join the dance. In an hour or so the report might pass around that the champagne was better at So-and-so's, and off we would go; a party was made or ruined by the ebb and flow of this bachelor tide. Finally, when the sun was well up, we would speed back to our lodgings. Milkmen and other early risers would turn to watch this strange flock of white-bosomed riders, each clutching a topper with one hand and a handlebar with the other, coat tails flying out behind.

Of all the parties those at Holland House, which belonged to Lord Ilchester, held the most enchantment. From the moment we turned in the great gates and started up the quarter-mile drive under the arching trees we seemed transported miles from London. The time-mellowed rooms had once heard the voices of Charles James Fox, William Pitt, and Thomas Babington Macaulay. Here, gathered about the witty and amusing Margot Tennant, were Arthur Balfour, Herbert Asquith, and other members of the "Souls," the intellectual coterie of the day.

If the Prince of Wales was expected at a party, the crowd was invariably larger. In spite of his mistresses and gay companions, he could establish a social reputation by a single word. One evening at the Duchess of Sutherland's ball at Stafford House I met him face to face. The royal family often went out of their way to make some friendly remark to members of the diplomatic corps, and he extended a hand, "I'm very glad to see you." As he passed on, I felt a tap on the shoulder. It was Davis. "Lord, some people are lucky. Here you've been in London only a few weeks, the Prince of Wales has spoken to you, and you've the foremost reporter in America to spread the news."

Davis and I were frequently together, and he was sure to be obsessed with some fresh romantic notion. Steeped in the atmosphere of Stevenson's *New Arabian Nights,* he lived in the belief that adventure was just around the corner. Whatever or whomever he saw became a possible scene or character for a book, of which someone like himself was the hero. He had been accepted by London society, knew who everyone was, and delighted in pointing out celebrities.

At Philadelphia parties you encountered the same group over and over again, but here you came across all sorts of outstanding political and literary figures, artists, sportsmen, country gentry, foreign visitors. Once I was introduced to a very agreeable older man whose name I did not catch. We started talking about this and that until suddenly he interrupted. "Why, how stupid of me. Of course you want to meet my wife."

"Of course I do," I agreed cordially, but without the faintest idea of who she might be.

He took my arm and led me up to a woman sitting on a sofa. "Here, my dear, is Mr. Griscom of the American Embassy."

Even after chatting for fifteen minutes I still had not learned who she was. As soon as I left her I made inquiries. "Don't you know? That's Mrs. Humphry Ward."

Apparently poor Mr. Ward just traveled around as her husband and could not conceive of anybody being interested in him.

Musicians and artists were always to be found at the salon of Mrs. Ronalds. One afternoon Sir Arthur Sullivan described with relish how, during a recent performance of "Utopia, Ltd.," he had handed his baton to his assistant and had seated himself in the stalls to test the sound effects. As one melody followed another he unconsciously began to whistle more and more audibly. Finally, the man beside him turned in exasperation, "Excuse me, Sir, will you please stop your whistling? I've come to hear Sir Arthur Sullivan's music, not yours."

The life of almost every social gathering were the young Guards officers. Once I fell into conversation with a subaltern of the Coldstreams. Compared with our West Pointers he seemed to have led a most pleasant existence. Like his fellows he had gone straight from public school to Sandhurst where life included week ends in London, polo ponies, and occasional interludes of hunting. Now that he had his commission everything was even more pleasant, because, unless there were a war or his regiment misbehaved, he was assured of being able to spend a large part of his time in London.

The seven regiments comprising the Guards — First and Second Lifeguards, the Horse Guards or Blues, the Grenadiers, Coldstreams, Scots, and Irish — took turns going on duty. Every evening the officers on guard, always excepting the unfortunate one stationed at the Bank of England, collected at St. James's Palace for the elaborate repast furnished them by the Queen. I eagerly accepted the invitation of my new acquaintance to attend a dinner as his guest.

At the end of the meal, prepared by one of the foremost chefs of England, the presiding major rose and the company rose with him. He lifted his glass; "Her Majesty, the Queen," he pronounced solemnly. And all around the table champagne goblets were extended; mine alone was empty. I was wondering why he did not give the signal to drink when I noticed his eye was on me, and out of the silence he thundered, "Young man, Her Majesty's health must be drunk in champagne."

Everybody remained standing at attention while a soldier hurriedly filled my glass. I drained it with the rest.

I apologized later to the major and tried to explain my arrangement with Father, but he reiterated that under no circumstances could anyone be excused from drinking the Queen's health. Luckily Father agreed with him.

After we broke up my host proposed, "Walk over to Buck House with me. I have to go on duty there tonight."

At the iron grille the sentry smartly presented arms, and I turned to leave. "Oh, come on in and see the guardroom."

Nothing loath, I accompanied him through the front door of the Palace into the room to the left, where the first thing I noticed was the printed sheet of military rules on the wall. To my horror I read something to the effect that no officer on guard, under penalty of court martial, should introduce any stranger into the Palace. That was enough for me. I did not intend to risk another scrape. Firmly I whispered, "You get me away from here as fast as you can."

The officer had had just enough alcohol to make him reckless and insisted that I stay. I was stubborn. "I'll walk out alone if you don't show me out."

Seeing I really meant it, the officer escorted me to the gate, but not until I was well beyond the grille did I breathe easily.

Every night in the week I went to a party, but all the gaiety halted for Sunday, a dreary day in London. No entertainment was offered unless after church you wanted to join the turn-out of society, parading up and down the footpath in Rotten Row, hoping for the Prince of Wales to pass by. When Lady Battersea was as good as her word and asked me to Aston Clinton, I was glad to escape.

The English branch of the Rothschild family, of which Lady Battersea was a member, had taken such fast root that a Government loan would hardly be successful without their backing. Their head was Baron Nathaniel Rothschild, who lived at near-by Tring, where I spent another week end. A section of the park had been set aside for young Walter Rothschild's zoo. With pride he displayed to me the team of zebras which he was trying to break in. As far as I could see they were doing all the breaking-in — standing on their hind legs and smashing the harness and carriage.

That evening, after the ladies had retired, four of the younger men suggested we play poker. Having no salary, I had to live entirely on an allowance of two hundred dollars a month; if I lost even a few pounds it would be a calamity. Much against my will I was dragged in to make up a game.

Observing that there were no chips on the table I wondered how we were going to ante; unconcernedly each of my companions pulled a fistful of coins from his pocket. My next shock was to find there was no limit. In all my poker experience I had never before sat in a game like this. The piles of gold and silver grew and grew until the table was covered, and when the currency gave out I.O.U.'s were scribbled and tossed in. I played my cards closer and closer to my chest.

I was a long while discovering that the rest were not, as I had supposed at first, really experts; they took incredible chances. By the end of the evening I had won seventy-five pounds. The man who owed me the greater part of this was the younger son of an impoverished earl. I thought, of course, he would write me a check, but instead he asked me as a special favor to allow him a few days in which to dispose of his library. To this I naturally agreed, realizing he must be on the verge of ruin; nothing could be more disagreeable for an Englishman than to request a delay in settling a gambling debt. If he did not pay me by the following Monday I could have him posted at his club, and he would be expelled instantly. Later I heard he had gone bankrupt and emigrated to South Africa.

The strain of all-night parties, which continued into August, made it very painful to rise early in the morning. I had rented a brand-new service flat at Number 3 Down Street, from which it was a short pleasant stroll across Green Park to the Chancery. Even so it was difficult to arrive on time. Larz Anderson, greeting me brightly, would inquire what had delayed me "up Down Street," and suggested that perhaps it had taken the general factotum at the flat, Owers, "hours and hours to rouse me out of bed."

Larz and I frequently walked to lunch together, each choosing a different side of the street, and counting the cats in our territory. The one with the lowest score paid the bill. I generally had a free meal, because Larz invariably kept to the cool shady side, and all the felines would be sunning themselves on mine.

In the United States businessmen met for lunch at clubs and restaurants, gulped their food, and hurried back to the office. In England the noon hour was a generous one, during which people gathered at private houses. There was usually an admiral, a general, a foreign service official, a colonial governor, and always somebody who knew something important. We would sit around and talk, and in this way I obtained much valuable political information I would never have acquired in any other manner.

Most amusing to me of all the anecdotes I heard were those which dealt with the remarkable career of Henry Labouchère, editor of the weekly, *Truth,* and a member of Parliament who cared not a whoop for anybody. Labby had been equally independent as a youth in the diplomatic service. On receiving an order sending him to St. Petersburg, he asked for his traveling expenses from Paris, and was told he would have to render the account after he had made the trip. Weeks went by and the English Ambassador wrote the Foreign Office from the Russian capital that he was very short-handed, because the third secretary had not arrived. Consuls all over Europe were directed to look out for the missing young man, and finally from one of the Baltic cities came a report that Labby was en route — walking. The Foreign Office was furious. Labby retorted most logically, "You wouldn't give me money for railway fare. The only way I could afford to go was on foot."

At Constantinople the Ambassador, Sir Henry Bulwer, Lord Dalling, used to hold each Sunday evening a formal dinner for his staff. Although the magnificent silver service would appear with all ceremony, the fare was meager. The steward in hushed tones would announce a famous vintage, but at the first sip everyone recognized it was nothing but common Greek wine mixed with prune juice to kill the flavor of tar — the Ambassador was economizing in preparation for retirement.

For several months Labby presented himself in evening dress, and then suddenly shifted to business clothes. At length Sir Henry called him aside. "Mr. Labouchère, my wife and I have noticed that lately you have not shown us the courtesy of dressing. Would you mind explaining to me why?"

"Well sir, I'd rather not."

"Come, come. I'm entitled to know."

"If you insist, Your Excellency, since I've been dining so often at your table my evening clothes do not fit me any more."

Labby, in the course of years, decided diplomacy was worth less and less effort. While on vacation in Italy he was appointed secretary to the Republic of Paraná, but before he could report for duty the Republic had ceased to exist. He spent some twelve months having a good time and when the Foreign Office demanded a report of his activities, he replied: "I've been searching diligently for any trace of the country to which I have been accredited, but so far have been unable to locate it. As soon as directions are sent me I shall hasten to my post."

The last straw came when Labby accepted an appointment to Buenos Aires provided he could superintend his duties from Baden-Baden. The long-suffering Foreign Office thereupon told him the diplomacy of England could be conducted without him.

These luncheon interludes did not make it easier for me to keep awake during the warm summer afternoons at the Embassy. Constantly I found myself drowsing over the archives or the other bits of drudgery which had gradually been transferred to me. As a result of the change in administration in the United States, every American consul in the British Empire was being superseded. No new appointee could exercise his duties until he had an exequatur, or official permit. I had to fill out dozens of applications and send them to the Foreign Office to be approved.

Consulships, being often rewards for political service, might be dispensed without regard to fitness — the Mayor of Podunk to be consul at Zanzibar, the editor of the *Smith County Herald* to be consul at Trinidad; even to the larger posts men were assigned who had never been outside the United States and had no adequate experience.

Ministers as well were likely to be round pegs in square holes. White recounted with relish the misadventures of some of our representatives. The State Department was once surprised to receive a formal protest that the United States Legation in Madrid was harboring a notorious Carlist leader. An investigation revealed that this rebel had rented a room from our enterprising Minister who, to increase his income, was taking in boarders. Located in the center of the city, his establishment was highly convenient for hatching plots and, because of our extraterritorial rights, quite safe for conspirators as long as they stayed inside. Our Government promptly interfered, and the Minister had to abandon the rooming business.

At Vienna, reputed the most exclusive court in Europe, one of our Ministers arrived with his son, recently graduated from dental school. He was anxious to have the young man get a good start, and opened an office for him. The time came when the Minister was invited to one of the Emperor Franz Josef's magnificent Court balls, and was presented to an archduchess.

With a polite bow he began, "Madam, you must pardon me if I make a personal remark. I can't help admiring your beautiful teeth."

"It's very kind of you," said the astonished lady.

"Anybody blessed with such teeth should take care of them." Here the Minister produced one of his son's professional cards and handed it to her. "My son is a member of the great profession of dentistry, in which America leads the world. Prevention is better than cure. Don't wait until you have trouble, but go to him now."

No American diplomat abroad could live on his salary if he wanted to entertain on any large scale. A rich envoy rented a mansion, but a comparatively poor man like Mr. Bayard had to find something he could afford. He had moved into a small house near Prince's Gate, just back of Kingston House, the residence of the Listowels. Every few days thereafter I could count on one interruption. The Ambassador would storm up to my desk, waving a paper covered with Mrs. Bayard's indecipherable hieroglyphics; she had sent the list of guests for that night's dinner with a request that the names be arranged in proper order of precedence. Mr. Bayard, stamping his foot with fury, would complain that he saw no reason why American women could not at least be taught to write.

I used to look for what I thought were the names in Burke, Whittaker, and the diplomatic list. The most deadly feud might arise from putting the Minister from Siam ahead of the Minister from Ecuador, who had presented his credentials two days earlier. Since new titles and new decorations were constantly being bestowed, the lists were never up-to-date, and I had to consult the Lord Chamberlain's office for verification.

Although I seldom went to the dinners, I always had to make a trip to Prince's Gate at the last moment to be sure no slip had occurred. One evening Mrs. Bayard received me at the door with catastrophe written on her face. I had prepared the seating on the supposition that she had asked the Earl and Countess of Pembroke; actually the Earl and Countess of Plymouth were about to arrive. Rushing frantically to the dining room I shuffled the placecards while the guests were kept waiting.

Between the British and American Governments there was but one important issue: most of the Embassy dispatches dealt with the Bering Sea controversy. For some time I considered it very dull — three-mile limits, *mare clausum, ferae naturae, res nullius,* and quotations from Pufendorf and Grotius. The live roots of the question were almost totally buried under verbiage. Once a year the seals returned to breed in the Pribilov Islands, and while thus engaged thousands and thousands of them were slaughtered; often they were dynamited wholesale. The United States was afraid there would be no sealing industry left and Mr. Bayard, when Secretary of State, had put forth the curious claim that seals were domestic animals and that, since Alaska stretched on two sides of the Bering Sea, we had jurisdiction over the entire body of water. Accordingly, we had seized British sealing vessels and the British Government had promptly demanded damages.

After years of bickering and volumes of correspondence, the dispute had been submitted in February to a Commission of Arbitration. Nevertheless, the dispatches continued to fly to and fro; one day I had to write eleven communications to Lord Rosebery and three more to the Department of State, all in longhand. There was a typewriter, although a very early one, and Frank Hodson had only reached the stage in which his letters and copies were smudged and out of line.

The Commission decided against us in August, and from that moment Mr. Bayard exhibited less and less concern about the minor matters that developed. Once he entered my room where I was laboriously inscribing a dispatch in the ponderous book. "What's that you're doing there?"

"Writing up the archives, sir."

"Oh, you keep them that way, do you?"

"Yes, sir."

"Hmmmmmmm. Interesting." And he walked out. Apparently he was not even aware that we preserved copies of dispatches. He never asked me another question as to how the business was run.

On the whole the Embassy seemed to be conducted on a very informal basis. Hodson would spend any amount of time talking about Mr. Bayard's predecessors. His hero was James Russell Lowell, who had been accustomed to scribble his instructions in verse on scraps of paper, every one of which Hodson had treasured. He was always producing them:

> Oh, Hodson dear, I greatly fear,
> The time is coming very near,
> When you or I must sally out,
> And tramp the London streets about,
> To find tobacco of a kind
> To soothe an old man's tired mind.
> So hasten forth, and drop your chores,
> And try the Army and Navy Stores.

From the beginning White had been my real instructor in diplomacy. He knew everybody, went everywhere, and never came back from a week end without some information of value. One day he summoned me to his room. "Here's a request from the State Department. Some Senator is making a study of postal methods, and wants to ascertain how many letters a day are handled by the London General Post Office. We've had a reply that it's not in the policy of the British Government to give out such facts. Do you think you could get them?"

"Well, I've just been on a house party where one of the other guests was the private secretary of the Postmaster General."

"All right, you go talk with him."

I called on my newly-made acquaintance at the Post Office. He greeted me pleasantly, and we discussed our fine week end. Then I showed him the questions and a copy of the Foreign Office refusal. "There isn't anything very secret about those statistics, is there? You know, it's a black mark for us if we have to write home and say we're sorry, but we can't find out."

"It does sound damn silly, doesn't it? Leave your paper with me, and I'll see what I can do."

A few days later I had a message that my friend wanted to see me. He handed me the answer, adding, "Don't let the Foreign Office hear about this."

When I told White how I had obtained the memorandum, he grinned. "My boy, that's what diplomacy is — personal relations."

CHAPTER V

THIS HAPPY BREED OF MEN

I came back one August day from the Royal Squadron Regatta at Cowes to find that the season had collapsed almost overnight. The Queen was leaving for Balmoral, the Prince of Wales for Sandringham, and everybody I knew was following their example and departing for the country. As I passed through the deserted streets of the West End, I observed shutters going up on houses. The Bachelors' Club announced that it was closing for overhauling. The Embassy showed no sign of animation; the Ambassador himself was succumbing to the charms of rural life, and Larz was on vacation.

When the Winningtons asked me for a full week to Stamford Court in Worcestershire, there was really nothing to prevent my accepting. Generous permission was always given me to take advantage of such opportunities.

"Don't forget," warned Lady Winnington, "that we live a long way from the station, and you'll want a carriage with two horses for yourself and your valet." I had never had a valet, but I had seen notices on the bulletin board at the Bachelors' Club, posted by members who had gardeners, butlers, and grooms not needed for the time being. I secured a good retainer, twice my age, who kept me very much on my dignity. He telegraphed ahead for a team to be ready — such arrangements were part of the stationmaster's duties — and we set off in state.

At the end of a twelve-mile drive over steep hills we halted before a great Tudor house, and I was ushered into a room filled with people. Lady Winnington offered me tea, but introduced me to no one. I had been reared with the fixed idea of not speaking without an introduction, and, since most of the others were older, I did not feel I ought to push into their conversation. In silence I stood, first on one foot and then on the other.

I was glad to be shown to my room, although as a junior bachelor I was not given a very good one; it was tiny and had neither stove nor fireplace to take off the chill on damp mornings. In one corner, resting on a piece of flannel to protect the floor, was a tin sitz-tub, high in back but so low in front that only your seat could ever be covered. Inside it was a tin of cold water, and, if I wished a bath, my valet brought me a small pitcher of hot. The single bathroom in the house was reserved for women; rain or shine the men had to use an outside latrine.

That evening some twenty of us, of all ages, in full evening dress, marched ceremoniously in to dinner and were placed according to our stations. Conversation was stiff. After the ladies had left I found myself listening to an Austrian count and a tall, self-possessed Russian nobleman, who were discussing the desirability of maintaining punctilious relations with one's wife. "I've been married ten years," said the former, "and have never yet visited my wife's apartment without first sending my valet to inquire of her maid whether she would receive me." They both agreed that formality between husband and wife made for the happiest marriage.

Gradually the strain of the new surroundings grew less. Neighbors from near-by estates dropped in for a little music. When the local talent was exhausted, somebody turned to me, "Sing us one of your American college songs." I started with "Solomon Levi," and soon they were all shouting "Tra la la la la la la" to the chorus. I taught them other refrains, and in a half hour they were roaring in the friendliest manner at what they thought my peculiar interpretations of the English language.

At about eleven our hostess retired, followed by all the ladies, and the men, changing to velvet smoking suits, gathered for cards or billiards. We did not stop until after three. As I was walking along the hall on my way to bed, suddenly from the room nearest me came a woman's scream, "Help! Help!" Without pausing to consider whether it was the proper time for me to rush in, I flung open the door.

In front of me, leaning comfortably back in the sitz-tub, was the courtly but obviously very intoxicated Russian, still in full dress. He was merrily splashing himself and most of the floor around, apparently deaf to the lady's protests that he was in the wrong room. Plunging into the spray, I grabbed him under the arms, and dragged him into the hall. Then I carefully propped him, dripping and playful, against the wall. As soon as I heard the key of her door turn in the lock I fled to my own room and locked it also.

The next morning I rang for my valet, and stepped into the passage to see whether the Russian had disappeared. He was gone, but my attention was caught by the strangest calls from below stairs. "The American Ambassador is wanted. The American Ambasador is wanted." At breakfast Lady Winnington told me that the servants sat at table according to the rank of their masters, and referred to each other by their employers' titles. My valet had announced that I was the American Ambassador, and, consequently, had taken a seat of honor next to the housekeeper.

We were left largely to our own devices, but there was always something to do. During the daytime we played cricket, rode horseback, drove over to view ruined castles or monasteries, had lunch at neighboring houses. In front of Stamford Court was an artificial lake filled with carp, its banks marked in numbered sections. One afternoon we were all given identical tackle, formed into teams, and assigned positions. Sir Francis fired a gun and we threw in our lines. Whoever caught a fish rushed to the scales to have it weighed, and then hurried back for another try. Each of us had put up a sovereign and the winning side divided the pot.

After the first night we drew lots for places at dinner. On one evening we all dressed in fancy costume, on another we had an indoor coasting party. Collecting all the tin trays in the house we gathered at the top of the broad oak staircase. With a terrific clatter and bang the most daring young man skittered over the edges of the treads, skidded across the polished floor, and brought up against the wall. I found it took great skill not to upset. Later, to make the game more exciting, we chose partners and went down two on a tray; there could not have been a serviceable one left in the house. Lady Winnington was the most accommodating hostess imaginable.

For the week of the Doncaster races I stayed with the Galways at Serlby Hall in Yorkshire. The guest of honor was the seventy-two year old Duke of Cambridge, cousin of the Queen and commander-in-chief of the British Army; his bald head with enormous Georgian side-whiskers made him look like the engraving on an old coin. We had constantly to keep jumping up and standing at his appearance.

About three quarters of the way through dinner the Duke's head began to wag from side to side. I watched in fascination as it drooped over farther and farther, until at last it came to rest on the shoulder of the lady to his right. Not at all concerned, she continued her meal, although with some difficulty, because she had to sit bolt upright. My dinner partner whispered that the Duke was always placed between two ladies who knew his habits. The only question was whether his head would fall to the right or left. His son, Colonel Fitzgeorge, woke him as the table was being cleared and a fingerbowl set in front of him alone. The Galways liked to maintain the ancient traditions, affecting to believe that some pro-Stuart guest might drink a health to the "King over the water."

When we rose, as the youngest present, I hastened to the door to open it. I twirled the knob; nothing happened. Lady Galway and the old Duke waited behind me. I fumbled and fumbled but it remained fast locked. "I can't think what the young American has done with the door, sir," I heard Lady Galway say.

I felt the Duke peering closely over my shoulder. Then, with a roar of laughter, he burst out, "By Jove, the young American is playing a joke on us."

Fortunately, no one could see my face. Lady Galway, entering into the Duke's humor, suggested, "Let's go out through the pantry and turn the joke on him."

"That's just what we'll do," agreed the Duke.

As the last of the procession vanished, I found a little catch underneath the knob which I must have tripped with my finger. I walked into the hall and almost collided with the ducal party completing its circuit.

"Ha, ha, ha," boomed the Duke again. "That was a good one. The young American made us go all the way around!"

Horrified because everybody believed I had done it on purpose, I slipped in line beside Lord Kerry. On the threshold of the drawing room one of us happened to touch Lord Powys in the ribs. He was still laughing and assumed at once we were continuing the fun by taking advantage of his well-known ticklishness. He grabbed us both, and in two seconds we were all three rolling on the floor, while the old Duke stood over us, clapping his hands in delight, and exclaiming, "That's right! That's right! Get him! Splendid!"

After dinner Lady Galway thanked me slyly for my efforts to lighten the party. She said royalty were always a problem and told me about what a time she had had with the late Duke of Clarence a year or two before. In a game of "Twenty Questions" the young Duke had been sent out, and the rest picked as a subject Lady Roberts, wife of General Roberts of Kandahar, who had a reputation for her sharp tongue and dominating disposition.

The Duke began his questions, "Is it animal?"

"Yes."

"Is it human?"

"Yes."

"Male?"

"No."

"Do I know this female?"

"Very well."

"Is she beautiful?"

A loud chorus of "No-o-o!" left no doubt on that score.

"Is she dictatorial?"

Everybody believed he had the answer and shouted, "Ye-e-e-es."

"Oh, I know who it is. My grandmother."

Silence enveloped the room like a pall. The assemblage was shocked at the idea that a royal duke would consider them so disrespectful as to describe Queen Victoria as ugly and disagreeable.

That evening we all played Spoonerisms, a game in great vogue. The scholarly Reverend William Archibald Spooner, Warden of New College at Oxford, had once accidentally given out the first line of a hymn as "Kinquering Congs their titles take." The mistake was received by the congregation with such approval that he was said to have lain awake at night inventing other transpositions. He was responsible for "I have in my mind a half-warmed fish" (a half-formed wish), "a shoving leopard" (loving shepherd), and he was supposed to have ordered the porter on the railway platform to take care of his "two bugs and a rag." Everyone was making them. "Filled with contrition" became "killed with fruition," and "divinely inspired" became "supinely desired." These may not sound so funny at this distance of time, but then they convulsed us.

The English loved good puns. The story was told of Lady Cardigan in her youth that she never would ride in anything but the smartest hansom with the highest-stepping horse and the best-looking driver. Once, after a particularly spruce outfit had swung up to her door, she handed the cabby a fare far too large, remarking, "Young man, your horse, your carriage, and you are so perfect I'd like to keep you always."

The quick-witted driver replied, "The same to you, Milady."

If it were a royal pun it was bound to be a success. Dr. Playfair, the court *accoucheur*, had just returned from Rumania, where he had safely delivered Queen Marie, daughter of the Duke of Edinburgh, of an heir to the throne. A family council was being called at Buckingham Palace to decide on the reward. His elder brother was already Lord Playfair. They could not agree on a title for him. Finally the Princess of Wales spoke up. "I know. Why not call him Lord Deliver-us?"

On one day during the week we did not go to the races and a rabbit drive was held. Rides were cut through the bracken and a gun stationed at the entrance of each. I stood in my place, ready for the exact second when the streak of rabbit should cross. Something flashed before my eyes, I pulled the trigger, my quarry fell.

There was a tremendous to-do, but no congratulations. I had committed the unpardonable sin of shooting a fox. Had I not been so young, and an American to boot, I might have been sent home in disgrace. To visit the MFH (Master of the Foxhounds) and kill a fox in his own park brought me most undesirable notoriety. Forty years later I was introduced to a woman who, taking one look at me, remarked, "Oh, I remember you. You're the American who shot the fox while staying with Lord Galway."

Lord and Lady Powys asked several of us to come back with them to Powys Castle just over the Welsh border. The fun continued even more unconfined because of the ingenuity of Lady Blandford, the daughter of the Duke of Abercorn, in devising practical jokes. Americans had to get used to the English humor in which someone customarily served as butt. All London was then laughing at the dinner contrived by a celebrated wag. The guests arrived

and the presentations began: Mr. Higginbottom, I should like you
to meet Mr. Bottomly; Mr. Winterbottom, I know you will enjoy
meeting Major Sidebottom of Nether Wallop; Parson Ramsbottom,
Mr. Wedbottom. All the "bottoms" he could find in London had been
invited on one pretext and another for this occasion. The *pièce de
résistance* was rump steak.

Lady Blandford soon selected as a victim Lord Powys, and enlisted Lady Powys and me as aides. After much plotting Lady Powys
announced that a certain Mrs. Goring had rented a house near by
and must be asked to lunch. Lord Powys assented, fervently vent-
ing the usual protests of a husband against social duties.

The morning of the luncheon we three conspirators retired to
the sewing room and the ladies set to work on me. They let down
as far as possible one of Lady Powys' dresses, a green silk with
frills, and, to round out their efforts, stuffed packages of cotton
inside the bodice. Then I had to sit and sit while they experimented
with paint and powder on my face. The stubble on my chin, however, remained evident, and at last they gave it up. A wig and a
plumed hat still did not disguise me enough, and they swathed me
in folds of veil.

A half-hour ahead of time I was spirited from the house by the
back door into a carriage, driven through the park, and deposited
at the front entrance. I minced into the drawing room, where Lord
Powys greeted me courteously and, after one disgusted look, turned
away. At lunch I was seated between him and Brown-Guthrie. I
tried to eat as delicately as I could under my veil, not encouraging
conversation, but Lady Powys was not going to have the fun spoiled.
At the first pause she leaned towards me, "Mrs. Goring, have you
any children?"

"Yes, three little dears," I answered in muffled tones.

"May I ask how long you have been married?"

"Two years," I replied without considering.

I felt every eye at the table shift in my direction. Only politeness kept the company from attempting to satisfy their natural
curiosity. I realized I would have to laugh and, to finish the prank
with a flourish, I hastily threw both arms about Brown-Guthrie.
On his face came an expression of utter horror; he thought I must
have gone mad. At that moment Lord Powys, catching on, let out a

furious yell, and made a dive for me. Brown-Guthrie joined in with a will. Off flew my veil, my hat, my wig, and in a second we were all three in a heap on the floor. I was thoroughly beaten up.

The moment that I landed in Dublin on my way to visit Charley Crichton, I discovered that humor bubbled over everywhere. The driver of my jaunting car jollied his acquaintances on the street, and at a full gallop turned around to shout a parting jibe. Then he started a race with another car, and off we rattled hell-bent neck-and-neck to the railway station. I had not had such an exciting ride since my trip to Trondhjem.

Mullaboden, some twenty miles distant in the Wicklow Hills, lay in the great hunting district of County Kildare. For a younger son, Charley had plenty of money, and saw to it that we all had a gay time. The house was filled with Irish girls — livelier, wittier, and more natural than any I had hitherto met in England — as well as with English officers from the Curragh, the military station a few miles away. In Charley's coach and four we drove to Punchestown, the merriest race meeting in the world, and the next day we went after otter, an exhausting ordeal. We had to run along the banks of a small river while the hounds splashed in and out of the water in chase of their prey.

My real introduction to Irish hunting life came when I stayed with the Listowels halfway across Ireland at Convamore on the Blackwater, near Cork; their eldest son, Lord Ennismore, was Master of the Duhallow Hounds. Instead of a valet I either had to bring a horse or hire one from Cork. A good hunter was expensive, but I found a gray which I thought would do. Early in the morning we gathered, all of us in top hats and some in scarlet coats — only those invited by the Master were entitled to "wear the pink." The hunt was a pretty sight as it streamed off through what was perhaps the stiffest hunting country in Ireland.

Suddenly I faced my first Irish bank, and my heart rose in my mouth. Fields were divided by two ditches, about five or six feet apart, and usually filled with water; between them the earth was piled in a rampart. My horse got his forelegs on the top of the bank, dug his hind ones into the slippery sod, hauled himself up, paused on the summit, and then plunged down and over the other trench.

I negotiated several small banks successfully and was beginning to feel a little more confidence in my mount when I was confronted by a gigantic one. I tried to rein in to look for the easiest place to cross, but my horse, abruptly taking charge, tried to "fly the bank" in one leap. His head cleared the ridge but he struck with his knees. His rear shot up and we somersaulted together. As he rolled on me, he kicked me viciously in the side of the head, and only my top hat saved my life. A few of the hunt stopped to find whether I had been killed; seeing me struggle to a sitting position they tore on, and my horse with them — I never laid eyes on him again.

For the moment I did not care. My head was throbbing. Blood was pouring over my face. Gently I patted it and discovered that a bit out of one ear was missing. I had no idea where I was, except that I was miles from home, but finally, after some of the dizziness had left me, I took my bearings from the sun and stumbled across the fields. At the first road I flopped down until a cart came along and gave me a lift into Cork.

The driver was delighted to have a hunting casualty as a passenger, and pointed me out to all his friends. By the time I had reached the railroad station an admiring crowd was following me and, as I mounted the steps of the train, my head still bloody and my topper smashed flat, they set up a rousing cheer. Later the English *Field* published a column describing the exploits of the wild American on the gray hireling from Cork.

To gamble to the limit, drink more than the limit, and start a brawl at the drop of a hat — that was the Irish idea of a perfect day. I had heard there was no better rough-and-tumble than the Tipperary races, and persuaded an English subaltern to accompany me on the long train journey. Farmers for miles around had collected, each with his corncob pipe, a bottle somewhere about him, and a few shillings jingling in his pocket.

Towards nightfall the subaltern and I crowded into a first-class compartment, intended for eight but already holding double that number, all Irish except ourselves, and fighting drunk. They recognized my companion as English, and with howls and yells they piled on top of us. Soon I was choking and gasping; the officer was limp and livid and had obviously fainted. Summoning my strength, I shouted, "I'm an American."

Those nearest me drew back at once, and I sat up, saying, "Look here! Haven't we Americans always been friends of you Irish?"

"What about that bloody Englishman?" muttered a surly voice.

Our assailants did let me get him to a window; I held his head out and he gradually came to. Continuing black looks and sullen curses made me afraid they were on the verge of roughhousing us again, and I knew my friend could not stand any more mauling. Acting on the principle that music hath charms, I proposed, "How would you like me to sing you an American song?"

They greeted this suggestion enthusiastically. I began with " 'Way down upon the Suwanee River . . . .," followed by " 'Twas from Aunt Dinah's quilting party . . . ," and then went on with everything else I could think of. The effect was far beyond my expectations. One red face after another fell back against the seat and, except for scattered snores, calm descended. Believing the danger was over I let my voice die away; instantly somebody awoke and grunted "Phwat are ye shtoppin' for?"

I started my repertoire anew, but my voice was cracking and we still had a long way to go. "What town are you bound for?" I croaked at the fellow beside me.

"Ballyhoura."

I managed to keep grinding out tunes until we slowed up for the next station. There I poked my head through the window and yelled in my best Irish accent. "Ballyhoura! All out for Ballyhoura!"

The compartment heaved, and the door opened. One by one our companions lurched onto the platform, and, pushing the last one out, we locked ourselves in with a sigh of relief. As the train gained speed I could see them looking around in bewilderment. I had no more idea of the real name of the station than they.

The parties at Convamore were boisterous and gay, but apparently they were pink teas compared with those of the old days. The Earl's sister, Lady Sophia MacNamara, one of the Queen's ladies-in-waiting, told me that in her girlhood her father expected every young man who came to a dance to get drunk; any who went home sober were not asked again. Once the male guests were prostrate on the floor, her mother herded the young women together; they lighted their candles, and, stepping carefully over the bodies lying about the hall and stairway, proceeded silently to their rooms. The next morning the men were gone, the house in order, and her parents congratulated themselves on a thoroughly successful entertainment.

Lady Sophia and I were walking in the garden one evening when she produced a short little black pipe. Leaning down, she scratched a match on a stone, and remarked she was sorry she was unable to strike it on the breeches in true Irish style. She puffed away expertly. "I'm trusting you, young man. Don't tell the Queen on me."

Everyone knew the Queen abhorred women's smoking, and Lady Sophia was sometimes hard put to it to enjoy a quiet smoke. At Balmoral she had a cubbyhole in the bookcase, hidden by a false backing of bindings, where she kept her tobacco. One day the Queen, who took the kindliest interest in her staff, and had a habit of paying surprise visits to see what they were doing, entered the room unexpectedly. "I hope, my dear, you have everything you want. I notice you have a fine collection of books."

Lady Sophia watched in terror as the royal eye roamed over the titles. If the Queen had tried to pull out one of the counterfeit volumes, her day at Court would have come to a speedy end.

After a week at Convamore all the young people traveled North to Crum Castle, the seat of the Earl of Erne, Charley Crichton's father. The plump, bald old Earl, head of the Ulster Orangemen, was a mine of amusing stories, and the Countess, though in appearance of ample size and stern demeanor, in reality had the gentlest and most lovable nature. A London wit had dubbed them the "Storied Urn and Animated Bust."

In the midst of our merriment at the first dinner the Earl rose to his feet, rapped on his finger bowl for silence, and then solemnly proposed the Orangeman's toast: "Here's to the great and glorious memory of the good and pious King William, and he who will not drink this toast, may he be rammed, damned, jammed into the big gun of Athlone, and shot into the furthermost corner of hell and the key of hell in the Devil's belly . . ." and so it went on. It struck me as the most ridiculous lot of balderdash, but I did not dare laugh.

At night we played hide-and-seek on the roof of the castle, dashing in and around the innumerable turrets and chimneys, inching along the ridgepoles, until the girls' dresses were grubby and torn. Almost every day we had a water fight; Crum was on Lough Erne, one of the largest and most beautiful lakes in Ireland, stretching for forty miles between the hills. Each boy scoured the place for any weapon he could find — a mop, a broom, a gardener's squirt that would throw a stream a dozen feet or so. Then, taking his best girl to steer him, he stepped into a canoe, and paddled forth to join one of the opposing lines. He singled out an opponent, set his mop in rest, his partner dug in her paddle, and the battle was on. Even if we tipped over we climbed on top of our canoes and continued the attack, jabbing at our enemies, trying to dodge in and tip them over also. The last crew left upright won the prize.

Sunday morning the entire countryside sailed to the church on the little green island in the middle of the Lough. At the chiming of the bells, from all along the shore boats of every description put out and converged on this same point. Ours bore the pennant of the Lough Erne Yachting Club, operated with the formality of the Royal Squadron at Cowes. I had been elected a member and wore my uniform with the rest.

The five sons of the Earl strode up the aisle and took position side by side in the front row. The clergyman, who was also their tutor and the Earl's librarian, began the service. The boys allotted him ten minutes for his sermon; when he had spoken for five they brought their watches out and held them open, one eye on the hands and one on the preacher. The moment the time was up — *Crack!* the covers snapped shut simultaneously. If he did not stop — *Crack!* they went again. After the second warning he knew enough to finish hurriedly.

The congregation dispersed and embarked once more in their boats. Back at the castle we watched the neighbors going home — scraps of white blowing across the blue below us, matched by bits of cloud in the sky above, and the ring of green between.

CHAPTER VI

HOLIDAY'S END

"Gie us a penny for the Guy," clamored the little boys in the London streets. With the coming of November, England was about to celebrate the anniversary of the Gunpowder Plot, and I my twenty-first birthday. Father paid me my thousand dollars, and Larz gave me a dinner to introduce me to alcohol and tobacco; we had claret which I liked, and champagne which I did not.

My birthdays always seemed to coincide with the end of good weather. Soon it was growing dark by three, even darker than in America because of the pall of smoke. One morning I awoke to find the fog had closed in during the night. I could see it and smell it in the room, and when I started for the Embassy the air was yellow with the smoke which could not escape. In Green Park everything familiar was swallowed in a flat, uninterrupted monotone — no paths, no landmarks, nothing. To keep my course I had to bend over double and run my hand along the cold wet iron railing, eight inches high, that bordered the path.

As I was crawling forward, practically on all fours, my head plunged into something soft. Startled, I jumped back and then my eyes focused on the gleam of brass buttons. The solid stomach of a bobby had stopped my progress.

"Bad weather," I remarked.

"It's bad and it's wet, sir."

"How can I get to Victoria Street?"

"Easy. Follow the rail until it ends. That's a cross-path. Pick it up on the other side and go on for two more paths; turn right and take your first left, and there you are."

For a full quarter of an hour I painstakingly obeyed his instructions. Then once more, without warning, my head collided with a yielding mass. "Sorry," I apologized.

"What, sir, you back again?" queried a voice I recognized. I had circled around to bump into the very same bobby.

On the next attempt I reached the edge of the park, where I had to climb a lamp post to make sure I was going towards Victoria Street. Vague figures loomed in front of me and vanished mysteriously. I held my hand tight over my wallet for fear of the thieves and pickpockets who, I had heard, swarmed out of the slums at such times, because they could snatch a purse and in a few feet become invisible to their victims. As I fumbled along the street, men with lanterns hugging the curb lighted the way for the great horse buses.

At the Embassy Larz and I now had all the work to do; White had resigned and his successor had not yet arrived. However, no new diplomatic issue arose to worry us; we had to rely for our excitement on the visiting Americans, among whom were always a certain percentage of cranks and lunatics. One day Hodson brought in a woman who insisted she must speak to the Ambassador. I thought I detected a strange glint in her eye, and advised him not to receive her. He was in a soft humor: "Oh, show her in. If she's in trouble I ought to see her."

Presently a scream and a call for help broke the silence. Hodson and I rushed to the rescue to find the woman with her arms locked about the Ambassador's neck, while he huddled in his chair exclaiming, "Mr. Griscom, get this woman out of here." We each took an arm and between us dragged her away. The Ambassador delivered me a generous piece of his mind for admitting her, but after that he was more inclined to follow my advice as to whom he should interview.

My turn to be mishandled came not much later. A powerful, wild-looking young fellow with his arm in a sling swaggered in and arrogantly demanded, "I want a ticket to New York."

"Are you a sailor?" I asked.

"I'm a prize-fighter."

"Sorry," I replied mildly, "the Government provides only for repatriating sailors stranded at a foreign port."

At this he grew very angry, bellowing, "Give me the money!" and the next instant I felt a huge paw around my throat. Still shouting, "Give me the money! Give me the money!" he banged my head against the wall several times, holding me so tight I could not even whisper.

Suddenly the pugilist's grip loosened, and he collapsed into a chair, white as a sheet. When we had both recovered our breaths, he said I must excuse him — he had not eaten for forty-eight hours. He had been brought over by his backers to face the English champion in his class. The fight had taken place two nights before in a London hall, and he had been knocked out. As day was dawning he had come to, completely alone on the platform, stiff with cold, his right arm throbbing with pain. At his lodging house he discovered his trainer and backer had already departed for America with the proceeds of the fight; he had not even sufficient cash to pay the doctor who had set his broken arm. Though the man had nearly choked me to death, I was very sorry for him, and arranged to pay his passage home from a private fund maintained for such a purpose by a number of wealthy American businessmen in London.

Often girls sojourning in England to study art or music were left penniless. One tall, slender, large-eyed young brunette, who would have been extremely attractive had she not been so haggard, told me a pathetic story: as a result of a cold she had lost her voice, her sponsor had stopped sending her money, and her parents were too poor to help. She had had no food for days, and unless we could assist, her only recourse was to go on the street. Upon investigation I learned her landlady had confiscated her baggage. Everything the girl owned was on her back, and she said she had not had a change of underclothes for two weeks.

The fund supplied enough for a ticket. "Would you rather have some of my old underwear than none at all?" I asked, and she accepted gladly.

I dug up an ancient and damaged portmanteau, initialed L. C. G. in bold black letters, and, with my undergarments packed in it, she set off, professing undying gratitude. She promised to let me know how she fared, but — as nearly always in such cases — I never had so much as a line. For some time I was worried lest my bag be recognized, and I wondered how her family would welcome their ewe lamb attired in ram's clothing.

To replace White in May arrived James Roosevelt Roosevelt,

known to his intimates as "Rosy." Soon afterwards his wife died and his cousin, Anna Roosevelt, Theodore's elder sister, came over to take care of his half-grown boy and girl, and to act as his hostess. She was intellectually brilliant, having no great claim to beauty but an abundance of vitality, and possessing an immense capacity for getting on with all sorts of people. Her friendship was one of the most valuable I acquired in England.

In the spring our battleship *Chicago* called at Gravesend, but we at the Embassy thought nothing particular of it until we received invitations for an official dinner by the English to Captain A. T. Mahan. "Who is this Captain Mahan?" we inquired. Our English friends were astounded that we had not heard of the author of *The Influence of Sea Power on History,* the volume which set forth and proved that England's eminence had been won, not because of the victories of Marlborough or Wellington on the battlefields of Europe, but because of her mastery of the sea.

Very curious, the Embassy staff attended the dinner *en masse.* A number of English praised Captain Mahan's book, and a little short man with a square beard rose to reply. Before he had been speaking five minutes I, like everyone else, was struck by his dry humor and originality of thought. I nudged my neighbor, "Who is that?"

"Why, that's John Hay," he answered, as though surprised at my ignorance.

You had to live in England to appreciate how rare it was to find Americans held in such high esteem as Captain Mahan or as well-known as Mr. Hay. Few English then traveled in the United States or had American friends. It was quite uncommon to meet one in English houses; the old Duchess of Buccleugh boasted that she had never had one under her roof and intended to die without doing so.

The longer I stayed in England the more I was impressed with the apparent permanence and security of its social structure. For generations England had been ruled by the landed aristocracy. At the top of the pyramid were the dukes, who owned a large portion of the land, and whose fabulous incomes were as yet not materially diminished by taxation. Socially they were set apart, not only from the lower classes, but from the knights, the barons, and even the earls. The Duke of Buccleugh, on his way out of an Edinburgh club, once asked the hall porter: "What do you think of the weather? Is it going to rain?"

"It might or it might not, Your Grace."

"Well, what does that little instrument up there say about it?" The Duke raised a tentative finger; anybody who sees a barometer wants to tap it.

"Oh, no, Your Grace. Come with me." And the Duke was conducted down a passageway to another barometer. "Here, Your Grace, this is the one."

The Duke tapped it. The needle shifted satisfactorily. As he was again preparing to go out he asked, "What's the matter with this barometer you have here by the door?"

"Oh, Your Grace, that's the one we keep for the members to tap; it hasn't registered for years."

The Emperor William of Germany used to remark that the position of an English duke was the greatest in the world. It was said that His Grace of Argyle had once turned his back on the Prince Consort rather than walk behind him. The entertainments of the Duke of Devonshire, one of the three wealthiest men in England, were bywords of magnificence; no one refused invitations to Devonshire House, and the Prince of Wales himself frequently was to be seen there. During the season of 1894 the effect of the panic was being felt by shops, hotels, and restaurants. One afternoon while the Duke was enjoying his regular rubber of whist at the Marlborough Club, the Prince accosted him, "I say, I'd like you to give a big party. Tradesmen are beginning to complain. It would stir up business."

"I'm sure my wife will be delighted, sir," agreed the Duke perfunctorily, his mind still on the cards.

"What about next Tuesday?" pursued the Prince. "We could dine with you then."

"Very good, sir."

"If I don't hear from you, I'll consider it settled."

"Quite so, sir. Quite so."

Late the following Tuesday afternoon the Duke's private secretary was stopping work for the day, when suddenly there came a message that the Prince would wear the Garter at dinner that evening — he was sending the usual warning so that the other guests would wear their decorations also. This news was a bombshell to the secretary. He knew of no dinner and rushed off, gasping, to tell the Duchess.

"Find the Duke," she ordered.

The Duke, routed out of his game at the Club, at first remembered nothing, and then, under pressure, recollected, "Yes, perhaps the Prince did mention something to me about a party."

Meanwhile, the Duchess's chef was tearing his hair, and her servants were running this way and that. Finally everything was arranged for — except the guests. The Duchess, looking over her invitations, found that Lady Londonderry was entertaining formally that night. "Will you help me?" she asked.

"Certainly," replied Lady Londonderry, "I'll bring all my guests to dine with you."

The Duke was sternly instructed not to be late. Actually, he descended the stairs adjusting his newly bestowed Garter as the Prince and Princess were ushered in the door. No one but an English duke would have forgotten that royalty was coming to dine.

However, the landed nobility of England were not a useless excrescence on society. They inherited the responsibility of caring for their tenants and, in the majority of cases, they and their families were loved and respected. The tenants liked to have someone to whom they could refer their problems with assurance of help. This patriarchal system had taken such firm root that it seemed impossible for any change to be effected.

I had seen the difficulty confronting any reformer in politics the previous September at the division in the House of Lords after the second reading of the Home Rule Bill for Ireland. The Commons had passed it the week before. Usually the place was absolutely deserted, but now, out of the five hundred and sixty members, four hundred and sixty were on hand; only a coronation or an impeachment could have caused such a turnout. Peers were standing in the aisles. According to the English press, some were in their dotage, some had to be wheeled or carried in, one or two were even slightly deranged mentally and were delivered at the entrance by their keepers. Nobody had to listen or understand. At the right time those who did not know what was going on could be pushed through the correct door and have their votes counted. Four hundred and nineteen voted against; only forty-one were for the affirmative.

The signs that this era of contentment was nearing its end were evident for anybody who could read them. I was in London when Asquith, the Home Secretary, opened up Trafalgar Square for the first time to labor meetings. I watched the procession tramping from the slums of Whitechapel and Rotherhithe under police escort. Although the marchers seemed to me like the miserable unfortunates of Hogarth's "Gin Lane," they were orderly enough — waved their banners, mounted their soapboxes in Hyde Park, and exercised peacefully their right to demonstrate. The wretchedness of the poor had not yet become a political issue; it was cared for by the devotion of private individuals and charities.

Nevertheless, in spite of its responsibilities, the English aristocracy lived a life of apparent leisure. There were always companions available with whom I could play tennis, shoot, hunt, amuse myself. We in America had plenty of men with more than wealth enough to spend their days in pleasure-seeking had they so desired, but most of them preferred work to play; they had never learned how to enjoy themselves. For years Father took time from his business only on Saturday afternoons and Sundays, and at most a two weeks' holiday in summer.

I began to wonder whether this existence, agreeable as it was, would really help me in my future career. I was perfectly well again. I could have stayed on with Mr. Bayard, but as soon as the next President was inaugurated I should probably be left high and dry. It was hard to think of tearing myself away from England. However, when Father came over in my second summer I told him I had made up my mind to resume my law studies that fall. He agreed. By this time, he was the directing head of a considerable fleet of vessels — he had bought the old English Inman Line, had added to it new ships, and shifted his headquarters from Philadelphia to New York. Galbreath Ward had joined with Randolph Robinson and Charles Hough to form the New York firm of Robinson, Biddle, and Ward; Father and I decided my best course was to enter their office, and to train there for the New York bar.

Early in September, 1894, I made my last trip to the Embassy, regretfully said good-by "until next season" to my friends, and sailed for home.

Before I had been on American soil twenty-four hours I had a commission from Father. The *St. Louis* was to be launched in December, and he wanted me to persuade Mrs. Cleveland to christen the first American-built liner. "If you've learned anything at all in diplomacy, you won't return from Buzzards Bay without an acceptance."

It seemed rather a severe test to me. I had never met either of the Clevelands, and everyone knew the President's dislike of publicity, especially with reference to Mrs. Cleveland — reporters had made his life unbearable during his honeymoon, spying on him from trees with field glasses. However, I set off for Cape Cod.

Only one hack was at the Buzzards Bay station. While I was telling the driver where I was going, a man tapped me on the shoulder. "We're both apparently bound for the same place. Do you mind if I ride with you?"

"Certainly not," and we climbed in together. My companion was Isador Straus; although a staunch Republican himself, he wished to talk to the President about his Democratic brother Nathan's candidacy for Mayor of New York. I was interested in the way the Straus family mended each other's fences. Oscar, the third of the trio, had turned Mugwump in the 1892 election, and been rewarded by President Cleveland with the mission to Turkey.

We were received by Mrs. Cleveland, who appeared scarcely older than I, and gave the impression of being a sweet and gentle person. Explaining that the President was fishing, she settled Mr. Straus comfortably to await his return, and then suggested to me, "We might as well go for a walk until the President and Mr. Straus have finished."

She showed me the bay and the fishing boats, and I described Father's efforts to put the American Merchant Marine on the high seas, and how much it would help if she would christen the *St. Louis*.

"Well, I'm not sure whether the President would let me."

"Don't you think you could persuade him? You know, you'd get a very nice present."

"I'd like to, and I'll back you up as much as I can."

We arrived at the house just as the President and Mr. Straus were ending their conference. Mr. Cleveland made everybody around him seem small; he was an enormous man with powerful face, penetrating gray-blue eyes, and heavy drooping brown mustache covering a firm mouth. He looked like a fighter; I should not have cared to be in his ill graces. Fortunately, the fish had bit well, and he was in a high good humor. Eying me quizzically as I made my request, he promised to make up his mind after election, and sent me off with a reassuring smile.

In due course I was established in New York. My days I spent in Robinson, Biddle, and Ward's office, earning ten dollars a week; most of my evenings were passed at the New York University Law School lectures. One December afternoon, however, I stood on the launching stand with Father and Mrs. Cleveland — and even the President himself was there. The supports were knocked out from under the *St. Louis,* the champagne bottle was smashed fair on the bow, the stern slid smoothly into the water, and Mrs. Cleveland walked away with her beautiful present.

Father thought a shade better of diplomacy.

CHAPTER VII

THREE GRINGOS

One evening in January, when the wintry winds were whistling up and down Fifth Avenue and dirty snow was heaped high along the sidewalks, I came out of the Croisic Apartments and crossed Twenty-sixth Street to Delmonico's restaurant. Since returning from London I had fallen into the habit of joining Dick Davis there for dinner, provided neither of us had any other engagement.

Nodding to Delmonico, who was sitting at one side where he could watch over his establishment, I walked through the mirrored room with its red hangings to the table which Dick always occupied. He was deep in discussion with a tall, good-looking boy whom he introduced as Henry Somers Somerset, a friend from England. I noticed that at sight of me the subject of conversation was abruptly changed. Somerset began talking about his trip through Athabaska — he had just written a book called *The Land of the Muskeg*.

All during dinner I observed Dick fidgeting, and from the gleam in his eye was certain a scheme was brewing. He managed to contain himself, however, until the waiter had brought coffee and gone. Then, leaning closer, he almost whispered, "If you can keep a secret I'll tell you something. Sommy and I are leaving tomorrow to expose the Louisiana Lottery."

The Louisiana Lottery was as familiar in those days as the Irish Sweepstakes now. In spite of the steadily growing moral condemnation of gambling in any form, advertisements appeared regularly in the program of nearly every theater in New York, urging readers to make their fortunes by buying tickets. Not much excited I asked, "How do you know there's anything to expose?"

"Well, it was a stroke of luck. A few nights ago a fellow whom I'd once met in a smoking car in Texas recognized me here, and said if I wanted a good story I ought to go to Puerto Cortes on the northern coast of Honduras. There I'd find one of the greatest frauds that ever existed. Lloyd, it's a really terrible thing," he continued. "The whole United States is honeycombed with the Lottery's agents. Thousands of poor people are putting their money in it and being cheated. It's a national disgrace."

Dick described how a quarter of a century before a group of unscrupulous promoters had procured a charter from the State of Louisiana, and, to make the venture seem respectable, had hired as directors two unemployed former Confederate generals, Pierre Beauregard, the captor of Sumter, and Jubal Early, the raider of the Shenandoah. The Lottery had been taking in hundreds of thousands of dollars from the public until finally the Government had forbidden it the mails. When Louisiana refused to renew the charter in 1890, its owners had decided to quit the United States. Honduras, which had a debt of such proportions that revenue from any source was welcome, agreed to let them use Puerto Cortes as a base of operations.

"The men who are running this won't stop at anything. If they discover we're trying to blow the lid off their lottery, it may be dangerous for us. We'd like to have another person along. Why don't you come?"

"Can't possibly. I have to study law."

"You can make up what you lose after you get back. From Puerto Cortes we intend to ride right across Honduras to the Pacific, and then cut through Panama and home by way of the Spanish Main."

I was greatly tempted; the thought of exploring the jungle, the chance of falling in with filibusterers and soldiers of fortune, the possibility of joining a revolution — that was what Central America meant to all of us. However, I was sure Father would never permit me to interrupt my law again for a pure pleasure trip. Suddenly I remembered that a few nights before Father had told me he had been offered the presidency of a company to build a canal across Nicaragua, a much shorter route to California than by way of Panama. Now it occurred to me that I might win Father over by suggesting I investigate the Nicaragua canal for him. The three of us composed a diplomatically worded telegram, containing the proposal. I had no real hope of success but to my surprise Father wired back: "GO AHEAD."

We sat up all night making plans, and next morning I dashed

around New York buying rifle, money belt, sola topee. Hurrying to Philadelphia I collected riding clothes and an emergency medical kit from Dr. Gerhard. To give me some standing among my literary companions, I persuaded Charles Emory Smith of the Philadelphia *Press* to certify me as a special reporter and, taking advantage of my diplomatic connections, secured a letter from the State Department recommending me to the good offices of all diplomats and consular officers I might meet.

Within a few hours, instead of being bound to my books at the law office, I was southward bound on another adventure. At New Orleans the three of us dined at Antoine's on oysters *à la Rockefeller,* and the following morning strolled down Canal Street to the wharves where the *Breakwater,* a small banana boat, was preparing to cast off. On the dock a cadaverous individual approached Sommy deferentially and said the baggage was all on board; it was his valet, Charlwood — I had never seen anyone who appeared less fitted for roughing it, but Sommy would not have dreamed of going without him.

We stood on the bridge and, shivering in an icy norther, watched the levees winding ahead of us. Over the tops we could see sugar cane plantations, and here and there a mansion house shrouded in live oaks and Spanish moss. As the sun set in flaming red and yellow, we steamed from the delta into the jade-green waters of the Gulf of Mexico.

Dick insisted that on the voyage we should not mention our mission to the other passengers, who, for all we knew, might be agents of the Lottery. They had the hard look of men who could handle guns. We heard that one had been hounded out of Honduras for murder, and was only returning because there had been a revolution.

After four days we dropped anchor off the tiny port of Belize, the capital of British Honduras. As a good British subject, Sommy departed to pay his respects to the Governor, Sir Cornelius Alfred Moloney, K.C.M.G.; as good Americans we went to present our letters to the American consul. With a bottle before him he was slouched over his office desk; the tropics had been too much for him.

Thoroughly shocked, we wandered back to the *Breakwater* to find Sommy already there — the Governor had been out. To console ourselves, we were planning for a wonderful dinner ashore when there was a swish in the water and a man-of-war's launch swept alongside, Union Jack whipping in the breeze, brass glittering, and gold-braided officers saluting. Sommy was invited to dine with the Governor. He rushed into his evening clothes and was whisked away, leaving Dick and me to the wretched ship's fare and visions of him reveling in luxury. The instant he stepped on board once more, very dignified in front of the crew, we made a dive for him. Each of us seized a leg, and we dangled him over the side by his heels, threatening to toss him to the sharks if he ever deserted us again. Not until he admitted that he had invitations for us also to Government House did we haul him up.

We lunched in state with Sir Alfred, sitting in great red leather chairs monogrammed *V.R.*, while liveried blacks served us curries and rice. From one month's end to the other the only Englishmen the Governor usually had to talk to were his secretary and a handful of British merchants. Greedy for every crumb of news from the outside world, he made us take all our meals with him during our two-day stay. As for the last time the launch ferried us to the steamer, he stood on the lawn wistfully watching us; we were sorry for him, chained to that God-forsaken spot.

To be able to say we had visited Guatemala, we went ashore for a few hours at Port Livingston, but by now our interest was focused entirely on what awaited us at Puerto Cortes. From the deck we scanned the harbor line, half expecting a row of sentinels would be on hand to keep off intruders. All that met our eyes was a native village of mud huts with thatched roofs, a customs house, a jail, a barracks, and a cluster of frame houses almost pushed into the water by the jungle.

Peering curiously about, we landed and joined a group of other passengers. As we started up the single main street, one of them pointed to a fairly large frame house with verandas, shaded by slender palms. "That's the Louisiana Lottery."

We stopped to stare at our den of iniquity — right by the road, no drawn blinds, no guards, merely a venerable gentleman with white hair and a goatee rocking on the porch. He noticed us and came to the gate. Dick recovered himself first. "Can you tell us where the hotel is?" he inquired.

"Just up the street, but we have plenty of room here. My wife and I so seldom see Americans that we would be delighted to have you stay with us."

Somewhat shamefaced, we were demurring when a little old lady hurried down and would not accept No for an answer. In a few minutes we were actually installed as guests in the house of the Lottery. Without our even asking, the couple showed us the glass wheel, as tall as I, and made us turn it; two of us could barely budge it. As we heaved at the handle, the hundred thousand small rubber quills with tickets inside bobbed and bumped and shifted.

Our host answered every question we could think of, his reports including the exact amount of profits and a description of how the winning numbers were picked out by a blind Indian girl. There did not seem to be the slightest chance for cheating. Instead of exposing a colossal fraud, we bought tickets ourselves and wrote letters home on the official stationery.

Still rather crestfallen, we proceeded to the hotel to make arrangements for crossing to the Pacific. The only railroad in all Honduras had been built inland from Puerto Cortes forty miles to San Pedro Sula, to carry bananas; beyond that we should have to fend for ourselves. While we were sipping planters' punches, we struck up a conversation with a thickset, powerful fellow, who said his name was Charles Jeffs, a mining engineer by profession, and on the side a colonel in the Honduran Army. He regaled us with tales of the revolutions in which he had participated during eleven years, and, on hearing about our trip, he offered to act as guide, procure us outfits, take care of everything. Without further ado we engaged him.

The next morning we watched Jeffs ride forth with his cavalcade — four *mozos,* or muleteers, and eleven mules, five for us and the rest for the baggage. We climbed on the last of the three cars of the train — no glass in the windows, narrow bare wooden seats piled with tortillas and bananas. The rusty old engine squeaked off at eight miles an hour.

Soon we grew tired of gazing at banana plantations, and searched about for something more exciting. Two negroes were sitting on the cowcatcher to sand the rails in slippery spots. At the first stop Sommy and I bribed them to give up their places to us. Dick as eldest pre-empted the sand box, and we scrambled up on either side of him, holding on as best we could. The conductor warned us to be ready to leap if the train jumped the track, as it often did.

Ahead of us the line was overgrown with vegetation and wobbled alarmingly; the instant we ran on a rail the far end rose several inches. It was a test of nerves to cross one of the wooden bridges, covered with moss, hung with lianas, and thoroughly rotten in appearance. Often for a hundred feet below us there was nothing but space. We closed our eyes, clinging tightly to anything we could get our hands on.

Every now and then the sun was shut off and we puffed through what seemed to be a tunnel. The coconut fronds arched overhead; higher still stretched gigantic sixty-foot sprays of the manaca palms. The green filtered light was streaked with flashes of yellow, blue, and red, marking the flight of tropical birds frightened by our approach. Marvelous orchids of unimaginable colors and fantastic shapes hung, drooped, clustered from the trees.

In front of the station at San Pedro Sula the station agent was waiting, a sheaf of waybills in his hand. "Good Heavens!" exclaimed Dick. "The last time I saw that fellow he was leading the cotillion at Newport. Later he took to drink, forged his father's name, and had to leave the country."

The agent pretended at first not to know Dick, but finally, realizing it was useless, acknowledged the greeting and ended by inviting us to supper. Outside his house two little half-breed children were tumbling about. A mulatto woman, who could not speak English, joined us at table, silent and apathetic.

Under Dick's prodding our host at length told us his story. After having been an actor in South America and a bootblack in Australia, he had ended up here. He declared proudly he had not touched a drop of liquor in two years, but we wondered whether alcohol were not preferable to "going native." All the three hours we were there the woman sat with unchanging expression and poked at a beetle, turning it on its back, letting it crawl over her hand.

With relief we departed for the hotel, run by a very nice middle-aged American woman, the widow of a botanist, who had accompanied her husband to Honduras to study the flora. His death had left her penniless and her great dream was to return to the joyous life of a Brooklyn boarding house. Although we could not afford to help her, we gave her our lottery tickets and wished her good luck. Later we saw the list of winning numbers. She had missed by one.

In four days Jeffs was ready with the mules and we set off, armed to the teeth; the only one who did not look like a brigand was Charlwood. Dick declared we were almost a revolutionary army in ourselves and should organize a government. Accordingly, he announced he would be Commander in Chief. Since Sommy was heir to the Beaufort dukedom he should be president; Jeffs naturally was the Military Attaché, and I, due to my Naval Reserve experience, was Chief of the Admiralty.

The main road and the mail route to Tegucigalpa, the capital, was a narrow trail which led straight up the side of a mountain, sometimes so steep that we had to ascend in steps hewn in the rock. The little mules were marvelously surefooted, and carried us unfalteringly over rolling stones and slopes where a man would find it difficult to find support.

We alternated mountain climbing with hacking our way through the jungle. In places the trail was so rarely used that we had to cut off overhanging branches and tangling vines with our new machetes — made in Birmingham, England. There were no bridges. When we reached a river, Jeffs would take the lead mule's rope and pull him into the water; the *mozos* would prod the others after him. Sometimes we were swept far downstream and had to slash a passage back to the trail through every conceivable kind of growth.

Crowds of chattering monkeys swung across the path, playing, breaking branches, throwing things, screaming like a lot of schoolboys. I shot one of them and it came tumbling to the ground, crying "Oh, Oh, Oh, Oh!" just like a baby that had been hurt. I hastened to put it out of its misery, but I was sickened and ashamed of what I had done. I never shot another.

So many creeping and flying things bit us that we were driven nearly mad. Each time we brushed against a tree our arms were sprinkled as though with grains of red pepper. These were the tiny ticks called *garrapatas,* which buried their heads in our skin, and, if we did not get rid of them, festered and formed small ulcers.

We would often ride ten hours, the mules plodding along at a snail's pace, a hard and wearing gait. Our saddles were ill-formed and rubbed us raw. Charlwood proceeded all day long in solemn dignity, not speaking unless addressed. Although we treated him as a friend, he could not forget he was the valet and butler, and it must have been painful for him to sit down and eat with us. To every request or order he replied invariably, "Very well, Sir," and was never too tired in the evening to clean our boots.

Exhausted as we were at nightfall, immediately on dismounting we had to pick off the *garrapatas,* and make a thorough search for "chiggers." We were cautioned particularly against this species of flea, which generally worked under the toenail and deposited a nest of eggs in a sac. As this grew the toe swelled and, if the sac broke, we were told the least we could expect was the loss of a foot. Once I was so tired that I flopped down on a wooden bench and leaned my head on the adobe wall. Suddenly I felt a sharp blow on the cheek like the stab of a knife, and looked around to see a scorpion darting back into his crack. The bite puffed up instantly, but fortunately it was not much worse than a hornet sting.

The *mozos* greeted us one morning with the news that a mule had gone lame from a poisonous spider bite. In a little while the hoof rotted away, sloughed off, and the animal died. A few days later we found another with a great hole in its neck and the blood running over its chest and foreleg. A vampire bat had attacked it, and had bled it so white that it could hardly walk.

One evening Sommy called us to inspect his great toe, which he complained had been itching. It seemed a little swollen and red. "Come over and look at this," we said to the *mozos.* With one accord they shouted *"Chigre!"*

We were horrified — out of reach of any possible help and Sommy in danger of losing his foot if not his life. He was the only one who did not appear worried. "You have the medical kit, Lloyd. You'll have to operate."

I discarded all the sharp instruments available in favor of my razor. While I was preparing a tourniquet and dressings a *mozo* started water boiling. Sommy stretched himself on a blanket, I rolled up my sleeves and planned carefully the direction of the incision — go in back of the swelling, round in a deep curve, out again the same distance away. The *mozos* pinned the leg fast to the ground,

I daubed the toe with antiseptic, dipped the razor in the boiling water, took a firm grip and a long breath, and sank in the blade. Sommy yelled and cursed bloody murder, but I kept right on and, with one slice, carved off a goodly portion of the big toe. Then, as quickly as I could, I tied on the tourniquet and bandaged the wound.

Even Sommy sat up to watch the autopsy on the hunk of tissue. I cut a slit, and there was the sac of minute, round, pure-white eggs, still unbroken — the operation had been successful. The next day Sommy was able to limp about and stay on his mule.

Up in the bare mountains the sun was blistering hot and we used to wait eagerly until we came to a stream. If inspection proved there were no steep drops Dick, a powerful swimmer, persuaded me to shoot rapids with him. To save our heads from rocks we would float feet foremost; soon the current would catch us and sweep us dizzily downward as though we were on a toboggan. Jeffs and Sommy would watch us from the bank, calling warnings that the alligators would get us; nothing would induce them to go in, and they jeered at us while we plucked off the inch-long leeches.

A few days after leaving Santa Barbara, the largest village on our route, we heard of a bullfight only fifteen miles off our road. It was an opportunity we did not intend to miss. As we rode into the outskirts of the village all the houses were hung with strips of colored linen. Women in their silk mantillas were hurrying towards the plaza which, barred by a seven-foot barricade of logs, bound together with vines, had been turned into a ring. We climbed to the upper rail and dangled our feet.

In a cloud of dust a group of horsemen galloped in, dragging a bull by its horns and heels. About a dozen men fell on the poor beast, tied his head to the lower rail of the barricade, and wound him round and round in a network of lariats. One of them, with spurs on his bare feet, settled himself on the bull's back, catching the ropes with one hand, and the animal's tail with the other. The lasso that held its head was cut, it scrambled to its feet, shook itself angrily, and tried vainly to reach its rider. The crowd howled, picadors darted in with spears and jabbed the bull. Bucking and pawing, it started up and off at a frantic gallop, but if it approached dangerously near anyone the man on its back, by some contortion difficult to follow, dropped a cloak over its eyes.

Dick could never sit on the side lines long. "Help me get a picture of this," he urged. Nothing loath, we dropped into the ring, hugging the bars in case of necessity. The bull's rider apparently was able to use the bull's tail as though it were the tiller of a boat, and the next thing we knew a whirlwind was charging at us. Dick's attention was riveted on the camera finder. "Tell me when it's close enough."

Imitating Dick's calm, Sommy and I waited until the beast was hardly more than twenty-five feet away. Then we yelled, and shot up and over the bars just as the bull crashed into them. The sight of us tumbling on the ground in our high boots and helmets sent the audience into roars of delight; obviously they took us for an added attraction. We glanced about to find Dick convulsed with laughter too. He had side stepped the bull's charge to snap a view of our rears disappearing across the rails.

After the bull was thoroughly played out, the matador strutted up and stuck in a *banderilla* behind its shoulder. No one thought of killing such a valuable animal; it had been imported from Spain and was needed for the next "baiting."

As we jogged on our way, we had constant talk of bandits and insurgents. Dick often drew Jeffs out, and on exhausting that well, started talking himself, squaring around in his saddle so that Sommy and I could hear. He was inventing a story concerning a millionaire American who had put his money in mines in the interior of Central America and engaged a very attractive engineer — you could not miss the resemblance to Dick — to go down and face the difficulties. In time, the owner himself arrived with his lovely young daughter on his big yacht to discover the country on the verge of revolution. Later this plot formed the basis of *Soldiers of Fortune*.

One night we were riding along in the moonlight, Sommy reciting from memory "The Walrus and the Carpenter" while we corrected. We had just reached " 'The night is fine,' the Walrus said, 'Do you admire the view?' " when suddenly from the shadows to our right sounded a sharp command, "Hands up!" At the same instant a bullet hit the ground near us and we saw a rifle muzzle gleam over a rock fifty feet distant. Popping off our horses on the far side Sommy and I started a fusillade at the rock.

In about thirty seconds we heard a familiar voice screaming, "Stop! Stop!" Our revolution turned out to be only Jeffs. He emerged trembling, and sheepishly admitted he had been trying to scare us.

It was almost three weeks before we rode down from the hills across a bare red stony plain and into the cobbled streets of Tegucigalpa. We passed house after house of adobe, with iron-grilled windows extending over our heads. The capital was a primitive place; clearly no tourists ever visited it, and there was no sign of business activity. We dismounted in front of the hotel and, to our surprise, some dozen people disentangled themselves from chairs and hammocks to investigate the clatter. Learning we were fellow Americans, they greeted us with open arms. Though we could not imagine what they were doing in this out-of-the-way corner, we accepted their invitation to a celebration banquet that evening.

Dinner started with tepid champagne — Honduras possessed no ice-machine — and under its warming influence tongues were loosened. We were informed that one of our hosts had been State Treasurer of Louisiana, and had absconded with several hundred thousand dollars; another was wanted in Chicago for the murder of his wife. All of them proved to be fugitives from justice, taking advantage of the fact the United States had no extradition treaty with Honduras. We found them very pleasant company, and so did our fellow guest, the Honduran Minister of Finance.

In a few hours we knew everybody in Tegucigalpa, and had a message from President Bonilla to call at the Palace at eleven the next morning. We made ourselves as presentable as we could, but the Chief Executive in his shirt sleeves gave us a remarkably informal audience. He began by showing us a bullet cut out of his arm during the revolution, which he carried on his watch chain. Afterwards he conducted us on a personal tour of the premises. In the big ballroom we noticed a number of holes, newly plastered, and he pointed proudly to the portrait of a uniformed figure which had been neatly decapitated. "I did that with my artillery," he boasted.

Since it was no more than a three-day easy ride to the coast, we said good-by to Jeffs and continued on by ourselves. On reaching San Lorenzo, a mere clump of huts on the Bay of Fonseca, we hired a native boat to transport us to the island of Amapala, where the steamer for Corinto, Nicaragua, was due. Through filthy streets we made our way to the steamship office, only to be told that the port was quarantined for yellow fever.

We had done many foolhardy things on our trip, but now we were really panicky. Yellow fever was worse than smallpox — horrible and swift and almost always fatal. We determined that, quarantine or no quarantine, we would get out even if we had to swim. We walked around among the fishermen by the water front, and finally located one who for a price would take us to Corinto. His craft was nothing but an enlarged rowboat with no deck, and did not look able to stand the Pacific combers. Nevertheless, he claimed it was seaworthy, and we preferred to risk shipwreck rather than yellow fever.

In the twilight we started — five of the crew, four of us, and a pile of canvas in the stern. The night descended pitch-black. We had no compass, but the steersman seemed to be confident of his own ability to guide himself by the stars, and we soon had something far worse to worry about than losing our way. As we neared the mouth of the bay, our bow began to spank the waves, and in no time we were pitching and rolling so that we could not sit on the benches. We had to huddle in the bottom of the boat, packed against the ribbing so tightly we could hardly move.

The churning motion made us all seasick. The waves splashed over the side but we did not notice them. The next thing we knew a woman emerged from under the canvas in the stern; our predicament became embarrassing. The one humorous note was poor Charlwood's unsuccessful attempt to maintain his dignity while seasick.

Dawn found us on the open Pacific, out of sight of land. The day wore on; although the waves died down, the blazing sun turned the interior of the boat into a pit of heat. If we looked over the sides the reflection from the burnished sea made us dizzy. We thought the voyage would never end, but at last, as the sun was dipping low once more, we rounded the point into Corinto Bay in Nicaragua.

Because we were arriving without health certificates from a yellow fever port in another country we hoped to slip up to the wharf unnoticed. However, the people on the dock spotted us immediately as strangers, and crowded round, sure we had been shipwrecked. They could not believe that in an open boat we had accomplished one of the roughest crossings along the coast. Unfortunately the word "Amapala" promptly brought a file of soldiers who marched us off to quarantine. We sent word to our consuls; on reading my letter from the State Department the American official arranged for us to stay at the hotel, provided we were tapped and jabbed for symptoms every day.

In order that I might fulfill my commission we obtained a dispensation to journey to Managua, the capital, where we were received by the President and the cabinet, and I talked to everybody about the canal. The consensus of opinion was that the prevalence of earthquakes would make the necessary locks impracticable.

We returned to Corinto to wait for a Panama-bound ship, and, to amuse ourselves, we crossed the harbor to the ocean beach where a magnificent surf was curling in. Dick challenged us to follow him and, quite undeterred by the warnings of the natives, we stripped and jumped in, diving over and under the waves. All at once a yell peeled out from behind us, and simultaneously we caught a glimpse of a dorsal fin cruising in our direction. With one accord we leaped shoreward. Panting, we saw the great shark swerve and glide out to sea. Again and again we dashed in, keeping careful watch, plunging to safety on the nearest comber each time a fin veered towards us. It was a daredevil game to try how far we could go and not lose a leg in a shark's mouth.

When the *Barracouta* put into Corinto I looked for her Plimsoll Line; it was several feet under water. Her decks were heaped high with lumber, and below there was scarcely room for us, because most of the cabins were filled to the ceiling with sacks of coffee.

The captain lost no opportunity to complain of his miserable ship. She should have been condemned years before. Her engines were so worn out she could make no more than six knots. He had informed her owners repeatedly of her unseaworthy condition, but their answer to every new leak had been to empty bags of cement in the holds. The entire bottom must have been from one to five feet thick with solid concrete. Not long after reaching home again I read in the newspapers that the *Barracouta* had sunk with all hands.

Luckily on our voyage we struck the most perfect weather — hardly a ripple except where endless schools of porpoises splashed and chased each other. Once we came to a stretch of sea covered with enormous turtles, fully three feet in diameter, which flippered lazily away at the noise of our approach.

Our trip was interrupted only by a short stop at Costa Rica and in six days we sighted the curving Bay of Panama, fringed with balconied houses set on piles. A few months previously, the second Panama Company had been organized by the French, who were trying to erase the memory of the de Lesseps scandal, and were planning to start operations again. Dick was prepared to write about dredges abandoned on the banks, engines rotting in the swamps, locomotives half-buried in mud, wrecks of deserted boats on the shore. Instead, the machinery had been raised from the ground and was protected by a great wooden shed; there were even signs of work going on. The sole mementos of the old failure were the rows on rows of crosses beneath which were buried the armies of laborers slain by yellow fever and malaria.

Finding no excitement on the Canal, we walked along the sea wall; underneath were dungeons for prisoners, many of them political. Leaning over the parapet, we could see, stretched out through the bars, a line of hands holding mirrors. In no other way could the inmates catch glimpses of the faces of their callers. We threw money down to them, and there was a tremendous scrabbling for the coins.

It occurred to me that if I could get in touch with revolutionaries who were still free, I might write an article about the Liberal Movement; and, leaving Sommy and Dick at the hotel, I paid a call on our consul general. He admitted a revolution was brewing but that was all I could elicit from him. However, I was more successful with his son, who said he thought he could arrange an interview for me with a leading revolutionist. We started towards the Bay, my guide glancing warily about him to be sure we were not observed. Finally he ducked into one of the houses overlooking the water, where a young man received us in an office lined with law books. The consul's son mumbled hastily, "Señor Rojas, Mr. Griscom," and disappeared.

My revolutionary was a Cornell graduate, and we had a common bond in diplomacy — he had been secretary of the Colombian Legation in Paris. Without urging he launched forth in a tirade against the existing Government, and was on the point of confiding his plans for the next attempt to overthrow it when suddenly a squad of soldiers burst into the room. "Señor Rojas, you are under arrest. You must come at once," snapped the officer in command.

"Where's the warrant?"

"We have none."

"Then under the Constitution you cannot arrest me."

The officer, grumbling, dispatched two men for the warrant; the others remained on guard in the outer office.

"Well, they've got me," Rojas announced philosophically.

This was better than one of Dick's lurid tales. "Anything I can do?" I asked.

"Perhaps you could send me some cigarettes at the prison."

I looked at the waves lapping at the piles beneath us. "Suppose there were a boat under this window. You could drop into it and row out to the *Barracouta*."

He brightened up. "Wouldn't that get you into trouble?"

"I've friends here. We'd like to try."

"It's too great a drop without a rope."

"I'll do my best to slip one to you."

Gathering together the incriminating papers on the desk, I stuffed them in my pockets and then, as nonchalantly as possible, I departed, on the way asking permission of the officer to bring Señor Rojas some dinner. He offered no objection.

I ran like fury to the hotel and breathlessly described to Dick and Sommy what had happened. They were not going to be left out of a revolution, and entered immediately into the spirit of the adventure. While they were ordering dinner I rushed off to buy a thin strong rope. This we wrapped around a big pie, covered the whole tray with a napkin, and bribed a waiter to carry it. Sommy, who did not put much faith in our own consul, told Charlwood to notify the British consul if we were not back by midnight.

The soldiers, I was afraid, would suspect something when they saw three of us, but we passed them unchallenged, trembling in our shoes lest they lift the napkin. Inside Rojas' office we blocked the doorway and motioned vehemently towards the tray. Rojas, still calm and unhurried, talked casually as he extracted the rope and hid it behind his law books. We thought he never would get it out of sight. Finally he scribbled on a piece of paper which he then handed over to me, "Don't come before dark or the harbor boats will stop you."

In the deepening dusk we hastened down the street to the wharves, and in a hired boat crept cautiously along under the overhanging balconies. We could not have been more than half an hour, but there were no lights in Rojas' office. Fearing the worst, we pushed close beneath the wall, and I gave a low whistle. Instantly rifle barrels protruded from the window and a voice called, "*Quién vive?*" We held our breaths until all was quiet again, then rowed silently away.

The next day we asked the consul's son to find out whether we could do anything for the prisoner. Rojas wanted nothing but cigarettes, and we sent him a thousand, doubting whether he would live to smoke them. Years later I noticed in an American newspaper a picture of Panamanian officials; one of them was Rojas.

The result of our dabbling in local politics was that we could not step from our hotel without being shadowed by swarthy figures. The consul advised us strongly to move on to Colón, where the warship *Atlanta* was in harbor and could protect us if necessary.

No sooner had we reached Colón than I was seized with the most awful dysentery. I ached all over, my head weighed like lead, my temperature was one hundred and five degrees. Dick, terrified, summoned a doctor who waved his hands, muttered "Chagres fever," dosed me with quinine and morphia, told Dick I had very little chance of living, and went away.

Dick and Sommy decided the single hope of saving my life was to smuggle me on board the small French liner sailing that night for La Guaira, Venezuela. They did not dare let anyone suspect what was the matter. Unable to stand on my own legs and only semi-conscious, I came-to just enough to realize I was being walked up the gangplank between Dick and Sommy, one of my arms caught over the neck of each and my head wobbling uncontrollably from side to side. Apparently everybody supposed me a merrymaker who had overcelebrated his departure.

I was brought to myself again by the sound of angry vociferations from a bearded man in a dressing gown who proved to be the ship's doctor, furious because when we were well at sea Dick had had him waked. Attempts to placate him being unsuccessful,

Dick too lost his temper. The doctor stamped out, slamming the door behind him, and refusing even to leave any medicine.

Things looked so queer and distorted that I wondered whether I were in my right mind. I could not sleep and asked Dick to tell me a story. Although I was barely able to follow him, if his voice ceased for an instant I begged him feebly to keep on. Tale succeeded tale, interrupted briefly for a drink of water or a few mouthfuls of food. At last some twelve hours later he said, "Well, Lloyd, I think that's the end of my true stories. Do you mind fiction? Did you ever hear about the time I was with the English regiment in Gibraltar?" And he embarked on a string of the most preposterous yarns.

Dick continued talking for twenty hours before I fell into a gentle sleep. The next day I awakened weak as a rag, but the crisis was past.

At Cartagena I peered out through the porthole at gray walls, gray church towers, the gray home of the Inquisition in the New World, and I thought of Amyas Leigh and Salvation Yeo and the other characters in *Westward Ho!* I was up and about by the time we steamed into the harbor of La Guaira, walled by precipitous mountains and dotted with the vessels of our Atlantic Fleet under Admiral Meade. The capital, Caracas, was only a short distance away over a railroad which had to go three miles for every one, around hairpin curves and across dizzy gorges.

Dick's literary fame had preceded him. The Venezuelans wanted him to do something to counteract their reputation for revolutions and absconding presidents who carried into exile enough millions to live in Paris happily ever after. By everyone, from President Joaquín Crespo down, we were feted and entertained. We spent some lovely days at haciendas in the country, and there we were introduced to a green and yellow fruit served in halves with French dressing. Dick's epicurean taste took to the avocado at once, and he arranged to have a basket delivered to his cabin on the steamer.

The climax of hospitality came when we were informed by the Minister of Foreign Affairs that the President had conferred on each of us the Order of the Bust of Bolivar, the Liberator, of the Fourth Class. Dick had heard of Bolivar, but neither Sommy nor I had even suspected his existence. Although we felt somewhat self-conscious about accepting decorations for which we had rendered no services, they made magnificent souvenirs.

Among the invitations was one to lunch with our Minister, a former mayor of Burlington, Vermont. He seemed a bit under the weather and surveyed us woozily with glaring eyes in which the pupils were contracted to pin points. In the middle of the meal he reached towards the castor, emptied the contents of the vinegar cruet into a glass, and swallowed the liquid. Apparently it made him feel better. We went away certain he must either be drunk or drugged.

The next time we saw our Minister was at his reception in honor of Admiral Meade and several hundred officers of the fleet. He looked very pale, began turning whiter and whiter, and at the height of the function collapsed and had to be carried out. The son of the Minister of Foreign Affairs told us that several nights previously he had been picked up in the street unconscious, and spent a night unrecognized as a drunk in the public jail.

The following day we were lunching with Admiral Meade on his flagship at La Guaira. He was shocked at the behavior of the Minister, and declared it was an insult to the Navy and a disgrace to the United States. He had decided to report it officially. "My difficulty is," he continued, "that the State Department's likely to regard a complaint from me as prejudiced. The Navy rarely gets on with diplomats. I want you, as American citizens, to perform a public duty and back me up in writing."

Dick and I were a little uneasy, but we did as he requested, and in the excitement of going home forgot about it.

Laden with machetes, knives, pith helmets, and other treasures, we boarded a Red D. Liner a few days later. All the way to New York Dick kept a watchful eye on his basket of avocados, and as soon as we landed carried them straight to Delmonico's. The best one was cut in two, the dressing added, and Dick watched anxiously until the old restaurateur's face relaxed in an approving smile. Delmonico was so enthusiastic that he ordered a regular supply for his restaurant, and in this way the alligator pear was introduced into America.

We had been back some months before we heard the end of our Central American trip. I received an official note from the White

House, saying President Cleveland wished to see me at once. Completely mystified, I took the train to Washington and was told that the President was in residence on the outskirts of the city.

When I reached the large grounds they were deserted — no Secret Service operatives, no workmen, no sign of life. I rang the bell but waited vainly for any response. The front door was ajar and, although it seemed odd to walk right in, I could think of nothing else to do. I clumped loudly into the hall, coughed, glanced in several rooms — no one there. Finally I opened a door and was confronted by President Cleveland, who was pacing up and down the library. He appeared startled. "Are you looking for somebody?"

"The President."

"I'm the President," he replied, obviously not recognizing me.

"Yes, I know. I rang but no one answered."

"That's the kind of house this is. Come in. What can I do for you?"

"I'm Lloyd Griscom. You sent for me."

Mr. Cleveland's face became serious. "I understand you've brought charges of improper conduct against our Minister to Venezuela."

I tried to tell the President what had happened, but he shook his head vigorously. "The Minister is about to sue you for libel. He is one of the distinguished citizens of Burlington, and has submitted irrefutable evidence of good behavior and regard. You say he took morphine. Well, you'll have to prove it. I'm bound to stand by my man until his guilt is beyond question."

Feeling as though a bombshell had exploded under my feet I hurried back to New York. It was some consolation to find that Dick too was being sued. An anxious letter arrived from Admiral Meade, hoping we would stand by him. In short order came a summons and a suggestion to Father's lawyer that we settle out of court for a fabulous sum. Dick and I had visions of most unpleasant publicity, and were thoroughly upset and nervous. The date for the trial was drawing very near when, like a bolt from the blue, a communication reached me from the State Department, announcing that the Minister to Venezuela had been removed from office, and thanking us for our public-spirited action.

It seemed the Minister had swaggered in for an interview with

Secretary of State Olney, and declared belligerently that he was going to exact full damages for the gross libel on his character. Suddenly, in the midst of a torrent of abuse, his head had fallen forward and he had dropped asleep in his chair; to brace himself for the interview he had taken an overdose of his drug. This had been his undoing, but Dick's and my salvation.

CHAPTER VIII

THE INS AND OUTS OF LAW

Nine o'clock. The office door at Robinson, Biddle, and Ward opened and shut a dozen times as we apprentices in the law hurried in, exchanging the usual morning quips. We hung up our coats, pulled down our books, and silence descended. Passing the examination for the New York Bar was a serious business, and in April, 1895, I had little more than a year in which to prepare for it.

However, we were rarely left undisturbed. A voice would call, "Griscom, Mr. Ward wants you to go to Jersey City and try to locate witnesses to the ferry accident where the man had his leg broken," or "Emerson, see what precedents you can find on such and such a point," or "Everett, will you carry Mr. Hough's bag to the Federal Court." Since our firm handled all the accident claims against the American and Red Star Lines, the Pennsylvania Railroad, the Third Avenue Street Railway, and other large concerns, we students earned our keep.

Running errands in an active law office gave a far more practical legal education than dry lectures on theory or abstracting cases. One day I arrived in court with a paper for Mr. Ward, to hear him cross-questioning a man with long gray hair and goatee. The venerable witness was testifying graphically that he had seen the driver of a particular horsecar deliberately whip up his animals as a child stepped in front of them. He told his story in such a straightforward manner that the jury swallowed it hook, line, and sinker, and assessed heavy damages against our client.

Shortly afterwards, I was in court during a case in which the plaintiff was seeking to collect damages for injuries from a sign which had blown down on his head. From all the evidence we could obtain our defendant could not have anticipated such an accident, and we expected he would be let off lightly. Suddenly, to our surprise, the prosecutor summoned to the stand that same old man with the gray goatee. With the same air of honesty as before, he related how he had been walking along the street, and had noticed that the hooks which held the sign hanging from the bar above him had spread very wide. In fact, the sign had seemed so insecure that he had turned around for another look; at that second a gust of wind had lifted it off, and dropped it on the plaintiff's head. As in the case of the horsecar driver, the jury was completely convinced of our client's gross negligence.

Mr. Ward suspected there was more than met the eye in the double appearance of this witness. He sent us out to search court records, and we found several other instances in which this man had just happened to be passing by when someone had been hurt. In brief, he was making a profession of calling on firms handling such claims, and offering to testify for a consideration.

As luck had it, the ubiquitous old fraud figured a third time in an accident case which we were defending. The moment he took the stand Mr. Ward started to cite chapter and verse. "You were a witness here, and here, and here." The jury was so angry that we won hands down.

Our legal education was helped considerably by the kindly interest shown by the partners in our progress. Once a week one of them would invite us to dine and afterwards test us in a particular branch of the law. The session usually ended with a general laugh at some of the classic legal anecdotes — such as that of a noted English judge who was interrupted during a trial by a huge mass of plaster which fell with a crash beside him; his only comment had been *"Fiat justitia, ruat coelum."*

The friendly and witty encounters of Edward Everett and Judge William Story, the two leaders of the Boston bar, were the sources of many other puns. On one occasion Story had spoken first, concluding his address with "Genius triumphs wherever it goes."

Everett sprang up: "Gentlemen, however I may strive or work I can never rise above one story."

Everett's grandson Leo was one of my fellow students at the office and shared my apartment at the Croisic. He had much of his grandfather's humor and was a fine musician; it was pleasant to return from lectures and hear him play the piano. Sometimes we spent an evening with Sam and Helen Bettle, who also lived at the Croisic.

Helen had been making a serious study of art, frequenting museums, galleries, and auctions, and was recognized as the expert of the family. She persuaded Leo and me to accompany her to the greatest sale of the winter, to watch the collectors bid against one another.

We squeezed into the gallery. Helen began pointing out artists and critics, and telling us what each painting ought to bring. Most of them climbed high in the thousands. From guessing the final prices, it was an easy step to joining in the early stages of the bidding. Leo was not very keen on the idea, but, since he had the loudest voice, he agreed to act as mouthpiece. When a Watteau started at a thousand, we whispered to him, "Go ahead. Say two." Somebody instantly topped it with three, and we dropped out. This was such fun that we tried the game again and again, each time getting a little bolder, because Helen always seemed to know where to stop.

Finally, a fairly small canvas was put up, showing a circle of naked nymphs dancing in a sylvan glen.

"What am I offered for this exquisite example of the art of Nicholas Lancret?"

"One thousand," came a voice from a corner. Helen remarked, "It's sure to reach twenty-five," and I directed, "Go on, Leo, bid." With our help the price mounted to eight, still a long way from twenty-five. "Give it a good jump," we said to Leo. "Ten thousand!" he shouted in stentorian tones.

Complete silence. In a few seconds the pause grew ominous. Without attempting to solicit other bids the auctioneer merely rattled off, "Going once, going twice, going three times. SOLD! — To the gentleman in the gallery."

We looked at each other in dumb amazement. Helen and I between us had not ten thousand dollars in the world. This was Friday, and we had to pay on Monday. We held a council of war in my room over scrambled eggs — Father was our only hope, we concluded gloomily. Accordingly, we planned a regular campaign to make him Lancret-conscious. Pulling out Helen's art books we spent most of the night memorizing everything they contained about him.

The next day the three of us arrived at Dolobran for lunch. Helen immediately launched into a description of the marvelous talents of Lancret. I chimed in, observing how well-suited Dolobran was to his country fairs and pastoral scenes, and Leo mentioned some of the high prices his works had brought at sales in the past. We seized every opportunity to drag Lancret into the conversation all Saturday, and up to the last minute on Sunday before we had to return to New York. Then Helen screwed up her courage: "Father, we'd like to talk to thee."

He took us into his den, probably supposing we were out of pocket money. "Father, we've a surprise for thee. At the sale last Friday we saw a wonderful Lancret which was exactly what thee needs for thy collection. If it had gone to its full value we would never have dared bid it in without consulting thee, but when it stopped at ten thousand it was such a bargain we felt we could not let it slip."

"You mean you've spent ten thousand dollars and you expect me to pay it," sputtered Father. "I never heard of such colossal cheek. Of all the damn fools!" But in the end, as he always did, he backed us up and paid the check. The Lancret was delivered, hung in a prominent position, and everybody was delighted with it.

Several years later Ned Berwind, a great art collector as well as a coal baron, dined with Father, and afterwards the two walked around the picture gallery. In front of the nymphs Mr. Berwind halted and pointed. "Good Lord, Griscom, you can't afford to own a thing like that. Why, I was at the auction where that was sold. We all knew it was bogus. You'd better get rid of it as fast as you can."

Father sent the painting off to his art dealer and it was disposed of further West. He never reproached Helen and me, or told us how much he had lost on it.

In New York, I did not stay up all night as in London nor did I try to include several parties in an evening. Since I was working hard, and had only a limited time for amusement, I preferred to pass my leisure with Dick and his friends — Edward H. Sothern, Stanford White, Charles Dana Gibson, Thomas Hastings, John Drew, Ethel Barrymore, Maude Adams, and Helen Benedict. Dick could not sell a story, receive a check, have an acquaintance come to town, without using the occasion as a pretext for a party. Often I arrived for tea before Dick's other guests, to find him sorting out

photographs from a bureau drawer. I would have to sweep clean
the shelf around the room, already lined with the faces of feminine
admirers, and help him arrange the new selection. The ladies to be
present would indubitably look to make sure that their pictures were
on display.

Dick's friends really comprised a remarkable group. Each was
an artist in his own field, but more than that each had his individual sense of humor, from the buoyant, rollicking high spirits
of Stanford White to the whimsical Peter Pan-ishness of Maude
Adams. One day I wired Maude according to my customary form:
"My son Lloyd wishes me to ask you whether you will lunch with
him at Delmonico's on Tuesday. CLEMENT A. GRISCOM."

My use of Father's telegraph frank had become a standing joke.
She wired back: "Maude says to tell Pansy to tell Augustus to tell
Lloyd that she accepts with pleasure" — and also signed it "CLEMENT
A. GRISCOM."

The witty Helen Benedict, who was one of the best women whips
in the coaching world, was responsible for some of our most original
parties. Her father, the old Commodore, had bought a plot of land
on Long Island Sound where he wanted to build a house. He
summoned wreckers to remove the tumbledown hotel already occupying the site, but instead of offering him something for the
structure, they prepared for him an estimate of how much he would
have to pay them to cart it away. When he had lost his temper and
sent them packing, Helen volunteered, "I'll tend to it for you if
you'll give me a free hand."

"Go ahead," he growled.

She invited thirty of us for lunch. Afterwards axes were distributed to the men, hatchets to the women, and we were turned
loose to break and chop and splinter as we liked. It was a delicious
feeling to walk up to a big mirror and shiver it to pieces, to pound
holes into a perfectly smooth plaster wall, to bring an ax down on
a bureau and see how many drawers could be smashed at one blow.
We kept at it until we were exhausted and then, at dusk, Helen took
a match and lit a gigantic bonfire. As the heavy beams crashed to
earth and the sparks flew, we cheered with all our might. Rarely was
the human craving to destroy so completely satisfied.

Dick's imagination was as busy as ever devising pranks. One

afternoon, having received a message to come to his rooms at Twenty-eighth Street, I discovered him and Robert Howard Russell, a publishing friend of ours, rummaging through the Central American trophies. Dick greeted me. "You're going with us to rescue John Drew from Harlem. I've just had a letter from him telling what a terrible time he's having there — eating all alone and cut off from his friends."

Harlem in the Nineties was another world; only a few pioneers lived as far north as Seventy-second Street. Since morning Dick had been preparing a Stanley-Livingstone party to venture into the wilderness beyond. At noon he had sent a telegram, "Natives from interior of Harlem report having seen Davis Relief Expeditionary Force approaching Central Park. All well." A two-o'clock message read, "Relief reached Eighty-fifth Street. Natives peacefully inclined. Awaiting rear column led by Griscom."

Even had Dick not already committed me, I would not have missed the fun for anything. Bobby Russell had his colored man enlist a friend, and we drew on Dick's Egyptian spoils to transform them into full-fledged African warriors — turbans, gold capes, sashes stuck full of swords and daggers. We three got ourselves up as explorers with sun helmets, high boots, long gauntlets, and bandoleers of cartridges over our shoulders.

Waving his assagai, George hailed an astounded cabby, and we piled in, shouting and brandishing our guns and revolvers. On the way north we stormed a telegraph station to transmit a final message of hope to John Drew, "If you can hold the audience at bay for another hour we guarantee to rescue yourself and company and bring you back to the coast in safety. Do not become discouraged."

Soon after ten o'clock we arrived at the stage door of the theater. The attendant thought we were lunatics and forbade us entrance with our weapons. Dispatching George with a note, we sat flourishing them, and in a few minutes some of the cast rushed out and escorted us in. Dick caught sight of John Drew standing in the wings, and in a few seconds the actor was locked in a tight embrace. He did succeed in extricating himself and answering his cue, but he was so overcome by amusement that he could not speak his lines. The manager had to ring down the curtain, leaving the audience to decide for itself how the play was to end.

As Drew retired offstage Dick stepped up and said, "Mr. Drew, I presume," and the reply was promptly returned: "Mr. Davis, I believe. I am saved." Then we all let out a yell and executed a war dance.

When the time approached for the bar examinations, Leo and I bought copies of the questions asked in other years, and started a systematic review of the subjects we expected to be quizzed on. Only on the last night did I discover to my horror that I knew nothing about bailments — that is, the law covering storage places. However, since according to the old papers our ordeal did not begin until ten, I stayed up until two cramming on it. We rose late, fortified ourselves with a specially good breakfast at Delmonico's, and strolled down Fifth Avenue, I with my pipe, Leo with his cigar.

For an examination morning everything at the Appellate Division Building was surprisingly quiet; not a soul was waiting outside. We walked through empty corridors to find the examination room shut. Feeling a trifle uneasy, we knocked. The door opened a couple of inches. Austen Fox, Chairman of the Examination Committee, and one of the prominent trial lawyers of the city, peered at us. "What do you gentlemen wish?"

"We've come to take the bar examinations," I explained.

Mr. Fox scrutinized us severely; over his shoulder I could see rows and rows of young men scribbling away for dear life. "Hmmm, I suppose you are acquainted with the rule that nobody shall be admitted more than an hour late. Perhaps you gentlemen think you require less time than the others?"

Leo, who did not recognize Mr. Fox, spoke up boldly: "Well, sir, there's no doubt about it. Mr. Griscom and I would not need so much time as the average student."

Mr. Fox was dumbfounded.

"Of course there's no chance of your passing, but as long as you're here you might as well come in."

We seated ourselves hastily, thinking what perfect asses we had been not to check the examination hour. My only comfort was that I could begin by putting down what I had learned on bailments. Many of the questions ended, "Which side would the judge find for? Write an opinion." After the examination Leo and I compared our answers. To our dismay they were in almost every case diametrically opposed. I said to myself, "Poor old Leo. He'll never get through," and he said to himself, "Poor old Lloyd. I mustn't discourage him." For two weeks we avoided the subject, each convinced the other had failed and not wanting to hurt his feelings.

Then we received the astonishing news that we had both passed. We were so delighted that we hurried over to thank Mr. Fox for admitting us. He grinned. "Well, I wouldn't have believed it, but you two gentlemen presented some of the best answers we read."

To celebrate my admission to the bar I booked passage for a vacation in England. Sailing day, the pier was packed with people waving flowers, some shouting "Bravo" and all trying to push their way nearer to the ship for a glimpse of Mme. Nellie Melba, my fellow passenger. I looked around curiously, but she was nowhere in sight.

On the prima donna's failure to appear in the dining room or on deck, I drew from the purser the information that she was resting and wished to see no one. It seemed to me that, as the son of the owner of the line, it would be a courtesy rather than a disturbance to inquire whether there were anything further we could do for her comfort; I rapped on the door of the bridal suite. It was opened by Mme. Melba herself, very regal and imposing. For a moment I was afraid she would not let me in, but then, with an abruptness which I later learned was one of her most engaging characteristics, she invited me to lunch. Afterwards we promenaded around the deck together.

Mme. Melba was surprisingly easy to make friends with. Once she was humming some aria or other and, without thinking how it would sound, I said out loud, "I'd like to go down in history as a man who has sung with Melba."

The idea struck her fancy, "Very well, what shall we sing?" and she proceeded to reel off a list of operatic duets. Not one was within my range. She also shook her head at the mention of each song in my repertory. Finally I suggested the popular hit, "Her Golden Hair was Hanging Down her Back. . . ."

"Let's try that," she said. "I've never heard it but you can teach it to me."

First I repeated the words several times: —

Oh, Flo, such a change you know,
When she left the village she was shy.
But alas and alack, when she came back,
She'd a naughty little twinkle in her eye.

One rehearsal of the melody was sufficient for Mme. Melba, and we began, I carrying the air, while her clear mellow voice ran effortlessly up and down the scale, filling in the harmony.

When we finished, she went to get something from her dressing case — such a worn, scratched object that involuntarily I exclaimed: "For Heaven's sake, that's not yours, is it?"

"Oh," she wailed. "For years I've been trying to persuade Alfred to let me buy a new one. There's a darling at Asprey's that would just suit me."

"Who's Alfred?"

"Alfred? Why, Alfred Rothschild. Most singers, you know, spend everything they make as fast as it comes in, and he told me how foolish I'd be if I did. He offered to take charge of my financial affairs if I'd turn over to him every cent I made. He sends me a monthly allowance for my living expenses, and, unless there's some emergency, I can have no more. I've shown him this old bag again and again. I've even pointed out that it's no protection for my jewelry. But all he'll say is, 'That bag's plenty good enough for you!'"

Mme. Melba died one of the rich women of the world.

Early one morning towards the end of the voyage my steward wakened me with the message that Mme. Melba wished to see me at once. Sleepily I slipped into my dressing gown and hurried to the deck above. The prima donna rushed out to meet me. With a wave of her arm worthy of her most dramatic moment in "Lucia di Lammermoor," she indicated a heap of towels and bathmats from which a thin thread of steam was rising. "The ship's on fire. All night long my maid and I have been fighting it. For fear it might cause a panic, I've been waiting for daylight before telling anybody. So far we've kept it down."

I had the presence of mind to refrain from revealing to Mme. Melba that she was fighting a leak in the steampipe, and hastened to warn the captain. "We must make Mme. Melba think we're taking this seriously," I cautioned him.

The captain came back with me immediately. "We can never thank you for your great service, Mme. Melba," he said. "The fire's already under control." At that moment we heard a clanging and banging from beneath. The wisp of steam disappeared.

To her dying day Mme. Melba was undoubtedly convinced she had saved the ship.

That entire summer I went wherever I wanted, and saw all my old friends — at Serlby Hall, and Convamore, and Mullaboden; and finally the two daughters of the Duke and Duchess of Abercorn invited Sommy and me to Baronscourt in the North of Ireland. The Duchess greeted me as a perfect stranger, not recognizing me as the young man who had returned her emerald three years previously. I did not mention it either.

The two girls demurely enticed me for a row on the lake not far from the house, and when we approached an island in the middle, they suggested I might like to explore it. I nosed in to shore and stepped to the bank, but, instead of disembarking, they seized the oars and shoved off. I had a choice — to swim to the mainland and in my wet clothes face the hoots of the house party, or sit patiently kicking my heels until someone rescued me.

I decided to wait and, after an hour, amid much laughter, I was fetched. It turned out that newcomers were always initiated in this way.

Before I left Baronscourt I had a more arduous initiation. Once a year some of the household lunched with a wealthy linen manufacturer of Belfast, who lived in the neighborhood, to sample the port from his famous cellar. Of late the Duke had avoided the ordeal, appointing substitutes to represent him. Accordingly, one day Colonel Edgecumbe, Lord Frederick Hamilton, Sommy, and I went bouncing over the country in a jaunting car, back to back, two on each side.

Our host welcomed us at the door, surrounded by his four sons, every one of them six feet five, the tallest group of men I ever saw. I had no idea of what we ate that noon; as soon as we sat down the butler solemnly filled our glasses with port twenty years old, and put the "dead man" on the sideboard.

The instant we had sipped the last drop, another bottle was brought of a vintage a little older, and took its place also on the sideboard. In rapid succession bottle followed bottle, each more cobwebbed than the other. My head was going round and round. All I knew was that I was drinking such port as I had never tasted — the final glass dated from the time of George III.

After nearly three hours at table we rose and faced the sideboard with its long row of dusty veterans. Nine voices counted in unison; the score was thirty-six.

As though from a great distance came the sound of the jaunting car being summoned. I recollect vaguely climbing into my seat and settling myself again back to back with Sommy. "Bring on the rope," ordered our host. A fairly short length with the two ends fastened together was slipped over our four heads and fitted snugly around our waists. Dimly I heard the echo of a cheer set up by the five giants as we jogged out of the courtyard. Then my head slumped forward.

I returned to consciousness, still with the echo of cheering in my ears. Now, however, we were driving along the avenue of Baronscourt, and what had roused me was a shout of approbation from a garden party on the lawn. We must have been a sight to gladden any Irish heart — dead to the world, heads rolling from side to side, bodies swaying to the motion of the cart, and held upright only by that loop of rope.

A footman assisted me to my room. I dropped on the bed, and the next thing I knew someone was prodding me to say I must dress for dinner. I was feeling a trifle shaky as I sat down by the Duchess. It would be just retribution, I thought, if I showed her the clipping from *Town Topics* which I had been carrying in my pocket for years. She laughed and passed it around; that night everyone was in high good humor because of the way we had maintained the honor of Baronscourt.

In London I stopped to see Mme. Melba at her hotel. "I've got it! I've got it!" she greeted me. "Alfred let me buy it this very morning." There on the table was a dressing case fitted with every conceivable bottle and brush. As pleased as a child, she displayed the gold and tortoiseshell decorations.

The prima donna was returning shortly to America and promised to lunch at Dolobran. I did not really suppose she would remember, but some weeks later she wrote me she was singing in Philadelphia, and she came out with her accompanist, Landon Ronald.

Mme. Melba was the sort of person for whom you put your best foot forward, and Mother made a big occasion of it. To top off the afternoon I told Augustus I wanted to drive our guest to town behind Father's fastest trotters. Pansy and Ronald occupied the rear of the light two-seater, Mme. Melba sat beside me, and we skimmed over the ground at twelve miles an hour. When we approached the zoological gardens Pansy remarked, "Lloyd, I don't know whether thee's forgotten, but these horses are terribly afraid of streetcars."

"Oh, heavens!" exclaimed Mme. Melba. "If anything happens to me so that I can't appear tonight, I shall have to forfeit ten thousand dollars."

I drew up the reins with a jerk, "You don't mean it! Well, in that case you'd better take the trolley from here."

Pansy was horrified, but Mme. Melba, her dignified bearing entirely unruffled, laughed and thanked me for the ride. As we turned around I had a glimpse of her waving from the corner where she was waiting for the next streetcar.

Although I resumed my work in New York, this time as a fully accredited lawyer, I did not feel that sitting at my desk gave me the experience I needed in talking on my feet, being heckled, and thinking quickly. To supplement my training I decided to enter politics. The fall of 1896 seemed an excellent moment; two years previously Tammany had been overthrown because of shocking disclosures of vice and corruption, and a reform administration under Mayor William L. Strong had been put in office. Supposedly the city was being run honestly rather than by machine politics.

Theoretically every good Republican was eligible to membership in his district club, and I visited mine several times. The atmosphere was frigid; in those days the organization was most secretive, and even the dates of primaries were hidden from the public until the last moment. I realized I would gain little by pursuing my intention of joining.

This repulse might have ended my efforts to get into politics; however, during the next few weeks I heard from a criminal court reporter of a vacancy in the Indictment Bureau as Deputy Assistant District Attorney under William M. K. Olcott. Since it was simply an administrative position, I believed I could fill it. I had Father ask the Senators from Pennsylvania, New Jersey, Ohio, and Maine to write the necessary letters on my behalf to Senator Thomas Platt, head of the New York State Republican machine. To make assurance doubly sure, we enlisted also the Pennsylvania Railroad, various New York bankers who had contributed largely to campaign funds, and finally the Vice-President of the United States himself, Garret A. Hobart of New Jersey. Such a bombardment completely overwhelmed Senator Platt. I was appointed with the comment, "What a waste of political ammunition! Why not make him Ambassador to London and be done with it?"

I arrived at the City Hall, a typical young liberal, full of enthusiasm, and ready to do my bit to give the city a clean administration. For the first few days I was occupied with the intricacies of making out indictments; I had no idea what a technical art it was. The omission of a single word or the failure to include the correct numbers of counts might cause a mistrial, and months of time and quantities of money spent in gathering evidence might thus be lost.

Daily I was interrupted by court reporters who were sent to extract what information they could. In an important case the return of a true bill by the grand jury could not be published until the indictment had been drawn; otherwise the criminals might escape before they could be arrested. A tip from the Indictment Bureau was worth its weight in gold, and in the past a good deal of gold had been exchanged for such tips.

The newspapermen had their own methods of ferreting out news. I was particularly warned against one who could read typescript upside down. He would brush through the bar in the outer office as though he owned the place, plant himself directly in front of my desk, and start talking to me. All the while I was conscious of his eye roving over the indictments on which I was working. It was undignified for me to cover my documents at his appearance, but more than once I opened his paper to find he had revealed an indictment, which meant that either the criminal or a principal witness would fly our jurisdiction.

Many of those who poured in and out of the office were going upon their lawful occupations — for example, the detectives who reported each morning to get orders for arrests. Shortly, however,

I discovered that certain important ward figures wanted to take advantage of our power to pigeonhole any indictment. Even in the smallest offenses pressure would be exerted, and, the bigger the case the greater it was. When a raid was staged on a notorious and wealthy Madam who numbered prominent bankers and politicians among her clientèle, I was bluntly informed it would be impossible to prosecute her.

As time went on I became more and more disturbed because papers and indictments mysteriously disappeared or never reached me; it seemed hopeless to put my finger on the leakage. The fact that any one of many clerks, detectives, and policemen possessed vital information gave enormous opportunity for the use of influence or the expenditure of large sums of money to defeat justice. In one of the back rooms I found several huge safes, and, on inquiry, I was informed they contained some five thousand indictments, mostly invalidated because of the Statute of Limitations.

To remedy conditions in the office would involve the overthrow of the whole system, a long-drawn-out and Herculean task. Fortunately, my anxieties were resolved for me. On the night of the Bradley Martins' fancy dress ball at the Waldorf-Astoria Hotel, I dressed myself in Cavalier costume of red velvet with knee breeches and white silk stockings and pumps. Feeling very foolish, I set out to walk the short distance from the Croisic. A fierce blizzard was raging; my legs were thoroughly chilled and wet, and as a result I contracted influenza which I could not shake off. The doctors ordered a change of climate, and I resigned my office and returned to Dolobran.

Dr. Gerhard, who was suffering terribly from asthma, suggested we try the healthful dry air of Arizona. As soon as Frederick Wistar Morris, a friend of my own age, heard where we were going, he decided his father's iron business could get along without him temporarily, and joined us. One March day we boarded the train for Phoenix, the capital of Arizona Territory.

CHAPTER IX

BUILDING IN THE WEST

Our first sight of Arizona gave us a sense of space and freedom — the wide flat main street of Phoenix with its few scattered trees, the hard hot sun sharpening every outline, the yellow desert stretching away to the ring of mountains. Breathing the clear crisp air we forgot we were supposed to be invalids.

Three abreast we set off to investigate the town. Its business consisted largely of saloons and gambling houses; one alternated with the other, open to the street, single-storied, with false fronts stuck on above. In our Eastern clothes we were conspicuous among the people passing up and down — stunted Mexican laborers, round-faced, dull-eyed Indians, cowboys in high-heeled boots, miners in red shirts and broad sombreros.

Impatient to explore, we hired horses immediately, and galloped towards the mountains apparently so near. We crossed fertile fields irrigated by ditches from the Salt River, which were being tilled by Mormon emigrants from Utah. When we spied the long-bearded farmers behind their yokes of oxen, we reined in to stare at them; back East people still shuddered at the mention of Brigham Young and the polygamous Latterday Saints.

Beyond, we were abruptly engulfed in the desert — dotted with greasewood, thorny mesquite, prickly palo verde, and evil-looking cholla cactus, which seemed to jump and fasten on us if we came too close. The peculiar birds known as road runners skittered away, and frequently we started giant jack rabbits the size of little goats. We had brought our guns and, to try our marksmanship, riddled the dead cactus stumps in the vicinity. Dr. Gerhard could have earned his living in a circus. Freddy and I tossed nickels into the air, and he never missed; he could even bend hairpins double. On our return at sunset we noticed enormous flights of doves overhead. Ducking under bushes by the side of an irrigation ditch we let loose at them as they darkened the sky above us.

Saturday afternoon the town began filling up, and by evening a solid line of horses with high Western saddles was tied to the rail in front of each saloon and dance hall. We made the rounds, watching the spinning roulette wheels, the croupiers raking in silver dollars, gold nuggets, occasionally small bags of gold dust. I saw one individual, better dressed than the rest, tear off his collar, write a check on it, and exchange it for chips. Miners and cowboys crowded up to the bars, gulping down the cheap rotgut which passed for whisky. We ordered beer, which we thought safer.

In the more pretentious places, painted, gaudily dressed girls were hopping about with the customers to tinny waltzes and polkas, thumped out on old pianos. Every now and then one of them would step up on a stage in the rear to sing some sentimental ballad of parted lovers or sons gone wrong.

Gentlemen, remember, the prisoner there's my son,
And gentlemen, remember, 'tis the first crime he has done.
Don't send my boy to prison, for that would break my hear-r-rt.

Another universal favorite was : —

There's a name that's never spoken,
There's a mother's heart that's broken,
There's a picture with its face turned towards the wall.

After several repetitions of this chorus, in which the audience joined, even the roughest and toughest among them were in tears.

A few nights in the Commercial Hotel convinced us we did not want to stay in Phoenix. Prices were very low — breakfast fifteen cents and dinner twenty — but the food was all fried and usually cold. Lobby and dining room were packed with salesmen, mine superintendents, and ranchers, arguing and emphasizing their points with jets of tobacco juice aimed at the spittoons.

Every room was taken, because the legislature was in session. The most influential of the politicians was Frank Murphy of Prescott, a heavy, gray-haired banker in his fifties, and an ardent booster for Arizona. Seizing at once on Dr. Gerhard he described to him a miraculous hot spring on Castle Creek, some seventy-five miles to the north in Yavapai County. Miners who came there doubled up with rheumatism were straightened out in no time. Murphy was anxious for a reliable medical opinion; if the spring had therapeutic value it would be a great asset for Arizona, and he kept urging us to inspect it.

By the end of two weeks we were feeling fit as fighting cocks and ready to see more of the country. We decided Castle Creek was as good an objective as any, and began collecting an outfit — a sturdy wagon to carry tents and blankets and supplies, a chuck box in the rear with a cover which let down to form a table, a draft team, and saddle animals for ourselves, big-footed, large-headed beasts, able to get us over the rough country. A wagon driver and a cook completed our equipment.

Once in the desert we encountered orange and black gila monsters, horned toads, ground squirrels and darting lizards, but we thought we were the only human beings for miles around. Our second morning out, however, we woke to find two of our horses had disappeared. We spotted extra hoof marks and supposed they had been taken by Indians. Armed cap-a-pie we tracked them as far as we could in a fruitless search; we had to retrace our steps to Phoenix to report our loss to the sheriff, buy more animals, and start afresh.

This time without misadventure we reached the Bradshaw Mountains, and followed the broad bottom of a canyon. On either hand sahuaro cactus lifted gaunt, twisted arms thirty feet skyward. Turning off the trail into a narrow side ravine, we passed through a group of cottonwoods, their yellow-gray branches covered with pale green new leaves, and dismounted near the spring.

After so many miles of arid desert, the sight of the water gushing from a slit in the rock made us feel dry and dusty. Pulling off our clothes we plunged into the pool. The temperature was as hot as we could comfortably bear, and when we joined hands, with the two end ones touching the rock walls, an electric current was set up. The power of the shock depended on the number of people in line; we did not care to experiment with more than eight.

Dr. Gerhard became so interested in the medicinal qualities of the water that he wanted to remain long enough to observe its effects on the miners. Rather than live at the boarding house, we chose a level spot where the canyon joined the ravine, and there built wooden platforms with wooden sides three feet high, over which we stretched our tents. The canvas did not shut out the cold at night or the heat during the day, but we were far better off than the miners below us. One afternoon we suddenly saw a solid wall of water driving down the ravine, turning the empty arroyo instantaneously into a raging impassable torrent. Some of the miners' tents were swept clean away as the result of this mountain cloudburst.

In a few days Murphy arrived to learn what we thought of his spring. Dr. Gerhard was already converted to its merits, and we all liked the place so much that we accepted Murphy's suggestion to go in with him and develop the springs into a health resort. The four of us organized a company: Murphy was President, I Vice-president, and Freddy, because of his business experience, was Secretary and kept the books; with Dr. Gerhard's help I persuaded Father to put up a fourth for my share.

To make our hotel accessible for guests Murphy, who was president of the railroad connecting with the Santa Fe at Prescott, promised to establish a station at the nearest point, from which we would construct twenty miles of road in to Castle Creek. Back to Phoenix we hurried to buy building materials, and there we were lucky enough to meet a wandering Easterner who was mason, carpenter, plumber, and builder into the bargain. We had no trouble getting workmen. Our valley was a main artery to a vast number of prospecting claims to the north and east of us, and many of the miners were eager to be grubstaked. They quarreled fiercely, and when drunk were entirely unmanageable. As sheriff, Freddy more than once had to drive out fractious cases with the aid of a revolver.

Day after day the ravine echoed with the pounding of hammers, the crash of falling rocks; we sawed and heaved with the rest. By the end of three months the hotel was framed and roofed, and the first stagecoach, with an armed guard for the mail, was bringing our letters from Morristown over a road of sorts.

The heat now grew so suffocating — one hundred and twenty degrees in the shade at noon — that we decided on a trip north to California Park in the Colorado Rockies, where we would find cooler weather and marvelous big-game shooting. We packed our wagon, hitched the horses, left our engineer in charge, and set off.

Once we were away from our canyon, there was not the slightest semblance of a trail; we simply steered by compass in the general direction of Flagstaff through a succession of mountains and monster piles of loose rock and shale, colored all tints of yellow and red. At precipitous grades we often had to unload everything, pull the wagon up by hand, and then laboriously carry our outfit on our backs.

In order to take a quick look at the Grand Canyon, we hired at Flagstaff a lighter vehicle and fresh horses, one a mare with a colt which ran free alongside. In spite of having to stop now and then to let it feed, we made the whole journey of seventy-five miles in one day, and the colt was apparently none the worse for it.

The Colorado River shone like a silver ribbon at the bottom of the Canyon; it seemed so close that we tried to throw stones into it to see the splash. To our astonishment, no matter how far we hurled them outwards, they disappeared directly underneath us. Not a single other tourist was anywhere about. When we discovered a boulder perched on the edge, we pried it loose, and it went ricochetting down, striking others and starting them rolling and bounding unbelievable distances. Soon we had launched a miniature avalanche that snapped huge pine trees like matches. It became a game to select an unstable rock, the bigger the better, and then all of us, working with stakes, would tilt it over and lie on the sheer edge to follow its course. None of us had dreamed the earth could contain a gash so deep and so wide.

Freddy Morris now had to go home, and for the rest of the trip we were joined by Dr. Gerhard's nephew Arthur, and a young friend of his named Hutchinson. At Glenwood Springs, Colorado, five guides and an outfit were waiting; we could not traverse this trackless expanse of forest and mountain alone. The head guide apologized for the horses. Rustlers had just made off with his others, which were the finest in Colorado, and he swore vengeance on the thieves if he ever caught them. Scanning the map, I thought his chances of carrying out his threats were very small.

Travel in Central America remained in my memory as the most exhausting imaginable. However, the uncharted Rockies made me change my mind. In places where there had been a fire, dead trees were piled together helter-skelter six or eight feet high. Often a horse would slip through a gap until its belly rested on a trunk; it would scramble over somehow. Occasionally a pack animal would run against a tree, burst its rope, gallop off, and scatter pots and pans and provisions along a mile or so. Occasionally another one would get its load twisted underneath, and would fight and buck to disentangle itself. Sometimes we were hours covering only a very few miles.

As far as food went we were always sure of a delicious meal — roast partridge or a haunch of venison for dinner, and trout from each stream. One evening our guide pointed to a lake by our camp, "All you have to do there is throw in your lines and pull 'em out. The funny thing is that every fish you catch will weigh exactly three quarters of a pound."

Smiling skeptically, I rigged up my line with three flies and made a cast; no sooner had they touched the water than I had a strike. In a second two fish were flopping on the ground beside me. Again I cast, and this time drew out three with equal rapidity. A few feet away Arthur and Dr. Gerhard were reeling them in with as little effort. This was an easy method of providing our dinner, but gave no chance for skill. A hungry mouth was ready to take whatever hit the surface of the water. To our amazement the guide was absolutely right; each fish weighed three quarters of a pound almost to a fraction of an ounce.

After about a week we rode into California Park, a broad upland plain, full of pronged antelope; the guide said deer of all kinds were out of season, but nobody would miss a few if we wished to try our hand. Approaching near enough for a shot was difficult since the animals were incredibly wary and swift. Years later Roy Chapman Andrews told me he had chased a herd of Asiatic antelope in a motor, clocking their speed. He was driving at sixty miles an hour when one passed him and crossed his bow — it must have been making seventy-five at least.

One morning on a fresh horse I started in pursuit of a young antelope which had broken from a herd. He would let me get fairly close, then put on a terrific burst of speed, and I would see his white rump disappearing over the next rise where he would pause again. Several hours elapsed before he began to slacken his pace, and at last he stopped, panting, his head down; I rode alongside and captured him alive.

The only reason we ever were able to shoot mature antelope was their habit of running in huge circles. Judging the diameter, we galloped across at right angles and intercepted them. We all left California Park with good heads.

Still traveling north, we struck through the mountains again and one day from our hillside camp we caught sight of a stranger some two hundred yards away, riding towards us. Our guide looked at him casually and suddenly jumped up, exclaiming, "By God, that's my mare. Grab your guns, boys, quick!"

We obeyed with alacrity and, pretending to be inspecting our rifles for spots of rust, sat ready to act at the guide's next command. The intruder was exactly my idea of a Western desperado, eyes close together, hard face, stubbly reddish beard that had not been shaved for weeks. He addressed the guide, "Pardner, can you spare any sugar and coffee? There's two of us and we're out of supplies."

"Don't worry about supplies. We'll take care of them. Hands up, you son of a bitch!" and instantaneously nine rifles pointed at the ruffian.

The guide delegated me to pull our captive's revolver from his holster, remove his rifle, and pat him for concealed weapons.

"I suppose you've forgotten that's my horse you're riding there. You know what we do to horse thieves. Where's your camp?"

"Five miles back," muttered the desperado.

We tied his arms and set off, the guide riding behind with his gun laid across his saddle. As soon as we came near the outlaw's camp I was left to guard him, while the rest advanced to deal with his companion. I tried to engage my prisoner in conversation, but he stared at the ground, ignoring me completely. I started to examine his revolver — Bang! off it went, and I just saved myself from dropping it. The trigger was so delicately filed that the slightest touch released the catch. My prisoner turned his head contemptuously. "When you're a little older, young feller, you'll learn not to monkey with dangerous weapons."

I made no mention of my ignominious mishap to the others, who speedily reappeared with their new captive and practically all the lost horses.

The five guides now began discussing what to do and in short order decided, "We're not going sixty miles back to find a sheriff. Nobody'll ask any questions if we string these bastards up here and now."

At this we four Easterners held a council and decided we could not be parties to a lynching. Dr. Gerhard announced to the guides that we had employed them, and although we realized these rascals deserved to be hanged, still we would not stand for its being done without a trial. The guides were furious, but in the end we hit on a compromise. We gave the prisoners the two worst horses, left them their money, and turned them loose. Even lacking food, guns, or fishing tackle, they seemed to us to have a sporting chance. They disappeared, followed by the guides' fervent assurance, "We'll hang you for certain if we ever lay eyes on you again."

We on our part continued north, occasionally shooting a deer for food. One morning while camped near the Wyoming border our breakfast was disturbed by the arrival of three visitors. " 'Morning, boys," said the leader; "I'm the sheriff. Just a little matter of inspection."

I noticed he was sniffing the venison frying over the fire, and glancing suspiciously at the haunch from which it had been cut. "Hmm. I suppose you know it's closed season." At this moment one of the deputies appeared with our antelope heads; we were caught red-handed. "Sorry, boys. I've got to take you to the judge," the sheriff said.

The evidence was loaded on a horse, and the seven of us proceeded to the tiny town of Hahn's Peak, which could not have contained more than twenty houses. On the roof of one, an old man with a gray beard, dressed in overalls, was hammering shingles.

"Come on down, judge. I've got some prisoners for you."

The judge peered at us curiously, then laid aside his tools, and deliberately began descending the ladder.

"Right this way, boys," invited the sheriff, and led us to the courtroom, furnished with a few benches and a desk with two books on it; one was the *Criminal Code of Colorado,* the other *Every Man His Own Lawyer.*

The inhabitants of the town had already filled every seat when the judge entered, pulling on a coat. He settled himself on the bench, solemnly adjusted his spectacles, and looked at us. "Sit down, prisoners."

We sat. "Strangers round here, ain't ye? We don't have many trials in these parts. Do any of you gents know any law?"

"A little, Your Honor," I volunteered.

"Then how ought we to start this?"

"Well, Your Honor, you have to charge us with something."

"That's right. Sheriff, do you charge these men with anything?"

"Yes, I do. They're in possession of game out of season."

"What do you do next?" the judge inquired.

"You might ask if we have anything to say."

This was a crucial moment. I had been calculating the maximum fine, which amounted to a thousand dollars; but if I could gain the good will of the court we might be given the minimum of two hundred and fifty.

I rose, bowed, cleared my throat, "Your Honor," I proclaimed, "the great hospitable State of Colorado (*applause*) wishes to have visitors travel here to spend their money. With knowledge of the kindliness of the people of Colorado, we journeyed here to make a trip across the beautiful mountains of this splendid state (*more applause*). Your Honor, while up there among those magnificent peaks, we had to live on salt pork and canned beans, except when the rivers and lakes gave us trout. Finally we came to a region where there were no trout but plenty of deer. Your Honor, the temptation was too much for us, and we did shoot game, but never more than we could eat. Your Honor, we plead guilty of transgressing the letter of the law of the great State of Colorado (*more applause*) but we appeal to the mercy of the honored court to consider the circumstances under which this misdemeanor was committed (*loud applause*)."

The judge focused his attention on the evidence laid on a bench in front. "Sheriff, what's the law say should be done with those haunches?"

The sheriff scratched his head. "Well, I'm not just sure, Your Honor."

"Let me look at your book, Your Honor," I offered, "and perhaps I can tell."

I sat down on the bench beside the judge and thumbed through the statutes. Finding the page, I announced, "Your Honor, I regret to inform you that any venison seized becomes the property of the court."

"Well, the court likes venison very much," grinned the judge, pushing his spectacles back off his nose. Then he rapped on the table and delivered the verdict. "In view of the frank admission of guilt on the part of the prisoners, I'm going to impose the minimum fine of twenty-five dollars a head." Here he whispered to me, "I have to do that, don't I?" and I nodded confirmation.

We paid over the money. The judge counted it carefully and handed half to the sheriff. "And now," he continued, "the court has carefully considered the disposal of the venison, and in view of the help rendered this court by the prisoners, and in spite of the court's fondness for venison, the court has decided to let the prisoners take it with them. If they're heading for Wyoming, they'll need it more than the court."

An enthusiastic cheer went up from the audience.

The sheriff now rose. "Your Honor, Gentlemen, Friends, and Prisoners. Since your sheriff has profited by this arrest, he now invites you all to join him in a drink."

Everybody, including His Honor, made a beeline for the door, and soon the saloon across the street was crowded with the entire male population of the town, downing their ponies of rye. Lustily they hurrahed for the sheriff, and speeded us back to camp with fervent good wishes.

Before reaching the Union Pacific Railroad in Wyoming we still had a long way to go through the wilderness. Bearded and bronzed, our clothes sadly in want of washing, we came out at a little town which boasted a Harvey restaurant, the most welcome spectacle for many a week. The presence of the trim, blond, Scandinavian waitresses, hard-working and attractive, undoubtedly accounted for the success of the chain of restaurants; since women were in a great minority, these had their pick of husbands and were said to be largely responsible for populating the West.

Leaving our guides we took the train for Yellowstone Park, our last excursion. As our huge, sight-seeing van lumbered up to the first station, we found terrific excitement; the sixty passengers of the stage ahead had just been waylaid and stripped of their valuables by two masked bandits. They were all exclaiming and gesticulating, trying to describe their assailants. The only clue on which they were agreed was that one had had stubbly red whiskers. We three had the same thought — our horse thieves! However, we never knew for sure, because the robbers were never caught.

Back at Castle Creek we set to work again with a will, and by winter our hotel was ready. Dr. Gerhard wrote to his old patients, Freddy and I canvassed our friends, and quickly we had our capacity of twenty-five guests.

In mid-February we received the news of the blowing up of the *Maine* in Havana harbor, and newspapers from the East were filled with talk of war. Suddenly we began to feel terribly far away from the center of things. Developing Castle Creek had been fun, yet none of us intended to go permanently into the hotel business. More and more frequently we discussed returning East.

Murphy pressed us to stay, and when the position of United States Attorney for Arizona fell vacant, he offered it to me with the additional possibility of my becoming Senator as soon as Arizona was admitted to the Union — provided I would settle there. The West was undoubtedly the place in which to rise rapidly, but I still believed I had a fair chance of making a career in the East near my family and friends.

In April, war broke out with Spain. I went home to volunteer.

CHAPTER X

THE LEGACY OF SPAIN

Instead of enrolling again in the Naval Reserve I decided to apply for a commission in the Army, which was being increased so fast that it badly needed officers. The Adjutant General, Henry C. Corbin, was a great friend of Father's, and in those days before we had any General Staff he more or less ran the Army. His office in Washington was bedlam, but I managed to get his ear for a few minutes, and he promptly declared, "If you know enough to be a lawyer in New York, you're certainly qualified to be a captain in the quartermaster corps."

The news of Dewey's May Day victory on Manila Bay made every American doubly eager to wipe out the disgrace of Spanish misrule at our door in Cuba — "Butcher" Weyler, *reconcentrado* camps, poor insurgents shot against the wall, Havana filth spreading yellow fever far and wide. I thought it a stroke of good luck when I was assigned as aide-de-camp to Major General James F. Wade, commanding the Third Army Corps in training at Chickamauga Park, Georgia. Because of his seniority it looked as though he would be one of the first to be sent on active service.

Equipped with my uniform of thick blue wool, an expensive aiguillette of gold cord for dress occasions, and a shining sword, I set off for Chickamauga. At the station the hot June sun was blazing down and soldiers were pouring from a troop train on the other side of the platform, mopping their brows and fanning themselves with their hats. I pushed my way through swarms of flies, clouds of dust, and a throng of sutlers, who were thrusting their wares under our noses. Only by a show of authority could I rescue a hack for myself and a ramshackle wagon for my baggage.

I had to ask several times for General Wade's headquarters before I was directed to the top of a knoll in a group of trees at least half a mile from the nearest regiment. The first person I saw was a friend of my Washington days, Benjamin Foraker, the son of the Senator from Ohio, a plump, amusing young man my own age, also a captain on the staff. He took me in to General Wade, who read my orders crisply, and then assigned me to a tent close by.

The camp was roughly a twelve-by-twelve-mile square which, at capacity, was to hold about forty-five thousand men. One of my jobs was to help meet the arriving regiments, mostly National Guard, and guide them to the sites assigned them. Daily I used to wait at the station in the ever-present heat and dust until my detachments had gathered themselves together. Some, like the crack Seventh Regiment from New York City, lined up smartly, others shuffled off sloppily, as though they had never learned the rudiments of drill. Occasionally we reached our destination to find it already occupied, and there was general confusion while sites were re-allotted.

Once the newcomers were settled I had to go back and check their equipment, often sadly deficient. One squadron was drilling earnestly with gray army blankets strapped around each man's waist instead of trousers; there was such a demand for uniforms that they could not be manufactured fast enough, and nobody seemed to know whether the home state or the Federal Government was responsible.

All of us had constant indigestion; for the first time I encountered the idea that a soldier ate what was put in front of him and did not complain. We had fried eggs for breakfast, for lunch and dinner fried ham supplemented by canned vegetables and fruits — never anything fresh. Our water was furnished by an apparently magnificent spring, but in a few days everybody was suffering from dysentery. Since the source was unsuspected, we were constantly being reinfected. Soon typhoid broke out, and the incoming patriots were laid low so rapidly that our inadequate force of doctors and nurses were absolutely swamped. Each nurse had fifty typhoid patients on her hands.

The Surgeon General's department collapsed completely. The sudden responsibility of taking care of these thousands of men had caught it unprepared. Lieutenant Colonel Hoff, our chief medical officer, was so overwhelmed by the paper work necessary in forming some sort of system that the health of the camp inevitably suffered. He and his superiors clung to the army tradition of not accepting outside aid, and refused the National Red Cross offer of supplies of ice, more trained nurses, and even money. Thousands died before this situation was remedied.

The regular Army's feeling of superiority over civilian soldiers permeated the camp. If the regulars wanted blankets, saddles, bedding, frying pans, they did not hesitate to "rustle" them. After things began to vanish from my quarters, I asked Father if he could not send me a steward who had seen military service.

Father made an excellent choice. Thomas, a champion boxer in the British Army, had been in the Black Watch under Kitchener in the Sudan. He had been known as "The Hangman" because, when volunteers had been called for to tie the noose in an execution, he had stepped forward. Not at all ashamed of his action, he commented to me, "I did not see why I should not do it, and I did, and it was a fine job I did." Tom was a born fighter. He had not been at Chickamauga twenty-four hours before he took exception to the insanitary dish-washing methods of the Headquarters cook; he promptly upset a pan of greasy water over the culprit's head and beat him up thoroughly. General Wade's good offices alone saved Tom from the jug.

Tom could outrustle any rustler in camp, and in short order he produced everything I needed to make my tent comfortable, including a pair of blankets which could only have come from the regular Army. The day after I mentioned in Tom's hearing that I lacked a box on which to stand my rubber washbasin, he presented me with one freshly painted a bright blue.

Lieutenant Colonel Hoff appeared at mess in a towering rage. "There are thieves in this camp," he announced, as though everyone were not already aware of this. He had just been to his tent where he had found his medical books and precious report forms all tumbled out of their box on the ground; nobody could have made a mistake, because his name was clearly printed on it. I thought immediately of my new blue washstand and kept very quiet. At the first opportunity I offered it to General Wade with my compliments, saying it was much too pretentious for a mere aide-de-camp. Later I told him how I had acquired it, and he was highly amused.

The staff, although mixed regulars and civilians, proved exceedingly congenial. I formed a great friendship with Second Lieutenant George W. Read, tall, strong-faced, handsome, who might have served as a model for one of Frederic Remington's drawings. He had been cadet captain at West Point in 1883, and was still waiting for those ahead of him to be moved up so that he could be promoted.

On formal parades I used to envy the way Read, while astride his prancing horse, could pull out his sword, salute, and with one deft motion replace it. Five minutes after the regulars had clapped their swords home smartly, most of us civilians would be sitting our mounts, our eyes fixed straight in front, holding the reins rigidly with one hand, and with the other making futile jabs for the elusive scabbard.

Hourly we were awaiting the summons to Tampa, where the regiments were gathering, but our hopes were utterly dashed when on June 25th General Brooke marched out with fifteen thousand picked men, leaving us to run a school for recruits. A week later we heard of the charge up San Juan Hill, and then of the destruction of the Spanish fleet at Santiago. The declaration of an armistice in August convinced us our chances to see the war were entirely gone.

Just at the moment of our keenest disappointment came the unexpected announcement that General Wade was appointed chairman of a commission of three to conduct the evacuation of Spanish troops from Cuba. Read and I, who were interested in languages, immediately buried our noses in a "Teach Yourself Spanish" course, so that we would have at least a smattering to use on arrival. The United States transport *Resolute* was waiting in New York, and in early September the commission assembled there, some forty-five in number, including clerks and stenographers.

We were a curious assortment. General Wade had been a brigadier in the Union forces in the Civil War. The other army member, the one-legged General Matthew C. Butler from South Carolina, had been a brigadier of the Confederacy. The Navy was represented by Admiral William T. Sampson. The Secretary of the Commission, General Clous, the army judge-advocate, was intensely jealous of Charles Gould, the Commission's very clever civilian counsel, who was supposed to guide the difficult political and legal negotiations with the Spaniards.

No sooner had we sailed than there was an eruption of the traditional feud so apt to spring up when the Army and Navy operated together. The naval officers tried to mark off half the afterdeck so that the Admiral could pace to and fro undisturbed, a reasonable enough proceeding because he was entitled to command at sea. However, some of the army officers planted their deck chairs within the sacred enclosure. Ignoring them, he would start his promenade, whereupon they would join him and remark conversationally, "Pleasant day, Admiral," or "What does that flag mean, Admiral?" or "Look at that porpoise over there, Admiral." The Admiral's gray beard fairly shook with indignation as he retired in dudgeon to the bridge or the seclusion of his cabin.

At sight of the tower on Morro Castle, everybody, with some apprehension, crowded to the rail. We were the first Americans to arrive in Havana since the beginning of the war. Spanish hatred of us was so bitter that the garrison might have been careless in sweeping up mines, and, if we were sunk, claim it was an accident. Cautiously we steamed through the narrow entrance, conscious of the guns frowning from the ramparts overhead and the scowling faces of the soldiers. The beautiful landlocked harbor seemed calm enough, but we heaved a sigh of relief as finally we dropped anchor a few hundred yards from the *Maine,* her masts, smokestacks, and bridge deck protruding from the water.

Nobody came out to meet us; obviously no arrangements had been made for our reception. I went ashore with the preliminary landing party to search for quarters. The quay was lined with Spanish soldiers and sailors, who stared at us sullenly. In answer to our inquiries, they shrugged their shoulders and drew aside.

We ventured into the city by ourselves. The streets were teeming with Cubans: walking skeletons, large-eyed, hollow-cheeked, half-naked, pock-marked, scabrous. They thronged around, begging for food, and when we shook our heads they fell back apathetically. They were obviously too cowed to show any signs of welcome or gratitude. The smell of filth and decay almost sickened me. I stepped up to give a penny to one woman carrying a baby, and my nostrils were hit by the most awful stench. I took one look and turned away — the baby had been dead for days, but the mother was still clinging to it.

In contrast to these scenes of misery, the hotels were filled with Spanish officers and beautiful women, enjoying music and dancing, good food and old wine; we could really imagine ourselves in Spain. Since there was no room for us, we hired horses and drove beyond the city limits to the suburb of the Vedado, where we engaged the Hotel Trotcha, a barrack-like building by the sea.

Our initial task was to make an inventory of Spanish troops and supplies, and I was one of the leaders of the detachment to examine Morro Castle. At the landing across the harbor we asked for the senior officer; he refused either to see us or to let us in. I was able to muster up enough Spanish to threaten that if he persisted in barring us we would bring a battleship and blow the place to pieces; the war was over and the principle, at least, of surrender had been accepted. In the end he gave way.

We discovered little of real value. Almost everything portable had been removed, and what was left irreparably damaged; even the bases of the cannon had been broken. We could hardly blame the Spaniards for their attitude. The garrison had never been defeated in battle, and could not comprehend why they should be capitulating. We completed our list as best we could, and then very willingly departed.

At the Arsenal the next day a junior Spanish officer denied me admittance and made an insulting remark about American pigs which he thought I would not understand. We had been warned to avoid any altercation, but this was too much. I told him to stand back and hold his tongue. He drew himself up haughtily and fairly spat at me: "You may expect my seconds to call upon you in the morning."

In a quandary, I submitted my plight to General Wade, but the only satisfaction I could get from him was that if I fought I would be court-martialed, and if I did not fight I would be a disgrace to the American Army. My knowledge of fencing was confined to the few flourishes which I had learned at the Haccius School; in any encounter I was certain to be properly punctured.

For several mornings I looked anxiously from my window, expecting to see a delegation, but none ever came. I was glad when I realized I would hear no more of the affair and that it was merely a Spanish gesture. However, so many other officers had similar disagreeable experiences that we had to insist that a Spaniard of high rank accompany us on our inspection duties.

In the course of our investigations we found at once that the Spaniards were working like beavers to make away with all public property before we could take charge. At the Arsenal they were actually loading neutral vessels, supposedly in harbor for cargoes of sugar and tobacco, with gold, silver, tapestries, furniture, ammunition, even old brass cannon dating back to the sixteenth century. What they could not ship off they were selling to private traders. We had to go through the cargoes and compel the masters to disgorge the loot.

Arrangements for evacuating the Spaniards advanced slowly. It was really a business proposition, and neither the Army nor the Navy was qualified to handle it. A civilian like Father would have drafted the necessary plans in a few hours, but the commission fell to wrangling with one another about how such things had been done in the past. Soon Gould and Clous were not speaking, and every suggestion of the Admiral was being voted down by the Generals. One day when it was urgent for me to consult General Wade, I opened the door of the conference room. "I'll raise you a dollar," I heard General Wade say. "I'll see you," replied the soft Southern drawl of General Butler. A fine exciting game of poker was in progress.

In spite of dissension, we were fairly well established at Havana by October, and it was decided to send members of the staff to pave the way for the departure of the Spanish garrisons in interior towns, choose camp sites for the American detachments that were to replace them, and pacify the Cuban rebels. Major Beebe was in charge of a group of some twenty dispatched to the great sugar town of Puerto Principe. Because of our knowledge of Spanish, Read and I were included. I was second in command, and he, now promoted to First Lieutenant, was under me.

A Government ship deposited us at Nuevitas on the coast, from which a little sugar railroad carried us into Puerto Principe. At the station we were met by the *Alcalde,* or Mayor, with a committee of a thousand or so "prominent citizens," and conducted to the house of the leading Cuban resident.

Major Beebe and I had to share a double bed. The screenless

room was alive with clouds of mosquitoes, buzzing, singing, and stinging viciously. We had brought no mosquito bars with us and tried pulling the sheet over our heads, but as soon as we fell asleep we were almost smothered; involuntarily we stuck out our noses for air and were straightway bitten.

The next morning we went to the barracks to ascertain the number of the garrison and the amount of supplies on hand. After checking all day we had to sit up late that evening toiling over a long report. During the night, Major Beebe was taken violently ill, with constant vomiting and a high temperature.

Our Army doctor pronounced it yellow fever and informed me I would undoubtedly come down with it at any moment. I had better make my will, because delirium would set in immediately and prevent my doing it.

I was angry. It was a doctor's business to tell his patients they were going to recover, not that they were going to die before they even had a symptom. Berating him for his unprofessional conduct, I assured him I had no intention of getting the disease; I had always suspected that my "Chagres fever" in Panama had really been a touch of yellow. Nevertheless, I could not help being distinctly uneasy in my mind for some time.

With Major Beebe incapacitated I was in charge. I had him put on a stretcher and sent him back to the boat while I, guided by principles I had learned at Chickamauga, picked out a camp site which had good water, good drainage, level ground, and shade. Then I inquired for the whereabouts of the rebels, who had not dared approach too near the town because of their fear of the Spaniards.

At their bivouac in the woods I had an enthusiastic welcome from a band of some thousand ragged patriots. All seemed bitterly intent on avenging their wrongs. Some had been hunted like beasts and had not set foot in a settlement for years. Others had been imprisoned in jails and *reconcentrado* camps with barely enough food to keep them alive. The result of their hardships was plain to see. Many of them were infected with malaria, syphilis, and even leprosy, introduced by Chinese labor on the sugar plantations. They were desperately in need of provisions, and we arranged for their emissaries to procure supplies from the town on condition they gave up their plans for Spanish pogroms and disbanded.

When we returned to the ship we found Major Beebe had died. Back at Havana we were greeted with the word that yellow fever had broken out among the Americans. Benny Foraker was one of the first of our staff to be stricken. Since, for the purposes of ventilation, the partitions of the rooms in the hotel only went part way to the ceiling, everybody grew panicky. He was transferred to a small wooden house a few hundred yards off and, feeling sure I was immune, I volunteered to nurse him. Thomas passed in food and books through the door, and once a day I walked alone around the Vedado. Nobody would even speak to me. Fortunately Benny recovered.

The city had to be cleaned up as soon as possible. Being still hale and sound, I was delegated to the unwanted job of inspecting the hospitals. The conditions were shocking beyond description. There was shortage of attendants and shortage of medicines, the pallets were packed so tightly there was barely space to move between them, the stench was so strong you could hardly stand it. The instant a patient died he was carted out, and a new one shoved into his place.

The epidemic had reduced the commission to skeleton proportions; nine of the forty-five died — twenty per cent. The result was that Read, who also escaped, and I were sent on the trips which had to be made into the interior, first westward through the rich tobacco country of Pinar del Río. En route the train encountered a terrific thunderstorm and the windows had to be closed. Suddenly the man across the aisle vomited. We knew this meant but one thing — yellow fever. Read and I did not so much as turn aside with disgust, but simply opened the window and let the sheets of rain pour through. The human power of reacting to horror had become exhausted, and we were tired of being frightened.

If we had not been thoroughly hardened we would never have finished our investigations. On our longest trip we had to visit eight cities in the central section of Cuba. The day we left we neglected to bring anything to eat with us and, having started at 4 A.M., towards noon we were famished. At a junction we bought cakes from a stand and began devouring them. They must have been about half gone when a Cuban leaned over from the opposite seat. "Excuse me, Gentlemen, did you buy those at the last station?"

"Yes."

"I beg you not to eat them. It is well known that the man who prepared them is a leper."

I was inured to revolting sights, but the idea of having eaten food touched by a leper was too much for my imagination. I dashed to the end of the car and lost my lunch; a minute or two later Read followed.

That night at Cienfuegos the hotel beds were separated merely by green gauze hangings. From the next cubicle I could hear a great moaning and groaning, but I was so fatigued that I fell asleep notwithstanding. In the morning, everything was silent and, wondering what had happened to the sufferer, I pulled aside the curtain. He was unconscious, in the last stages of smallpox; where his face should have been was only a hideous mass of pustules. All I could do was abuse the hotel manager.

At Santa Clara the hotel was filled as usual with Spanish officers, who, seeing our uniforms, turned their backs, the first instance of such discourtesy outside Havana. As we were retiring, a Cuban merchant whispered to us, "Some of those drunken Spaniards are talking about assassinating you. Better watch out."

Believing such threats must be bravado, we were not concerned, but we had hardly closed our eyes when a knock came on the door. The proprietor of the hotel begged us to move our rooms. He assured us the Spaniards really intended to strike a last blow at the American Army.

Still not convinced, we did as he asked. However, before going to bed again, I glanced casually out the window, then beckoned to Read. Below the room we had just left shadowy figures were assembling in the courtyard, creeping stealthily to make no noise. One of them climbed on the shoulders of another and heaved himself carefully over our sill. In a few seconds he reappeared. There was a shaking of fists and an angry murmur, but finally the group dispersed; as in the case of the duel, we heard no more of it.

Sancti Spíritus, also in the interior, was a relic of the Middle Ages. The streets were paved with great stones worn smooth from centuries of use, and so narrow no wagon could get through. They were dark from the overhanging buildings and smelly from the drainage. Walking from our house to the hotel where we had our meetings was a hazardous undertaking, particularly at night. Suddenly a window would open above us and without warning a pot of filth and slush would come showering down. At best we were well splashed, and we always had to clean ourselves off afterwards and even change our clothes.

On our return to Havana we had covered a thousand miles in sixteen days. In every city we had seen the same striking contrast — lordly, well-dressed, well-fed Spaniards and starving, diseased, oppressed Cubans. We had never dreamed that people could suffer so and still exist; we were glad those Spaniards were to be ejected.

On January 1st, the Spanish flag was lowered for the last time, the American flag went up in its place and the work of the commission was over. I had witnessed so much misery that I was anxious to get out. Many of the staff were half-sick and I myself was run down. General Wade offered to recommend me for a captaincy in the regular Army, a far higher rank than a captain of volunteers, but I had had enough of military life and I declined.

Nevertheless, when I reached home, I found I had not as yet the energy to start in again at law. My friends kept suggesting "Why don't you go back to diplomacy for a while?" Ever since my experience in England, I had been bitten by the idea of entering the diplomatic service and I decided there was no harm in putting in an application. Both Pennsylvania Senators promised to recommend me to the new Secretary of State, John Hay, whom I had come to know well in Washington.

In the meantime, I had made another friend in the person of the all-powerful Senator from Ohio, Mark Hanna, who was heart and soul with Father in building up the Merchant Marine. He was a chunky powerful man, almost as broad as he was tall, with a full face and an expression which left no doubt that he would fight to the last ditch for anything he had determined to obtain. His morning appearance in the lobby of his Washington hotel was like a royal levee. As he proceeded to the door, at least four people were holding to his coat tails and a half-dozen more trying to whisper in his ears. Unless you saw it yourself you could not believe human beings would so openly seek offices.

In the summer I accompanied Father to take the cure at Aix-les-

Bains, and Senator Hanna joined us in London. Whenever we had a party he used to hand his wallet over to me with the remark, "You know how to spend money better than I. You ask the people you want, go to the best places, and pay the bills out of this."

I had never had such a pocketful of money, and I made certain it was disposed of to the best advantage.

At Aix, J. P. Morgan met us. I was much amused at the way the trio of old gentlemen "submitted" to the so-called "rigid" regimen. They consented to appear at the baths in the morning, where they were pummeled and punched, and had warm water squirted on their livers from hoses so potent that the force almost knocked them down. However, in the afternoon, they drove comfortably through the beautiful environs, and at night there was always a dinner party.

The doctor said to Father, "I'm sorry, Mr. Griscom, but I have to forbid your eating any strawberries."

"All right," said Father.

"And, Mr. Griscom, I absolutely forbid you to eat any tomatoes."

"Very well, but a little champagne won't do any harm, will it?" asked Father.

"Of course not. Of course not."

So every evening at table Father availed himself to the limit of the wonderful French cuisine, and drank at least a pint of champagne; he ate everything but strawberries and tomatoes. Afterwards the three health-seekers stayed up into the small hours watching plays brought from Paris, or the gambling in the Casino.

Father skipped the customary *Nachkur* in the Tyrol or Switzerland, but I went off to the Engadine with Charley and Leila Crichton. In the midst of mountain climbing and water color sketching there came a cable from Washington. I was offered the position of Secretary of Legation at Constantinople.

CHAPTER XI

THE SICK MAN OF EUROPE

Bag and baggage I was on the Orient Express which pulled out of Paris September 12 — en route to report to our Minister to Turkey, Oscar Straus, now returned to the Republican fold and rewarded with a second mission to Constantinople. We wound around the wooded mountains and high grassy valleys of Bavaria, speeded past the white villages and blue lakes of Austria, rumbled over the muddy Danube into Vienna, and headed for Budapest and Belgrade, the gateway to the Balkans.

In the dining car I inspected my fellow passengers curiously. The authors who concocted the thrillers of the Nineties constantly used "the Orient Express" as a setting for their plots. I wondered whether the man opposite me were a prince in disguise, whether the beautiful lady across the aisle were an adventuress, whether the two men at the corner table were secret service agents weaving plots against the peace of Europe.

I was scarcely surprised when in the middle of the third night we jarred to a stop, and through the window I saw flickering lights reflected on the rocky sides of a defile. I thought Balkan bandits were holding us up until the conductor came by to say there was a cave-in ahead; we would have to change trains. The sleepy passengers, each clutching a pitch torch, followed him over a great heap of debris, boarded handcars, and started through a tunnel. Sometimes a sudden draft made the flames leap up, and out of the darkness momentarily sprang into view the white skirts, the colored headdresses and swarthy mustached faces of Serbian railwaymen.

Climbing into a compartment on the new train, I found it already occupied by a trim lean Englishman beside whom stood two enormous leather pouches. By the tiny golden grayhound dangling from his watch chain I identified him as one of the Queen's Messengers who carried the diplomatic correspondence of the Empire

— England did not trust the regular mails. Presently he chained the pouches to his wrist and went to sleep; in the morning he had his breakfast sent in rather than leave them. I was sure they must contain the secrets of British policy in the Near East.

My companion had made the trip often and was quite ready to comment on the points of interest along the way. Beyond the Bulgarian border, the track began to twist snakelike over the country in the most fantastic manner, never going up the slightest grade if it could go around. This section had been constructed on a kilometric basis by the Viennese bankers, Hirsch Brothers. The longer they could stretch out the railroad, the more money they could collect from the helpless Turks.

Near Constantinople we ran over a flat arid expanse and then, without warning, we passed through a gap in the decaying walls of ancient Byzantium and were swallowed up in Stamboul. We skirted the hills on which the city was built, so close to the shore that I could see the masts of ships tied at the wharves. On the left rose sharply masses of unpainted, yellow-gray, wooden hovels with grilled windows and flat roofs. All patched and falling to pieces, they bulged crazily into narrow, crooked streets which cut like gullies in every direction. Far above I glimpsed dark cypresses and slender minarets against the sky. The train swung around a great curve by the Golden Horn, and we had arrived.

The platform of the little wooden station was hung with red, white, and blue, and crowded with people, grouped by a red carpet. The strains of the "Marseillaise" blared in through the open window. "The French Ambassador, M. Constans, is coming back to his post," said the Queen's Messenger. "In an out-of-the-way spot like this half your life will be spent seeing members of the Diplomatic Corps going off and returning again." And he waved good-by as he strode away, keeping within arms' length of his pouches.

I tried to pick out someone who might be there to meet me, and finally caught sight of a fierce-looking individual in a skirt covered with gold lace; his belt bristled with Circassian knife and revolver, and in his hand he carried a short whip with a wicked thong. It was hard to believe this apparition from the Arabian Nights belonged to the American Legation, but the two men standing near him proved to be John Riddle, the departing secretary, and our dragoman, or Oriental secretary, Alessandro Gargiulo, a gray-bearded, emaciated Italian with a hooked nose.

Riddle explained that all the diplomats had left Constantinople for the summer and that Mr. Straus was at Therapia, some ten miles up the Bosphorus; after breakfast the Legation launch would take me there. He then made a gesture towards our retainer, "Mahmoud will get your baggage." The minute the Albanian appeared in the customs house, every Turkish official dropped whatever he was doing and went scurrying in search of my bags. In no time they were being loaded into the Legation carriage. Noticing my astonishment, Riddle observed, "A Legation kavass is a privileged person. Mahmoud's responsible to the Turkish Government for the safety of the Minister and all his staff. If anything happens to us he might lose his head. Like most Albanians he knows how to handle the Turks."

Mahmoud's methods were efficient but decidedly brusque. Springing to the box, he screamed and swung his arms until the people who had closed in around the carriage reluctantly gave way. I was afraid we would run somebody down as we charged ahead through the crammed and jammed street — men in the costumes of a hundred nationalities, women veiled and unveiled, gilded and inlaid sedan chairs on the shoulders of bearers, horses, oxen, donkeys, and everywhere the most horrible dogs. Some were limping on three legs, some had lost an ear or a tail, some had great open sores and lay in the sun licking them. Many were nosing in piles of filth, seeking something to eat.

"Doesn't anybody do anything about those dogs?" I asked Riddle.

In Turkish eyes, he answered, they brought luck. The Government had once removed five thousand to an island, but immediately a disaster had descended upon the city and everybody had said, "Those dogs ought never to have been taken away." Since then they had scavenged unmolested.

My nose told me the scavenging had not been very thorough. At my sniff Riddle remarked, "Oh, don't mind the smell. You'll get used to it. When Lord Byron was here he made a census of stinks and counted seventy-five separate ones." I caught a few pleasant whiffs of coffee, tea, and perfume, but "stink" was the only term that fitted most of what came to my nostrils.

Turning sharp right, we clattered across the rickety old wooden bridge of Galata, which spanned the Golden Horn, and started up-hill along the broad paved Grande Rue de Péra, where the Europeans lived. Riddle pointed to the second-story windows of a shabby building with a dentist's sign on the first floor. "That's the American Legation. Not very prepossessing, is it?" Altogether he seemed rather disillusioned about the diplomatic service. He had spent three years learning Russian in the expectation of being stationed at St. Petersburg. The State Department had considered his application, and then had sent him to Constantinople.

We breakfasted at the Cercle de l'Orient, to which all the diplo-mats belonged, and which had the reputation of being one of the greatest gambling clubs in Europe. Afterwards we drove to the Turkish Arsenal dock on the Bosphorus, and Gargiulo and I em-barked in the Legation *bateau mouche*. Straightway we were in the midst of a water life as varied and picturesque as the street scenes of the city. We passed ferries shuttling back and forth from Scutari on the Asiatic shore, tramp steamers Odessa-bound, fishing boats with dirty red sails, and open coasters that might have carried the Argonauts. Pointed, slender caiques, painted every color, darted swiftly here and there, manned by two, four, six, eight, ten oars, according to the importance of the owner. I saw one with twelve rowers in red fezzes, blue tunics, and broad white trousers, rhyth-mically swinging along together.

A launch flying the German flag approached, and an imposing, heavily-built man sitting in the stern rose and lifted his hat. "You must return his bow," said Gargiulo. "That's the German Am-bassador, the Baron Adolf Marschall von Bieberstein."

This was my first experience of what an official position did for you. I stood up, somewhat self-conscious, although I realized the salute from the former Foreign Secretary of the German Empire was not given to me, but to the flag which indicated a representative of the United States.

As we proceeded, I tried to draw Gargiulo out on diplomatic affairs. He was as close as a clam, merely scrutinizing me with his sleepy black eyes while he identified the edifices which lined the shore. Most impressive of all was the imperial palace of Dolma Bagché, an incredible quarter-mile façade of domes, columns, balconies, courts, and ornamented gates from which flights of white steps led into the pure blue water.

The current pouring out of the Black Sea grew stronger, and we drew nearer and nearer to the bank. Our prow cut through the reflections of pink and white villas, palaces, and tall green trees — and where the channel narrowed to about five hundred yards we came practically within touching distance of the quai wall. Above our heads rose the ancient ruined battlements and three square towers of Rumeli Hissar, the Castle of Europe. Beside them were the modern buildings of Robert College, erected and maintained by the American missionaries. Then once again the Bosphorus widened, and in the sweeping curve to our left nestled little villages, one of which was Therapia.

At the foot of Mr. Straus's garden was a wharf, and there the Minister was waiting, a small, scholarly-looking man with a straggly, sandy beard. Both he and his wife did their best to make me feel at home. As soon as we had finished lunch we went for a drive in the cypress-covered hills of the Forest of Belgrade behind the town. Carriage after carriage rolled by with a big black eunuch on the box. In the back of many were veiled ladies in silks and brocades, and when we were well into the country some of them lifted their *yashmaks,* — the cloths which concealed their faces, — ogled, smiled, beckoned us to follow. Mr. Straus warned me never to show any interest because they meant nothing by it, and whoever made advances to a Turkish woman ran the risk of being immediately attacked by any Mohammedans who witnessed the insult.

Towards evening, the Strauses left me at my hotel in Therapia. While from the balcony of my room I watched the fading light on the purple-shadowed hills of Asia across the Bosphorus, a band was playing Viennese music in the garden below. I fell asleep convinced that Turkey was going to fulfill my utmost expectations of romance and adventure.

I reported for duty early the next morning and Mr. Straus at once set me at my old job of writing up the archives; to my dismay they had been far more neglected than those at London. I found it a dull occupation for a beautiful morning. Through the open door I could see the garden and the sun shining on a spreading tree loaded with ripe black figs, a fruit I particularly liked. About eleven o'clock the temptation became irresistible. I sauntered out and looked up; they were just beyond reach. Quickly I pulled myself into the tree, and, with my mouth full, was swinging my legs happily when I heard a great voice booming, "Mr. Griscom, I expect the secretary of my Legation to attend to his duties and not spend his time eating figs in the garden."

I had to swallow hastily before I could reply meekly, "Yes, Mr. Straus." I felt I had made a bad start.

Thereafter it seemed to me I had a time clock on my every minute. Quite unlike the Embassy in London, this Legation was conducted as though it were an office with regular hours. Mr. Straus had received an excellent business training in the family crockery-importing concern at 42 Warren Street, New York City. The discipline did me a world of good, and his profound knowledge of international law was extremely helpful.

It did not take me long to discover that American relations with Turkey had run into difficulties. Every diplomat kept a list of questions under discussion in his pocketbook, and as soon as one was settled it was scratched off; Mr. Straus's list had virtually not a scratch on it.

Trade between the United States and Turkey was negligible; the Legation's real purpose was to protect and advance the interests of the hundreds of missionaries scattered throughout the country — an American in Turkey was practically synonymous with missionary. In the Armenian massacres of five years earlier, much property had been destroyed and the payment of the resulting ninety-thousand-dollar indemnity claim was our chief issue with Turkey.

In proportion to the relatively small sum involved, the stir in Washington was tremendous. The missionaries had been among the first to learn how to exert pressure in politics — even the head of our State Department used to quake when the head of a Bible Society walked in. Almost every instruction to the Minister included an exhortation to "get that Armenian indemnity."

The Turks had their own reasons for declining to pay. They had refused steadfastly to admit responsibility for the massacres, which they said had been perpetrated by "wild people" over whom they had no control. However, the underlying reason was the natural Turkish antagonism to missionaries. Originally these had come to educate, and, if possible to convert, Mohammedans — but instead their schools were now filled with Greeks, Bulgarians, Armenians, and Syrians, who belonged to Christian subject nationalities, and were frequently leaders in revolts against the Turks. Although no proof had ever been brought that the missionaries had encouraged rebellion, every conceivable obstacle was placed in the way of their activities.

Before any building could be erected, the legation had to obtain an imperial sanction, or iradé, which took months. If an exequatur was requested for a consul in an Armenian district, the Turks kept putting it off, pointing out the sole excuse for stationing an American consul there was to help the missionaries. The Turks not only refused to pay any indemnity, but also stood firm against reconstruction of the ruined buildings — which irritated the missionaries more than the unpaid money.

Shortly after my arrival Dr. George Washburn, the head of Robert College, called on Mr. Straus to learn what progress had been made. Of all Americans in Turkey, he was the most influential, and his position was increased at the moment because he was a cousin of John Hay. In his forty years at Constantinople he had amassed an immense knowledge of Near Eastern affairs; the best articles on these subjects in the leading American and European reviews were his. In England also his prestige was great; the single piece of advice a new Ambassador received from Lord Salisbury was "Cultivate Dr. Washburn." He was known as the "Father of Bulgaria"; seven out of the nine members of the Bulgarian Cabinet had been his students, and in every crisis they hurried down to ask him what to do. The dream of his life was to educate enough young men in liberal ideas so that in time they could assume the task of reform.

From the conversation between Dr. Washburn and Mr. Straus I gathered that the missionaries were growing extremely impatient at the long delay. Mr. Straus admitted his helplessness. The Turks were procrastinating to the limit, even in the most inconsequential matters.

The person who was really responsible for the stalemate, and the only one who could alter it, was the Sultan Abdul Hamid. There was a Grand Vizier, a cabinet, and an army, but not one of them counted for anything. The diplomatic corps was accredited officially to the Foreign Office in charge of Tewfik Pasha, a complete figurehead, because foreign policy, like every other branch of government, was conducted by the Sultan from his palace, Yildiz (Starry) Kiosk, outside the city.

An envoy's success depended on whether he were *persona grata* to the Sultan, and Mr. Straus had accomplished much on his first mission. Abdul Hamid was once asked whether he objected to the United States' having sent a Jew.

"Not at all," he had replied. "I'm delighted to receive one. In my mind there's no difference between a Jew and a Christian. Both are infidels."

Friendly as the Sultan had been in the past, he was now showing his displeasure in the most marked manner. Every Friday occurred the ceremony known as the *Selamlik,* literally "the place of salutation," during which Abdul Hamid drove to prayers while the diplomatic corps looked on from a pavilion. Afterwards the favored ambassadors and an occasional minister were received in audience. For six months he had not summoned Mr. Straus.

Due to their peculiarly Oriental methods, the Turks had Mr. Straus at their mercy. The papers concerning every little affair were scattered among the different departments of the Sublime Porte, the name given the Turkish Government building, because in the old days justice had been administered by the Sultan at the gate of the palace. Each paper had to be moved progressively from the lower departments to the higher, and almost always it took three to four months before one was finally approved. No department would ever settle anything itself, but would pass it on to another.

However, I soon found that American claims were infinitesimal compared with the designs of the Great Powers of Europe who many years previously had constituted themselves the surgeons of Turkey. "We have on our hands a very sick man," Nicholas I of Russia had remarked in 1853 to Sir George Hamilton Seymour, the English Ambassador at St. Petersburg, "a very sick man. It will be a great misfortune if, one of these days, he should slip away from us before the necessary arrangements have been made."

From the Western point of view Turkey was indeed sick, — with dissatisfied subject nationalities, different religions, a corrupt bureaucracy, and a weak government. Immediately upon his accession Abdul Hamid had been engaged in a disastrous war with Russia over the Bulgarian Massacres. The other Great Powers thereupon had called a consultation to prevent Russia from operating alone and at the Congress of Berlin the carving up of Turkey began. As her share England took Cyprus and in a few years Egypt as well — actions which turned Turkish trust of Great Britain into profound suspicion. Russia, Austria, France had helped themselves to slices, and Italy was sharpening her knife for Tripoli.

In marked contrast to the attitude of the other physicians, Germany's medical staff was prescribing a regimen of kindness. She had asked for nothing at the Congress of Berlin, had sent General von der Goltz to reform the Turkish army, had supplied arms and munitions from Krupps, and her Emperor had paid a visit to Constantinople the year after his accession. Only recently he had made a second visit, and everybody was still speculating as to what he had meant by his famous statement at Damascus, "May the Sultan and the three hundred million Mussulmans scattered over the earth be assured that the German Emperor will always be their friend." No wonder the German doctors were the only ones who were collecting their bills in full — the concession for the final link which took their Berlin-Bagdad Railway, on paper at least, to the Persian Gulf had just been signed.

Since the Powers considered it essential to keep a finger on the Turkish pulse, they sent diplomats of the first rank who were now in residence in and around Therapia. Germany was represented by her ex-foreign minister, the Baron Marschall, whom Abdul Hamid received more frequently than any other ambassador. Signor Pansa of Italy, an urbane Latin, was also a favorite of the Sultan. M. Constans of France had accomplished the feat, impossible in any but a republican country, of rising to his position from that of a *vidangeur,* or cleaner of cesspools. Baron de Callice of Austria was our dean, and with the elderly M. Zinoviev of Russia, worked to maintain the status quo in the Balkans. Gargiulo, in one of his rare moments of loquacity, told me he had seen Maximov, the Russian dragoman, unload bags of gold from his carriage and openly distribute it in handfuls to the Palace servants; innumerable Turkish officials, high and low, were said to be in Russian pay.

Sir Nicholas Roderick O'Conor, the British Ambassador, was a taciturn Irishman of long experience in Bulgaria, China, and Russia. It was natural for me to make friends among the English staff — Maurice de Bunsen, the Councillor, was an intimate friend of Harry White; next in rank was George Barclay with an American wife. Instead of hiring foreigners for their dragoman service, the British had a special branch, the members of which were trained in the language and manners of the country where they were stationed. Adam Block was chief dragoman, and his assistant was Gerald Fitzmaurice, a leading authority on Turkey.

A notable distinction between the British and American foreign services was that our envoys were instructed to restrict their reports to events in the country to which they were accredited, while the British, on the other hand, reported everything they could get wind of. They picked up many strange stories which, although sometimes exaggerated, were often amusing. One of their choicest dealt with a Cabinet meeting held by King George of Greece shortly after his arrival in Athens in 1863. To illustrate a point he walked to a huge map on the wall, leaving his watch on the table. A few minutes later when he resumed his seat the timepiece was gone. He looked around and said, "Will whoever has my watch please return it?"

The circle of faces stared blankly at him. The King still could not believe the disappearance was intentional. "Well, gentlemen, I'm not accustomed to this type of joke. I'd like to have my watch back."

Nobody spoke or moved.

The King announced firmly, "I'm going to put out the light while I count sixty. If I find the watch again on the table, the incident will be closed."

In the darkness he called the seconds out loud, and turned up the light. His silver inkstand had vanished.

Work for everybody was generally over at three o'clock, and the chief recreation was to go galloping across the hills, sometimes in small groups, sometimes in a long cavalcade. Riding among the mountains of Arizona had been exciting, but here there was always an added spice of danger. We all had stallions which were ready to fight at any moment. Many times I had to rein up sharply to avoid a pair of hooves flashing before my face. If we had the misfortune to meet a mare pulling a cart, our mounts began to foam at the mouth, leap about wildly, and rear on their hind legs.

We often encountered groups of three or four Turkish soldiers, fully armed and accoutered, who eyed us disagreeably. Because of the Moslem hatred of Christians, we were warned to avoid provocation of any natives. The hills were filled with shepherds guarding their flocks; their great crooks made them resemble illustrations from the Bible. If we approached too near, their fierce dogs would fly at us, and we would spur up our horses and escape as fast as we could. We knew that if we tried to beat off the animals, the shepherds would pull out their knives, and once a row started every Moslem in the neighborhood would be ready to lend a hand against the *giaour*.

Once a half-dozen of us were invited to have lunch with Aziz Bey, an aide of the Sultan, in a lovely little garden restaurant not far from San Stefano, some thirty miles out of the city. Thinking sixty miles was too long a ride, I had arranged for a groom to take back my horse while I returned by train.

In many places the railroad track paralleled the road, and as we went along I kept a careful watch for my companions. During a momentary delay near a military arsenal, I saw them come galloping at full speed across a wide stretch of open country, apparently not noticing the signs *Yassak* (forbidden) which were posted all around. Suddenly, springing out of nowhere, appeared a squad of Turkish soldiers. They surrounded de Bunsen, who was in the lead, jabbed him in the thigh with a bayonet, and dragged him and the others off their horses. Aziz Bey dashed up and, angered by the treatment of his friends, lashed at a soldier with his crop. In spite of the aigrettes he wore as a Sultan's aide, he too was roughly pulled to the ground, and, as my train puffed away, the whole party was being herded into the guardhouse.

When I met de Bunsen again he said ruefully, "This is a fine mess I'm in — a bayonet scratch on my thigh, and a first-class rumpus with the Turkish Government — and to think you escaped only because you had a sore tail!"

Whatever ride we took, and we went in a different direction almost every day, somebody assured me it was Lord Byron's favorite. Although the poet had stayed only two months, he seemed to have covered the country thoroughly, and everywhere in Constantinople you heard anecdotes of him. At one party he had defied anyone to give him a word on which he could not make a pun. "Mephistopheles," somebody suggested. Unhesitatingly Byron had clenched his hand and replied, "I can double up Mephistopheles." ("My fist awful easy.")

On another occasion Lord Byron put on a charade. The curtain rose to disclose a stage bare except for an unpainted clotheshorse of pine, known in England as deal, and, when no one could guess what it meant, he prompted, "An island in the Aegean." Still no light dawned. Finally he had to explain that the answer was "Delos." ("Deal 'oss.")

Again the curtain lifted to reveal the identical scene. "Another island," Lord Byron announced. The audience had to be told it was "Samos." ("Same 'oss.")

For the third time the curtain unveiled the same setting. Strangely enough no one was sufficiently clever to suggest "Naxos." ("Next 'oss.")

The most talked of Englishman ever in Turkey was Stratford Canning. In 1810 at the age of only twenty-three, he had been left alone in Turkey as Minister Plenipotentiary. His home Government had been too busy waging an almost single-handed conflict against Napoleon to bother with instructions for him. Setting his own wits to work, he saw that if Turkey, only half-friendly to France, could be persuaded to make peace with Russia, then the Russians, also lukewarm to France, might feel strong enough to break with Napoleon. Without authority he opened a secret correspondence with the Muscovites, and at the same time pounded away at the Sultan with demands, persuasions, reminders, and threats.

For two years he kept this up. Finally, in June, 1812, due almost entirely to his efforts, Russia and Turkey signed the Treaty of Bucharest. The Russian Army of the Danube was hurriedly called north to Moscow, and arrived just in time to make certain the rout of the *Grande Armée*. Thus a young man of twenty-five, forgotten by his own Government, had been a decisive factor in the downfall of Napoleon.

Again and again Canning had tried to retire, but in each crisis England had sent him back. Although he had now been dead two decades, to Englishman and Turk alike he still remained the *Buyuk Elchi,* the Great Ambassador. He was the model for every young diplomat in Constantinople — we were all going to be Cannings.

CHAPTER XII

THE UNSPEAKABLE TURK

In October, when the weather grew cool, the diplomatic corps moved back to town. Mr. Straus lived on the Grande Rue de Péra, and I rented a charming house at the very summit of the hill. One of the *hamals,* or porters of Constantinople, famous for their strength, took my heavy trunk on his shoulder, and walked up the steep grade to the Rue Siraselvi as though his load were a feather-weight. I hired two Armenians, — Bedros to cook and Balthasar to do the rest of the work, — and moved in immediately.

The noises of the city floated faintly through my window — the cries of cab drivers and street vendors, the snarling of dogs, the creaking of wheels, the shrill call of the muezzin from the turret of the little mosque below. Beyond the roofs and minarets I could see the cypress-clad hills, most beautiful tipped in white after a slight fall of snow, and in the distance the blue sweep of the Bosphorus.

At night the city watch clumped by, banging their staffs, and making such a commotion that any thieves in the neighborhood had ample warning. The money that each household was expected to contribute to their maintenance seemed to me an utter waste until I learned that, if I did not pay my share, the thieves would be notified that nobody was watching my number.

Each morning I arrived at the office to find Gargiulo gathering himself together for another attempt to move papers at the Porte — he was one of the laziest human beings that ever breathed, yet one of the shrewdest. In the course of his long experience at the Legation he had become expert in following the tortuous ins and outs of the Turkish mind. During ex-President Grant's visit to Turkey in 1878 on his world tour, Abdul Hamid, a young man only two years on the throne, had presented him with a pair of magnificent black Arabian horses. The General, taking one look at them, snorted,

"Spavined! Both of 'em! Not worth a damn! Send 'em back!"

Realizing what a fearful insult this would be, Gargiulo suggested, "Let me see what I can do at the Palace."

He sought out the Sultan's secretary and, after the usual politenesses, remarked, "I've come to thank you for the horses."

"I trust General Grant is pleased."

"I've come to thank you for the horses," repeated Gargiulo.

Sensing something amiss, the secretary inquired, "Anything wrong with the horses?"

For the third time Gargiulo reiterated, "I've come to thank you for the horses."

The secretary now smelled a rat. "Tell me what's the matter," he insisted.

"We've investigated the records and we find no precedent for an ex-President of the United States to be drawn behind a pair of black horses."

"Oh, then the Americans are superstitious?"

"All I can say is that no ex-President of the United States has ever driven behind black horses."

"Leave it to me," replied the understanding official.

The next morning an unblemished pair of grays was substituted.

As far as settling any of our questions was concerned, Gargiulo's efforts were fruitless. I found I had time on my hands to spare. Knowing my French needed improving if it were to stand the strain of diplomatic conversation, I engaged a teacher, a tall, good-looking Turkish Jew who had been educated in France. At my first lesson I asked him about his life in Turkey. Instead of answering, he shifted the subject. I persevered: "Have you ever seen the Sultan?"

Instantly he put his finger to his lips, walked to the door and glanced up and down the hall, crossed to the window and peered out, even made sure no one was underneath the sofa. Then he whispered in my ear, "Whatever you do, I beg of you not to express any view on the Empire. Do not even mention His Majesty or any public question in front of your servants. Just speak French. Nobody can tell who is a paid agent. One hint from a spy and I may go to some jail and never reappear. My people have no influence and no defense. Many of my friends and relatives have already vanished, and no trace of them has ever been found."

At Therapia I had not realized so clearly the methods by which Abdul Hamid maintained his power. His extraordinary spy system stretched throughout the Empire, and he was aware of a plot almost before it was hatched. We had not been back in town more than a few days when a loiterer attached himself to me openly and boldly — not because anyone cared what I did, but because the Palace wanted to know what Turks associated with us. At the Legation Mr. Straus warned me not to leave any papers on my desk; one of our employees undoubtedly reported to the Palace all that he saw and heard and the contents of any letters he could read. I should not even talk in loud tones because someone might be listening at the door.

I was quite ready to believe any of the fantastic accounts of the tyrannic rule of "Abdul the Damned," "The Red Sultan," "The Great Assassin." As a safeguard against plots no two Turkish officials dared dine together except at a foreign embassy, in which case they had to secure permission and make a point of arriving and leaving separately. Moreover, if any Turk's dossier showed too much familiarity with any foreign diplomat, he was automatically suspect.

With reason the Sultan was terrified of attempts on his life. All but foreign diplomats had to approach him with hands crossed in front to show they carried no weapons. He virtually never left Yildiz, and, when he went the few hundred yards to *Selamlik,* he took with him in his carriage Osman Pasha, who had so valiantly withstood the Russians at Plevna that he had become the idol of the people. The Sultan apparently believed that anybody who wanted to throw a bomb would hesitate if he had also to murder such a hero.

For fear of poison, every morsel Abdul Hamid ate was prepared by his mother, and handed to a trusted Palace official who was always stationed behind his chair to serve him personally. In case of revolution, the Sultan kept a carriage perpetually hitched and waiting inside the Palace gate, and his yacht lay at anchor offshore with steam up, ready for instant flight.

Among the high Government officials were three men in whom the Sultan apparently trusted. These three did not dare be disloyal; they knew that they would be the first to fall if anything happened to their master. From the diplomats' point of view the most important was Tahsen Bey, the Sultan's *Bash Kiatib,* or private secretary. He was a first-class businessman and a shrewd planner, who was credited with being largely responsible for the Sultan's foreign policy. Complementary to him was Izzet Bey, head of the Secret Service, the practical man of action, the reputed organizer of the Armenian massacres. Cruel and heartless, he was the most dreaded individual in Turkey. Last of the trio was Hassan Pasha, the Minister of the nonexistent Marine, the wealthiest official in the Empire by virtue of being the Sultan's favorite. His annual salary was increased by such side revenues as the three hundred and fifty-four thousand dollars from the tolls of the Bridge of Galata.

With these helpers Abdul Hamid carried out his measures of cruelty and suppression. Fitzmaurice described to me how once at Yildiz he had been talking to an imperial secretary, while from the next room were echoing the terrible shrieks of a man in torture. The official went serenely on, merely raising his voice loud enough to be heard over the tumult.

One day I learned that a new *Vali,* or Governor, of Tripoli had been appointed. I naturally supposed that he was being accorded a great honor, but Gargiulo sardonically remarked, "There won't be anybody on the pier to wave that fellow good-by, and before many months we'll be reading of his unfortunate illness and death. An aide-de-camp accompanies him who, some fine morning, will drop poison in his coffee. Then some other poor wretch will be elevated as *Vali.*"

Another time I was told that Izzet Bey's police had come in the night to the house of a prominent citizen, roused him from his bed, and dragged him off. Weeks elapsed, and nobody could ascertain what had happened to him. Perhaps he had been advanced to power through some female relative who had risen to favor in the harem, and when she had been supplanted by a rival, he had fallen with the rest of her faction.

Nobody had accurate information as to the fate of those who disappeared, but occasionally some ugly discovery was made. Several years prior to my arrival, the seawall in front of Dolma Bagché Palace had caved in, and a diver had been summoned from England to repair the damages. No sooner had he reached the bottom on his first descent than he signaled frantically to be pulled up. Anxious helpers hurriedly removed his headpiece. His face was white as a sheet, and it was some time before he could utter a word. "You won't get me down there again," he gasped; "it's nothing but a bloody cemetery."

The diver had opened his eyes to find himself surrounded by enormous sacks, their rotting tops swaying gently back and forth in the current. He put his hand out to touch one and it dissolved, disclosing a skull on top of a heap of bones. Looking closer he distinguished more bones protruding from the others — all that remained of men and women who, for some reason or other, had incurred suspicion and had been done away with.

Naturally I was eager to explore this mysterious city. Every time I gazed from the Chancery window I saw something interesting. Frequently eunuchs off duty, reminding me of big puffy capons, paraded by in twos or threes. I was told they lived for food, and that their conversation was devoted almost entirely to their marvelous dinners. You could not believe that such thin little squeaks of voices could come out of such huge bodies.

Sometimes my attention would be attracted by a noise in the street, and I would glance down to be confronted by the face of some dead Greek, staring up at me as he joggled by on a hearse or on the shoulders of bearers; the Greeks never closed their coffins before the cemetery was reached. In Stamboul we were always running across Turkish funerals bound for one of the graveyards outside the city walls. As the cortège progressed along the street, tailor, cobbler, butcher stopped work, left his house or shop to replace a bearer, and continued until someone in turn replaced him. In the heart of the city he might have to go only a few yards; farther out, as much as a half mile. It seemed to me a pleasant custom that, however poor a man might be, on his death he too would be carried to his grave without cost to his family as a reward for the help he had given others during his lifetime.

Different nations had their own holidays and customs. On the Greek Easter, every Greek flocked to congratulate the Patriarch at his Palace on the Golden Horn. Every one greeted everybody else with *"Surrexit"* ("He is risen") and a resounding kiss. I observed one smartly dressed fellow accost fifteen girls in this way.

Not an able-bodied Greek woman in Constantinople stayed inside on Easter.

After the rains came the streets were seas of mud, and often we had to wade or duck out of the way to avoid being splashed. I was a long time getting over my surprise at the inverted sense of modesty of the Turkish women. At every mud puddle they hoisted their skirts up to their waists, revealing stockings, bits of bare thigh, and good old-fashioned drawers. If they allowed their hair to be seen they were disgraced, but apparently they had no feeling about displaying their legs.

When some American friends of mine visited me, they too poked about the city and unearthed an ancient Greek portrait of a feminine nude. As they were leaving Constantinople, the Turkish customs officers refused to let it pass. It seemed my friends were going to lose their treasure until one of them quick-wittedly saved the day by pinning a handkerchief over her face. Immediately the officers smiled and bowed them through with the picture.

Curiously enough the Turks combined with their fierceness a remarkable naïveté. By the Admiralty Dock in the Golden Horn the remains of Abdul Aziz' navy rested in the mud — laid up by the present Sultan for fear of a revolt; caretakers were growing flowers on the decks. There was a charming story in circulation of the Turkish gunboat which had once put forth to sea, and in the Mediterranean encountered bad weather. Being poor navigators, the ship's officers lost their bearings. The captain was ashamed to ask for his position, but finally sighted a tramp flying the British flag. "She's bound to get to a port. We'll follow her," he decided. The British vessel steamed through the Pillars of Hercules and into the Channel, the Turkish gunboat close behind. Right up the Thames to Tilbury docks the Turks pursued her — and then hired an expert English navigator to take them home.

The most fascinating place in Constantinople was the Grand Bazaar, great stone buildings with vaulted roofs covering miles of streets — some broad enough for a carriage or camel train, some so narrow you could barely squeeze through. Here and there they opened out into squares with mosques and fountains. Knots of thirty or forty Turks would be gathered around one of the professional readers, listening intently to extracts from the newspapers or the Koran, and frequently stories. The Turks rarely showed amusement in ordinary life, but they loved an amusing tale, and suddenly young and old would throw back their heads and burst into laughter.

Fitzmaurice said many of the anecdotes dealt with the doings and sayings of the peasant philosopher, Nasr-ed-Din Hoja, and he retold some for my benefit. Nothing could have illustrated better the peculiar biting Turkish humor. On one occasion this farmer borrowed his neighbor's copper kettle. The owner appeared to reclaim it, and was surprised to find, inside, a second kettle, a miniature of his own. "This doesn't belong to me," he said.

"Yes, it does," Nasr-ed-Din assured him. "I've good news for you. Your big kettle has given birth to this little one."

The neighbor did not stop to probe too deeply into how this miracle had come about, but hurried home delighted.

A few months later Nasr-ed-Din once more asked for the loan of the kettle, and the neighbor was only too ready. On calling for it, full of anticipation, he was met by Nasr-ed-Din, wearing a mournful expression. "Friend, I've sad news for you. Your kettle has died."

"What nonsense! Don't try to make me believe a kettle can die!"

"Anybody who can believe a kettle can have a baby can believe a kettle can die. Good-by," retorted the philosopher.

Another time Nasr-ed-Din borrowed an ass. When the owner came for it, the farmer shook his head. "Too bad. Too bad. My son has it in the next valley across the mountain, and I can't return it now."

"But, I need it very much."

"I'm sorry. It isn't here."

Just then resounded a loud bray from a near-by shed. "Oh, Nasr-ed-Din, you've lied to me," cried the neighbor. "I hear my ass."

"Neighbor," demanded Nasr-ed-Din, drawing himself up proudly, "do you mean to say you'd take the word of an ass against mine?"

The darkest corners of the Bazaar were alive with color — red fezzes, green turbans of the Hajjis who had been to Mecca, white turbans, bright awnings, garish new rugs spread out so that the tread of passers-by might age them. Every street was a bazaar in itself — one each for gold, silver, copper, perfume, pipes, carpets, arms. In addition there was a street of shops which sold accumulations of treasures and junk from all the countries of Europe and Asia — old German engravings, rare French prints, furniture left behind by members of the foreign colony, sequined dresses stolen from the wardrobe of a famous actress, rings and jewelry given by a prince to some favorite who had pawned them when he lost his master's favor.

The old Turks would sit impassively in the back of their shops, puffing away at their narghilehs, waiting for Allah to direct a customer to their doors. Every purchase was a ceremony. In one shop I asked about a beautiful silver-handled knife; without replying, the merchant offered me thick syrupy coffee in a V-shaped cup set in a metal holder. The grounds were supposed to fall into the V, but I could not help swallowing some of them. After we had sipped silently a few minutes, he named a price, far too high. I demurred and offered him one far too low. He shook his head. I rose and thanked him for his hospitality — unfortunately I was a poor young man with little money, and could not afford to possess such a valuable object.

"Do not go yet," urged the merchant. "I like you so much that I'll make you a better price." He poured a second cup of coffee, and we parted on terms of friendship.

In a few days I returned for more coffee and conversation, and again went home without the knife. It was several weeks before I finally secured it. Sometimes I was conducting negotiations in five or six establishments at once.

Purchasing things was one of the chief amusements of the Diplomatic Corps. We all turned out for the sale of the effects of the Sultan's deceased Grand Chamberlain. I happened to be standing next the Secretary of the Belgian Legation, Fritz van den Steen de Jehay, who told me the history of several sets of china. One marked with an N. and a crown, which I bought, had been a gift from Napoleon III. Another of my bargains was a set of plates, each decorated with a painting of a Swedish castle, originally sent by the King of Sweden as a birthday present to the Emperor Franz Josef of Austria; after some years in a storeroom at Schönbrünn they had been packed up again and dispatched to Turkey for the Sultan's birthday.

Van den Steen had been King Leopold's private secretary, and his first duty of the morning had been to supply a list of sovereigns and royalties whose birthdays had to be remembered. For a lesser prince or grand duke a telegram would do, but for emperors, kings, and crown princes, presents had to be selected. King Leopold kept shelves stocked with gifts he had received, and the two would choose an appropriate one, Van den Steen checking to make sure it would not go back to its original donor. Sometimes a set of china would spend years traveling around Europe, and eventually by mischance a monarch would find himself once more the owner of an object which he himself had started on its rounds perhaps twenty years before.

Since the foreign colony was not very large, social life lacked variety. The wives of Ministers and Ambassadors all had afternoons at home which secretaries were supposed to attend, and now and then, to liven things up, there were formal balls. The most amusing feature of these was the sight of the younger and more attractive ladies of the Corps in their *décolletage,* which disclosed their arms spotted black and blue. The method employed by the Turks to show admiration for European women they passed on the street was to reach out and pinch them. The nearer the woman approached the Turkish ideal of feminine beauty, the more likely she was to be marked. Although the pinches must have hurt, the bruised ones seemed rather pleased with their scars.

If I wanted some exercise I could usually procure a companion at the British Embassy; work there was so well organized that somebody could always get away. Wherever they were, the English would not forgo their shooting. We had fine sport with the little Egyptian migratory quail, which came by the million round the Eastern end of the Mediterranean. With Claud Russell, one of the younger British secretaries, I hired a two-acre wheat field some fifteen miles distant by the Sea of Marmora, which we could reach by launch any afternoon in the right season and obtain enough birds for dinner. The extraordinary thing was that the next day the patch would be just as full of them as ever.

Riding up and down the country, we were amazed to see Turks with hawks on their wrists; apparently the ancient art of falconry had never died out. Managing a falcon looked easy enough; it sat until it was unhooded and then, with a twist of the owner's wrist, it soared into the air, swooped on the quarry — and there you had a quail. Russell and I were so enthusiastic that we sent to London for books on the subject, and soon became nuisances around the British Embassy with our talk of mews, jesses, stooping, waiting on, imping, casting, and mantling, and the relative merits of eyases and tiercels, peregrines and merlins.

We inquired for a well-trained bird and located one priced at five pounds. Having watched her work, we were given a stick with a white cloth at the end, and shown how to lure her back after she had made her kill. Then we secured directions for food and care, and brought her home.

The very next morning we sallied forth to our wheat field. Russell, who had a leather gauntlet, carried the bird, very gay in her crested hood and bells tinkling on her legs. The hood slipped off without ruffling a feather. However, the minute we stretched out a finger to unloosen the jesses, or leather thongs around the feet, our hawk bit at us viciously. The quail were getting up constantly, and we were afraid we would miss them. Only after several tries did Russell manage to shake her free, and we both shooed her on with a good old English view halloo. To our consternation our falcon, instead of circling into the air, as she had done with her former master, flew straight to a tall dead tree near-by, and perched on a limb.

We waved the lure frantically, but the falcon ignored us completely. Russell pulled out a red cloth and brandished that. Again no result. For about a half hour we lured, and lured, and lured. The bird merely preened her feathers, seeming to laugh at us. Finally, I remembered that one book had advised lying on the back and kicking the heels in the air. By this time I was willing to try anything and painfully lowered myself on the prickly wheat stalks and kicked with all my might. Still the falcon remained morosely perched on the limb.

Obviously the only recourse was for one of us to climb that dead tree. Russell volunteered and I boosted him up. He moved as cautiously as he could so as not to frighten the bird, and I was quite hopeful when he reached the branch on which she was sitting and gingerly started to creep out. It quivered dangerously, but the bird, although eying Russell suspiciously, allowed him to come near. Holding his breath, Russell very slowly extended his gauntleted hand. Just as I thought he had our costly falcon in his grip, she spread her wings and flapped nonchalantly away. We never saw her again.

Too late we learned that a falcon would not work for a new master without months of breaking-in.

Meanwhile at the Legation, as uneventful weeks went by, Mr. Straus was becoming more and more convinced that his mission was hopeless. He had gallantly decided, at the sacrifice of his personal popularity, to do what he could for his successor. Accordingly, he had deliberately adopted a policy of being disagreeable, making his notes stiffer and stiffer, hoping the Sultan would find anyone else such a welcome contrast that the United States claims would be settled.

Mr. Straus had avoided *Selamlik* for some time, and I had been in Turkey three months before, on December 15th, I drove with him to Yildiz Kiosk on its hill above the Bosphorus. Near the walls the road was lined with soldiers in white uniforms and red fezzes — the Sultan's own Albanian bodyguard, the most loyal troops in the army. As we dismounted in front of the pavilion to join the rest of the corps, a squadron of the White Horse Lancers, each rider bearing a red banner, flashed by us to assume their positions farther down the hill. Ibrahim Pasha, the bearded master of ceremonies, showed us to seats.

Exactly at noon I heard a fanfare of trumpets, and out of the gateway on our left emerged two white horses drawing an open barouche carrying the Sultan — and Osman Pasha. I had expected to see a spidery little man crouched in a corner. On the contrary, there was nothing furtive or cowardly or weak in the Sultan's large penetrating eyes, or sharp aquiline features covered with a graying beard. He was dressed with the utmost simplicity in a red fez and black coat, tight around his neck like a military stock.

I could only glance briefly at the Sultan, because my gaze was riveted on the extraordinary rout of officialdom which scuttled higgledy-piggledy after the carriage, fat and thin, tall and short, old and young, all in full regalia, spurs jangling and swords clattering about their ankles. Gargiulo whispered in my ear, "Those two fat fellows in front are the Grand Vizier and Hassan Pasha. The bearded thin one on this side is Izzet, and right behind him is Tahsen."

Here were the most feared and the most important individuals in Turkey, those who had power over thousands, trotting along like a drove of cattle. The Sultan never looked in their direction. His only motion was to bow several times towards our pavilion as we stood at attention with our hats raised.

Some fifty yards farther on Abdul Hamid turned into the Mosque of Hamidieh, and, while he was at his prayers, coffee and cakes were served us. Emin Bey, the Sultan's chamberlain, appeared through the covered gallery which led to the Palace, and spoke to Baron Marschall, Signor Pansa, and one or two others — he never came near us.

After half an hour the Sultan drove back, followed again by his retinue. *Selamlik* was over, and there was nothing for us to do except go home. Mr. Straus seemed more discouraged than ever.

A few days later the Minister entered the Chancery hurriedly. "Mr. Griscom, Mrs. Straus and I are sailing for New York in three days and I don't know how long I'll be away. In my absence you will be chargé d'affaires of the Legation."

CHAPTER XIII

TALKING TURKEY

From the station platform I waved good-by to the Strauses, feeling very solemn at being left as the chief representative of the United States in Turkey. From now on it was up to me to grant or refuse all the requests which people were constantly making of the Legation. Moreover, I was answerable for the lives and property of the hundreds of missionaries in the Empire. Inevitably I had a sense of elation, but on the other hand the responsibility was sobering; it was easy for anyone in authority to forget he was only the representative of power — not the power itself.

My first official duty was to attend an afternoon musicale at the German Embassy. Mahmoud strode through the streets in front of me, swinging his whip and, delighted at the opportunity to glorify his own position, shouting, "Make way for the *Buyuk Elchi*." When some idler moved too slowly out of the way, the kavass's face turned black with anger and he knocked the offender sprawling. Like everybody else the man showed no resentment, merely shrinking respectfully aside and looking at Mahmoud as though to say, "He must serve a very great man."

Self-conscious as a new boy at school, I walked into the magnificent German Embassy and heard myself announced, "Le Chargé d'Affaires des États Unis." After the music the Baroness asked me to sit beside her on the sofa. *"Sie sprechen Deutsch, nicht wahr, Herr Griscom?"* she began amicably.

"Nur ein bischen, Eccelenz," I replied.

"Then we must talk German," she insisted. I had not spoken that language since the days of the Haccius School, and before I had struggled through three sentences, I had inadvertently used the familiar *du*. She took it as a huge joke, but every German within hearing was horrified. I was thoroughly deflated at having addressed the German Ambassadress as *"du"* on her own sofa.

Inexperienced as I was, it was fortunate that I assumed my new position at a moment of comparative inactivity for the diplomats. The Christmas holidays were succeeded by Ramazan, the movable Turkish month of atonement during which Mohammedans were supposed to fast daily from the time the light permitted them to distinguish a white thread from a black thread in the morning to the time they could no longer do so at night. Being half starved, the Turks were irritable, easily provoked, and crotchety. No one who could avoid it dreamed of attempting to do business with them. However, I was anxious that during Mr. Straus's absence there should be no falling-off in order and discipline at the Legation. Towards the end of the celebrations I summoned Gargiulo for a council of war. Laying Mr. Straus's list on the table, I said, "Let's run over these questions and see what's the status of each."

Without much enthusiasm, Gargiulo put on his spectacles, pulled out a mass of documents from his pocketbook, and selected one. It was divided into squares, each showing the location of a paper at the Porte and the date on which it had been last moved. Several of them were being held up at the office of the Foreign Minister. "We ought to make an effort to push some of those through somehow," I urged. "Why don't we go see Tewfik Pasha together?"

Accordingly we drove across the Bridge of Galata to the old dilapidated buildings of wood and stone known as the Sublime Porte. Gargiulo led me along dusty corridors to the office of the Foreign Minister who received me with a cordial handshake, offered me coffee, and we conversed — he could speak French fluently enough to dispense with an interpreter. However, if I attempted to corner him on something specific, he took refuge in generalities. I departed with the feeling that no matter how well-disposed Tewfik Pasha might be, he was helpless to make an important decision without authority from the Palace.

Although I knew the heads of missions did not go to Yildiz unless for *Selamlik* or an audience with the Sultan, I proposed to Gargiulo, "How about my talking to Tahsen Bey myself?"

A gleam of interest flickered over Gargiulo's countenance. "It's never been done, but I believe it's a good idea."

Together we chose three items which the Turks could grant with no loss of face. Gargiulo arranged the interview, and I went out to Yildiz. Tahsen Bey was a charming-mannered, gentle-looking Turk with the characteristic large, doelike eyes, crisp mustache, and soft voice. He was obviously surprised at my youth, and I had the impression I was being sized-up very carefully.

We drank the inevitable coffee and then I said, "You know, Tahsen Bey, I'm left alone in charge of the American Legation, and if there's anything that would help to smooth relations between our Governments I'd like to do it. The United States is deeply concerned that nothing's being done about our long-standing issues. If a few questions were settled, I'm sure American sentiment would become more friendly towards Turkey."

At this point I handed him my list. "Nothing there involves a European crisis. Some day you'll grant these anyhow; why not now?"

Tahsen Bey laughed, took the paper, and the interview ended with the customary flowery and meaningless Oriental phrases.

Apparently more had been in Tahsen Bey's mind than he let appear, because Gargiulo returned from his next visit to the Palace with an unusual air of animation. The *Bash Kiatib* had suggested that I pick out one request that he could submit to the Sultan, and, selecting a permit for the missionaries to rebuild their hospital at Cæsarea, we duly submitted it.

A few days later Gargiulo actually hustled in. "Do you know what's happened? The Porte is going to issue an iradé for the Cæsarea hospital."

Mr. Straus's policy of self-sacrifice was bearing fruit rapidly. In my excitement I wanted to cable the news to Washington at once. "Oh, no," warned Gargiulo. "Don't do that unless you're willing to pay for it out of your own pocket. The cable is a last resort." I contented myself with a dispatch.

Eager to strike again while the iron was still hot, I collared our dragoman the first thing the next morning. "Now Gargiulo, what about that permit to construct an outbuilding to the missionary college in Erzerum?"

"Oh, don't let's bother with that today."

"Yes, Gargiulo, get out your pocketbook and see where it's being held up. You old rascal, you know you can do it if you want to."

He grinned and answered, "All right, I'll try."

To our great surprise, for the second time our request was promptly granted. Without my urging, Gargiulo exhibited his list, saying, "Well, my boy, which question would you like put through tomorrow?"

I named one. "You can consider it settled," he declared, and we celebrated with a good lunch and an afternoon off.

No one would ever have believed that old Gargiulo could have become so co-operative in the space of a few short weeks. Thoroughly amused at our success, he almost hurried as he set off on his rounds. At the Porte he would even make a reluctant official rout out a forgotten document and then carry it in person to the office higher up. The Porte quickly sensed the attitude of the Palace, and one by one I crossed items off my list.

The Palace had done something for me, and soon it was to be my turn to do something for the Palace. One morning Gargiulo announced that an important official of the Sultan's privy purse was in the anteroom. Presently a long-bearded old Turk in a flowing, quilted gown bowed himself in, and without a word began clanking on my desk buckskin bag after buckskin bag, taking some from the right side and some from the left side of his robe, like a magician producing rabbits.

"His Majesty wishes you to buy him a thousand pounds' worth of American pianos."

"What make?"

He shook his head.

"What kind has he already?"

Again he shook his head.

"I can't spend so much of His Majesty's money unless I know what piano pleases him. Let some eunuch go into the harem and look at the name on the lid. If he can't read English, at least he can make a tracing of the first few letters."

The old fellow threw up his hands in horror, "Oh, Sir, Excellency! It is quite impossible! His Majesty has ordered American pianos. He must have American pianos. Once His Majesty has given an order nobody can ask for an explanation."

At this point he started for the door, but Gargiulo and I sat him down in a chair while we opened the bags and sorted the yellow coins into piles of ten. We had little heaps all over the office — one hundred of them.

Not until we were satisfied that the count was correct did we let him go. Remembering that mother had a Steinway, I wrote a letter to the head of that firm. A reply came promptly. The Sultan should have his pianos at cost, lavishly inlaid to suit Oriental taste. I never saw them, but months later I received a decoration to be forwarded to Mr. Steinway in token of the Sultan's appreciation.

Because of the renewed activity at the Porte my hours grew longer and longer, and when I left the Legation it was usually part of the day's work to go to a dinner or reception. Each Embassy or Legation entertained its visiting nationals, and the arrival of a Russian royalty or Austrian archduke meant a round of festivities which might last a week at a time. The most interesting people appeared at the British Embassy, among them Valentine Chirol, the Foreign Editor of the London *Times*. It is not easy now to realize the prestige of that paper's European representatives four decades ago; de Blowitz, the master of them all, really altered history by ferreting out and publishing secrets of state. In Constantinople Edwin Pears was almost as influential as the diplomats themselves, and the British always consulted him in a crisis.

Although I enjoyed meeting these people, the mornings after were a struggle and I considered hiring a secretary at my own expense. Most opportunely for me, Philip Marshall Brown, a former instructor at Robert College, was eager for the chance to embark on a diplomatic career. I invited him to live with me, and he became indispensable at the Legation. The diplomatic corps smiled at the cards I had printed for him: "Philip Marshall Brown, Sécretaire du Chargé d'Affaires des États Unis."

Just as in London, queer things kept happening and queer people kept walking into the Legation. A steady stream of archeologists applied for permits to excavate in various parts of the Empire. One man had spent his life collecting references to the Golden Calf and was now certain he could find it. Another was headed for Ur of the Chaldees, armed with kegs of castor oil. He treated every Arab chief who called on him with a large goblet full, which his visitor downed as though it were champagne, smacking his lips at the pleasant flavor. According to his account, one had drunk three glasses— without apparent ill effects — and then had furnished him all the diggers he could use. I concealed my incredulity and procured him the permit.

One day two Mormons with enormous beards applied for an iradé to carry on missionary work. Our colony of Protestants would indubitably resent this intrusion, yet, since my visitors were American citizens, it was not for me to discriminate between religions. It seemed amusing that Mormons, whose faith allowed more than one wife, should seek converts among the Mohammedans who shared this belief with them.

Frequently I had to interfere on behalf of some American sailor who, celebrating his shore leave, got into a drunken brawl and was thrown into jail by the police. In the unspeakably filthy and disease-infected Turkish prisons he ran a good chance of not living until his trial. Provided his crime was not serious, I used to order Mahmoud to go down, take possession of him, and have him rowed out to the first boat in the harbor due to sail. I never included this in my report to the State Department, but I knew that all the other legations and embassies employed their kavasses in the same way to protect their nationals.

I was interrupted one morning by the hasty entrance of a short, swarthy, slant-browed fellow who said his name was Volpi. His life was in danger. Spies had followed him even to my office. He was a naturalized American. I must get him out of the country.

"What sort of trouble are you in?" I inquired.

Somewhat incoherently he told me his story: having learned in Austria of a plot against the Sultan's life, he had offered to sell the details for a price. At the invitation of the Palace he had journeyed to Constantinople, but, instead of being rewarded, he was sure he was going to be killed.

I noticed his pockets were bulging suspiciously, and asked him, "What are you carrying that knife and revolver for?"

Rather unconvincingly, he explained he was only conforming to the custom of the little Sicilian town where he had been born. Under further questioning, he admitted he was an anarchist. Skeptical of his whole explanation, I advised him to go back to his room at the Péra Palace Hotel, and stay there until I communicated with him. Then I telegraphed to our consul in Palermo, Sicily, for Volpi's record, and sent Gargiulo to investigate at the Porte.

When the dragoman returned without enlightenment, I felt

uneasy and walked over to the hotel. At the desk I was informed that Volpi had locked himself into his room, and refused to come out. The manager and I pounded on his door, called, and pounded once more. No reply. Finally it had to be broken in. The room was empty and the window by the fire escape open.

Mahmoud spent two days vainly making the rounds of every jail in Constantinople. Eventually the American Hospital on the Golden Horn notified me that one of their patients answered my description. I jumped into a hack and dashed across to Stamboul. A band of excited doctors and nurses met me. Only a few moments before a police boat had churned up to the hospital pier, officers in uniform had forced their way in, and Volpi had been carried off struggling.

Every department of the Government denied any knowledge of Volpi; every effort to trace him ended in a blank wall. I never heard of him again. On receiving word from Sicily that he was wanted there for murder, I was much relieved; but the fact remained that not even the Legation could always prevent a man's being dropped into the Bosphorus if the Turks decided he was dangerous.

In the spring cruise ships began to arrive with American passengers. As a result of the steamship companies' advertisements, "Visit Constantinople and see the Sultan go to prayers at *Selamlik,*" some three hundred tourists at a time would storm the Legation, demanding their tickets. With difficulty I made arrangements to shepherd forty or fifty of them in a group, hoping the disappointed ones would not cause me trouble on reaching home.

On one occasion I settled my charges in the space allotted to them in the garden by the door of the diplomatic pavilion, and joined my colleagues. Suddenly Ibrahim Pasha rushed up to me, saying I must come at once; something very serious had happened. I hurried out to find that a young American girl of eighteen, not satisfied with craning her neck with the rest of the crowd, had climbed a tree and was ensconced on a limb directly over the road.

Should the Sultan emerge to behold a female *giaour* in such a position of vantage, the officials were afraid they would lose their official heads, but they had hesitated to precipitate an international incident by pulling her down themselves. I tried to explain to the girl that she ran a serious risk of being hurt. Still she refused to abandon her perch. It was nearly noon and there was not a second to lose. Resolutely I laid a hand on the trunk of the tree and announced, "If you're not down here in ten seconds, I'll be up after you myself." This threat sent her scrambling to the ground.

Among the visiting cruise ships was the *Augusta Victoria,* bringing Charles Gould who had been on the Cuban Commission. He introduced me to his fellow passengers, Mr. and Mrs. Frederick Bronson of New York and their daughter Elizabeth, dark-haired, brown-eyed, with lovely coloring and slightly tip-tilted nose. She had been educated abroad and spoke French and German with an ease that made me envious. I guided the Bronsons through the bazaars, gave them a dinner, went with them on a tour to the Black Sea, and took them to *Selamlik.* Miss Bronson seemed delighted with diplomatic life. We agreed to write to each other and planned to meet on my first leave.

By the time the Bronsons sailed away, most of the minor questions on my list had been disposed of. So far neither the Porte, the Palace, nor I had mentioned the Armenian claims. I hesitated to bring them up, especially since I had no idea how long I was to be left in charge; Mr. Straus had not resigned or notified me of any intention to return in the near future. Finally, I consulted Dr. Washburn, who urged me to see what I could do.

It seemed to me the chief obstacle was the Sultan's unwillingness to acknowledge his responsibility for the massacres. Therefore I wrote Mr. Hay, to ask whether he would object if I could get the payment without an admission of the principle. While waiting for a reply, I felt out the ground by pushing our request for an iradé to rebuild the college at Harput, where most of the damage had been done. Gargiulo and I worked up a series of arguments — the advantage to the Sultan of having such an intellectual center in his Empire, how gracious it would make him appear in Western eyes, and so on.

Gargiulo had presented a number of our points to the Palace without apparent success, when one day in early April I encountered Baron Marschall. He remarked, "I think the Sultan intends to grant you an audience." I smiled politely, thinking he must be joking — it was almost unheard of for chargés to be thus honored. I had quite forgotten the incident by the following Friday, April 12th. Then, as

I was drinking my coffee at *Selamlik* with the rest, Emin Bey tapped me on the shoulder. "The Sultan hopes you will remain afterward."

Gargiulo was even more excited than I. While three ambassadors were being received ahead of me, he overwhelmed me with instructions: I would speak in French through an interpreter, but I must remember to be as careful as though I were addressing the Sultan himself, because he was said to understand that language perfectly. Above all, I must not strike a match; the noise would suggest a firearm to the nervous monarch. More than once on such an occurrence he had risen and immediately terminated the interview.

Before Gargiulo had entirely finished cautioning me, Emin Bey appeared to usher me into the little reception room. I bowed; the Sultan extended his hand, an amused expression on his sharp wrinkled face. The thing I noticed first was the squeaking of his incredibly tiny patent leather boots. He had a most dignified manner; the carriage of his head and his gestures betrayed a heritage of great race. Inviting me to sit down, he offered me a cigarette from his black gunmetal case and, leaving me no opportunity to wonder what I should do for a match, struck one himself and held it for me.

The Sultan maintained a lively conversation, never touching on business, but discoursing at length about his new water works and their effect on the typhoid fever rate. He described shooting expeditions he had made in his youth, and when I left he asked me to be sure to come to the next *Selamlik*.

Just as after the interview with Tahsen, I could not gather from the Sultan's manner what impression I had created. However, Gargiulo returned from his next trip to the Palace with an iradé for Harput College. Dr. Washburn and all the missionaries now urged me to broach the subject of the Armenian indemnities.

At this moment arrived a note from John Hay in his own handwriting, "You may make as unprincipled a settlement as you please."

The elements for a solution were already at hand. Some time previously, the Sultan had let it be known that he was in the market for a cruiser to form the nucleus of a new navy. Mr. Straus had thereupon communicated with Cramp's shipyard in Philadelphia, which had sent out General Williams to compete with the English firm of Vickers-Maxim for the contract. The Minister had said to him, "If I can get you the order for this cruiser, and if I can persuade the Turks to add the Armenian indemnity claims to the price, will you pay the first installments to the State Department?"

"I certainly will," he had agreed enthusiastically.

However, the plan had come to nothing; for months General Williams, as well as his English rival, had been warming the chairs in Tahsen Bey's anteroom. I decided to revive Mr. Straus's strategy.

I realized that before I could make any progress I must convince the Sultan that the United States was in earnest. One of my friends was a fellow member of the Constantinople cricket team, a young Englishman named Ferguson who was temporarily in charge of the all-powerful Reuter's Telegraph Agency. Any dispatch from him was distributed throughout America by the Associated Press. I knew the Sultan had forty translators at Yildiz working on foreign press comments, and anything I could get published would be sure to reach his ear. I invited Ferguson to lunch, and proposed to him a partnership — I to furnish news, he to put on the wires some good rousing copy.

An older man would have refused to listen to such a scheme, but Ferguson jumped at the idea; then and there we mapped a campaign. To begin with, we composed a note to the Porte in language sharp enough to provide lively reading in American papers. April 24th I delivered it to the Porte, and Ferguson cabled a spirited account. Immediately headlines, far more lurid than I hoped for, sprouted out in the United States. "Turkey May Make Missionaries Suffer." "Troubles of Sultan Multiply." "United States Will Not Allow Further Delay." The editorial writers picked it up. "Ordinarily the United States waits forever, but when it starts you can never tell what may happen. It has no respect for precedents, no traditions, no diplomatic manners, and it is liable to do anything."

Ferguson was showered with demands for more Turkish news. Even the correspondents of the London *Times* and *Telegraph* were asked for paragraphs. Rumors flew about that the *Kearsarge, Kentucky,* and *Massachusetts* were on their way to Turkey. In Washington Mr. Hay, sensing my purpose, refused to deny them, and in fact subtly encouraged them. At the Porte, where I called every two or three days, Tewfik Pasha assured me, almost trembling, that he was trying his best to persuade Yildiz that we meant what we said.

Nevertheless, whether the Turks were frightened or not, they showed no signs of paying. May 23rd I submitted another formal demand to the Porte, this time threatening an ultimatum. The Foreign Office countered by stating they would have to await the return of Admiral Ahmed Bey, who was at that moment in the United States inspecting cruisers. For years the Sultan had been getting ultimatums to settle for this and settle for that, and he had never paid unless he had no other alternative. Obviously, with summer upon us, nothing more would be done until fall.

By the beginning of June, everyone was moving out of Constantinople. Instead of following the rest of the corps to Therapia, I selected the beautiful island of Prinkipo in the Sea of Marmora, and there I rented a villa on a bluff overlooking the water, complete with tennis court, stables for horses, stone landing, and boathouse. The pungent scent of salt water, pine needles, roses, and heather filled the air.

My holiday was delayed by one disagreeable duty — the delivery of the Commencement Address at Robert College. I had never made a public speech in my life, and it loomed as a great ordeal. For my subject I chose "The Renaissance of Hellenic Ideals of Physical Culture in American University Life," and wrote what I considered a very fine speech.

One sunny warm afternoon found me sitting on the platform, surrounded by venerable missionaries. The student body filed in, and the exercises proceeded. I was last on the list of speakers, and it seemed a long time before Dr. Washburn introduced me. Rising, I started to read with as much animation as I could. After the first few pages I glanced up, and imagined I saw a few heads nodding in the front row. Believing I must have been mistaken, I launched into my tribute to the "courageous band of men and women who were now bringing back to its native soil the seeds of culture, which had been taken from the East to the West to be planted, nurtured, and expanded."

A page or two more and I risked another quick glance. This time there could be no doubt that many heads had fallen forward. I had just reached the point which I intended to be the climax of my speech — "In spreading the seed of modern knowledge, let the seed of physical culture not be lost sight of." Instead of shouting it out loud and strong, I mumbled my conclusion hurriedly and, in great mortification, resumed my seat. The first four or five rows were apparently slumbering peacefully.

As soon as the exercises were over, I apologized to Dr. Washburn.

'Why, you said just the right thing."

"But, Doctor, I put at least a third of the audience to sleep."

"I should have warned you, Mr. Griscom. Those boys in front were newcomers who did not understand English. We placed them there hoping that, if they sat near enough, they might catch a word or two."

CHAPTER XIV

A BATTLESHIP TO PLAY WITH

The summer slipped by in riding and swimming and yachting. At my return from Prinkipo in October I found a remarkable transformation in my position. The Shah Muzaffar-ed-Din of Persia passed through that fall; the Sultan gave a state banquet for him, at which I was seated only four places from the Shah. Nine heads of mission were absent; I was the ranking chargé, years younger than any of the rest.

At the end of dinner we lined up for the presentation. The Shah, looking very bored, made lengthy speeches to the Ambassadors and Ministers. Then the interpreter announced, "The Chargé d'Affaires of Yenghi Dunia (New World)." The Shah muttered three or four words, whereupon to my astonishment the interpreter delivered me a flowery address inquiring about the health of President McKinley, the welfare of Mrs. McKinley, and the general condition of the United States.

Later I questioned Gargiulo, who had a fair knowledge of Persian, "Exactly what did the Shah tell his interpreter?"

Gargiulo grinned. "He said, 'Tell the American Chargé d'Affaires the same old thing.' "

I still had no idea how long I was going to be left in command. With the exception of that one note from Mr. Hay, I had had no other instructions from the State Department. Nevertheless, I determined not to abandon my campaign for the cruiser purchase and payment of indemnities as part of its price, and I cast about for a trump card to play. Remembering the stir created by the report that our battleships were en route to Turkey, I wrote again personally to Mr. Hay; perhaps he could persuade the Secretary of the Navy to arrange for a United States cruiser to include a Turkish port in its itinerary. I assured him nothing unpleasant would happen, and

I was certain I could get him his payment. Had I been older I would never have taken such a risk.

Ferguson, Gargiulo, and I went into consultation at the Legation, a new note was dispatched to the Porte, and in a few days the same ominous headlines of the spring began to crop up in the American papers. The Turkish reaction was unexpected. A Palace courier appeared with a message that His Majesty wished me, as a favor to him, to have the American press stop making disagreeable remarks about him. I replied with equal politeness that His Majesty must understand the United States was a republic, and by our Constitution our Government must allow freedom of the press; it was as powerless as I to order a newspaper to change its tone.

The result of being firm with the Sultan was that at next *Selamlik,* November 18th, I was given an interview and invited to the Palace the following evening for some music.

The Sultan's private opera company was famous. Abdul Hamid never tired of listening to Verdi, Rossini, and Gounod, and for years had kept his own troupe. Some time ago the report had come to him that his sopranos and altos were having affairs with the tenors and bassos. The Sultan, who from the Mohammedan point of view was a man of the highest morality, pronounced immediately: "I will not have any loose women in my palace." Next day the company went out, lock, stock, and barrel.

After an all-male cast proved unsatisfactory, the Sultan had another idea. "Get me a one-family opera company," he ordered. For months his agents scoured Europe, and finally in the north of Italy located a troupe composed of a grandfather and grandmother in their seventies, their children, their children's wives and husbands, and even grandchildren. A degree of relationship might have been stretched here and there, but the Sultan did not inquire about this too closely.

At the strange and inconvenient hour of six-fifteen, Signor Pansa, Gargiulo, and I were ushered into the royal box of the small, square theater which had been built into the Palace. In boxes to the left were Cabinet Ministers and Marshals of the Empire; to the right were grilles through which women of the harem might peek. The opera was "Faust." The Sultan apparently was quite familiar with it, because he talked loudly to Signor Pansa and me. Gargiulo, who was sitting behind us, had to keep sticking his head forward to interpret.

Mephistopheles appeared from underneath the floor, set to work tempting poor Faust, and in due course revealed to him the vision of Marguerite, seated at her spinning wheel. *"O Merveille,"* exclaimed Faust, and Signor Pansa and I opened our eyes wide. The supposedly innocent young maiden was dressed in a long Mother Hubbard affair falling to the ground, which failed to conceal the fact that she must have been at least eight months *enceinte*.

The garden promenade of the two lovers in the third act was so ridiculous that nobody could possibly have been disturbed about Marguerite's fate, and by the time Faust tried to embrace his beloved through the open casement of her bedroom window, Signor Pansa and I were having difficulty holding in our laughter. The Sultan heard us chuckling and said to Gargiulo: "Will you inquire of His Excellency, the Italian Ambassador, and the young American Chargé d'Affaires what they find so diverting. I should like to enjoy the joke."

Signor Pansa answered, "It is very hard for us to see, Your Majesty, how Marguerite is going to be seduced."

Abdul Hamid laughed outright. "I understand why you are so amused, but actually I am much pleased. It means that soon I shall have one more member of my chorus."

No one could be more gracious or charming than the Sultan if he chose. We were served an excellent supper and escorted home by a squadron of cavalry galloping in front and behind our carriage. On the way I asked Gargiulo, "The Sultan isn't really as bad as he's painted, do you think?"

In response Gargiulo described a similar opera performance he had attended with our former Minister, A. W. Terrell, an ex-Confederate Colonel from Texas without diplomatic experience or inhibitions. At his first audience he had told Abdul Hamid that all Turkey needed was a representative constitutional government on the American plan; the Sultan had taken a fancy to him and invited him to the opera. There Mr. Terrell had leaned back, his jaws working steadily on his plug of tobacco; every now and then he bent forward to spit, frequently striking the superb gold brocade which hung over the front of the royal box. Each time Gargiulo had noticed the Sultan shudder. Finally Mr. Terrell had remarked genially, "How did Your Majesty like that Virginia tobacco I gave you recently?"

"Excellent."

"Why isn't Your Majesty smoking it now?"

"I find the American tobacco so much stronger than the Turkish, that I smoke it in a pipe and only in the garden where I am free to spit."

At the first opportunity Mr. Terrell had asked Gargiulo, "You heard that remark of the Sultan's about tobacco. Do you think he meant anything personal by it? Do you suppose he didn't like my spitting?"

Gargiulo had smiled ironically. "I think, Mr. Terrell, that was the impression he intended to convey."

A few days after our opera party a coded cable came from Mr. Hay. "The battleship *Kentucky,* now at Villefranche, will proceed to Smyrna for a four-day stay en route to Manila."

I waved my cable around the office — Gargiulo and Brown ran to see what was the matter. Ferguson was summoned. The *Kentucky,* Captain Colby M. Chester commanding, was one of our newest warships, equipped with superimposed fighting turrets which increased her formidable appearance. There was not a minute to lose, but we could not afford a mistake. We had to frighten the Turks enough to make them sign, yet not stir them up so that they really would defy us.

I sent two open cables which I knew everybody would read. One was to Captain Chester at Villefranche: "On arriving at Smyrna please take no action until hearing from me." The other was to our consul at Smyrna: "Battleship *Kentucky* will arrive within few days. Please proceed immediately on board and request Captain Chester to take no action without consulting me."

However, we tempered our first announcement to the press by a statement: "The *Kentucky* has at present no hostile intentions towards Turkey."

If ever I had any doubt of how closely my colleagues kept track of each other's business, it was promptly settled for good and all.

At once, in their various ways, they did their best to discover what the United States was up to. Trying to slip out of their attempts to pin me down was excellent training as well as a lot of fun.

Gargiulo was horrified but fascinated. He made only weak protests when, after allowing time for the Turks to be impressed, I dispatched him to the Palace with a blank contract. "Tell Tahsen Bey it would be advisable for him to order Hassan Pasha to fill in the price, being sure our ninety-thousand dollar indemnity claim is added to it, and then sign it."

I set to work with the code book to cable the State Department, a laborious process. Words and phrases in common use were represented by numbers, but the authors of the cipher apparently had not believed the word "Cramp" would fall within the vocabulary of a diplomat, and had assigned it no number. I might have put each letter into code separately; however, having been imbued with the necessity of saving money, I printed "Cramp's" in full. That night Sir Nicholas O'Conor sent Adam Block to the Palace to enter a formal protest against Turkey's purchase of a cruiser from the United States.

Excitement increased with the answers to my cables. The consul at Smyrna (carefully coached in advance) assured me his launch was ready, and the moment the *Kentucky* sailed over the horizon he would dash on board and try to prevent Captain Chester from taking any violent measures. The Captain, grasping the situation and playing up marvelously, cabled he was sailing immediately, and understood his orders — the implication being that he was to force the Dardanelles and crash through the Sea of Marmora before the Chanak Forts could fire a shot. He could not imagine why I should ask him to stay action. "However, since your telegram seems positive, I will withhold my hand."

To relieve the strain I went out to play polo on the Maidan, and was galloping back and forth in the first chukker when Balthasar, heedless of flying hoofs, appeared in the middle of the field, looking as though death itself were at his heels. He waved his arms wildly, "Excellency! Excellency! Hurry!"

"What's the matter, Balthasar?"

The Armenian lowered his voice to a whisper, "Izzet Bey with his cavalry is at the house and demands to see you."

To increase their own importance, Orientals always made visitors wait, and I decided this would be the best treatment for Izzet Bey. "Don't worry," I said to Balthasar. "Go serve His Majesty's representative as many cups of coffee as he will drink. Say the American Chargé regrets being delayed in a polo game. Meanwhile will he please regard the American Chargé's house as his own."

We finished in about half an hour, and I reached home to find that Bedros and his fellow servants, believing my end had come and theirs was soon to follow, had fled to the cellar. Balthasar alone, almost green with terror, remained above stairs. I was still perspiring heavily, and, instead of joining Izzet Bey at once in the drawing room, I directed Balthasar to ask him to be patient while I had a bath and changed my clothes.

Izzet Bey was pacing irritably up and down as I entered. The minute he saw me he burst out, "His Majesty has sent me to you because you are his one great friend in America. The Governor of Smyrna has telegraphed that he fears his city is about to be bombarded. His Majesty wants to know from you what he should do."

"I'm sorry, but unfortunately things have gone beyond my control. I warned the Sultan many times that the patience of my Government would soon be exhausted, and now I fear painful consequences are inevitable. However, a contract is now lying on Hassan Pasha's desk. His signature might have an admirable effect. This is my only suggestion."

Izzet Bey accepted this grandiloquent pronunciamento quite seriously. His air of gloom did not lighten, as he took his departure amid a clatter of hooves. The press carried rumors of ruptured relations and the Turkish Cabinet met to decide how to cope with the situation.

December 2nd came the report from Smyrna of the dramatic arrival of the *Kentucky,* cleared for action — her crew lining the decks, her bulwarks down, her guns run out. Instead of stopping at the regular moorings a mile off shore, Captain Chester steamed slowly up and anchored within two hundred yards of the seawall, so near that the giant turret guns dominated the city. The roads out were clogged by panic-stricken inhabitants, fleeing with their donkeys, mules, carts, and baggage.

I expected the Turks to make some sign, but after two days without even a word I began to count the hours that the *Kentucky* still had to remain. With difficulty I restrained myself from a trip to the Porte, knowing if I seemed too eager I would betray my hand. My nervousness was capped by the receipt of one of Dick Davis' characteristic postcards: "Few boys of twenty-eight are given a battleship to play with. Be very careful it doesn't go off."

The silence was ultimately broken by a message from Yildiz; the Sultan would like to show his good will towards America by buying a cruiser from us. He thought Cramp's was an excellent firm. Did I approve the idea?

I replied that, if he cared to, I would arrange for a contract.

At once he countered, "To save objections from other powers, why not finish the matter right away?"

General Williams, shaking with excitement, set off for Hassan Pasha's office. In his absence came another communication from the Sultan. He had just learned that an American battleship was in Turkish waters; why had I not told him before? As an indication of American amity "Admiral" Chester and the *Kentucky's* officers must be his guests at Constantinople.

The Sultan was apparently willing to settle the indemnity claim if I would save his face publicly. Unfortunately, the *Kentucky* was to sail in forty-eight hours. Urgently I cabled Mr. Hay, "Contract with Cramp's about to be signed. His Majesty absolutely insists Captain Chester pay a visit of friendship."

Quickly the welcome word was returned, "Secretary of Navy consents that stay of *Kentucky* be extended."

Meanwhile, General Williams had waited at the Ministry of Marine for hours, only to be told the signing would be postponed until later, since the Navy had to prepare for the reception of "Admiral" Chester. He was greeted with all but royal honors. The entire Turkish Navy was drawn up at the Arsenal. Escorted by the crack Marines, we drove through the Grande Rue de Péra at the head of a long line of carriages. In order to make a show Captain Chester brought every one of his officers, except a few unhappy boys who had to be left in charge.

The climax of the visit was the official banquet at Yildiz, December 10th. Captain Chester was on one side of the Sultan and I on the other. Glancing round the table I was proud of the fine appearance of our officers, and the Sultan must have been impressed also because, nodding towards a particularly nice-looking ensign, he said to me, "If that young man will enter my service, I'll appoint him an admiral."

After dinner I informed the officer of the Sultan's offer. At first he thought I was joking, but on being convinced he could indeed be a Turkish admiral if he wished, he refused flatly. I modified his rejection by explaining to the Sultan that the young man felt he had definitely committed himself to the American service by accepting an education at Government expense.

Before we left, the Sultan shook my hand warmly, and declared he was very pleased with me. Obviously, he did not resent the pressure I had brought to bear on him, and somehow he had worked it out in his Oriental mind that I had done this face-saving as a personal favor to him.

I went to bed congratulating myself that the fight was over. Even the next day, when still no contract was delivered, I was not particularly worried. The following day again there was no word, and a message arrived from the Navy Department saying the *Kentucky* had to be on her way. Overnight my pendulum swung from confidence to the depth of depression. I kept waiting for the miracle; no miracle happened; and a week after the banquet, the battleship sailed.

Should the Turks back down now I was lost. I pretended not to be disturbed, but inwardly I thought my colossal bluff was about to be called. General Williams was certain that further efforts were futile, and started packing. Once he had gone there would be no contract to sign.

I made a desperate decision. At six o'clock, Christmas Eve, I descended on Tewfik Pasha at his house. In the plainest language I gave him my opinion of Turkish methods, Turkish officials, Turkish honor. Turkey was playing fast and loose with a great nation and would find it a dangerous game. My utility in Constantinople was at an end, and there was nothing to do but ask my Government to recall me. I must know his intentions by midnight.

De Bunsen and Fitzmaurice came to dinner, and I could hardly eat. We sat down at the card table. Gargiulo and I revoked so often that our guests, who considered bridge a serious matter, damned us roundly. Every time we heard a noise we jumped out of our seats. Our hopes had all but vanished when at eleven a message was handed me that an Imperial iradé had ordered the signing of the contract at ten o'clock the following morning. The Turks had never retreated from such a definite arrangement.

I took my pencil and crossed off the last item on my list; I could not imagine a better Christmas present. Rarely had anyone been more lucky — to have had the ground prepared by Mr. Straus, the steadying hand of old Gargiulo, the advantage of Dr. Washburn's wise advice, the coincidence of finding a young man of my own age in charge of Reuter's, a friendly diplomatic corps which regarded my efforts in the nature of a joke, the confidence of John Hay who trusted me with a battleship, and lastly the good will of the Sultan, who had been well-disposed from the start. All these contributed to my attaining the dream of every diplomat — a clean slate.

Because of the Sultan's kindness to me, I was naturally prejudiced in his favor; I could not help liking him in spite of his reputation. His name had been such a byword for cruelty and misuse of power that his virtues were lost sight of. People failed to realize his methods of terror and suppression had always been employed in Turkey. On the other hand, he was a hard worker and early riser, he did not squander the public purse on his own pleasures, and he was devoted to his wives and to his children. He was keenly interested in sanitation and measures for improving health. Unfortunately, any reform he started was nullified by the greedy bureaucracy, which sucked up every penny it could lay its hands on.

Besides these virtues, the Sultan had the form of courage which, once the danger was tangible, enabled him to confront it fearlessly. Early in 1901 was celebrated the great four-day festival of Kurban Bairam, during which the Sultan visited Dolma Bagché Palace to honor the relics of the Prophet, and to receive the homage of the dignitaries of his Empire. With the rest of the Diplomatic Corps I climbed many stairs to a high gallery, far above the vast central hall. Below I could see the Sultan enter to the strains of the Hamidieh March. He advanced to the throne and took his seat. Marshal Fuad Pasha, standing by his side, held out an embroidered scarf. Field marshals, pashas, beys, valis, ulemas, glittering with decorations and jewels, formed in line about the room. The Grand

Vizier stepped forward first, salaamed, kissed the scarf, and, still salaaming, backed away. The other members of the Cabinet followed him; Abdul Hamid looked on with the same contempt he showed at *Selamlik*.

Suddenly I felt the rail against which I was leaning quiver. While I was still wondering whether it could be an earthquake, it shook harder. In the middle of a bar the band broke off. Directly in front of me chunks of stucco and plaster detached themselves from the ceiling and crashed. The central chandelier, one of the largest in the world, swung and clanged, and the crystals shivered to pieces. Screams and cries burst from the assemblage, and a wave of people surged towards the doors. The walls of the building kept on swaying, more patches of ceiling fell; pandemonium was complete.

The only exit from our gallery was a narrow staircase, and, seeing this was hopelessly jammed, I turned back and joined Colonel Ponsonby, the British Military Attaché. Abdul Hamid was sitting perfectly unmoved except that he did lean over and speak to the priest nearest him, who immediately began to recite the prayer for earthquakes. No one heeded him. Unable to approach the blocked door, a fat pasha hit with his sword the plate glass of one of the tall French windows, and dived after it. In no time every window was smashed by dignitaries who could not wait to open them.

Half the assembly had escaped when abruptly the Sultan stood up. His voice rang out above the confusion, commanding the people to be calm. Every person in the room stopped, turned around, and sought again his place in the line. As the priest intoned the last words of his prayer, the quakes died away, and the procession moved uncertainly forward. I could not honestly blame those who had fled, but they were ruined men.

February 11th after *Selamlik* I had my final audience with the Sultan, the eleventh in fifteen months. Soon afterward, our new Minister, John G. A. Leishman, arrived — and I was free to go home on leave. Gargiulo, Brown, some of the missionaries, and many of my other friends came to the train. To the wonder of everyone on the platform there appeared Ibrahim Pasha, who never saw off anybody less than an Ambassador. The Sultan had sent him to wish me a speedy return and thank me again for "my great service."

CHAPTER XV

HONEYMOON TO PERSIA

At the State Department Mr. Hay looked at me from behind his desk. "As head of our foreign service, Lloyd, I suppose I ought to reprimand you for some of those chances you took." Then he smiled quizzically, "You know we might have landed in a lot of trouble."

I grinned, saying I had had a few qualms myself, and described Izzet Bey's visit, and my Christmas Eve interview with Tewfik Pasha. At the story of the Sultan's opera party, Mr. Hay laughed outright. From the first time I had met him I had admired him wholeheartedly, and it was reassuring to have a chief who salted his profession with a grain of humor. Nevertheless, I departed with as little idea as I had had on entering of what the future held in store for me.

While I was in the United States I was eager to pick up the threads I had dropped two years earlier; even this short absence made me feel out of touch with my former life. Father's offer of a private car for a trip to the Pan-American Exposition at Buffalo afforded a fine opportunity for me to gather together a group of my friends — Senator Lodge, Anna Roosevelt and her husband, Commander William S. Cowles, who had been Naval Attaché when I had been in London, Rosy Roosevelt's daughter Helen, and finally Mrs. Bronson and her daughter (Mr. Bronson had died shortly after leaving Constantinople). Being much attracted by Miss Bronson, before the party separated I fixed a rendezvous with her later in the summer at Innsbruck for some mountain climbing.

I went on to the Rosy Roosevelts' at Hyde Park, whence a party of us set out to drive to the Cowles place at Farmington, Connecticut. Helen Roosevelt and I sat on the front seat of a smart trap; Mrs. Cowles and Bob Munro Ferguson occupied the rear. Drawn by two fast cobs we bowled over the green hills of Dutchess

County, through elm-shaded New England villages, fragrant with lilacs in bloom, and on the evening of the second day reached Old-gate. A telegram from Mr. Hay was waiting for me. "The President directs me to offer you the position of Minister to Persia. Do you accept?"

Did I? Twenty-eight and a mission of my own? I was on top of the world. Marvelous! Wonderful! No adjectives could describe my elation.

The news spread in Farmington and to Miss Porter's School that the Cowleses were entertaining the new Minister to Persia. That afternoon the famous headmistress sent a message to my hostess, saying the girls would be most interested to hear a talk by an experienced diplomat. Could her distinguished guest spare time from his much-needed rest to address the school?

I had many friends among the girls at Farmington, but in those days you could not call unless you were a relative. The invitation promised a perfect entrée, and Mrs. Cowles, delighted at the implication that I was a decrepit, fatherly old creature, asked Miss Porter to tea. At five o'clock she was shown in. She looked me over, up, and down, sipped her tea, commented on the pleasant weather, and took her departure. Not a word was said about my addressing the girls.

Probably it was as well that the lecture never came off; my knowledge of Persia ended with Alexander the Great. I was not even sure how to get there. Suspecting it might be a complicated journey, I stopped off at Cook's in New York to make inquiries for the best route to Teheran via Constantinople, so that I might have a chance to close my house and collect my belongings. The clerk appeared dubious. "Just a minute, Sir," and retired for consultation. Finally he returned, shaking his head — he could not help me.

"But you arrange trips all over the world, don't you?"

"Not to Persia. Nobody goes there."

Rather taken aback, I proceeded to Washington for the required thirty days of instruction in my new duties. The colored elevator man prided himself on recognizing every Ambassador or Minister who entered the huge, old-fashioned building; without a halt he shot me to the floor of the Secretary of State — if a head of mission were on the way to see his chief, whoever wanted to get out in between had to ride up and back.

Mr. Hay introduced me to the various officials. Sydney Smith was then in charge of the Diplomatic Bureau; it used to be said a Secretary or Minister could judge his standing with the Department by the degree of cordiality shown him by Mr. Smith. Although acquainted with diplomatic procedure from A to Z, he had nothing to tell me about Persia. I then presented myself to Alvey Augustus Adee, the Second Assistant Secretary of State, who had been there nearly twenty-five years, and knew by heart the terms of every treaty in United States history. Because of his deafness, I had to shout my queries, but his answers shed little light on my post. Our Government had no questions at issue with Persia, and virtually no trade. All I could learn was that I had sixty days' travel allowance to reach it.

Long before my month was up, I had tried in vain all the sources of information I could think of, and I boarded the train to Philadelphia. On the way, by great good luck, I met Herbert Bowen, my predecessor at Teheran, and I arrived at Broad Street Station with several pages of notes on necessary supplies and equipment, as well as an itinerary. From Constantinople I must go up the Black Sea to Batum, cross by rail to Baku, take another steamer down the Caspian Sea to Enzelli in Persia, and then drive for days over the Elburz Mountains and through the desert. I felt as though I were bound for the last frontier.

In England, acting on Bowen's advice, I made vast purchases, and as soon as I saw them safely packed in fifty cases of a size suitable to a camel's back, I hastened off to join the Bronsons. From Innsbruck we went by coach to a small inn on the bare, wind-swept Stelvio Pass, the loftiest in Europe.

While Elsa and I spent our days mountain climbing, Mrs. Bronson, who was not interested in athletic exercise, and never altered her routine for anything or anyone, stayed at the inn. She was a born ruler and organizer, and every minute of Elsa's life had been planned. Deciding she could provide a more thorough education than a school, she had engaged the best tutors she could find, and gathered some of her friends' daughters at her house, among them Elsa's cousin Katherine Duer, May Goelet, and Consuelo Vanderbilt. Afterwards Elsa had been taken abroad, perfected in French and German, and piloted through so many art galleries that she knew the location of each picture in Europe.

Although Elsa had led about as sheltered an existence as a girl could, she adapted herself to roughing it with remarkable rapidity. Mountain climbing quickly developed our feeling of companionship into one of intimacy. I would have asked her then and there to marry me, but I did not see how I could, because I had no time for a wedding, and believed it wrong to ask a girl to remain engaged for the indefinite period of my absence in Persia.

The last day of a glorious week we ascended a fine snow peak, and the view was so beautiful that I removed my dark glasses. Only a few minutes after returning to the inn, I was seized with a splitting headache, and everything went black before me. While I was helpless with snowblindness, Elsa refused to abandon me. She and her mother hurried me to Milan, the nearest city, put me to bed, and nursed me until I was well.

My leave being nearly up, I suggested that we go on to Vienna for a round of farewell parties. There we were met by the news that President McKinley had been shot by the anarchist Czolgosz. Since he was expected to recover, we were undeterred, and set out to enjoy Vienna in the heyday of its gaiety — dinner at Frau Sacher's, where you had to be introduced to get a meal; dancing to the Strauss waltzes; driving home in the morning through the Vienna woods. This was the jolliest time I had ever had in my life.

September 14th, we were thunderstruck to hear that President McKinley had died. My letter of credence was now worthless, and in case President Roosevelt might wish to appoint someone else, I cabled for orders. Receiving no reply I cabled again that I would await directions at Paris, and accordingly departed thither with the Bronsons.

It seemed almost as though events had been arranged so that I might have an opportunity to get married. I proposed. In a few days I sent a third cable to Washington, asking for extra leave for my wedding.

We could not return to New York, and chose London because we both had friends there. Father, Mother, Clem, and Pansy hurried to England; Charley Crichton was my best man, and Sommy Somerset was an usher.

In England it was illegal to be married later than three; in the good old days a gentleman might well be drunk after that hour, and not in a condition to know what he was doing. A little before one o'clock, November 2nd, 1901, Sommy and I arrived at St. Margaret's Church in the shadow of Westminster Abbey, and, being early, sat on the rear steps smoking cigarettes. Sommy tried to keep my mind off wondering why the Bronsons did not come by reminiscences of our narrow escapes in Central America.

In no time the ceremony was over, the wedding breakfast was over, and Elsa and I were off to Bournemouth for a week at Lady Theodora Guest's villa. Then the Guests insisted we pay them a short visit in Somersetshire. The tiny railway station was bright with garlands, and the whole village was on hand to welcome us. We mounted into a victoria, the coachman picked up his white reins, the white-ribboned horses swung under a triumphal arch, and we rode through the street with the church bell ringing and flowers falling in front of us.

Our honeymoon really began when we found ourselves at last on the Orient Express, headed for Constantinople. As we pulled into the station, there on the platform were Gargiulo, Brown, Fitzmaurice, and Russell, brimming with accounts of the negotiations for ransoming Miss Ellen Stone, an American missionary, kidnapped by Turkish bandits. It was like the Harput indemnity all over again.

Busily we packed up my belongings — our final array of baggage consisted of a hundred and forty-five pieces and a baby grand piano. Balthasar and Bedros both asked to be taken with us, and they, added to Elsa's German maid, Marie, and my Scotch butler and valet, William, an ex-footman at Dolobran, made a considerable retinue.

The Sultan had sent a special message for Elsa and me to come to *Selamlik* Friday, and there he invited us to dinner and the opera the next night. During the performance he was his old self, interrupting constantly with conversation. He was sorry I was not to stay in Constantinople, but if I had to go anywhere else it was a pity I was being isolated in such a rough, uncivilized, and even dangerous country as Persia. His shrewd, black eyes snapped as he continued in the same tone: "You know, I am told that in the wilder parts of Persia they are much troubled by brigands, who actually kidnap foreigners. Turkey is very fortunate in having no brigands." I looked around; nobody was smiling.

After the curtain had fallen the Sultan offered Elsa his arm, while Gargiulo and I followed them into an anteroom. As we entered, Ibrahim Pasha stepped forward and hung on Elsa's neck the Grand Cordon of the Chefekat, a plaque of diamonds and small rubies at the end of a broad red and green ribbon. Elsa thanked the Sultan, and I was about to make my farewell bow when he drew me aside. Once well out of hearing, he pulled me down until his lips were at my ear, and then, in perfectly good French, whispered: "*Adieu, mon cher, et bon voyage*" — the first time to my knowledge that the Sultan had ever uttered a foreign word or admitted he knew French. At the same instant he pressed into my hand the gunmetal cigarette case which he had carried for ten years. The next minute he had shaken hands and was gone.

Immediately Ibrahim Pasha, Emin Bey, and other court officials crowded around, begging to be allowed to examine the gift. They held their breaths while I lifted the lid, marked with the Sultan's monogram in diamonds: Abdul Hamid, El Ghazi ("the conqueror"). Inside were several rolled cigarettes, together with loose tobacco and papers.

We trotted back to the Péra Palace Hotel behind a jingling escort of cavalry. If I had planned the evening to order, I could not have contrived for Elsa a more picturesque introduction to diplomatic life.

In contrast, our actual departure, November 25th, was a dash of cold water. An outbreak of bubonic plague forced us to sail on the little Austrian Lloyd freighter *Polluce,* which had no first-class accommodations. Two hundred steerage passengers were sleeping on the deck, cooking their own food. The stench was so fearful that we retired to our cabin. There Elsa unpacked a portable alcohol stove and made us some tea, all either of us felt like drinking, because a stiff norther was rocking the ship.

Thirty-six hours of tossing brought us off Ineboli. The captain, to show he was familiar with the etiquette to be employed with an envoy on board, was flying the American flag at the foremast. An official launch promptly came out to invite me ashore to visit the *Kaimakan,* or Vice Governor, arrived from Constantinople only an hour before. When I had downed the inevitable coffee, he requested to see the Sultan's cigarette case and was as awestruck as the court officials. His wonder knew no bounds at my sending a telegram to congratulate Abdul Hamid on his birthday. There was a similar sensation at Samsun where I received an answer. At each Turkish port news of the cigarette case had preceded us; every official asked to examine it, although not one dared touch it.

From Batum we took the train to Tiflis, and then on through a forest of oil wells and tanks to Baku. There in the old, flatbottomed, side-wheeler *Tamara,* we set off southward for the two-and-a-half-day journey along the coast of Azerbaijan. As we drew near Enzelli, we began wondering about the great reception which Bowen had predicted I would have — the firing of guns, the Governor of Ghilan on the royal yacht, and a guard of honor. Unfortunately the wind was blowing stronger and stronger. The captain became more and more pessimistic, saying the *Tamara* would probably have to anchor in an open roadstead and, in order to land, we had to cross a huge bar; in a heavy sea no boat could get out to take us off. On a previous trip he had seen one capsize and everybody on board drown.

In a gale and pouring rain we lay to a half-mile offshore, watching the Shah's yacht in the distance. Discouraged by the sight of the bar exposed with every comber, it turned around and disappeared upriver. The captain shook his head and told me gloomily that sometimes diplomats trying to reach Persia had had to sail to and fro on the Caspian for a month before they could disembark.

Our hearts were in our boots at the thought of having to retrace our course; but now struggling towards us we perceived a broad, open rowboat, with a dozen men at the oars and a steersman in the stern. Pointing to it, our Finnish mate called, "If you want to chance it, I'll get you on board. As long as they've come out, they can probably make it back."

The wind seemed to be growing worse, the waves mounting higher every minute, and the boat dancing about like a pea on a hot shovel. However, with very little discussion, Elsa and I agreed we would rather die by drowning than by seasickness. We offered the serv-

ants their choice of risking their lives with us or staying on the
Tamara; with one accord they said, "We'll go with you."

Our hand baggage was tossed down while we tied on life preservers. A rope ladder was flung over the side; we had to climb
to the end and drop when a wave lifted the boat close enough. Elsa
started first; I held the ladder and tried to lend her a hand; it was
almost impossible to keep the ropes steady. In a few seconds she was
soaked with rain and sea water, and her wet skirts were tangled
around her ankles. Somehow she landed safely. I scrambled after
her, the servants after me, and we all rolled together in the bottom
of the boat. The old, gray-bearded coxswain motioned a command,
the oars dipped in, and, one minute swallowed in the trough and
the next perched on a peak of foam, we lunged towards shore.

As we drew near, the spray leaped high and the noise grew deafening. Above the din, the steersman, still calm and self-possessed,
shouted an order. The oarsman gave way, the crest of a five-foot wave
caught us, we swept dizzily ahead. Suddenly I saw bare sand, and
we were sucked onto the bar with a grinding bump. The following
comber loomed over us; if it did not break before it reached us we
would be smashed to pieces. Sharply the stern heaved up, and we
were heaved forward; then *bang!* — down we thumped once more.
A second towering white sea appeared about to engulf us; again
we lifted and banged. "Poor Elsa," I thought. "What a honeymoon
for her!"

It seemed a miracle when the next wave hurled us into quiet
water. We rowed up to an empty dock; not a soul was visible. Shivering, bedraggled, and thoroughly miserable, we mounted some
steps, and pushed open the door of the Customs House. A Belgian
official looked curiously at the pair of forlorn young intruders.

"Where have you come from?" he asked.

"I'm the American Minister."

"Impossible. I've just returned from the official welcoming party.
On account of the high seas, His Excellency was unable to land,
and his steamer has gone back to Baku."

Our dripping clothes and a few words of explanation quickly
convinced him. He built a fire so that we could dry out, and soon
we were filling our oft-emptied stomachs with scrambled eggs. Like
magic our seasickness left us; our spirits were completely recovered,

and we were laughing at our own ludicrous appearance by the time the Government barge arrived.

As we stepped aboard, the gaily dressed crew of twelve up-oared, saluted us, and then rowed us to a little island. Bugles blew, drums rolled, cannon fired, and between two rows of soldiers we walked towards a white stucco palace, where, in a large garden planted with orange trees, we met the Vice Governor. We had to sit through long apologies and a longer luncheon; afterwards, back in state we marched to the barge to set off for Resht on the mainland and another welcome, this one by the Governor.

We progressed across the broad, reedy lagoon, alive with cormorants, pelicans, cranes, swans, snipe, and many other birds I did not recognize. Once more we had to change boats before we at last nosed into a muddy bank.

Instead of the expected Governor we found a small man in a misfitting uniform, who deluged me with excuses: that very morning his master had been called to a distant section of Ghilan by a dreadful murder. There was no sign of Tyler, our Chargé d'Affaires, but an Armenian named Benjamin announced he had been sent by the Legation to aid us. Finally a Persian, who said he was a nobleman, introduced himself to us as the Shah's representative delegated as my official escort to Teheran.

We climbed into carriages, and behind a file of cavalry started for Resht, some seven miles away. On each side of us ran four men in scarlet gold-braided tunics, white turbans, and white stockings, all carrying long black staffs, with which they laid about them at the outskirts of the town, shouting loudly, "Make way for the Vazir Mukhtar!" ("The Great Minister!") Night had already fallen as we crossed the bazaars. By the lights in the shops we could make out swarthy faces, garish costumes, heaps of strange foods and merchandise.

Foreign ministers passing back and forth were, according to custom, entertained at the house of the richest landowner of Resht. Tired as we were, that night we had to appear at the banquet in his huge hall, lit by hundreds of candles and carpeted with beautiful Persian rugs. Neither the interpreter nor I had opportunity to eat, because the moment we sat down the many guests began hurling questions at me.

"Is your father a high nobleman in your country?"

"Of course," I assured them. "Among the highest."

"Is he an official in the Government? Is he a large landowner?"

"He runs ships across the Great Ocean."

"How valuable are they?"

When I had apparently satisfied their insatiable curiosity on that point, I thought it was my turn to make a few personal inquiries. I asked my host, "What's your annual income?"

He answered frankly, adding that he would like to be Governor of Resht, but doubted whether he could extort any profit from the position above the two hundred thousand tomans (roughly equivalent to dollars) which he would have to pay out in bribes to secure it.

Before I could continue, I was assailed from another quarter. "How much dowry did your wife bring you?"

Since wealth in Persia was measured by villages, from which the owner extracted as much revenue as he could, I made a rapid count of all the houses belonging to my mother-in-law — including the stables and cow barns — and then announced boldly, "Twenty-five villages." Immediately the whole table gazed admiringly at Elsa. She was a great heiress indeed — almost the owner of a province.

In Turkey I had discovered how important it was for success that the Oriental should consider you a personage, but I was totally unprepared for the battles royal waged over prestige by the Persians. The next morning my eyes were opened by the British Vice Consul. He told me the Governor of Ghilan had not been called away, but was merely trying to show his underlings how little he cared for foreign officials. If I did not demand the definite formalities prescribed by treaty, the news would spread, and during the entire journey to Teheran I should be expected to submit to indignities without protest.

It was hard for an American to realize he had to keep insisting on his exalted position. Nevertheless, I summoned the minor officials, informed them I intended to report to the Foreign Office, the Grand Vizier, and the Shah himself the rude manner in which I had been received by a low-down Vice Governor. Up to that time the Persians I had seen had moved very slowly, but I found that when frightened enough they could move very fast. Within a few minutes came a

message that luckily the Governor had just returned and was prepared to receive me at his Palace. I drew myself up haughtily.
"Say to the Governor that if he wishes to see me, he may call here,
and I shall consider receiving him."

Again there was a scurrying; presently a clatter of hooves sounded
in the street, and the Governor of Ghilan was announced. I had
won the first round.

Meanwhile, I had to make my arrangements for the five-day trip
by carriage across the mountains to Teheran. The Shah's "nobleman" knew only Persian and proved utterly useless, but Benjamin,
who had a smattering of English, haggled over prices, set different
carriage owners bidding against each other, and finally secured for
us two ancient but roomy landaus and three baggage wagons. The
piano and heavy boxes were to follow by camel caravan.

At once the Shah's representative sprang to life. To guide us,
he must ride in our carriage. However, Benjamin told me this official already had been given an expense allowance, and I should not
let him impose on me. As we were about to start, December 10th,
he tried to climb in with Elsa and me. I waved him aside, saying he
was much too low in rank to travel with us, but if he wished he
could get in with the servants. Before the tropical jungle closed in
behind us, I looked back to see Scotch William, German Marie, our
two Armenians, and the Persian, laughing, joking, and talking in
sign language.

The road was so muddy that again and again we bogged to the
axle; all of us had to lift and push. By changing horses at post-
houses every twenty miles or so, we had ascended by nightfall into
forest country, and stopped at a square caravanserai surrounding
a courtyard. The place had been used as a lodging for hundreds of
years with a minimum of cleaning. The instant our feet touched the
ground fleas began hopping up and down, and the hopping continued
the entire way to the *balakhaneh,* the balcony suite reserved for
travelers of rank. The sole furnishings were two iron beds, on
which we sat while the servants were setting up our own cots. With
one accord the fleas made for Elsa; as fast as she could brush them
off, more jumped on, and in a few minutes she was well bitten.

We were so exhausted with the day's travel that as soon as our
beds were ready we fell into them, but in less than half an hour

there was an exclamation from Elsa. Her sheets were specked with fleas. Since I had not been attacked, I exchanged beds with her, and we both settled down again. I was just dozing off when I was conscious of Elsa's tossing and scratching — the fleas had rediscovered her. For the rest of the night we shifted regularly at thirty-minute intervals.

Probably we slept more than we thought, because we were quite refreshed as shortly after daybreak our cavalcade started again. For that day and a part of another we climbed upward through the forest, and then suddenly the trees ended and we continued over luxuriant grass. At the topmost pass of the Elburz Mountains, six thousand feet high, the grass also ended in a line as sharply demarcated as though it had been sodded to a tape. All the moisture rising from the Caspian was cut off at this point, and ahead of us was only bare sand and rock — not a tree, bush, or any trace of green.

The air was now so clear that we could see miles across the red, yellow, gray desert. Some distance from Kasvin, the single large city between Resht and the capital, we could make out a reception party assembled on the road. However, there was no Governor of the Province — merely the Vice Governor saying the Governor was waiting for me at his palace. By this time I had learned my lesson. I would not shake hands with him, would not drive in his carriage, would not even listen to his argument that the Governor was a Royal Prince and not subject to treaty obligations. Turning my back, I mounted once more in my own carriage.

At the gateway of the city the Royal Prince put in an appearance, and I consented to ride with him. Nevertheless, when he announced a banquet was being prepared, I refused to attend unless he called upon me first, and, furthermore, if he were not at my caravanserai in half an hour, I would not receive him. At the last moment came a great rattling in the street outside; a large body of cavalry reined up before the door; the infuriated Governor stalked in. Instead of advancing to meet him, I stood at one end of the room and let him walk the whole way. He mumbled a few words of welcome, sat down, took one swallow of coffee, one nibble from a biscuit, and in three minutes departed.

The Governor had now admitted my higher rank. Therefore,

after a proper interval, I drove to his palace, walked the length of his reception room, bowed, shook hands, sat, accepted coffee and a sweetmeat, and in a little less than three minutes, to his utter astonishment, rose and departed without mentioning the banquet.

My position being no longer in question, presents were bestowed upon me, and also an honorary guard of ten soldiers who stuck to me like leeches. Every time I repaired to a certain very private place, they escorted me across the garden and stationed themselves at attention outside the door. Then came the military march back. Louis XIV never suffered from this ceremony as I did; he was used to it.

At Kasvin we joined the main caravan route, and our road was crowded with a fascinating assortment of traffic — a huge wagon loaded with pilgrims, an old sheik leading a donkey which carried two baskets, one on a side, each containing a wife, trains of donkeys laden with Russian goods and, most exciting, the files of camels, sometimes a quarter of a mile in length, from Afghanistan, Turkestan, Baluchistan, Kashmir, and even China. As the leader passed, its yellow head swinging back and forth and its bell jangling, our noses were assailed by a rank smell, and as the others followed, our ears were filled with a raucous chorus of wheezings, screechings, groanings, and grunts.

From the *balakhaneh* of the caravanserai that evening we watched the camels lurch into the courtyard. Boxes and bales were hauled off to the accompaniment of shouts and curses from the cameleers, squawkings, squeals, and hideous noises from the animals, which bit and kicked. The bedlam continued all night as the caravans went in and out; most of them preferred to travel in the dark because it was cool.

We ourselves suffered the next morning from the dust and heat of the road, and stopped for tea at a small *chapar khaneh* or inn. Noticing an objectionable odor, evidently arising from oblong parcels leaning against the wall, we inquired what they were and discovered this was a halting place for corpses. The Persians had a horror of cremating their dead, and one of their worst oaths was, "May your father be burned." Instead, they wrapped the body in the best rug they had and set out with it for interment at some shrine. Among the commonest sights in Persia was a group of two or three men on foot, leading a donkey laden with the family corpse.

With a fair wind they could be detected half a mile away. Those who could afford it traveled across the border into Turkey — to distant Kerbela, the Holy City, the burial spot of the martyred Hassan and Hussein, founders of the Shiah Mohammedan sect to which almost all Persians belonged. The dealers there did a very good business buying, washing, and exporting these funeral rugs.

When we went on we knew we were nearing our destination, since we could see ahead on our left the perfect cone of Mount Demavend, towering solitary from the plain, over eighteen thousand feet high. Benjamin told me that, although the British often climbed it, the Persians believed it could not be scaled because Feridun, their ancient hero, had chained to its summit the tyrant Zahhak whose spirit drove off rash invaders.

We halted at Mehrebad, some four miles outside the capital, where we met Tyler, our Chargé d'Affaires, Oriental Secretary, and Vice Consul General, an indeterminate Englishman of about sixty — as well as the entire American colony, which had driven out *en masse* in seven carriages. They took charge of Elsa, while I retired to a little villa to change into evening clothes for my official entrance.

This final reception surpassed any of the others. Two gorgeously attired officials, representing the Shah and the Minister for Foreign Affairs, escorted me to a royal carriage. Drawn up in front of the six white horses were two hundred of the Shah's Russian-officered bodyguard, the so-called Cossacks, wearing bright red tunics down to their knees. Before us jutted out of the desert the medieval battlements and towers of Teheran, looming up bigger and bigger and bigger as we approached. At a snail's pace we passed under the Gate of the Horse Races, the *Darvaszayeh Aspdovan,* down a broad, shaded avenue, lined with soldiers and crowds of dark-complexioned townspeople, across the Great Artillery Square, the *Maidan-i-Top- khane,* up another avenue between high mud walls, and finally through a huge arched gate by which stood five Cossacks presenting arms — the Legation Guard.

We stopped under the portico of a large white house with columns the whole length of the façade. Elsa was waiting at the top of the steps. Our journey was over.

CHAPTER XVI

TAMASHA

Although our journey was over, our troubles were by no means ended. The winter dusk was settling down as the glittering retinue departed. By the light from oil lamps which smoked and poured out soot we walked through the spacious rooms, empty except for a piano and a set of drawing room chairs upholstered in white satin. We shivered in the cold, but no wood had been brought for the fire. We wanted to wash our hands, but there was no water; in fact there was no plumbing of any sort. We could not even examine the premises, because the owner was still in possession.

The only note of cheer was Tyler's announcement that our landlord was providing us dinner. When we entered the dining room a great, fat, bearded Persian, smelling strongly of alcohol, motioned us to be seated, seized for himself a bottle of wine, and passed one to each of us. Without more ado, he fell upon a joint of lamb, wrenched it apart, and, between swallows, stuffed it in his mouth. Then he doffed his astrakhan kula, the bowl-like native hat, set it in the middle of the table, and began rubbing his hair with both hands. This was too much for Tyler. "That's the worst insult a Persian can offer," he exclaimed. "We can't stay here."

Elsa and I had to retire to our rooms, chilled and supperless. It was a discouraging first night.

In the morning, as soon as our landlord had left, we made a quick tour of inspection and found we had not fathomed the depths of Persian discomfort. Our kitchen resembled a root cellar, below the level of the ground, with dampness oozing from the flagged floor. The stove consisted of two stones supporting a small grate over a charcoal fire; a tin box served for oven.

To see what provisions could be had, Benjamin took William to the bazaar, some two miles off. Our Highlander returned with a long face. He had tried to buy white bread, but the Persians did not know what it was. Practically the only food he recognized was rice and lamb; pork was forbidden, and there was not enough grass to raise beef.

Officials of the primitive water company notified us we would have the hours from nine to twelve on Mondays in which to fill our tank and fountains, wet down the trees, clean the courtyards. Water was the most precious thing in Teheran, coming all the way from the Elburz Mountains; however, after running through open ditches in the streets, it was unspeakably filthy, and we could not bring ourselves to drink it. Fortunately, at this moment a boy appeared, carrying a huge skin of water from the spring in the grounds of the English Legation. Even this had to be boiled and filtered, so it tasted flat.

The problems of housekeeping were a challenge to Elsa's New England instincts. Leaving her to cope with them, I went to make my official call on the Foreign Minister, the Mushir-ed-Dowleh. He had very little to say for himself, except that the Shah Muzaffar-ed-Din would receive me the following day.

When the three royal carriages arrived, I searched in vain for the official who was supposed to escort me. No one had any idea of his whereabouts; there was nothing for it but to get in alone. Tyler occupied the second vehicle and, not to waste the empty space, William and Benjamin brought up the rear.

A few blocks farther on in the main street, an old man, looking like a tramp, signaled to the coachman, who pulled up obediently. While I watched in surprise, the ragged coat was exchanged for a splendid uniform; and lo and behold, to the admiration of the assembled crowd, the tramp was transformed into a court chamberlain. He climbed in beside me and on we rode.

Driving under a gorgeous gate, we alighted and proceeded along paved walks, bordered by streams of water running over blue and white tiles, to the main door. To our left was the façade of the Palace, marred in places where the plaster had fallen off. The effect was one of mixed grandeur and neglect.

In front of the entrance to the Hall of Diamonds a pair of galoshes was standing; in the case of diplomats, the rule of "shoes off" for a royal audience was amended to "shoes covered." I slipped my feet into them, and next there was a solemn conference as to whether I should wear my top hat; according to the Persian custom I should have kept it on. Finally they decided I should remove it.

The instant the door was open, I was dazzled by the reflection from the thousands of diamond-shaped mirrors which lined the walls. Against this scintillating background was revealed an incongruous group of figures, dressed in every conceivable type of uniform down to cashmere dressing gowns, barely hiding the dirty day clothes beneath. In their midst I discovered the Shah, leaning on a piano. Under his waving aigrette flashed the famous diamond *Darya-i-Nur,* the Sea of Light, sister to the *Koh-i-Nur,* the Mountain of Light. Slanting across his chest was a leather band, studded with dozens of other diamonds, each of them larger than any I had ever seen worn.

At the Shah's beckon I walked forward, stopping three times on the way to bow. He did not offer to shake hands or sit down, merely gazing at me blankly out of a pasty-gray face, as expressionless as when I had seen him in Constantinople. I presented my letter of credence; languidly he passed it on to the Foreign Minister. I delivered my short prepared speech in French about doing everything in my power to maintain cordial relations. Still he did nothing but stare at me. The pause had become almost embarrassing before he collected himself enough to make the customary inquiry, "How is the health of the President of the United States?"

"Excellent!" I replied.

"And how is the health of the wife of the President of the United States?"

"Excellent," I repeated.

Then, with the first show of interest, the Shah asked, "Is it true your President is fond of shooting?"

I assured him Mr. Roosevelt was a mighty game hunter.

"I should like to visit America and shoot with your President."

"The President would be delighted to have you as his guest."

Thus stimulated, the Shah began to cross-question me in regard to America. "Have you any streams of water that go on and on and on, and never dry up?"

"Many of them," I said.

The Shah looked doubtful. "Is there any part of your country, such as my provinces of Mazanderan and Azerbaijan, where blades of grass grow so thickly they make a solid plot upon which you can walk?"

"Miles and miles of it."

The Shah looked even more dubious. The rulers of Persia had been lied to for centuries, and he was consequently suspicious of anything out of the ordinary.

"How do you get to America?" he demanded abruptly.

"You must take a ship across the Atlantic Ocean."

The Shah appeared displeased. "I will not go by sea. I am always seasick."

Apparently he thought I was trying to prevent his making the trip, because he turned away, the only sign by which I knew the interview was terminated. I backed out with my three bows, kicked off the galoshes, and drove home. The Kajar Dynasty had certainly outlived its virility; it seemed to me I was returning from a thousand years ago.

My impressions were little changed in the next few days, during which I called on all the royal princes. In each case the routine was the same. I would alight before a glorified villa — many doors leading into stately halls, much glass, tiled walls, decorated in patterns, figures, and scenes, a succession of courts with green or blue tiled pools. The master of the house, seating himself on a French gilt chair, would listlessly ask me to follow his example, and proffer me coffee and dusty-looking cakes while Tyler interpreted inconsequential questions and answers.

The only Persian who did not strike me as being a relic of the past was the Grand Vizier; for his services, he had been given one of the greatest historic names in the country: the Ata Beg. His enormous body was directed by a remarkably acute mind.

A few months previously, a traveling French balloonist had invited the Shah to watch an ascent. Crowds had gathered outside the city walls and exclaimed with amazement as the balloon rose jerkily from the ground. The Shah was enchanted, but said he would not believe the evidence of his own eyes unless the Ata Beg went up; if anyone so heavy could soar in the air, then he would be convinced.

The Ata Beg, though terrified, did not lose his presence of mind. Thanking the Shah profusely for the honor to be conferred upon him, he walked across to the aeronaut. "Five hundred tomans if you can postpone the ascent twenty-four hours."

The quick-witted Frenchman spied a small cloud resting over Demavend, a rare event for that season. He lifted his glasses and, scrutinizing it carefully, declared, "Your Majesty, I regret that cloud will preclude another demonstration today. We must wait until tomorrow."

That evening the Ata Beg sought the court astrologer; the Shah never started his day without having his dreams of the night before interpreted. "A thousand tomans if you can prevent my going up in that balloon."

"Consider it settled," said the astrologer, pocketing the tomans.

The first thing the next morning the Ata Beg was summoned to the Palace. "My astrologer," said the Shah, "has just predicted that the most shining ornament in my kingdom is in danger of sudden death. This can refer to no one but you. You must on no account trust yourself to that balloon."

The Ata Beg thereupon fell on the floor, wailing and complaining of His Majesty's cruelty in withdrawing this great honor. The Shah was so affected that he forthwith sent for his Treasurer, and handed the Grand Vizier several sacks of tomans, a sum far exceeding in value the outlay to the Frenchman and the astrologer.

Meanwhile I had also been paying my respects to the Diplomatic Corps, beginning with the Dean. Most of the Ministers were already elderly, and it had taken them years to reach this rank; that I was coequal at twenty-eight was sometimes naturally resented. However, Elsa and I made friends quickly. The arrival of a new envoy excited considerable interest and an envoy on his honeymoon was rare indeed.

Although one and all assured me Persian was hopelessly difficult to learn, Elsa and I decided to make the attempt, and Tyler recommended a teacher, or *Mirza*. First, we had to master an alphabet more than twice the length of our own. Then, on opening a book, we were faced with the most impossible combinations of consonants. Since vowels were omitted, you could not tell whether mn meant man, men, min, mun, mean, mine, or mon. It was a light in the darkness to recognize a few of the Sanskrit roots which had penetrated to the English language — father was *pidar*, mother *madar*,

brother *biradar,* daughter *dukhtar,* store *magzan,* and man *adam.*
Elsa, who was a born linguist, left me way behind. Nevertheless,
I persevered, convinced that knowing Persian was essential for
travel and in gaining the good will of the government officials.

Persian respect continued to be dependent on my maintaining a
show compatible with my "exalted" position as Minister. We had
to have a tremendous household. Benjamin, whom we made *Nazir,*
or head servant, procured for us a coachman, a groom, and a gardener. Several applicants for house servants declared they were
descendants of Nasr-ed-Din, a claim which I was inclined to doubt
until I was informed the late Shah was reputed to have over five
thousand living descendants; most of them had been cast upon the
world to make their way in it as best they could. One applicant,
named Achmet, gave the British Legation as reference. I consulted
Sir Arthur Hardinge, the Minister, who said the only reason they
had let him go was because he had murdered a fellow employee.

"In that case I don't want him."

"Why not? His family has bought him off and he's had thorough
instruction here."

We took him on and never had any complaint to make of him.

When our staff was complete, I purchased a roll of cheap scarlet
cloth and had a tailor make it into tunics, supplemented by American
eagles embroidered in gold on the shoulders, gold braid facings
down the front, blue trousers, and military top boots. Our strange
assortment of servants presented an imposing array, provided you
did not inspect them too closely.

Although our retainers were well trained for Persians, they tended
to be slovenly, greasy, and buttonless. Unless constantly watched
they were always vanishing, usually to be found after fifteen minutes' search contentedly sunning themselves in some distant corner. They took advantage of us at every opportunity. Like other
Persian grooms, ours kept poultry in the stable which he fed from
our supplies. Furthermore, he enjoyed the perquisite of selling the
horse manure back to me, to use as fuel to heat my bath.

Worst of all, each one of the servants pilfered. Benjamin had
to guard the horse feed under lock and key, measure it out three
times a day, and then remain while the animals ate it. Otherwise
the groom would sweep it from beneath their noses and peddle it

in the bazaar. In the house the most astounding things were sometimes filched, among them Mrs. Bronson's photograph, which disappeared from the mantel. The servant responsible was told to produce it at once. He swore it was lost and proceeded to search the room, opening cupboards, looking back of cushions, finally turning up a corner of the carpet and pointing. "You see," he said, "it just fell there by accident. It was not stolen at all."

The ladies of the harem paid a good price for pictures of European women which showed the latest style in clothes and coiffure. The wives of the Diplomatic Corps who visited them recognized many of their female relatives lining the walls. Whatever the article taken, if not missed soon it was gone forever.

Coming in one day after a long ride, I ordered a bowl of buttermilk, but before I could drink it I was called away. When in a few minutes I returned, it was nearly empty. I shouted for the servant, a big, black-mustached fellow.

"Where's my milk?"

"I do not know, Sahib."

Taking a little hand mirror I held it in front of him. He cast one glance at the white frill of curds on his upper lip and grew pale as a sheet. "Oh, Sahib. Forgive me. It shall not happen again."

I could have summoned the public bastinador to set up his stocks in my courtyard and whip the soles of the culprit's feet. However, I was so amused that I let him off with a warning.

Thievery in Persia was so common that it could hardly be regarded as a crime.

One afternoon Benjamin announced that the head of the royal stables had brought a present from the Shah. I hurried to the courtyard. There, led by a gold bridle and covered with gold brocade, stood a magnificent-appearing Arab stallion, his small pointed ears pricked forward on a slender head. The delegation from the stables were waiting expectantly. This time I did not grudge them their pieces of gold; never had I dreamed of owning such a horse.

The instant they left, Arshak, my Cossack Corporal, and I went to the Maidan to try out the stallion. I swung on to his back prepared to dash off at a gallop. He did not move. I dug in my heels; he bounced up and down almost in the same place. Arshak examined his knees; they were permanently injured and so stiff he could not bend them. When I inspected the gold bit more closely, I discovered some of the gilt had already been chipped by his teeth. I scratched the facing on the bridle with my fingernail — nothing but gilt.

The Persian officials had substituted this worthless crock and these gimcrack trappings for the animal worth two hundred tomans stipulated by treaty. Sir Arthur Hardinge told me I ought to complain at once, but I had not yet been in Persia long enough to look a gift horse in the mouth, and he remained in my stable.

The Oriental mind rarely explored below the surface; to the Persian all that glittered was gold, and the value was estimated by the *tamasha,* or show. The very high officials I called on sent me presents, which, with the exception of superb carpets from the Mushir-ed-Dowleh and the Ata Beg, were nearly all paste and tinsel. Nevertheless, each involved a return gift, a severe drain on my personal exchequer. The British Government furnished Sir Arthur Hardinge with a chest from which at need he could pull out a silver box, cup or piece of jewelry. I had to hunt around the bazaars and pick up trinkets at exorbitant prices. Eventually, it occurred to me to cable to Father for some electric fans and candles run on storage batteries; these cut my expenses and were enthusiastically received.

The Persians were like children in many ways. In exchange for the stallion, I tendered the Shah one of the newly invented Luger revolvers; you kept your hand on the trigger and it kept on shooting. He scarcely gave me time to demonstrate the mechanism before he snatched it away and hastily terminated the interview.

The next day the English court doctor cursed me roundly. As soon as I had left, the Shah had invited him for a drive, and beyond the city gates had started to shoot my revolver at the glass insulators on the telegraph poles. Disgusted at failing to splinter a single one, the Shah aimed the weapon at some peasants in the fields near by, popping it off like a machine gun, exclaiming with delight to see the dust fly close to the mark. By this time the English doctor, in fear of his life, had slumped into the bottom of the carriage, where he huddled until the Shah's ammunition was exhausted.

Unlike Abdul Hamid, who had a theory of government, Muzaffar-ed-Din had but one aim in life — to gratify his own whims and caprices. Of all the superstitious Persians, he was the most superstitious, and this made him an easy mark for any cock-and-bull story. Once he had a letter from a citizen of Shiraz, who claimed to be disturbed by dreams. In repeated trips to Paradise he had observed multitudes of happy men surrounded by plump houris — one alone was tearing his hair and moaning.

"What's the matter?" asked the visitor.

The miserable wretch answered, "On earth I was the Shah Nasr-ed-Din. I am now suffering the tortures of the damned because my son, Muzaffar, has not made the pilgrimage to Kerbela that my soul may rest in peace."

To every pious Shiite of Persia a trip to Kerbela was as important as a trip to Mecca for a Sunni Mohammedan. The Shah, troubled and terrified, sent a fast messenger to Shiraz with five hundred tomans to pay the expenses of the dreamer if he would go as a substitute to the Holy City. Back came a refusal — such a sum might do for an ordinary man, but for one who was to represent the great and mighty Shah it was utterly inadequate. The Shah immediately doubled his offer.

Such episodes constantly recurred and, combined with the Shah's extravagances, kept the treasury empty. The only way he could fill it was to borrow from some European country which would be willing to lend, and since he had no intention of repayment, the only lenders were those who wanted concessions of some sort. The result was that Persia had degenerated to a mere sphere of influence in dispute between Russia and Great Britain. The Russian zone lay north, the British south, and they met at Isfahan.

The Shah saved himself from being a complete puppet mainly by changing his banker periodically. The heads of the Anglo-Persian and Russian banks were really political agents, each trying to take advantage of the Shah's foibles. On one occasion the signatures alone had been lacking to a Russian loan when, without explanation, the Shah abruptly refused to go on with it. As usual, he had had a dream, this time of a beautiful moon in the sky which suddenly fell and hit the earth, crashing into millions of small sparkling pieces.

The astrologer declared this moon was Iran, and the brilliant fragments were money. "Your Majesty," he predicted, "something is about to happen which concerns gold, and this will cause Persia to break to bits."

The astrologer's palm had been crossed.

However, the Russians were having rather the better of it. The Tsar had executed a master *coup* by securing permission from Nasr-ed-Din to organize the Cossack Guard, which was now the backbone of the Persian army. Their commander, General Kossagovski, was the dominant personality in Persia, and he looked the part — at least six feet five inches tall, broad-shouldered and muscular, seeming in his uniform like a heroic statue.

The question absorbing the diplomatic world at the moment was who should advance money to the Shah, so that he could repeat his trip to Europe of two years previously. Russia's price for the loan, which Sir Arthur Hardinge was doing his best to block, was permission to build a road from Tabriz to Teheran with elaborate property rights on either side; someone had smelled oil.

All the information I could muster was included in the customary review of the political situation which I sent to the State Department at the end of two months. Although, in the absence of American interests in Persia, I did not expect anybody to read it, I had learned that all diplomats warned their Governments of every conceivable contingency. If anything developed later, their Foreign Office could never complain, "Why didn't you let us know about this before?"

I did not have enough business to tie me down to the Legation and neither did most of my colleagues. Fortunately the Shah opened to those of us who liked shooting a section of his game preserves in the Elburz Mountains, some half-day's journey from Teheran. Among the high peaks roamed the ibex and moufflon, so prized by game hunters that many journeyed all the way from Europe just on the chance of a shot.

To avoid conflict, each member of the corps was allotted a specific time. When my turn came, I took Elsa and, so that she should be sure to have good luck on her first trip, we hired beaters. Early in the morning they scattered to round up the animals and drive them towards the butts in which we were stationed at the bottom of a dry, bare ravine. It was exhilarating to be out in the clear sparkling mountain air, and we waited patiently until the shikari pointed upwards; less than a third of a mile away I could distinguish a little beast about the size of a goat silhouetted on a pinnacle of rock. "Ibex," said the guide.

In a few moments I could catch glimpses of a group of females and their young, racing in spurts along the slope, halting frequently while from some crag the leader surveyed the landscape ahead. Finally he was outlined against the horizon not more than two hundred yards away. It was a long shot but a sporting one. Aiming carefully behind the shoulder, I pulled the trigger. He leaped in the air and then rolled down the hill.

More and more animals followed, and as soon as one came near enough, I said to Elsa, "Now thee try." She lifted her gun like a veteran, held it steady to the mark, and killed her ibex.

Shooting driven big game never appealed to me, because the odds were entirely against the animal; it was a different matter to use your own skill and endurance to get within range. Anxious to see what I could do if the quarry and I were on more even terms, I left Elsa at the lodge, and set off on a day's stalking.

The going was hard — beginning with an ascent of three thousand feet across broken rock and loose shale which slid with every footstep. I could not detect a sign of vegetation, and wondered on what the animals fed. At last we spied an ibex in the distance and then the real work commenced. Once the lookout was alarmed, the whole herd would start running, and that would be the end of the day's shooting. My bearer and I had to make a tremendous circuit to approach him up wind, scrambling over ridges and down hollows, down hollows and over ridges, and often having to go back and try another route if we wanted to keep out of sight. At length we reached the top of a steep rise from which I had a perfect shot at a hundred and fifty yards. Just as I was about to fire, there reverberated a loud explosion to my left and my prize tumbled.

Completely dumbfounded, I jumped to my feet. So also did a figure close by. As angry as I had ever been in my life, I hurried towards the intruder. Who should it be but the Bavarian cook of Count Rex, the German Minister. I asked him what business he had there, rated him soundly, and the minute I returned to Teheran reported the incident to his master — who, I thought, ought to know that his cook was surreptitiously making shooting expeditions in the diplomatic preserves.

The Count, a noted *bon vivant*, looked very sheepish. "If you insist, I shall have to dismiss him, but in that case my whole health, life, and happiness will be gone. At home he was a great poacher, and unless he is allowed to shoot, he will not stay in this outlandish place."

The Count was almost in tears; the whole incident appeared ridiculous and my annoyance vanished. "All right, I won't say anything, but you'd better warn him not to interfere with anybody else again."

Having so much leisure, we were making excellent progress with our Persian, and were soon proficient enough to translate simple folk tales. Many of them resembled the stories of Nasr-ed-Din Hoja, only, instead of the peasant farmer, it was the court fool who pointed the epigram. For example: He saw the Shah mounted on a beautiful ass, and immediately roared with merriment.

"What are you laughing at?" demanded the Shah.

"I do not like to say."

"What is it?" This time more sternly.

"I was just thinking how funny it was for one ass to be carrying another."

In every case the ending was *Padishah ruhid ve inam dad* — "the Shah laughed and gave a present."

On the whole, our closer acquaintance with Persian literature did not increase our respect for the Persians. In another anecdote a cadi found a treasure which, in order to enjoy it, he hid in his bed. In his endeavor thus to keep it for himself, he had numerous amusing adventures which on the surface were suitable reading for any child, but when the *Mirza* informed me the treasure was a woman, they acquired the most bawdy significance imaginable.

This system of double meanings was far more elaborate in poetry. The highest art of Persian writers was to veil their true thoughts under a mass of symbolism which many European scholars passed by unsuspecting. How was the foreign reader to know whether a beautiful tree in a garden referred to the tree of life, or the tree of knowledge, or some other tree? Often the references were sexually significant; the moon might represent one part of a woman's anatomy, the stars another. Tyler told me Omar Khayyám was held in greater repute for his lewdness than for his poetic talents, and Persians, who could not be made to realize that Fitzgerald's translation surpassed the original, repeatedly asked me why we admired Omar so much in the West.

In addition to pornography, the Persians exhibited a particularly callous streak of cruelty. One day Elsa was shopping in the bazaar, accompanied by Arshak and two other Cossacks. Suddenly she heard a distant uproar, and then the sound of running feet. The crowd about her shifted uneasily. Arshak questioned the man nearest him, "What is going on?" — and at the answer swung around quickly, saying to Elsa, "We must get out of here as fast as we can."

Before they could move, people pushed in from all sides so that every passage was blocked, and Arshak pulled Elsa into the shelter of a shop. Although out of the way of the shouting and jeering rabble, she could not avoid seeing, in their midst, led by the Governor of Teheran's servants, a stark naked man. Slits had been cut in his flesh, and in each bleeding orifice had been inserted a lighted wax taper. The stench of seared flesh, the streaming blood, the moans of agony, haunted Elsa's memory for days.

On my inquiry, it was explained to me in the most matter-of-fact manner that the culprit had invaded a harem and raped a young Mohammedan girl. This punishment had been specially devised as a warning to others. No one I spoke to seemed shocked.

Almost all justice was administered by Governors and Vice Governors, who every morning heard cases in their courtyards. Their decisions were absolute, and, to avoid the expense of keeping prisoners, sentences were carried out at once. Torture and mutilation were the common method, and when a hand or ear was removed the spectators would approve heartily, "That's a good punishment."

In March Blair Fairchild, my private secretary, arrived. He was good-looking, talented, popular, sang well, performed like a professional on the piano, and became much interested in collecting Persian folksongs. One day while he was talking to a wandering minstrel in the garden, the wind whipped the man's long hair back from his head and disclosed little holes instead of ears. Under questioning he frankly admitted he was a thief. At his first offense in Hamadan he had been set free on condition that, if he were ever apprehended again, he should lose both ears. Undeterred, he had reverted to stealing, been arrested, and off they had come. "Quite right, too," he agreed.

Many hands and ears were saved because every official could be bribed. Even though the family could not redeem their black sheep entirely, they might raise enough money to secure a reprieve, in which case he could seek sanctuary or *bast*. A variety of places were recognized as inviolable, including the royal stables and a raised stone platform in the *Maidan-i-Arg* (Citadel Square) on which stood a large gun mounted on wheels. During our polo games we used to see refugees sitting there, waiting until evening for some relative to come and feed them.

It had been an accepted custom that, when a Grand Vizier fell, his successor caught and killed him if he could. Recently, however, he had been allowed a few hours to escape. The Ata Beg had already spent two years at Kum, one of the greatest sanctuaries in Persia, where he had built himself a fine house, still kept in readiness should he need to return there again.

To the Westerner the most annoying trait of the Persians was their incurable lack of initiative. Turkey had been a land of rush and bustle compared to the repose of Persia. Since this was my first post as head of mission, I wanted to accomplish something if I could. I observed that the Persians apparently liked American wares; the Germans did a brisk trade by sending sewing machines labeled "Singer" and watches branded "Waltham" and "Elgin." The Ata Beg suggested there would be a good market for our agricultural machinery. Enthusiastically I wrote home to Father, who asked how I expected to have them shipped.

Undiscouraged, I opened a discussion of the various difficulties with the Foreign Office. I had to wait and wait for an answer and, when it finally came, it was addressed to "His Excellency, the Honorable, Glorious, and Mighty Acceptor of this: My desirable friend, my greatest friend, and my dearest friend, Griscom, the Minister of the High Government of the Republic of America. To the Big House to be given attention." And inside were nothing but more flowery phrases.

The next possibility that occurred to me was railways; the single line in Persia ran a few miles from Teheran to the Mosque of Shah Abdul Azim. The Ata Beg assured me railroads were quite out of the question; the superstitious Shah regarded them as the work of the Devil, and only the Powers of Darkness could be responsible for making a steam engine go. In an attempt to console me, the Ata Beg continued, "Perhaps you've noticed that big ruin crumbling to pieces outside the city. Some years ago Belgian capitalists built a factory to refine the sugar beets grown in the neighborhood. Promptly on its completion the peasants stopped growing them. They said to themselves, 'We'll be in our graves soon, so what does it matter?' "

Any effort to stir up the Persians seemed hopeless; inertia was an integral part of their character. One of the stories I read with the *Mirza* concerned a merchant who was seated in front of his shop. Along came a rascal who grabbed his turban and sprinted off. The merchant leisurely rose and began walking in the opposite direction.

A passer-by called helpfully, "Hajji, where are you going? The thief went the other way."

"I'm going to the cemetery."

"But why?"

"All I have to do is wait there long enough and he is bound to come."

CHAPTER XVII

AMONG THE BAKHTIARI

Often when I found myself in my office with nothing more serious to occupy me than the map of Persia, my eye was drawn over and over again to one section of the country west of Isfahan, marked "Bakhtiari." Now it showed no settlements and no roads, although in ancient times through that wilderness of mountains and rivers went one of the old trade routes of Cyrus and Darius.

Few unexplored spots were left in the world — parts of Afghanistan, Tibet, Brazil, Arabia, and one of the least explored of them all, the land of the Bakhtiari. The nomads who inhabited it were fierce warriors; "No Bakh dies in his bed" was a tribal adage. They were their own masters; they allowed no Persian within their borders, and paid only a nominal tribute to the Government. Nevertheless, the Shah had arranged to employ a regiment of their young men in his bodyguard, and he sat more comfortably on his throne because, once their loyalty was pledged, they could be counted on to fight to the bitter end.

To see to the welfare of this regiment there came to Teheran that winter the principal chief of the Bakhtiari, Hajji Ali Khuli Khan. The monotony of our life was broken by an invitation from the Ata Beg to meet him. The *Ilkhani* was quite different from any Persian I had yet encountered — stocky but sinewy, square of forehead, keen blue eyes in a bronzed and sunburned face.

Having spent two years at Paris, he spoke excellent French and conversed with most un-Oriental frankness. He had won supremacy over his people by what sounded to me like a feudal struggle of the Middle Ages, in which one chieftain made war at will on his neighbor until finally peace was enforced by the stronger. For the effete and corrupt Persians of the plains, he had the profoundest contempt; each of his five thousand mounted and armed tribesmen was worth ten of them.

I made a remark about the reputed hazards to travelers in his country. Hajji Ali regarded me seriously. "For my friends there is no danger. If you and your wife would care to visit me, I will guarantee your safety."

The promise of such an adventure seemed like a gift from the gods. Only a handful of Europeans had ever been among the Bakhtiari: after early explorations by Sir Henry Layard, Mrs. Isabella Bishop had made a trip in the summer of 1891, and recently Sir Mortimer Durand, then British Minister at Teheran, had made another.

We saw Hajji Ali often during his stay, and each time he renewed his invitation. The single consideration that caused me to hesitate for an instant was the thought of Elsa's safety. I consulted Sir Arthur Hardinge, who assured me the word of a Bakh chief was as good as gold. Fitzmaurice, who had come out from Constantinople to spend his holiday with us, urged me not to miss this unparalleled opportunity. Before Hajji Ali left, it was agreed we should go. The main carriage road led to Isfahan; there his messenger would bring exact instructions how to find the armed escort which would meet us at his borders.

At once we began forming our plans. Rather than follow the same route back, we decided to make a real exploration — strike north from Hajji Ali's castle through uncharted territory to Sultanabad. On such a trip there would be no inns, and few sources of supplies. We would have to have a caravan of our own and be completely self-sufficient.

If possible, we wanted to secure a guide who knew the route. Accordingly, I sent Benjamin to the Bazaar, the gathering place for the *charvadars,* or muleteers. Hours later the *Nazir* returned alone to report some of the old-timers had been as far as caravans went — to Kalgan, Medina, Samarkand, Bagdad, and Damascus — but none had ever been to the land of the Bakhtiari. Furthermore, at the very suggestion of going, one and all had shaken their heads; they had no desire to risk their skins. Eventually Benjamin produced Ali Hassan Akbar, taller than I, his white hair and beard stained with henna; for double the usual number of tomans he consented to venture with us.

Under Ali Hassan's supervision twenty-seven mules with muleteers to tend them were engaged. At this moment the Shah, having come to terms with the Russians for the much-discussed loan, announced he was leaving for Europe. In one night all the idle pack animals in the city were driven by their owners into the mountains for fear of being impounded into the royal service. We had to dispatch Arshak to escort Ali Hassan back, and for several days our caravan wandered contentedly about our garden, not daring to poke a nose outside.

Our last public appearance was on the Persian New Year, March 22nd; as part of the celebration it was announced the Shah would review his thirty thousand troops. Knowing that the entire Persian Army only numbered five thousand men, we wondered what magic wands the Persian officials would wave to fill the gaps.

From our tent in the palace gardens the Diplomatic Corps had a perfect view of the Shah, reclining in front of a window in the Hall of Diamonds to show his people how ill he was and how greatly in need of a journey. Beside him was a small table, covered with moneybags and heaps of loose coins.

The trumpets sounded. Through a gate at one end of the field the first band entered, looking so like pouter pigeons that I commented on it to Sir Arthur Hardinge. He smiled. "My dear Griscom, you see before you all the bands in the Persian Army. Those fellows have on three uniforms, one over another. The minute they are out of sight they can peel off the top layer and dash around to be ready for their next appearance."

After the band advanced the first regiment — brilliantly attired in the uniforms of Napoleon III's cuirassiers, complete with horse-hair plumes. They halted while the colonel stepped forward and received a bag of tomans. Next followed a regiment of Prussian Uhlans, and then a squadron wearing what I was sure must be the helmets of the New York Fire Department. Apparently the Persian Army had bought up the discarded uniforms of the world.

Five regiments paraded by, each receiving its New Year's present, and we supposed this would be the end. Not at all. A fresh regiment came in — Zouaves this time — and at its heels another. As one regiment marched out and vanished with its money, the men tore off the uniforms they were wearing, buttoned themselves into others, and a new colonel took his place in the lead. The procession never stopped until we had seen the whole thirty thousand, a miracle that could have happened only in Persia. We were identifying familiar faces under strange feathers long before this *opéra bouffe* was finished.

A few mornings later, by different gates, two caravans wound out of Teheran, one a mile in length bound for Europe, and the second, much smaller, heading south on the road to Isfahan. In addition to Elsa and me there were Fitzmaurice, Fairchild, the *Mirza,* two Cossacks — Arshak and Ali — Achmet the murderer, William, and Balthasar. Peach and apricot and cherry blossoms were hanging over the high mud walls as we left the city behind.

We all had saddle horses; the caravan would start early but we would get up at our leisure and gallop across the desert, sometimes chasing graceful gazelles, sometimes stopping in the heat of the day for a rest at some *chapar khaneh.* As we approached Kum, the Holy City, we saw glittering in the distance, framed against the background of blue and purple mountains, the great gold dome of its mosque. With particular interest we inspected the house of the Ata Beg.

At Kashan I bought for Elsa a *takhtravan* (moving throne), a sort of sedan chair suspended on poles between two mules. It was lined with cushions and big enough to sit or lie in, and I had a carpenter cut windows so that she could look out. The only flaw in this luxurious arrangement was that, as we toiled up and over the Korud Pass, the *takhtravan* swung back and forth so like a ship in a storm that Elsa was seasick.

Outside Isfahan we were received by the Sepoys of the British Consul and a guard sent by the Governor, the Shah's elder brother, the Zil-(Shadow)es-Sultan. We had expected to stay at the *chapar khaneh,* but instead we were conducted by the Zil's deputy, the Fath-ul-Mulk, to a palace of endless courtyards and gardens filled with lilacs and nightingales. A row of servants salaamed as we entered. Elsa and I exchanged glances. We knew what that meant — presents. The inn would have been cheaper.

The next morning was the Tenth Moharrem, the Shiah day of mourning for the martyrdom of Hassan and Hussein. Although at this time the people were often roused to a pitch of fanatical frenzy, we drove with the Fath-ul-Mulk to view Persia's ancient capital.

Traces of its glory still lingered in blue stone pillars, tiled arches, arcades, minaretted mosques and marvelous three-storied bridges with covered galleries in the middle.

On our way back we were passing by the Bazaar when we heard a rhythmic chant of "Hassán! Hussein! Hassán! Hussein!" punctuated by shrieks and howls of human agony. The Fath-ul-Mulk ordered the coachman to pull up. Suddenly around the corner reeled a procession of young boys in long white robes like nightgowns, splashed and stained with gore. Every time a mourner called out "Hassán! Hussein!" he slashed himself on the head and shoulders with his sword. The sickish smell of blood was revolting.

In the midst of the flagellants we were horrified to see our sixteen-year-old Cossack Ali, as spattered with red as any of the others. As they came abreast of us, one of our startled horses knocked over a table of sweetmeats set up as a sacred offering to the dead, and in a few seconds our carriage was surrounded by an infuriated mob. The Persians, although timid individually, were cruel collectively, and there was no telling what they might do. The Fath-ul-Mulk, pale, trembling, and frightened almost to death, managed to lean from the carriage window and make profuse apologies and explanations. With many ugly looks in our direction the crowd melted away.

We had been back at the palace for some time before Ali slunk in, pretending he had a miserable toothache. Arshak, eyeing him sharply, demanded, "What's that blood running down your face, you son of Shaitan?"

Ali had to confess and Arshak beat him soundly. At first we rather thought he deserved a punishment for getting himself entangled in such a demonstration, but then we discovered he had several gashes in his head, one of them five inches long, and he had lost so much blood he could hardly stand. Elsa fetched her sewing outfit; I daubed the wounds with iodine while she stitched the edges together. Finally, we bandaged him and, thoroughly humiliated at having had to submit to treatment at the hands of a woman, he disappeared.

That afternoon I called on the thick-set, moon-faced Zil. Again our sight of an Oriental despot was disappointing. To illustrate how nearly some of the attempts on his life had succeeded, he kicked off his slipper and swung his left foot on the table for our inspection of the scars. At the moment his chief interest was in his medical outfit, particularly his collection of dental forceps. He was using his harem women for practice. If he found a tooth that withstood his first efforts, he tugged a little each day to loosen it; he had rarely encountered one that resisted more than a week.

Our second day at Isfahan the expected messenger arrived with Hajji Ali's instructions. We were to travel by an appointed route until we reached a cleft in the mountains through which ran a broad, rapid river. This we should follow for ten miles, then at a certain bend we would find the escort waiting. Accordingly, we loaded the caravan and, a little nervous at leaving civilization behind, we set off westward towards the mountains. Fitzmaurice, whose vacation was nearly up, rode out with us to the edge of the desert, where we said good-by.

For two days we went over mountain and plain, the population growing sparser and sparser. I began to wonder whether I had been wise in trusting so entirely the word of a man I had seen so few times. My suspense increased when we came to the cleft and started along the narrow valley, the high hills close about us. At last we recognized the bend in the stream which had been set for our rendezvous and, rounding a point of rock, we saw lined up across the road a body of some twenty dark-skinned and blue-eyed horsemen, each with rifle on back and knife in belt. Their leader galloped to meet us. He said he was the tutor of Hajji Ali's children, and welcomed us in his master's name.

At a command the troop split, half taking position ahead and half behind, and we proceeded through gray mountains alternating with oak forest. The few tribesmen eyed us curiously, but at the sight of our escort drew aside. On the third day after leaving Isfahan, we reached a fertile, well-watered, rolling valley, in the center of which rose a mound crowned by a medieval stronghold with crenelated battlements and tower.

From the walled village at the foot of the fortress a crowd rushed out to meet us, the women peering in the windows of the *takhtravan* and dropping flowers between the curtains. They accompanied us as we clattered through the arched gateway into a vast open court where Hajji Ali, like a feudal baron before his keep, stood to greet us. Servants jumped to our horses' heads; we dismounted and followed our host up the steps to the *balakhaneh*. He poured us tea and departed, saying he would see us the next morning after we were rested.

The illusion of being in a medieval citadel had to be modified somewhat as we inspected our suite of rooms — walls covered with pink flowered silk, furniture upholstered in red plush, the three windows curtained respectively in red, green, and blue. Our bedroom was pasted solid with pictures from French and English illustrated weeklies, mainly scantily clad ladies from *La Vie Parisienne,* grouped about an enormous chromo of Lillian Russell.

At dinnertime, Hajji Ali's servants brought to our own dining room *kababs,* or lumps of lamb on a skewer roasted over charcoal, *pilau* of rice mixed with chicken, sour goats' milk cheese, and a drink like curds and whey served in a hollowed lump of snow ice.

We were getting ready for bed when Elsa suddenly asked, "What's that?" I listened. It sounded to me like Marley's ghost clanking its chains, but the noise did not seem to draw any nearer and we went to sleep. We woke to the same sound. I hurried to the window. Hajji Ali was stationed on a little terrace, and prisoners with shackles were being hauled by the scruff of the neck from the dungeon underneath us. The *Ilkhani* never hesitated. Each case was heard and sentence delivered within a few minutes. Some prisoners had their shackles knocked off, some were dragged away, apparently for punishment, some were thrust back into the dungeon.

The court having adjourned, I asked Hajji Ali about the prisoners. A few were murderers, most had stolen sheep or horses, the ones who had been returned to the dungeon had robbed a caravan under his protection and were being detained for a meeting of the chiefs. He let us look down at them. They were in a cell without windows below the ground level, chained to giant rings in the wall. Then he showed us the rest of his premises. The castle seemed equipped for siege — the water supply was protected, the vast cellars stored with food, pens prepared for sheep and goats, blacksmiths, saddlers, and armorers working in their shops.

Hajji Ali had arranged a round of entertainment. In the daytime we had an excursion, picnic, or a shoot. Whenever we rode abroad with him we were attended by several hundred warriors and innumerable sons and nephews, each with his retainers. One of his young sons, a black-eyed urchin of four, dressed in red velvet, was perched high on a mule with silver trappings, lording it over a half-dozen horsemen who held him on if necessary. At lunch we found a village of tents, completely furnished even to the rugs on the floor and open towards a river so that we could enjoy the sight of the tumbling water.

While we lunched, our host had dancers perform for our diversion, and native musicians played for us the harsh and barbarous songs of the camel drivers. Later, storytellers recited exploits of the tribe, which Hajji Ali translated. None of the tales seemed to take cognizance of the passage of time. Some which were supposed to have happened a few generations ago obviously dated from the era of Cyrus and Darius.

We had planned to remain only a few days, but one morning I woke with fever, and for almost a week was flat on my back. During my illness Hajji Ali never left the house. "How can I absent myself when my friend is ill under my roof?" he said.

This brought home to me what it meant to be sick in a country without doctors or medicines, and I wondered what I should do if anything happened to Elsa. Furthermore, the feudal atmosphere was proving too much for my following. The *Mirza* in particular was perpetually shaking with fright, begging me to leave; the timid muleteers dared not address the Bakh servants. On the other hand I was constantly afraid lest Arshak and Ali, who themselves came from fierce fighting Kurdish tribes, would precipitate some fracas.

Hajji Ali urged me not to hurry, but I was anxious to be away. On the morning of our departure, May 9th, we came into the courtyard to find extra mules loaded with barley and other food, and a gray-bearded *gholam* to guide us. As I shook hands, Hajji Ali gave me letters to various chiefs whose territory lay between us and Sultanabad.

Never had there been a more generous host.

Saying farewell to the Middle Ages, we set off through a trackless wilderness. Every evening we pitched our tents; from most ancient times the Persians had been masters of the art of tent-making, the trade of Omar. Wherever we camped a regular village sprouted from nowhere. Elsa and I had a most elaborate affair, white water-proof outside and an inner lining for insulation. Dining room and kitchen were separate; the servants occupied small tents of black goats' hair; the *charvadars* slept under flaps of canvas slanted across a pile of bags.

At first Hajji Ali's name was all-powerful. On the third day, however, the *gholam* rode ahead, and that night we discovered our camp was surrounded by as ruffianly a crew as I had ever beheld. The *gholam* reassured us, saying we need have no alarm because he had merely bribed the worst characters in the village to act as guard; this was the only way to be certain the troublemakers would not bother us.

Here and there we chanced upon encampments of nomad Ilyats, three or four black tents and a white one for the chief. Some were definitely unfriendly, and surlily refused our requests for food. If the *gholam* explained we were under Hajji Ali's protection, they retorted: "Who is he? We do not know him. Strangers are not allowed here." We moved on as fast as we could.

The farther we went, the more suspicious the tribesmen became, and the less knowledge our *gholam* had of the trails. In the wild country of the Baghi Nazen, a mile and a half high, I was riding in the lead with Balthasar and the *gholam,* when abruptly the stillness was shattered by a burst of rifle fire from the mountain on one side. It was promptly answered by a volley from the other. I stiffened to attention, and the *gholam* reined in. The crests to right and left as far as we could see were bristling with men, at least a thousand.

"Watch out! They're shooting at us," cried the *gholam*.

No sooner were the words out of his mouth than little puffs of dust were kicked up right beside us. One bullet pinged against a stone at my feet. I looked back. The rest of the caravan was strung along behind, the *takhtravan* lumbering prominently in the midst.

The *gholam* excitedly gestured towards a little ravine to the right. "There's a trail around the mountain. Let us go that way."

"But I must wait for the *takhtravan*."

"No!" he said firmly, and turned his horse. "No time for that. Besides, it's too heavy to keep up with us."

"You don't think I'd save myself and abandon my wife, do you?"

The old man pulled impatiently at his beard. "Of what importance, Sahib, is the life of a *khanum?* Always remember there are as

many wives as grains of sands in the desert, but only one of you.
Now come along!"

Apparently the rifles were too ancient to carry accurately at
that distance, because during this argument we had been standing
still, offering perfectly good targets. Meanwhile, the *takhtravan*
trundled up, and the *gholam,* grumbling under his beard, helped to
herd it into the ravine. But before we had gone more than a few
yards the path became too narrow, and we had to halt.

If we tried to go back we were afraid the warriors might pursue
us; we could not go forward without being picked off. Our only
hope was to get word to our assailants that we were friendly travelers.
A short way off a man was tilling a small patch of soil, quite un-
worried by the battle. I pointed to him: "*Gholam,* there's our one
chance. If that man will take a message to the tribesmen, perhaps
they'll let us through. Give him this toman and tell him he can have
another when he returns."

Like an ibex the messenger went scampering up the mountain
side. The firing ceased, and in an incredibly short time he returned
breathless to claim his reward. It seemed we had intruded in a
tribal quarrel. Two men had been killed the previous day, and the
battle was being waged for revenge or blood money. What right
had we to interfere in their affairs? However, both sides would
agree to a truce long enough for us to hurry through.

Not losing a second, we piled out of the ravine and whipped the
mules forward as fast as we could. In a few minutes we heard behind
us the echoing shots as the combat was resumed. Realizing our hair-
breadth escape, I warned everybody to be particularly careful to
avoid altercation with anyone we met.

Towards one evening we sighted a large settlement of some five
hundred inhabitants, perched on a high rock on the far side of a
stream. While we were making camp, curious villagers, some carrying flails, some scythes, some shepherds' crooks, began crossing
the river on steppingstones. At first they did not try to annoy us
beyond getting in the way, but then they grew bolder — picked up
things, and peered into our bags. Paying no attention, our men
continued setting up Elsa's and my tent.

Finally, one of our visitors started spreading out the contents
of the food box. Our cook, a powerful fellow, lost his temper, seized

a tent peg, and stepped forward, waving it menacingly. The villagers promptly brandished their weapons and prepared to assault him. Arshak tried to treat the affair as a joke. "Are we a pack of monkeys that you should stare at us so?" At this the shepherds turned on the Cossack, who drew his knife.

Anything might happen now. I shoved Elsa inside the tent and stood at the door, shouting to the men not to use their weapons; if a shot were fired we would be annihilated. The terrified *charvadars* fled to the shelter of bags and cases as the young shepherds commenced hurling heavy stones. One of them, narrowly missing me, whizzed into the tent.

Achmet, swinging back and forth the big heavy mallet for driving in tent pegs, cleared a space around himself. A mountaineer stabbed Ali in the side, and was about to deliver another blow when I flung a rock, hitting him on the arm so that it dropped limp beside him, and he ran howling from the fight. We dodged the flying stones as best we could, but many of them found their mark; Arshak was knocked unconscious. Our assailants were being held back literally at the bayonet point; every moment we expected to be overwhelmed by sheer numbers.

All at once we heard screaming and calling, and looked up to see the women of the village dashing across the river *en masse*. Each made straight for husband or son, and took hold, pulling with might and main. Close behind came graybeards, mollahs, and a little man in a blue coat, all haranguing loudly. Gradually the individual scuffles ceased, and the aggressors retired with muttered threats and menacing gestures.

Not knowing whether the attack was to be renewed, we kept a sharp eye on the villagers. Shortly, a deputation of elders approached and their leader announced: "We cannot restrain our young men long. Many have been hurt. They are determined to kill you when morning comes. If you will leave before daylight, we will send you a guide to conduct you into the next valley." Battered and bruised as we were, we gladly accepted.

We ate the rescued remains of our dinner in the dark, and lay down to rest until the fires burned low in the village. Then the tents were struck and packed, the bells muffled, and in the starlight we silently passed our sleeping enemies, stumbled up the mountain, pushed through a great stretch of white snow at the top, and descended into new country.

As soon as we thought we were safe from pursuit, we stopped while Elsa and I set to washing, bandaging, dressing wounds. The muleteers were the only ones who did not need attention. We were relieved to find we were not far from the Eastern Portal of the Bakhtiari land; and, with no further mishap, we drifted gradually into Persia.

By the time we joined the highroad to Sultanabad we had had enough of danger and hardship, and traveled at full speed through the heat of the day to the city. From there it was an easy trip to the capital. We were delighted to be back. The Bakhtiari country was no place for strangers, even under the protection of one of its greatest chiefs.

Not long after our return, Benjamin reported that two Bakh horsemen were in the courtyard with a message for me. They were covered with dust, and their panting horses seemed about to drop from exhaustion. One of them pulled a letter from inside the folds of his tunic. It was very brief. Hajji Ali had heard of the discourtesies shown us in his country. He wanted us to know that the offending village had been rebuked. In the future, that section would be safe for his friends.

I ordered the messengers given food and rest, and in the morning extracted what details I could. Hajji Ali with a thousand horsemen had attacked the village, sacked it, burned it, killed every male inhabitant, and carried off the women and children for distribution among his men. This was what the *Ilkhani* of the Bakhtiari termed a "rebuke."

In the June sun, Teheran was so hot that the thermometer would not register; the narrow streets were like ovens. With the rest of the corps we moved to the foothills of the Elburz Mountains, some fourteen miles due north. For several hours at midday I had to lie down for a nap without a stitch on, and still the perspiration rolled off me. However, towards five a cool and delicious breeze blew from the mountains, and then we would drive to the tennis court for exercise.

As the weeks went by and I still had nothing to do, I began to have the feeling that the world was moving and I was being left

out; it took months even for letters to reach us. At first Persia
had been an adventure; now the adventure was wearing thin. Elsa
and I had to confess to each other that we were growing lonely.

Fall found us once more in Teheran, just in time for the return
of the Shah. The most extravagant reports of his doings had preceded him. He had been on a purchasing spree, the spoils of which
included fifteen automobiles, dozens of rifles, shotguns, and revolvers, cases of jewelry, and several motion picture machines. In
Paris his staff had poured down enough champagne to float a battleship; his bill at the hotel had been five thousand dollars per day. His
last exploit had been to summon the women of his harem to meet
him at the frontier, but he had changed his mind and sent them back
at a cost of seventy-five thousand dollars.

Curiosity brought everyone out early to see the Shah's approach.
The Diplomatic Corps assembled in one of the royal gardens beyond the walls. Soon we saw a cloud of dust, and from it emerged
the household guard, the fire brigade, the royal jockeys mounted
on the royal race horses, an elephant, green and white turbaned
mollahs, and finally the Shah himself, who withdrew to a tent to get
ready for the reception. We waited an hour before being herded
through to felicitate the monarch on his homecoming. He seemed
little altered.

Sir Arthur Hardinge regaled us with a sidesplitting account of
the Shah's journey. King Edward had given a great ball in
Buckingham Palace and the Shah, with Queen Alexandra on his
arm, led the procession. The Persian entourage followed to the edge
of the raised dais and there milled around, at least fifty of them.
When the Head Chamberlain requested, "Please move over to the
side. Dancing is about to begin," they shuffled away, but, to the
horror of all the Gold and Silver Sticks, one Persian nobleman,
calmly carrying an ordinary china chamberpot, remained obstinately
in front of the dais.

Posthaste Sir Arthur was summoned to inform the Persian he
must leave the ballroom. The offender vehemently asserted he was
Hereditary Royal Pot-bearer to His Majesty, and it was as much
as his job was worth to be more than forty feet from his master.

Rising to the occasion, Sir Arthur had said, "Get hold of some
young chamberlain, and tell him he has been appointed Hereditary

Royal Pot-bearer. He must make his Persian colleague understand that in England a special position is set aside for possessors of this high office."

A candidate was immediately selected, and with a screen of helpers the two Hereditary Pot-bearers were run down the line, and thrust through the first door into an anteroom, where they remained for the rest of the evening.

Another major crisis had almost been precipitated on account of my casual remarks to the Shah concerning a visit to President Roosevelt. He had proposed to go to the United States on a shooting trip. The Ata Beg, having bought a new Government yacht, offered to sail his master to America. However, Muzaffar-ed-Din, who had been desperately seasick crossing the Channel, would have none of it. Instead he ordered a caravan to be prepared.

The Ata Beg ventured timidly, "Your Majesty, I do not believe there is any caravan route to America."

The Shah, suspecting his Grand Vizier of wanting to prevent his expedition, spoke sternly: "What nonsense! Hasten to the bazaars and stay there until you find a muleteer who knows the caravan route to America."

A command of the Shah could not be disputed. "Yes, Your Majesty," replied the poor Ata Beg.

The next day he returned and told the Shah he could discover no muleteer in the London bazaars who had ever been to America. At this the Shah was certain he was being put off; there was no place on earth you could not reach by caravan if you went round far enough. He had gone round the Caspian, round the Mediterranean; why could he not go round the Atlantic?

Greatly disturbed, the Ata Beg consulted Sir Arthur, who also had a solemn interview with the Shah. Maps were spread out — the Shah did not comprehend. All he understood was that everyone was conspiring to block his visit to President Roosevelt, and in the face of this combined opposition he had to abandon the idea.

The Ata Beg was so glad to be back in Teheran that he secured permission for me to shoot in the Shah's own preserve, a very special privilege. I thought that, if I could accomplish nothing else for my country in Persia, I could at least secure a prime specimen of ibex for the Academy of Natural Science in Philadelphia. I rode off forty miles into the foothills, where I spent the night at the royal lodge.

After long and arduous search and endless clambering, I caught sight of a magnificent male — the biggest mountain goat I had ever seen, his thick horns curving back a yard from his forehead — keeping guard on his point of rock. All morning I stalked him, crawling, creeping, climbing, stooping, wriggling, barking my knees and elbows, and finally I had my shot. To my delight, down he came.

We started eating lunch with relish while the shikaris were skinning the carcass on the rocks in front of us. One of them said, "Sahib, watch far up. Do you see that bird?"

I scanned the heavens. They seemed perfectly clear.

"No, Sahib; take your glasses."

I swept the sky with them and still could not distinguish a speck.

"There. Look there!" he pointed.

Nothing but spotless blue.

He was impatient. "It's right there," he insisted. At last I could make out a minute dot in the heights. It was as though living in civilization had dulled our eyesight; the mountaineer's naked eye could penetrate farther than I with the aid of my glasses.

Soon we could identify the speck as a vulture, swooping earthward with incredible speed. Within the next three or four minutes others appeared and also circled about our heads, lower and lower, until they were barely a few hundred feet above. Then they settled silently around us on the rocks; the instant we moved away they waddled clumsily towards the kill.

Suddenly the shikari pointed again, this time downwards. With my glasses I could pick out a figure zigzagging up the mountain, running where he could, climbing rapidly where the going was harder. When he was close enough for me to recognize Achmet, my heart missed a beat. Only in case of extreme emergency could Elsa have dispatched a special messenger. I hurried to meet him, my hand extended for the envelope long before he was near. Snatching it from him, I ripped it open.

If I had not had to uphold my official dignity, I would have set up a cheer. Just after I had killed the biggest ibex in the Elburz Mountains John Hay was offering me the post of Minister to Japan.

I could hardly wait to get back to Teheran for a jubilation with

Elsa. Although Japan was not regarded as a post of first-rate importance by the State Department, it seemed to us the opportunities in the Far East would be greater than at some small post in Europe where, from the political point of view, the United States was still regarded in the category of Denmark, Switzerland, or Sweden: We played no part in Europe's shifting balance of power. On the other hand, in the Orient our prestige was mounting. We were the nation which had introduced the modern world to Japan, and had established the principle of the Open Door in China.

Like every other envoy, the minute I was appointed to a new post I found my mind turning away almost instantly from the problems which had been occupying it. Elsa and I felt our roots in Persia were cut off, and we wanted to leave as soon as possible. In no time we were packing up. Our friends were genuinely sorry to see us depart; we were young and our house had been gay. After warm farewells to them and perfunctory ones to the Persian officials, again we bounced and rattled over the road to Resht. Now there were no receptions and no guards of honor; we were no longer of interest to the Persian Government. We did not care, our only desire was to get home.

We had a mill-pond voyage across the Caspian, and at Baku we said good-by to Balthasar and Bedros, who returned to Constantinople. We ourselves took the Moscow express. In midwinter, we landed in New York.

Already impressions of the dirt, fleas, and hardships of Persia were fading. We remembered only the swaying caravans, the sound of running water in the shaded gardens, the stately pillared palaces, all that made it more romantic than any country we had ever seen. We promised ourselves that someday we would go back, but deep down in our hearts we knew we never would. Persia was too far away.

CHAPTER XVIII

THE RISING SUN

"Glad to see you back, Lloyd. How are you, Elsa?" Mrs. Cowles, cordial, energetic, efficient as ever, greeted us as we entered the White House door. Being an old friend, she felt responsible for us and introduced us to Mrs. Roosevelt, our hostess of the week end. Then she briskly led the way upstairs; at the top we were almost bowled over by young Quentin Roosevelt, brandishing a big bow and bundle of arrows, just given him by his father.

On my return from Turkey I had followed in the wake of Senator Hanna through the same door and up the same stairs to call on President McKinley in his offices on the second floor. At that time I had had an impression of faded curtains, worn carpets, heavy mahogany, golden oak, red plush, and horsehair, the accumulations of half a century of indifferent tenants. Now the interior had been lightened and brightened and the offices swept out to a new wing, so that the overflow of visitors no longer occupied the family living rooms. The coming of the Roosevelts had blown a blast of fresh air through the stuffy old mansion; it had become a home as well as a house.

Before lunch we joined a group of guests in the reception room, among them Speck von Sternberg, the German Ambassador, Mr. Hay, Albert Shaw of the *Review of Reviews,* and several newspapermen. The President was late and Mrs. Roosevelt kept sending messages to hurry him. Finally, he burst in, smiling broadly, teeth flashing. There was a flurry of salutations and then, obviously hungry, he marched ahead to the dining room.

The food was simple but plentiful, and the President did it justice, stoking up prodigiously, as though he were a machine. All the while he managed to talk a blue streak, starting with the topic most on his mind at the moment — a proposed visit by King Leopold of the Belgians. "We've no court and we're democrats. If we don't show foreign royalties the respect to which they're accustomed, they're offended. If Leopold comes to the St. Louis Exposition and adds to the scenic effect, that's one thing, but he shall not come now." Here the President banged the table for emphasis. "Twice I've intimated to the Belgian Minister that we don't want him. If he asks again, he must expect a frank refusal. It's a great responsibility to have royalty. Some stupid fellow might take it into his head to try to kill him. Now, if the German Emperor wished to come, I should be sorry to refuse him. At least he's a man, and, if he were a plain citizen of New York, he'd be leader of his ward. As for Leopold, he's a dissolute old rake!"

Apparently Mr. Roosevelt put no guard on his tongue even in the presence of the German Ambassador and members of the press; he assumed that any guest would respect his confidences, and rarely was a President less betrayed.

Mr. Roosevelt had a remarkable faculty of adapting his conversation to his audience. He used to say you could not repeat too often variations on the old themes, "Be good and you'll be happy," "Be kind to your mother," "Love your country." That afternoon we watched him receive a thousand Daughters of the American Revolution. He put such emphasis and sincerity into his familiar moralities that they appeared profound truths instead of sentimental commonplaces.

Nothing the President did seemed to diminish his boundless vitality. At night he held forth to an entirely different set of guests, and the next morning, when Elsa and I descended for eight o'clock breakfast, he was already there. This early hour he considered ideal for doing business; he was at top form, whereas his visitors were inclined to be sleepy.

He started to volley questions at me about Persia, but, before I could answer, he launched into a monologue on the Great Empire from the rise of Babylon to the invasion of the Moguls under Genghis Khan. He paused long enough for me to begin an account of ibex shooting but interrupted to send for the rifle with which he had hunted in the West; he wanted to show us the marks of a cougar's fangs on its butt. Then he suddenly switched to Japan — what an opportunity it was for me, and how he himself had always been fortunate in making the most of his own opportunities. The changed atmosphere I had noticed in the White House reflected the refreshing influence he had brought into politics with his energy, directness, and forcefulness.

Only a few days after this week end I met the railroad builder, E. H. Harriman, whose daughter Mary was a friend of Elsa's. Fundamentally he was as dynamic a personality as Mr. Roosevelt, but in appearance and manner he was the very antithesis of the President — a quiet, rarely smiling, little man with a drooping mustache who spoke in a soft voice, with no striding into the room, no pounding the table for emphasis, no coining of phrases, no quality of being picturesque.

During dinner Mr. Harriman explained the basic principles of the "Long Haul" on which he had constructed his railroad empire; by cutting his operating costs under those of his competitors, he had provided cheap transportation to the public. First, he had reduced grades so that engines could pull increased loads. This led naturally to designing freight cars of greater capacity, which in turn meant laying heavier tracks, strengthening bridges, enlarging tunnels. Ultimately, he had bought up railroads and combined them so that freight could travel without the cost and delay of frequent loadings and unloadings.

Although Mr. Harriman controlled the Pacific Mail Steamship Company, which operated steamers to Japan, he had never been there. As we left I remarked casually, "You ought to see what's at the other end of your line. Why not come out to Tokio and visit us?"

Quick as a flash he answered, "You may be getting more than you bargain for. It sounds like a good idea to me."

This time my thirty-day instruction period was no farce; half Japan's commerce was with the United States and there were several disputes of long standing. For example, the American Trading Company had been filling Japanese orders for the cheapest grade of whisky, known as "white whisky," which the purchasers mixed with *sake,* or mild rice wine, and then sold in large quantities to the public. Anxious to protect their people from this deleterious blend, the Japanese Government had seized the entire stock of "white whisky" in Japan, destroyed it, and refused to pay damages. The same summary treatment had been accorded other American businesses: the

Japanese, having decided tobacco would make a lucrative monopoly, had taken over American factories and trade names, offering in exchange so small an indemnity as to amount to confiscation. Similarly, such severe restrictions had been imposed on American life insurance companies that they had to operate at a loss.

In Mr. Hay's opinion my most delicate problem would be Japanese resentment over their exclusion from California. He saw nothing critical in the advance of the Russian Bear in Manchuria, although Russia, having consolidated her position there, seemed preparing to push the Japanese from Korea. Japan — less than fifty years before a collection of clans fighting for supremacy with medieval weapons — would never dare challenge the Russian Colossus, with its mighty army and navy, huge size, and limitless resources.

Most Americans still thought of Japan as a flowery fairyland inhabited by little people in kimonos, carrying fans and parasols. Not until we had sailed on the *Siberia* from San Francisco did I begin to realize that this was not the Japan to which I was bound. Since 1868, when the feudal regime of the Shogun, a species of Mayor of the Palace, had been overthrown and the reigning Emperor Mutsuhito restored to power, Japan had been reorganizing her government on Western lines; now she had a Constitution, a Prime Minister, a Cabinet of nine, a Parliament of two houses, a liberal party and a conservative party.

Our first sight of Japan bore out the traditional poetic conception — a scallop of mountains on the horizon, lifting higher and higher above the sea, and then the magnificent stretch up Tokio Bay with the perfect cone of Fujiyama in plain view. We were brought back to earth at the Yokohama dock, where the Foreign Office officials met us in top hats and frock coats, like diplomats anywhere in Europe. The entire Legation staff was on hand — Huntington Wilson, First Secretary; John McIntosh Ferguson, Second Secretary; Ransford S. Miller, Oriental Secretary; and the Military and Naval Attachés. Reinforcing them were hundreds of American missionaries and merchants; the major part of the American colony lived in Yokohama.

For the eighteen-mile journey to Tokio we settled ourselves in a car which resembled one of our old-fashioned trolleys. On the long seat opposite us were several Japanese families, who bowed and smiled; soon from neat baskets they drew forth bowls of rice, and took turns dipping in expertly with their chopsticks. Beyond the city, the most terrific stench rolled in through the open windows. When it showed no signs of blowing away, I asked Miller what it was. "Fertilizer," he answered, and pointed to little men in blue tights with handkerchiefs tied about their heads who were hurrying up and down the green rice paddies, pouring liquid human excreta from tin cans with spouts. Green and lush as the landscape appeared, it had an unfurnished look which puzzled us until we noticed there were no cows or sheep to be seen. Miller explained the sharp edges of the bamboo grass cut their stomachs so that they could not be allowed out to pasture.

At Shimbashi Station we were greeted by more officials, more merchants, and more missionaries. Climbing into the Legation victoria, we set off down the Ginza, the principal highway of the city, threading our way among ricksha-men with bulging calves, who were running in all directions. Then we drove under arched cherry and plum trees, and finally, turning into the Legation grounds, halted in front of a white frame house that would have fitted perfectly in the suburbs of any American city. After inspecting the drab interior, we were glad we had brought along our own wallpaper and plumbing fixtures.

The next morning Wilson, who had every detail of Legation business at his finger tips, introduced me to the Chancery, located in a connecting wing. Chancing to glance out of the window, I saw a Japanese in flowing kimono walking towards the door. It was Iwasaki; since we had said good-by in London twelve years ago I had not heard a word from him. I dashed out to greet him, telling him he was a bad lot not to have written me. He only grinned and said letters were very hard for him. He had come to ask us to dinner to meet his family, and, before leaving, offered in his shy, reserved manner to supply us with milk and cream from his imported herd. Elsa and I were delighted because we both had taken a dislike to the extract of corn which the Japanese used as a substitute.

As soon as Iwasaki had gone, I started for the Foreign Office to call on Baron Jutaro Komura, who — at forty-eight, very young for a Japanese — had been made Minister of Foreign Affairs. He was thin to the point of emaciation; his sharp alert eyes and quick gestures indicated extraordinary vigor. Having graduated from Harvard, studied law in New York City, and served as Minister to Washington, he knew the United States well. I had the impression of a mind remarkably Western in its comprehension of world affairs.

On the way home my carriage was authoritatively waved to the curb by a policeman in Western uniform, who opened the door and signaled me to get out. Perceiving no reason for such unprecedented conduct to a head of mission, I hesitated. However, my Japanese coachman, an old servant of the Legation, begged me to comply. The Emperor himself was approaching. No one must look down upon him, even from the slightest elevation; the curtains in all the windows along the street were drawn. As I stood there, every person in the vicinity bowed to the ground at sight of his coach and remained in that position until he had passed.

The spontaneous reverence for the Japanese ruler was beyond anything I had seen in Turkey or Persia. Information concerning his private life was almost unobtainable, because to discuss him in conversation was shocking to the Japanese; they would no more have dreamed of talking about the simple details of his daily existence than we would talk about what God ate for breakfast.

My interview with the Emperor on the morning of June 22nd was hedged around with most elaborate court ceremonial. Elsa and I, riding in an imperial carriage, felt we were on the threshold of a Holy of Holies. The Palace grounds were cut off from the encircling city by a huge moat and an earthen embankment like a Mississippi levee. We crossed a double bridge, and drove up a broad avenue lined with saluting soldiers, then over another bridge into an inner enclosure, where we alighted.

In Japan the temple was the home of the priest as well as the place of worship; the Palace decorations were such as you might see in Kyoto or Nikko. We were conducted through a succession of great halls, the carved beams and ceilings of which were lacquered in gold, green, and red. The furniture was an odd combination of native and European — gilt and heavy oak contrasted with brilliantly painted screens depicting formalized scenes from Japanese history.

Leaving Elsa in an antechamber, I was shown into the throne room. At the far end, surrounded by court officials, stood the Emperor on a red-carpeted dais in front of a gilded armchair. I made the prescribed three bows as I walked towards him, and he, on his part, half stumbled forward a few steps, holding out a limp hand for me to shake. His contribution to the conversation was limited to a series of inquiries carefully prepared for him in advance. He replied to my formal speech in soft Japanese gutturals, pitched so low I could hardly distinguish the sounds. His only movement was to shift his weight from one foot to the other; his face expressed neither interest nor indifference.

At the end of a few minutes he stretched out his hand again, and with my three bows I was back at the door. Just before it closed, he turned and started in his curious shuffling gait off the dais. I had the feeling that he was being protected at every point of contact with the outside world; the Japanese considered it an inestimable favor for an envoy to be admitted to his presence.

Afterwards Elsa and I were received together in another room by the Empress Haruko, a tiny doll-like creature who, although she spoke in a voice barely above a whisper, had the same type of dignity as Queen Victoria. I could not help thinking what a lovely picture she and her ladies in waiting would have made if, instead of being clothed in European dress, they had worn their native costumes.

The conviction that a veneer of foreign manners concealed the real personalities of the Japanese deepened with every one of my official calls on the royal princes — Arisugawa, Kanin, Fushimi, Higashi-Fushimi — and also on the Prime Minister, Count Taro Katsura. It was not until I made the acquaintance of the four *Gen-ro,* or Elder Statesmen, that I felt I was talking with men whom I could meet on anything approaching common ground. Marshal Aritomo Yamagata, Count Matsukata, Marquis Kaoru Inouye, and Marquis Hirobumi Ito, who had played leading parts in the modernization of Japan, were beyond and above all convention and could converse with me frankly. I formed an invaluable friendship with Marquis Ito, whose gardens adjoined ours; he was more like an American than any other Japanese I ever saw.

One of Marquis Ito's innovations had been the employment of European experts to train young Japanese in every field — military, financial, economic, even artistic. For years the Foreign Office had employed as adviser an American, Henry W. Denison. Wilson immediately gave a dinner so that I could meet him, and I liked him at first sight — a burly, genial fellow with a keen sense of humor and fingers gnarled and twisted as the result of playing professional baseball in the days before gloves were used.

I had arranged in tentative order my list of questions to be taken up with the Japanese Foreign Office, and naturally seized the opportunity to ask Denison for suggestions. Casting no more than a glance at my paper, he became very serious. "Mr. Griscom, I'm not now in a position to give you more than a hint, but I'm betraying no confidences when I say that Japan is concerned with only one thing — keeping the Russians out of Korea." Japan's population, he continued, was growing at the rate of a half million a year. She was already cultivating every possible inch of ground; one bad crop of rice and she was faced with famine unless she could be assured of food from the mainland. Russian outposts were already on the Yalu, the Korean frontier; the new fortifications at Port Arthur were supposedly impregnable. The Japanese Government had decided this was the moment to meet the Russian threat and was taking steps accordingly.

It was hard to adjust my mind to the full import of Denison's words: that Japan was ready to pick a quarrel with Russia. Although he had opened up a startling train of thought, he would say no more, but promised to keep me informed. Rather than risk a prediction to the State Department, which was interested only in facts, I decided to wait until some definite step had been taken.

Among my colleagues I heard not a whisper of any impending trouble. Our Dean, Baron Albert d'Anethan of Belgium, MM. Harmand of France and d'Ambro of Austria, Count Arco-Valley of Germany, Baron Sweerts of the Netherlands, Sweden, and Norway, all seemed to look upon Japan as a place for recuperation after strenuous activity elsewhere. The British Minister, Colonel Sir Claude Maxwell MacDonald, had been Governor of the Oil Rivers on the West Coast of Africa, supposedly the most unhealthy spot in the British Empire, and had led the defense of the Legations in Peking against the Boxers. In spite of the alliance concluded by Great Britain with Japan the year before, neither Sir Claude nor his secretaries were perturbed about the possibility of friction with Russia. None of the Corps was in higher favor with the Japanese than Baron and Baroness Rosen of Russia, who had been in Tokio for years.

At the Foreign Office I found nothing which indicated its officials were engaged in any absorbing negotiations. As a matter of fact it was impossible to know what they really were thinking. The aloofness which I had sensed at my first meetings with the Japanese did not diminish on further association. In my case I had a particular difficulty in winning Japanese confidence, because in Japan only old men usually attained high position. For the United States to send a youth to deal with their graybeards might be construed as a mark of disrespect or a reflection on their importance. Baron Komura, who knew America, did not share this skepticism, yet even he would turn into a stolid Oriental as soon as business was mentioned. If I could introduce the subject of Harvard, his face lighted up, but his smile faded again if I tried to obtain some definite concession. He, like many Japanese, appeared apprehensive lest somebody might get the better of him.

In Persia knowledge of the language had been of immense benefit. However, it was useless to consider learning Japanese; ordinary correspondence required knowledge of five thousand characters, and in addition the student had to master an elaborate system of honorifics. For example, a Japanese always depreciated what was his and praised what belonged to anyone else. His own house was a hovel, but that of his friend was invariably a fine, glorious mansion. A son delivering a message from his mother would say, "My disgusting, pig-dog parent charges me to say to your beautiful, honorable, august parent, that . . ." And the reply might be, "It is an immense honor for my low-down wretched mother to receive a message from such a gracious, illustrious, noble person as your parent."

Among a people who surrounded themselves with so many bars to understanding, Westerners were isolated. Although the Japanese gave us lavish banquets and entertainments, they did this not for social purposes but because it was an official duty. Outside of business they shut themselves in their homes and we never saw them. Americans had lived twenty years in Japan without being invited to a Japanese house; even Wilson, who was popular with the Japanese, had been asked only once, for a week end, by a Government official with a German wife — and he told me he had been uncomfortable during his entire stay. By the time we were to dine with Iwasaki, I realized my friendship with him was almost unique.

At the moment Iwasaki was living at Komagome, one of his great residences in the heart of the city, the grounds of which seemed nearly as extensive as those of Central Park. We trotted along between pines, cryptomerias, sweeping lawns bordered by feathery willows and maples, cut here and there by streams, pools, and bridges. The house before which we stopped was a brown frame structure resembling the Legation.

Iwasaki and his wife greeted us in a reception room furnished in pure Western style, including the pictures on the wall. Instead, however, of asking us to be seated, they led us back through a passage into a second house, their real Japanese home. We had entered another world. In the corner of a room, open on two sides to the garden, stood a priceless Satsuma vase holding a single lily. On the wall beside me hung a delicately colored *kakemono,* a painting on a long strip of rice paper shaped like a narrow window shade. A circle of guests rose from their mats on the floor and bowed almost to the ground. Then we all settled down, I curling my legs under me as best I could.

Immediately nine geishas filed silently in, each with a tray and covered bowl. Lifting the lid of mine, I was confronted with the body of a fish floating in broth, its glassy eye gazing up at me. A little dubious, I took a swallow of the liquid, and was rather surprised to find it delicious. The first tray was whisked away to be replaced by one on which stood an empty cup. Iwasaki, seating himself opposite me, filled mine with *sake,* drank my health, and then moved around the circle, enacting the same ceremony with the rest.

During the four-hour dinner we tasted many of the delicacies of the Japanese cuisine — raw fish sliced to knife-edge thinness, tasting much like chicken, which we dipped in soy bean sauce; eels soaked in rich custard; bamboo shoots; and the most delectable species of lily bulb. I seemed to be able to consume a tremendous amount without feeling overstuffed, because the early courses were digested long before the later ones appeared. The only flaw in my enjoyment was the acute agony from my doubled-up knees; I had been warned it was the height of rudeness to stretch out a leg even for a moment.

At intervals the geishas entertained us, always in new costumes, and always doing something different — dancing, playing their *samizens,* telling stories, or conversing with us. In addition, Iwasaki had engaged parasol dancers and jugglers. It was as though a whole theater company had been performing for our benefit alone.

So much had been crowded into the first few weeks in Japan that we had disregarded the summer heat which, combined with the dampness of the rainy season, was making Tokio more unbearable every day. We had to keep our clothes in tin-lined cases to protect them from the mold that formed overnight. For comfort we absolutely had to have a parasol and a fan, and I carried them with me everywhere; I did not feel conspicuous, because everybody used them. Most of the diplomats spent the summer at Lake Chuzenji near Nikko, and we rented a house there for a hundred dollars for the season. Prices were low, and the exchange was all in our favor; fifty cents went as far as a dollar at home. I had never had such a sense of prosperity.

Anxious not to leave Tokio without the last word on Manchuria, I stopped to see Denison. He told me that Japan, pursuing her determination to settle the issue once and for all, had proposed to Russia a complete discussion of the Manchurian question. This positive step made me decide I was warranted in cabling a warning to Mr. Hay, in which I indicated that war was a possibility. Naturally I could give no authority. Unfortunately Mr. Hay was in New Hampshire, and Assistant Secretary Loomis was not impressed at my making statements without proof.

The next day we took the five-hour train journey to Nikko, the city of temples, where we engaged *kurumas,* or rickshas, to carry us the seven miles to Chuzenji. At an amazing pace, our *kurumayas* whirled us along, one boy running between the shafts, another fastened to the crossbar in front of him by a strip of cloth, and a third pushing behind. This last "boy" appeared about forty, far too old, I thought, for such strenuous exercise. We passed buckwheat fields, rice paddies, cottages of mud and thatch, and then, without slackening our speed, began slanting up and up through the woods, bordering a mountain stream which often tumbled over steep cliffs and struck the rocky bed in a tumult of foam and spray.

We reached a teahouse in a clearing; our runners dropped the shafts, scurried inside, washed down a bowl of rice with tea, and started off again. We had gone no more than a few yards when the *kurumaya* in the rear slowed up, tottered to the side of the road, and collapsed, completely done in; apparently his overstrained heart had failed him. I called to the others to halt, which they did, laughing as though this were a great joke. They wanted to abandon their comrade, but I insisted they wait. As soon as he could stand he made a move to continue on. I would not hear of it. Impatiently they declared, "Oh, he should have stopped long ago. We all have to come to this end sometime. By staying on he's only interfering with young men who need jobs."

To me it seemed a tragic conclusion to a career.

At the outlet of the lake were the Great Falls of Chuzenji, Kegon-no-taki, two hundred and fifty feet high. We descended to examine the rock from which annually numbers of young Japanese committed suicide. A student would compose a romantic poem about the charms of death, hang it on a near-by tree, and then leap off and be dashed down with the beautiful falling waters. Hundreds would be inspired by this example, and a wave of suicides would follow throughout the Empire, thousands during a year.

Passing between the brilliant blue lake on one side, and on the other the vivid green sacred mountain, Nantai-san, more than a mile over our heads, we finally reached our house. It was like a box, divided evenly into four rooms upstairs and four down, with sliding walls of paper through which every whisper was audible.

We led a pleasant life that summer, racing on the lake in our sailing canoes, playing bridge, dining with the rest of the Corps, going on picnics. One August morning we were awakened by the sound of tinkling bells; the pilgrims were arriving for the yearly ascent of Nantai-san. By afternoon the town was crowded with thousands of white-clad figures in huge straw hats, eating, drinking, bathing. At midnight, each, with lighted lantern in hand, began the climb. We could trace the route by the yellow pricks winking through the darkness.

The event which we had been anticipating all summer was our visit to Iwasaki, in the hot-spring country of Ikao. We made the journey an excursion, walking or riding in *kurumas* where we could, and taking the train only when necessary.

I had never felt so much in the public eye as on the first night at a Japanese inn. While I was soaking in the bath, dainty little maids appeared with more hot water. Once they were there, I thought they might as well make themselves useful, and had them empty the buckets over me. Before I finished, virtually the whole personnel found some excuse for coming in to see all there was of an American Minister.

The last six miles we traveled by *kuruma* up a green valley. The air was filled with the song of nightingales and larks, and heavy with the fragrance of auratum lilies. The road grew steeper, and, as we entered Ikao, the village street was merely a flight of steps between the terraced houses on either hand. At the top we passed through an old Japanese gate, and stopped in front of a large house built on the side of a cliff.

Everything had been done for our comfort, beginning with a European chef to cook for us the food to which we were accustomed. Instead of the single short thin pads which the Japanese slept on, the Iwasakis had procured for us dozens of extra long comforters, which were heaped on top of each other, and, as a final touch, made up with sheets and blankets; we sank into them as though they had been feather beds. We had never enjoyed more luxurious arrangements for bathing — a complete Turkish bath with every variety of nickel-plated sprays and douches, and a monster tub into which was piped water from a neighboring spring of a constant temperature of one hundred and five degrees.

In our rooms were laid out complete sets of Japanese clothes, on which Iwasaki's mother had been working for weeks; we wore no others while we were there. On walks I flopped along like a scarecrow, holding hard to my sandal strap with my big toe.

The hour before dinner was given over to the children, who were all learning English from their beautiful and talented mother. Every evening, Miki, the eldest, used to command me to get down on the floor, and, the instant I was within reach, the whole five pounced on me like Lilliputians climbing on Gulliver. When tired of jumping and tumbling, they invariably demanded a story. I described to them my ibex shoots and my experiences with the Sultan of Turkey, repeated the fables of Nasr-ed-Din Hoja, and, after those were exhausted, resurrected what I could of Aladdin, Ali Baba, and Sindbad the Sailor. As they were dragged off to bed they always chorused, "Oh, you'll tell us more tomorrow, won't you?"

CHAPTER XIX

A WAR OF NERVES

When we returned to Tokio in September, my first visit was to Baron Komura. He seemed tired, asked me perfunctorily about Chuzenji, parried with his usual skill my attempt to discuss Japanese-American affairs, and then paused. "Perhaps you've heard, Mr. Griscom, that Japan has been trying to open negotiations with Russia over Korea?"

"Yes," I said. "Are they making any progress?"

"None," he declared promptly and with unmistakable irritation. "Russia either ignores our proposals or evades answering them."

His statement brought me up sharp. I was as sure as though he had spoken the words that he meant, "Tell your Government how reasonably Japan is conducting herself and how impossible Russia is to deal with." Realizing that a Foreign Minister did not go out of his way to complain deliberately of the actions of one power to a third without some ulterior purpose, I asked him whether Japan had decided upon her next step. He replied by saying public opinion in Japan was gradually being aroused, and ended with the definite assertion, "Some action must be taken."

It seemed to me I needed no more trustworthy confirmation of Denison's warning that Japan would stand by her demands. If Russia pursued her intransigent policy, the negotiations would lead inevitably to war. Again I cabled Washington, this time giving my authority.

One fact was evident. In a few months Tokio would be a center of world interest, and the mission to Japan would offer far wider opportunities than anyone had ever suspected. The minute war was a serious possibility, Washington would want all sorts of information. Unless I were to be a mere mouthpiece for Baron Komura, I must have my own news sources. Taking a hint from British practice, I wrote at once to Ministers Horace Allen in Seoul and E. H.

Conger in Peking, and to Ambassador Robert S. McCormick at St. Petersburg, suggesting we keep each other posted about what was going on in our respective capitals.

Also I made up my mind to talk to as many influential Japanese as possible; and entertaining was the most efficient method of accomplishing this purpose. Under my predecessor, the Legation had been a sleepy old place; we determined to liven it up. Our first banquet was in honor of Prince and Princess Kanin, the highest ranking royalty allowed to dine with foreigners. We chose white as the motif for our decorations. Our two-acre garden was aglow with hundreds of white lanterns, hanging from every tree and bridge. Elsa ordered special moss and ferns from Kyoto to serve as a background for a gorgeous table display of white camellias. A band played the national anthems. The Legation had never seemed so bright and cheerful. When the last guest had stepped into his carriage, we went to bed feeling distinctly puffed-up.

A day or two later an imperial chamberlain called on me. He said the Court appreciated our party very much, and only let out gradually the surprise caused by our manner of receiving the Imperial Prince and Princess. "Perhaps you do not know, Your Excellency, that among our people white is the color for funerals." We were the laughingstock of the Diplomatic Corps and were properly deflated.

Soon we found that Japanese etiquette had other quirks. One afternoon we were preparing for a dinner in honor of Count Matsukata. The house was in confusion — furniture being moved around, Elsa arranging flowers, both of us in day clothes. Suddenly the Elder Statesman walked in, all dressed for the evening, smiling amiably, and evidently intending to stay. A member of the *Gen-ro* could not be left alone. I had to sit with him until Wilson came to the rescue and allowed me an opportunity to dash up and change. Wishing to pay us a compliment, he had arrived an hour or so ahead of the time for which he was asked.

We enjoyed especially having Marquis Ito as our guest at the Legation. He had a keen sense of humor and was famous for his practical jokes. While we were in Tokio, one of his friends shipped him a model of a beautiful naked girl made by Mme. Tussaud's waxworks. This suggested to him an idea. He sent for Dr. E. Baelz, the bearded German who was physician to the European colony. The worthy old man entered his patient's room to find it so darkened that he could barely distinguish a form in the bed. "Very sorry, Sir, to hear you are ill," he began sympathetically, and stopped short. By the side of the Marquis he had discerned a set of blond curls and a bare white shoulder. He drew himself up with dignity. "Sir, it is contrary to all principles of respect for my profession that you should ask me here to treat you while you are in bed with a woman!"

Marquis Ito burst into laughter, threw the bedclothes off, and jumped up, disclosing the wax dummy. His visitor was terribly injured.

Three or four times a week Elsa and I had to attend formal dinners, given either by other members of the Corps or by Japanese officialdom. The most magnificent were the Emperor's rare banquets to the Corps, served in the European style — china, table linen, cutlery, all marked with the exclusive imperial crest of the sixteen-petaled chrysanthemum. At my first one I was rather surprised to be offered a whole fried fish, which looked to me at least the size of a cod from the Grand Banks. I ate a small portion, and it was removed. When I left the Palace, I discovered in my carriage a number of packages, neatly tied with ribbons. At the Legation Elsa and I opened them. One was a silver bonbonnière full of little candies, another was the *sake* cup from which I had drunk, the biggest of all contained the remains of the fried fish.

Our servants, who knew the custom that guests at the imperial table should take away some food, had waited up for us and now gathered round expectantly; I had to divide the fish on the spot. Each received his share with the utmost respect. The desire to have something which had once belonged to the Emperor was overpowering. At my departure from Japan I should have had eleven *sake* cups; I came home with but one, all the others having mysteriously disappeared.

Every American had an intense curiosity to see the Emperor, and at the approach of the fall garden party for the Blooming of the Chrysanthemums, the Legation was besieged with requests for invitations. Since we were supposed to keep our list within reasonable bounds, our supply was quickly exhausted. However, this was not the only difficulty. Top hats and frock coats were *de rigueur,* and very few of those who wanted to attend ever seemed to have one. Even though the secretaries and I pooled our resources, we could not begin to fill the demand; most of the guests had to hire theirs.

From my position in the presentation line, I looked back at my countrymen, doing my best to conceal my amusement. Never was there a stranger sight — tall hats, short hats, hats with broad brims and hats with narrow brims, shiny black ones and rusty green ones, — hats mildew-stained and hats moth-eaten, — hats that perched on the head like thimbles, — hats that came down like pails over the ears. Every cast-off topper in the world must have made its way to Tokio.

The greatest strain on my endurance as a host developed from a most unexpected quarter. One morning the telephone rang. Wilson answered it, listened for a moment, then summoned Miller. He confidently said "Hello" in Japanese, then shook his head in bewilderment. "Apparently someone wants you, Sir, but I can't understand a word." No sooner had I picked up the receiver than my ear was bombarded with a stream of Persian. It was the secretary to the Ata Beg; my friend, the Grand Vizier, had already fallen from power, and was on an enforced tour of the world.

Like all Persians, the Ata Beg had to be entertained, no simple task in Japan. We heaved a sigh of relief when, after a busy week, his ship sailed, and I set to work catching up on my mail. Among the letters was a plaintive appeal from Yokohama. A certain Pinky Thompson was in serious trouble, and would go utterly to the bad if no help came from me. I showed the letter to Elsa. "Why, Lloyd," she said, "thee can't let a girl go on the street for lack of a few dollars. Thee must do something!" Rather skeptically I sent off a contribution.

A few days later Miller stuck his head around the door and announced, "Pinky Thompson is here to thank you."

"All right. Show her in," I replied, assuming a benevolent smile. Instead of the anticipated damsel in distress, I beheld the most nasty, pimply-faced, emaciated young lad imaginable. Miller had difficulty restraining his mirth until I could get rid of my caller, and my aiding Pinky to keep her virtue became a stock joke in our Legation.

During the fall I visited the Foreign Office regularly, and was never allowed to forget that, although the Japanese were steadily pressing the Russians for a reply, Russia was still acting as if there were no issue in dispute. The Japanese continued to exert every effort to win American good will and sympathy, yet, curiously enough, discussions of all my trade questions were apparently making no headway whatsoever.

One day in mid-December the Foreign Office telephoned that Baron Komura would like to see me at once, so unusual an occurrence that I hurried over as fast as I could. Baron Komura announced without preamble that an entirely unsatisfactory reply had been received from Russia. Manchuria was utterly ignored; its status must be settled before Japan's interests in Korea could be safeguarded. He was going to ask Russia to reconsider. In conclusion he requested me outright to inform the State Department of what he had told me; Sir Claude MacDonald was already sending a similar report to Downing Street.

This was my opportunity. "How do you expect our State Department to be friendly when you consistently refuse to discuss any of these questions?" I asked, pulling my list from my pocket.

"Let me see them," he said. I was sure from the way he spoke that no such trifles were longer to be allowed to prejudice American public opinion.

From then on I talked with the Foreign Secretary almost daily, and each time he handed me a memorandum of what he wished me to report to the Secretary of State, I immediately countered with a query as to how my business was progressing. Shortly I was able to report to Washington that the Japanese Government was capitulating on one claim after another.

Realizing the importance historically of my conferences with Baron Komura, and unable to take notes, I used to hasten home and from memory set down the conversations as accurately as I could remember them. In the beginning the exact phraseology was difficult to reproduce, but gradually it became easier and easier for me to record not only an impression but the precise wording.

In all our interviews Baron Komura was scrupulously careful to observe the proprieties of what I, as a neutral, could do, and there was a tacit understanding that I would add comments of my own to his statements. Nevertheless, the result of his deliberate propaganda was that Japan's position was placed before the State Department in the best possible light.

During the last ten days of December a remarkable change came over Baron Komura. His emaciated figure seemed literally to contract to a shadow; a joke about Harvard no longer brought a smile to his face. Among the Corps also the spirit of unrest was spreading. Sir Claude MacDonald's carriage and mine had been so conspicuous driving back and forth from the Foreign Office that all sorts of rumors were current, even that he and I were urging the Japanese to fight. Often on joining a group after dinner, I noticed the topic of conversation was immediately changed. The Rosens, who had been very friendly to us, now hardly spoke.

New Year's Eve Baron Komura told me Japan had gone the limit in concessions, and that, if Russia did not reply satisfactorily within four days, an ultimatum would be sent. Denison declared only a miracle could preserve peace, because the *Gen-ro* had at last become convinced that war was the single solution. Next to the Emperor the Elder Statesmen were held in greatest reverence and esteem. The Government heeded their opinions, just as a President of the United States would respect the advice of George Washington, Thomas Jefferson, Alexander Hamilton, and John Adams, should they be brought back to life.

At the imperial reception next day, the atmosphere was electric. The Diplomatic Corps lined up in the throne room while the Emperor passed along to greet us. Usually during this ceremony there was a rustling and whispering, but, as His Majesty approached Baron Rosen, every eye was focused on them in tense silence. Whoever expected drama was disappointed. The Emperor's face was never anything but a mask, and Baron Rosen was too finished a diplomat to display any emotion.

All January 4th I expected to hear of a Russian reply, but nothing came. Passenger liners were called off their runs and taken over by the Government. In the bazaars pictures of Japanese soldiers thrusting swords through Russian flags were being sold; no effort was made to stop them.

Three days late the Russian answer arrived — a renewal of the proposed neutral zone in Korea and mutual nonintervention in Manchuria. On the 12th Baron Komura handed me the reply — a rejection, which still did not shut the door entirely. Although Japan insisted on a recognition of her sole right in Korea, she was willing to allow Russia an equally free hand in Manchuria. Due to the promptness with which I received the memorandum, I was able to have it on Mr. Hay's desk before it reached St. Petersburg.

I was now reaping the benefit of Japan's desire to make a friend of the United States. In quick succession I secured from her an agreement to purchase the properties of the American Tobacco Company at a suitable price; to pay full indemnity to the American Trading Company for the white whisky claim; to permit the insurance companies to remain, on payment of a small deposit; even, with many protests, a promise to sign a copyright treaty. Thanks to extraneous circumstances rather than to my powers of persuasion, by the beginning of February I had, for the second time in my career, a clean slate.

One day towards evening the agent for the Standard Oil Company, a leading American merchant, came rushing to me with the announcement that the Diet had suddenly enacted a new tariff, which would not only throttle the American oil trade in Japan, but also, incredible as it might seem, act to the advantage of Russia. "If the Emperor approves it, our business is ruined," he concluded.

Waving the bill in my hand, I almost ran to Baron Komura's office and repeated what I had learned. "That's impossible," he said.

"Here's the bill," and I thrust it under his nose. "Can't you get the Diet to recall this before it adjourns?"

"That's never been done before, but — just a minute!" He reached for the telephone and, after a series of staccato explosions, interpreted, "Count Katsura is to see us at once."

We drove to the Prime Minister's house. He also read the bill, grew very angry, and more explosions crackled over the telephone. While I waited, an amendment was carried to the lower house, passed, carried to the Peers, passed, and delivered at the Palace for the Emperor's signature.

It was now apparent to everybody that, unless Russia backed down, and did it soon, war was only a matter of days. February 6th I was summoned earlier than usual to the Foreign Office. Baron Komura was alone; he sprang up, his face pale with excitement. "The Japanese Government has reached the end of its patience. We are recalling our Minister from St. Petersburg. Baron Rosen will be handed his passports."

"Then that means war, Your Excellency?"

"We have no choice."

Throughout January everybody had been saying, "Oh, they'll find some way out. They won't fight." But now they were going to fight — no more talk about neutral zones, rights, concessions, paramount interests. The only remaining question was how, when, and where hostilities would begin.

"Will the Japanese armies act without a formal declaration?" I asked.

"No!" was the emphatic reply.

I had the most important news in the world in my possession, and left at once to wire it to Washington, on my way out passing Sir Claude in the corridor. "There's going to be a rush for the cable," I thought. Never was a dispatch more quickly coded and hurried off.

That evening it was hard to talk and act as though nothing had happened, especially when I had to sit through a dinner at the French Legation with my colleagues around me, obviously still ignorant that in a few hours the guns would be firing. I looked across at Sir Claude and envied him his superb British phlegm.

After dinner I cornered him as soon as I could, "Well, at any rate we all know where we stand now," I said.

Sir Claude put down his coffee cup. "What's that? What do you mean?"

"Why, Komura must have told you this afternoon."

"Told me? Told me what? He didn't tell me anything."

That Baron Komura should have confided in me and said nothing to Sir Claude was inconceivable. "There must be some mistake," I exclaimed. "You'd better get hold of Komura."

Sir Claude, mumbling a farewell to his hostess, made one of the speediest exits ever achieved by a dignified Scot. Running Baron Komura to earth, he taxed him with treatment unbecoming an ally. The Baron's excuse was, "I forgot to tell you." He had indeed been so mentally exhausted that this was the simple truth.

The whole world was waiting for the declaration of war when suddenly on February 9th came two startling reports: first, that Admiral Togo with a mosquito fleet had attacked by surprise the

Russian ships in Port Arthur and bottled them up; second, that near Chemulpo, the port of Seoul, where the Japanese planned to land their armies, the Russian war vessels *Variag* and *Korietz* had been destroyed. Japan had, by a lightning stroke, gained the all-important control of the sea, without which she would have been beaten at the outset. It was unfortunate for me that I had already cabled to the State Department Baron Komura's definite statement that Japan would make a formal declaration before starting hostilities. This followed two days later.

For the Rosens, the war was a personal tragedy; the members of the Corps who had once been their friends now remembered they were Russians, and in this affair deserved no sympathy. Because of the obvious American partiality for Japan, I was not looking forward to paying the customary farewell call. Since I was sure Sir Claude must dread it as much as I, I drove around to the British Legation, hoping he would back me up. No one was there but Thomas Hohler, the second secretary. "How about our going to the Rosens' together?" I suggested. "They can't do more than throw us out."

When we entered the Rosens' drawing room it was already filled with diplomats, uneasily holding teacups in their hands, and not knowing quite what to say. We expressed our regrets to Baron Rosen, who listened politely enough, but, the moment we turned to the Baroness, she burst out, "How did you dare pretend to be our friends while you were knifing us all the time in the back?" She spoke so loudly that not a person in the room failed to hear the remark, and the conversation died abruptly. To bridge the awkward silence, Baron Rosen hastily offered us tea. We gulped it down, and departed as soon as possible.

"Thank God, that's over," muttered Hohler, as we sank into the carriage seat.

The next day the Rosens departed, the first casualties of the war.

CHAPTER XX

DAI NIPPON BANZAI

The start of a great war is a dramatic period in the history of any country. Almost overnight we at the Legation had to adapt ourselves to a changed world. We were immediately besieged by hundreds of American missionaries, merchants, and travelers throughout the Empire — every one wanting his particular question answered. Would Russia conquer Japan? What was to happen to their ships? How were we going to protect their interests? Would we help them sell munitions to the Government?

All these and endless other demands were listed on a long sheet of paper which lay on my desk. After each appeared a letter — "W," "M," or "G," — indicating whether the matter was to be attended to by Wilson, Miller, or me. Soon we added "S" for George Scidmore, who had practised law for many years in Japan, and "L" for Irwin Laughlin of Pittsburgh, my new private secretary, who arrived to take Ferguson's place. All were efficient, highly trained, willing to do anything, and paid no attention to hours. The lights in the Chancery were rarely extinguished.

Our work was made more complicated by the necessity of maintaining a strictly neutral attitude. Elsa and I had to be careful not to be present at patriotic meetings, although we could be sponsors for the Red Cross or other purely humanitarian undertakings. Americans in Japan were rampantly pro-Japanese, and, believing the United States was on their side, the Japanese frequently greeted our entrance at one of their gatherings with cheers and the playing of the "Star-Spangled Banner."

In contrast to this popular enthusiasm, there was a sudden reserve in official circles. The State Department was calling for news, but now I was hard put to it to find any. Whenever I mentioned war plans to Baron Komura, he murmured something about "the military not having decided," or "the military would announce in a few days." I had the impression that the Foreign Office was taking orders from the Army.

Soon I was aware that a well-organized spy system, inevitable in war, was in operation. I mentioned to Hohler that we were receiving many complaints from Americans that their baggage was being ransacked and that they were being followed. He said the British were having the same trouble, and related the amusing experience of a Scotland Yard man who had come to Tokio to learn single stick from the Japanese police. During one morning's practice his stick slipped, hitting his instructor across the left cheek. While dining that night at the British Legation, he happened to glance at the servant in livery who was pouring his wine, and almost dropped his knife and fork; across the fellow's left cheek ran a great purple welt.

We ourselves had a very efficient Japanese butler, who one day without warning or reason gave me notice. I asked why. He merely repeated he was sorry, he had to leave. I urged him to change his mind, but he shook his head. Miller told me he was undoubtedly a police agent shifted to another duty.

The surveillance was apparently so thorough that I wondered more and more whether our dispatch bag was being tampered with. The United States Government had a singularly childish trust in the sanctity of the mails. For economy's sake, we employed no special courier to carry our diplomatic pouches to and from Yokohama. We did not even stipulate that they should travel on an American vessel; we simply delivered them to the Tokio Post Office.

I was assured the Japanese Secret Service had a collection of the seals of every country, which enabled them to open and shut a dispatch bag without showing a trace. As a test, I included in one report a deliberate misstatement of fact. Within a week Baron Komura remarked he was afraid our Government was receiving an erroneous conception of a certain matter which he wanted to correct. After that episode I began to look for Americans on their way home who could act as temporary special couriers.

A humorous aspect of the Japanese interest in our correspondence was that, throughout the war, letters from President Roosevelt reached me by the regular mail in a White House envelope, often bearing only a two cent instead of the required five cent stamp. He

usually expressed in the most outspoken terms his detestation of
the Russians — very awkward if his undiplomatic language had
become public property. Curiously enough, as far as I could see, not
one of these communications was ever intercepted.

By the end of February Japanese soldiers by the thousand were
being transported to Korea, and there under General Kuroki were
being assembled along the Yalu River ready to invade Manchuria.
At the same time, each incoming ship was bringing its quota of
foreign war correspondents. Among the Americans were John Bass
and Stanley Washburn of the Chicago *Herald,* Robert Moore Collins
of Reuter's, Frederick Palmer of *Collier's,* James H. Hare, his staff
photographer, John Fox, Jr., of Kentucky and New York, and
dozens of others. Martin Egan arrived from the Philippines to
manage the Associated Press Bureau, and employed Willard
Straight as his assistant.

Although the world was clamoring for news, a censorship of unparalleled strictness blacked out all reports from the mainland. Hardly
a day went by without some veteran American newspaperman turning up at the Legation and protesting, "Here, what is all this? I've
been to the War Department and they won't give me a pass to the
front. It's preposterous. How's anybody going to know about this
war?"

I explained to Baron Komura that these fellow countrymen of
mine represented the leading American papers, that upon their reports depended American public opinion, and that nobody had ever
tried to keep war correspondents away from the front before.

Baron Komura hemmed and hawed, mentioned military exigencies,
said Japanese success hinged on surprise, arrangements would be
made as soon as possible.

The correspondents were somewhat put out, but at first were satisfied to wander all over Tokio with copies of Murray, collecting atmosphere, writing laudatory accounts of Japanese character, and
describing Japanese gardens, street scenes, personalities. Some took
advantage of the delay to travel through the country, but again
promptly encountered restrictions.

One day I had a frantic appeal from Jack London. He was in jail;
I must have him released immediately. Investigation showed that
he, with his camera, had strayed by mistake into one of the fortified

areas along the Inland Sea; and on my assurance that he intended no harm, the Japanese released him. However, he returned to Tokio, sputtering with wrath because his valuable camera had been confiscated; he could not replace it; it was essential to his livelihood; a war correspondent without his camera was like a plumber without his tools.

On my next visit to Baron Komura, after I had gone through my other business, I brought up the matter of the London camera. He was in a rather irritated mood, and said that he did not see how he could grant this request, but to make certain he would summon the legal counsel of the Foreign Office. I knew very well that when a Foreign Minister rang the bell for his legal adviser, it meant he needed support, and I would not get what I wanted.

The counsel arrived, an extremely clever lawyer, who, according to the quaint Japanese custom, had sat on the bench for many years to gain experience before being allowed to practise and have clients. As soon as the case was put to him he answered, "What you ask, Your Excellency, is absolutely forbidden. The statute declares that the weapon with which a crime has been committed becomes the property of the court."

"There you are," Baron Komura said to me.

"Does that apply to every crime?" I asked the lawyer.

"Yes, to every crime of every description."

I turned to the Foreign Minister. "If I can name a crime to which this does not apply, will you release the camera?"

Regarding me doubtfully for a few seconds, Baron Komura replied, "Yes, I will."

"Well, what about rape?"

Baron Komura's Oriental stolidity dissolved in a shout of laughter. "That's a good one. Wait until Count Katsura hears it."

Later the Foreign Minister called me on the telephone. "Mr. Griscom, your story broke up the Cabinet meeting. Mr. London gets his camera back."

I was beginning to wonder where Dick Davis was when, one morning about the middle of March, he and his wife Cecil burst into the Chancery. "What a war this is going to be! What luck that I'm not too late for the start! Come on over to the Imperial Hotel, Lloyd, and look at my outfit."

Dick's ideas of equipment had grown since Central America. Spread on the floor of his room was the most amazing collection of pith helmets, campaign hats, field glasses, canteens, wash basins, a rubber tub — everything an Arctic and African explorer combined would have needed for several years away from civilization. In spite of seeing his fellow correspondents all kicking their heels in the hotel lobby, he was sure that he at least would be leaving in a few hours to join Oyama and Kuroki.

I asked Dick to bring some of his friends to dinner. They were in fine humor during the meal, swapping stories and anecdotes. Over our brandy and cigars, however, they made a concerted attack on me. "Why can't you get us passes to the front?"

All I could think of to reply was, "There won't be a front until the Japanese cross the Yalu."

One of them piped up, "Well, then, while we're waiting, why don't you have us put aboard Admiral Togo's flagship, where we can have a view of the sea fighting?"

After other mutterings of discontent, Dick chimed in, "This would give you and your staff something to do, Lloyd, besides drinking tea in the afternoon with the wives of the nobility, and going to banquets every night and trying to extract state secrets from each other.

"You diplomats certainly do enjoy yourselves," he finished.

As the secretaries arrived the next morning, one by one they exploded with indignation at Dick's disparaging remarks. The result was we decided to show him an evening he would not forget. We invited him and Cecil to dinner, this time alone, and devoted that afternoon to making preparations.

All of us were letter perfect in our parts when the unsuspecting Davises were ushered into the drawing room. I put down a sheaf of papers to greet them, but at that moment Laughlin hastened in with a cable. Tearing it open, I frowned and handed it back with the curt injunction: "Please take care of this." Laughlin promptly left on the half run. With an apology I turned to the Davises.

No sooner were we settled than Miller appeared, and thrust another cable under my nose. "Sorry to interrupt you, Sir. This is marked urgent." I read it, muttering, "Yes, this is very important. It must be answered at once." Miller shoved a pad in front of me on which I scribbled rapidly. "Code that as fast as you can, and send it off." He too hustled away.

Before Dick could utter a sentence, Wilson entered and spoke to me in an inaudible voice. In what I imagined to be the language of a true Davis hero, I gave instructions: "Inform Minister of Foreign Affairs Baron Komura that my Government will not tolerate such conduct." Off Wilson rushed to the telephone.

Dinner was announced. As I was about to offer my arm to Cecil, Laughlin and Miller returned, hauling a diplomatic pouch. The keys were brought. While dinner waited, I solemnly unlocked it and dumped dozens of dispatches and letters on the floor. The whole staff plumped on their knees and began to separate the contents into piles — one to Wilson, another to Miller, another to Laughlin. I seized the envelopes marked "*Immediate!*" and, after one look, shook my head apprehensively. "This is disastrous."

Meanwhile, Dick sat on pins and needles, obviously dying to help, but we made no move to ask him.

Finally, we went in to dinner. I swallowed a few mouthfuls of soup, was handed another cable, glanced at it, and passed it on to Miller, who left the room. Every ten or fifteen minutes one of the staff hurried in or out on some errand or other. Towards the end of the meal a second dispatch bag appeared. "Shall we interrupt dinner?" asked Wilson.

"Let's take a chance and wait until we've had coffee," I replied.

I could see Dick's eye wandering to the dispatch bag in the corner. As we rose from the table, he exclaimed, "Really Lloyd, I had no idea of the pressure you fellows are under. We'd better leave since you have so much to do."

"Oh, this is nothing," I deprecated. "An everyday affair. Don't go. We must have some relaxation."

We insisted they stay for an hour longer, speaking mysteriously in stage whispers about "the cipher," and once I pounded the table and announced, "We must stand up to the last for our citizens."

When Dick departed he was very humble, and afterwards wrote some charming tributes to the hard-working Legation staff. He never found out how we had toiled, salvaging old envelopes, retrieving used telegraph forms, even raiding scrapbooks. Actually the second dispatch bag had been identical with the first. Miller had remained outside sealing up what had already been torn open.

Unfortunately the atmosphere of good humor did not continue; irritation increased as week after week of inactivity followed. The correspondents pestered the War Department with complaints, but only towards the end of April was permission given for the first contingent to leave. Jubilation was quickly replaced by gloom at the discovery that they were to be chaperoned as closely as children at kindergarten. They had to wear foreign clothes and display the name of their paper on their left arms, they could go nowhere without escort, everything they wrote had to be passed by a censor. Such restrictions had never been heard of.

Nevertheless, one and all were glad to be off, and some of them agreed to let me know if they learned anything of particular importance. I made the same arrangement with American military observers who were to accompany the various Japanese columns — among them General Arthur MacArthur, Colonel Enoch Crowder, Colonel William Crozier, and Captain Peyton C. March. To complete my news-gathering service I promised to give Egan and Straight what information I could in exchange for their co-operation.

The first reports that came to me described the splendid behavior and endurance of the Japanese soldiers. Physically they were like athletes unused to luxuries. Men who had spent their lives toiling in the fields on a diet of rice found it no hardship to plod along all day with heavy packs on their backs. The Japanese were probably the greatest marchers in the world. During the Satsuma rebellion a Choshu regiment in full medieval panoply had advanced seventy-five miles, and then without rest fought and won a battle. At the crossing of the Yalu, May 1st, the infantry had run three miles to extricate the cavalry from a difficult position.

The one absolute necessity for the Japanese soldier was a hot bath. At home in winter he took three a day to keep warm. In the field provisions were made to have water heating appliances and wooden tubs attached to each unit. Crowder wrote me he had often seen the soldiers dig a hole in the ground, fill it with hot water, and then, one after another, get in, regardless of mud or the number that already had used it.

Of plans of campaigns we still heard nothing — only accounts of *faits accomplis*. By the end of May General Nogi had landed on the Liao-tung Peninsula, isolating Port Arthur, and in June the Japanese columns had begun to move forward into Manchuria. Many of the correspondents were discouraged; they were never allowed near the front even to observe a skirmish, and never saw a battlefield until the battle was over. For Dick there was no romance in a war of which he knew less than I back in Tokio. I was not surprised to learn he had given up in disgust and returned home before a major engagement had occurred.

That summer of 1904 it did not seem advisable to go as far as Chuzenji. Instead, we rented a house at Kamakura, looking out over a long beach open to the Pacific. The town had once been the center of the bronze casters, armorers, and sword makers of Japan. In medieval times no artist was more revered than the swordsmith, and a blade of Kamakura could leave its mark on other steel, or cut through a pile of copper coins unnicked. When a Japanese took in his hands a masterpiece of Munechika or Muramasa, he put a handkerchief over his mouth in order not to defile the "living soul of the samurai" by breathing upon it. Now, Kamakura's chief claim to fame was its *Dai Butsu,* the colossal bronze statue of Buddha, which stood in a tiny valley a half-mile away.

At the end of August I was recalled to Tokio by the news that Kuroki had engaged Kuropotkin in a terrific battle at Liao-Yang; a half million troops were involved, the greatest concentration since Gettysburg. Many did not believe the Japanese could win. For eleven days — August 25th to September 4th — the struggle continued, until at last the Russians withdrew. The victory for the Japanese was complete but not decisive, because the Russian force was still intact; the final outcome had to await the spring.

The unanimous support of the people at home, evident from the beginning of the war, showed no signs of diminishing under the perpetual strain. Prices did not rise appreciably; there was no profiteering. Although five hundred thousand young men were away, their fields were tilled by relatives or neighbors; the rice crop was the largest in history. Everybody from the highest to lowest contributed to war loans. Iwasaki's name headed the subscription list with ten million yen, five million dollars; a month later he subscribed a similar amount, and again a third time, a total of fifteen million dollars out of his own pocket.

The war was uppermost in everyone's thoughts, yet it seemed the Japanese went out of their way to play it down. The news of the battle of Liao-Yang, and the siege of Port Arthur, the arrival of trainloads of wounded, the departure of fresh levies, roused no visible emotional reaction. A Japanese considered it a sign of extreme weakness to admit he was in mental or physical pain. One morning my head Japanese servant came to me, smiling and grinning, with a request for three days' leave. "What for?" I asked rather sternly.

He burst into a little titter. "My mother died yesterday."

I looked at him in surprise, and it took me a few seconds to realize that this assumed merriment was merely the prescribed cloak for his intense grief.

Japanese stoicism was partly due to ancestor worship; a soldier gladly risked any danger, because he knew nothing would be more pleasing to his forefathers than his honorable death on the battlefield. Conduct was also partly regulated by *Bushido,* the Way of the Knights, a code open in feudal times only to samurai. It ordained unquestioning devotion to the chief, unflinching bravery in the face of certain death, and complete self-discipline. At the break-up of the Japanese feudal system, *Bushido* became the standard for the whole nation. The people were taught to obey their Emperor implicitly, to think no sacrifice for their country too great, and to scorn all display of feeling.

The Japanese idea of a patriotic demonstration was characteristic. On the Emperor's birthday, November 3rd, the entire Corps went to Aoyama Field to watch him review his troops. Thousands of citizens had been standing there since dawn to make sure of having good places. Cheering the Emperor was forbidden, but I expected some demonstration as he drove up in his red and gold barouche. There was no sound; silently the crowd bowed almost to the ground as he passed.

So that the Emperor's halting gait would not be noticed, he alighted and walked slowly to his coal-black horse. Accompanied only by the Crown Prince Yoshihito, Count Katsura, Prince Arisugawa, and Marshal Yamagata, he circled the field and took his position for the review. The band struck up a French march as long lines of infantry, company front, advanced with quick nervous pace. Opposite the Emperor the officers raised their swords; the troops snapped their heads sharply towards him, then snapped them back. Artillery rumbled by, and behind trotted squadrons of lancers, guidons fluttering gaily in the breeze. Still no applause, no cheering, came from the crowd — all we heard was the music of the bands. There was something about the expressionless faces of the soldiers and the hushed calm of the spectators that gave an impression of inexorable force.

After two hours the last man passed, and the Emperor, painfully dismounting, returned to his carriage. The assembled thousands again bent double and remained so as the Imperial barouche disappeared from the field. Then at the same instant they all straightened up, hands shot into the air, and three tremendous cheers burst forth. *"Banzai! Banzai! Banzai!"*

That winter there were no military surprises. The Russian Fleet, which had left Libau on the Baltic in October, was on its slow progress around the world. The chief event was the long-expected fall of Port Arthur. I knew President Roosevelt would be eagerly awaiting the news, and arranged to have my cable take precedence. When the flash came, I sent it off on the instant; the President received it as he was about to greet his guests at the New Year's reception and thus enjoyed the pleasure of announcing it to them.

One morning in late winter a tall, well-built officer in American uniform, with as perfect a military carriage as I ever saw, was shown into my office. Saluting smartly, he announced, "Captain John J. Pershing, Sir. I have the honor to report for duty as Military Attaché." He departed at once to join the observers at the front, leaving behind his pretty bride, the daughter of Senator Warren of Wyoming. In a few months he returned, and the two proved welcome additions to the Legation. She was jolly and friendly, and he was thorough and efficient. My only complaint was that I could never induce him to talk enough of his adventures with the Indians or Moros.

As spring approached, we all watched for news of the inevitable clash between the two waiting armies. Kuropotkin had concentrated a quarter of a million men at Mukden, and there, Febru-

ary 20th, Oyama attacked with his five armies. It was another protracted battle. Seventeen days passed before we knew the Japanese
were victorious.

Paradoxically, this victory, and every advance the Japanese made
thereafter, put them in a worse position, because they were at a
greater distance from their base of supplies. The war was costing
far more than had been anticipated, and their financial structure
was feeling the strain. There was even a possibility that they could
not afford to pursue the contest if the Russians clung to a Fabian
policy and simply withdrew further and further into Asia.

However, from all reports, the Russians were in a sorry plight.
Their constant defeats, their loss of Port Arthur, the collapse of
their service of supplies along the Trans-Siberian Railroad, the
weakness of the Government in St. Petersburg, and the universal
corruption made their prolonging of the war a difficult matter.

To bring about peace between two warring powers is the dream
of every president or ruler, and President Roosevelt was no exception. I received intimations from Washington that I should be
on the lookout for the timely moment. It had to be carefully chosen;
if the mediator offered his suggestion too soon, he ran the risk of
a humiliating rebuff.

After Mukden, the only question remaining was whether the
Russian Fleet, now nearing Japan, could wrest back control of the
sea. Until this issue had been decided, the Russians were adamant
against peace proposals. The Japanese, on the other hand, were
willing to state their terms; I sent a rough draft to Mr. Hay in the
middle of May.

May 29th came news of Admiral Togo's overwhelming victory
in Tsushima Straits. Of the thirty-two Russian vessels only two
protected cruisers and two destroyers escaped to Vladivostok. Two
days later, Japan proposed informally that President Roosevelt act
as mediator.

All during the war the Japanese had held themselves in, but
when June 1st was set aside for a great *banzai,* they gave vent to a
burst of excitement and joy such as we had never witnessed in
Japan. On our way to the elaborate program of singing and dancing
arranged for the public at Hibiya Park, we saw bands playing
everywhere, and the sky was dotted with kites; across the streets,

and from the tops of buildings, floated streamers filled by the breeze into shapes of monkeys, lions, tigers, and giant fish, some fifty feet long.

Before we started home it was dark, but the city was radiant with light. Every sampan in Tokio Bay carried a colored lantern; the burning of a Russian ship was enacted in fireworks from a float. The square in front of the Imperial Palace was so jammed with thousands of people that we could not get through. Here and there tar barrels were blazing, and the flickering light waved across a sea of upturned faces, while over and over again from hoarse throats broke exultant cries of *"Dai Nippon banzai!"*

CHAPTER XXI

HANDS ACROSS THE SEA

An aura of peace was in the air on the morning of the 9th of June, 1905. The sun had just cleared the rim of mountains and was sparkling on the blue water of Lake Chuzenji; hardly enough breeze was stirring to fill the sails of a sampan, drifting by almost under our windows. Elsa and I watched it idly as we dallied over our breakfast.

The calm was ruptured by the arrival of a messenger boy with a telegram from Baron Komura. He must see me at once. No explanation. I was looking up train schedules when the boy returned with another wire, this time from the Legation — Martin Egan had received a cable from London stating President Roosevelt had volunteered his services as mediator. A few seconds later the telephone bell jangled. Tokio was on the line. I scarcely recognized Wilson's voice, usually so dry and precise, but now cracking with excitement. "A cable's here for you from Washington. Hay wants to know what time you delivered his previous message to Komura. No such message has come. What shall I do?"

"I'm taking the next train."

In fifteen minutes I was tearing down the long grade to Nikko. Did this mean that Russia had accepted the mediation offer? Why, of all moments, did the cable have to fail now?

Wilson was on the station platform in Tokio. "Is it here?" I asked. He shook his head. "Drive to the Foreign Office," I said to the coachman.

Baron Komura knew no more than I, except that two days before President Roosevelt had sent for Ambassador Takahira to inquire whether Japan would be willing to appoint plenipotentiaries to meet directly with Russian envoys for peace discussions. Japan had assented. Apparently Russia also had agreed.

I hurried to the Legation, where the staff were gathered. We sat for an hour until at eight o'clock the lost dispatch appeared. Laughlin took the code book and Wilson began writing — "The President feels that the time has come when in the interests of all mankind he must endeavor to see if it is not possible to bring to an end the terrible and lamentable conflict now being waged. . . ."

In two hours I delivered the translation to Baron Komura's messenger, and then we settled ourselves to wait for the Japanese reply. It was handed to me at one. Again we turned to, with the code book, and towards dawn the Japanese acceptance was on the wires to Washington. All of us found it hard to believe this was the end of the war.

With the choice of Baron Komura to head the Japanese peace delegation, interest shifted to Portsmouth, New Hampshire. Calm descended on the Legation, and at length after many months Elsa and I could seriously consider the prospect of a vacation. I was looking forward with particular eagerness to going home, because I had been offered and had accepted an appointment as First Assistant Secretary of State. More than anything else I wanted to work with John Hay. His policy of reasonableness rather than aggressiveness, his ability to understand the other side, had made even European nations regard our conduct of foreign affairs with a respect they had never hitherto shown. I admired him as a statesman, and the charm of his gentle, poetic, whimsical personality remains unique among the holders of high office in this country.

July 1st came a brief cable that the Secretary of State had died. A few days later there arrived in the mail my last communication from Mr. Hay. Some months before I had sent him a poem composed in his honor by the old court poet, Takasaki, and this was his reply, written in his own hand. It was curiously apposite as a valedictory for the man who had done so much to build friendly relations between East and West: —

> I, a gray poet of the Sunset Land
> Greet you who sing by Nippon's shining strand.
>
> Out of the shadows of a day that's done
> I hail you, Poet of the Rising Sun.

My plans for the future were entirely changed. Naturally the new Secretary of State, Elihu Root, wished to select as his principal assistant a man whom he knew personally. I applied for leave but was asked to wait until the peace negotiations had been concluded.

The summer was not so quiet as I had anticipated. Suddenly I had word that our Secretary of War, William Howard Taft, was to stop for two weeks on his way to the Philippines. One or two important visitors were a responsibility at any time; Mr. Taft was bringing with him a party of seventy-five, among them Sereno E. Payne, Chairman of the House Ways and Means Committee, Frederick H. Gillett, the rising power from Massachusetts, the silver-tongued orator General Charles H. Grosvenor of Ohio, and his junior, Nicholas Longworth, the reform Republican leader of New York County, Herbert H. Parsons, and Senator Francis G. Newlands of Nevada, the champion of reclamation.

The Congressional mission had a serious purpose — to report on our Philippine experiment. World-wide interest was aroused by the presence of Alice Roosevelt, who was accompanied by Mabel Boardman and several of her other friends. To make sure each step of the progress should be recorded several photographers and newspapermen were included.

From the time the members of the expedition stepped ashore until the gangplank was hauled up behind them, every minute had to be apportioned according to schedule. Fortunately, the Japanese at once seized on this unparalleled opportunity to cultivate American good will, and together we laid out a program — a reception by the Emperor, a dinner by Prime Minister Katsura, a luncheon by Minister of War Terauchi, a geisha entertainment by the Mitsui, and a monster garden party by the Legation. The Japanese wanted Alice and Mr. Taft to stay at the Shiba Rikyu, one of the smaller royal palaces. As delicately as I could, I intimated it might be embarrassing for the President of a democracy to have his daughter accorded the honors of a royal princess. I accepted for Mr. Taft, but Alice would visit us.

To the popping of fireworks and the fluttering of American and Japanese flags the *Manchuria* steamed in to Yokohama, July 24th. Laughlin had ascertained who was in which room, and before anybody landed, he and his assistants dashed on board with prepared baggage labels and tagged each piece; we were determined that not a hat box should be mislaid. Mr. Taft marched on to the pier, smiling his famous smile and carrying his great bulk with agility. After him appeared Alice, waving and calling greetings, and then followed the others, gazing about them with wonder.

Our journey to Tokio was a triumph; the locomotive of our special train was draped with bunting; peasants in the fields lifted their arms in salute, and faint *banzais* floated in the window. In Tokio bands played us through the streets to the Legation. The Japanese were firmly convinced that Alice was the Princess Royal of America, and at sight of our carriage the men shouted *"Bei-ko-ku banzai,"* "America for a thousand years," while the women bowed double again and again. Alice clutched my arm and exclaimed, "Lloyd, I love it! I love it!"

The Legation was a bedlam of reporters, merchants, delegations with gifts, ladies' committees. Nevertheless, we managed to sort out our visitors and send them off to their destinations; every one of them was delivered safely with every piece of baggage. Our own guests were shown to their rooms.

Elsa and I were racking our brains in the effort to work out a seating plan for lunch when white-bearded old General Grosvenor walked in. I asked him his advice. He gave me a comical look, "Ho-ho, young man, don't you worry. You have the dinner bell rung. We'll tend to the rest."

I took him at his word. At the opening of the doors, Elsa led the way with Senator Newlands, and, without hesitation, all the other senators and representatives made a dash for their wives. At the threshold a rapid sifting process occurred, and each couple passed in according to seniority. I remarked to one of the representatives that in the Diplomatic Corps it was regarded as a terrible blunder if a husband and wife were placed together. "I married my wife so as to sit with her at my meals," he commented laconically.

At eleven the following morning, long before I had had time to memorize names and faces, I found myself at the head of the line, presenting my guests to the Emperor. Luncheon was served, and afterwards, to my great amazement, the Emperor offered to let us see his own private garden, hitherto never exhibited to foreigners. We climbed into imperial barouches and drove through a narrow gate in a high green fence surrounding a beautiful park. In front of us was a lake, covered with pink flowering lotus. We walked across an old mossy stone bridge, sharply curved in the middle, and reached a forested island, crisscrossed by little trails. The nightingales were singing, the first time most of the party had ever heard them.

Viscount Chinda, who was acting for Baron Komura at the Foreign Office, said neither he nor any of the other Government officials present had ever expected to be admitted to this garden. He was very grateful to us for getting them in.

The powerful merchant banking family of the Mitsui gave a most elaborate banquet at the Maple Club, all in the Japanese fashion — shoes off at the door, no chairs, no cutlery. Mr. Taft vainly attempted to achieve the squatting position, until finally a polite Japanese rushed up with a padded stool from which he looked down majestically on the rest of us.

Our party scrutinized the Japanese food with interest, but on the whole they did not eat much. When, instead of a juicy steak and black coffee, they were presented with a box from which protruded the head, wings, and tail of a quail, still feathered, they drew back in alarm. Even the familiar rice was elusive, they could not hold the grains between their chopsticks. After dinner the best geisha dancers in the Empire entertained us, and then a sigh of pleasure went round the famished audience at the sight of sandwiches, cake, and champagne.

While everybody was making up for lost time, Alice, who was next me, tapped me on the shoulder. "Do you see that old, bald-headed man scratching his ear over there?"

"Do you mean Nick Longworth?"

"Yes. Can you imagine any young girl marrying a fellow like that?"

"Why, Alice, you couldn't find anybody nicer."

"I know. I know. But this is a question of marriage."

We had all heard rumors of such a possibility, but here was the first confirmation.

The luncheons and dinners kept on and on, each with its own special features. Prince Fushimi arranged a series of bouts between the great wrestlers of Japan — men in such magnificent physical condition that they could sit outside in the dead of winter without other clothing than their loincloths, and could not enter a house without dripping with perspiration. The national champion strode up solemnly to be introduced. As the two monumental figures shook hands, everyone, including Mr. Taft himself, roared with laughter.

Before leaving Japan, the delegation decided to hold a celebration of its own for Mr. Taft, and bought a huge porcelain Satsuma bowl which General Grosvenor, as the most famous orator in the party, was elected to present. The afternoon of the dinner I came in to find the General studying the bowl with an air of deep puzzlement. "What am I going to say about this thing tonight?"

"Well, it's the finest Satsuma porcelain and can no longer be reproduced."

"Tell me that again."

I explained once more, and he nodded his head, although he still looked somewhat doubtful.

That evening the old-fashioned eloquence of the General's tribute brought tears to the eyes of the delegation. Every face was turned expectantly towards him as he lifted the bowl and addressed Mr. Taft. "And now, beloved friend of all of us, on behalf of us all, I have the honor to present to you — " He started to hand over the bowl, then hesitated — "I have the honor to present, beloved friend, this — " "I have the honor to present." He coughed. "This — this — this — Beloved friend. I have the honor of presenting to you this — splendid specimen of carved and painted crockery."

A perfect howl of delight went up as Mr. Taft, bowing and smiling, accepted the gift.

Our efforts to see that the legislators had a good time were apparently successful, because at their departure they showered us with so many compliments that everybody on the hard-worked staff was confident of being an ambassador in a few months.

The Japanese outdid themselves in their farewells. From Legation gate to railroad station the streets were lined with crowds, shouting "*Banzai!*" and waving red and white lanterns, and throwing bouquets at the daughter of the Peacemaker. The square at Shimbashi Station was so tightly packed that the police had to force a way through. The special train pulled out to the thunder of innumerable *banzais*. Never had there been such a demonstration for foreigners.

No sooner had the Taft party sailed away than I had word other visitors were approaching — Mr. and Mrs. Harriman, their three daughters, two sons, Mr. and Mrs. Robert Goelet, R. P. Schwerin,

Vice President of the Pacific Mail Steamship Line, Mr. Harriman's personal physician, Dr. Lyle, a tutor, three stenographers, several valets and maids. August 31st the Legation was again swarming with guests.

Ostensibly Mr. Harriman was coming on a pleasure trip, but at the same time he had a weather eye cocked for the welfare of the Pacific Mail Steamship Company. Among the Japanese dreams of Empire was apparently a design to compete for the carrying trade of the Far East, because they were trying to buy new steamships in the United States and subsidizing their own. Mr. Harriman, anxious to determine whether or not Japan was seriously threatening to sweep the United States off the Pacific, wanted to meet and talk with as many of the Japanese officials as he could. As one of the greatest railway men in the world and as the embodiment of business success, Mr. Harriman stood to the Japanese for everything they admired.

Another round of festivities had barely begun when the report came from the United States that Japan had withdrawn her demand for a Russian indemnity, and the peace treaty was about to be signed. Japan's paramount interests in Korea were recognized, and Russia was to restore Manchuria to China. However, the Japanese people had been led to believe they would receive at least a half billion dollars from Russia to help pay for the war; most of them expected far more. In their eyes the southern half of the island of Saghalien, accepted in exchange, was a poor substitute. The terms were regarded as a national disgrace.

The day of the signing, September 5th, I was surprised by the arrival of an officer of the Imperial Guard, who said he was stationing two squads of troops in front of the Legation. He explained that a mass meeting of protest was being held that afternoon in Hibiya Park, and, although the public anger was aimed at the Government, precautions were being taken. The idea of hostility to Americans seemed ridiculous. Feeling no apprehension whatsoever, we and the Harriman party set off to dine with the Minister of Finance, Baron Sone.

We noticed at once that the streets were more full of people than usual, and we passed many carrying flags draped in black crape. Some turned around and started to follow our carriage, hooting at us. We were glad to reach our destination without further unpleasantness.

During every pause in the dinner conversation we were conscious of a dull roar coming from outside, and kept wondering whether the mob were getting out of control. Suddenly the room went black; a servant scurried in to say the electricity was off all over the city, and bands of hoodlums were running wild, burning wooden police booths, soaking trams with petroleum and setting them afire.

We jumped to the windows and pulled aside the curtains. Here and there from the darkened city sprouted tongues of flame. We decided not to wait any longer but to go home as soon as we could. A detachment of cavalry arrived from the Ministry of War and we started out behind them through crowds which had become distinctly menacing. Several stones whizzed by our heads and one struck Dr. Lyle on the neck. As we approached the Legation, we saw a police box five hundred yards away in flames. Our street was lined with troops, bayonets fixed, who pushed back the shouting, gesticulating rioters so that we could pass. Our garden was dotted with the campfires of the troops who were bivouacked there.

The evening had been nerve-racking, but the Harrimans accepted it as a matter of course, and seemed to be thrilled at the idea of being witnesses of history in the making.

It was not until next morning that we realized our narrow escape. Some fifty people had been killed and hundreds wounded. The demonstrations had taken on a particularly anti-American tone. President Roosevelt's picture, which adorned many Japanese houses, was turned to the wall. I had quite a number of anonymous letters saying the mob would shortly again visit the Legation to express appreciation for the part we had played in depriving Japan of the fruits of victory.

I would not have left the Legation that day if I had not had to deliver a personal message from President Roosevelt to the Emperor; I was escorted to and from the Palace by mounted police, riding before and behind my carriage. No sooner was I home than one of the guard rushed in shouting, "Where's the Minister? The mob's on the way." This proved to be a false alarm, but such interruptions continued all night and the servants were frightened half to death.

In a few hours the anger of the Japanese shifted from us to

their own officials. The editor of one of the principal newspapers told me he had received over a thousand letters, recommending that the responsible Ministers commit suicide before they were assassinated.

On the third day the mob stopped throwing stones, and our guard was reduced to a sergeant and twelve men. I happened to mention to Marchioness Oyama that even such precautions were ridiculous, because "Nobody would harm the American Minister." This remark grew and grew, and in a few days I heard that I had risen at a dinner and announced: "I require no force of arms to protect my person. The American Minister needs no other guard than the people of Japan." The popularity of the Legation mounted from the depths at least twenty per cent.

Meanwhile Mr. Harriman, quite oblivious to the uproar, continued making the acquaintance of important statesmen and financiers. I noticed he was becoming quite preoccupied, and was spending a great deal of time perusing the papers and examining maps. One evening, without a hint of what was coming, he began abruptly: "Griscom, there's no doubt about it. If I can secure control of the South Manchuria Railroad from Japan, I'll buy the Chinese Eastern from Russia, acquire trackage over the Trans-Siberian to the Baltic, and establish a line of steamers to the United States. Then I can connect with the American transcontinental lines, and join up with the Pacific Mail and the Japanese transpacific steamers. It'll be the most marvelous transportation system in the world. We'll girdle the earth."

From the lips of anybody else such a scheme would have seemed a pipe dream, but, as Mr. Harriman put it into words, it sounded quite feasible. When I asked him how he proposed to meet some of the obvious obstacles — the fantastic capital required, the necessity of relaying track and reducing grades, the different gauges, he replied, "The way to find out what is best to be done is to start doing something. You know all these Japanese. I want you to help me."

I was in a quandary. The feud between President Roosevelt and Mr. Harriman over the dissolution of the Northern Securities Company had caused a sensation; my diplomatic future was dependent upon the President's good will. On the other hand, if Mr. Harriman could put through his deal, American trade in

Manchuria and Korea would advance by leaps and bounds. After thinking it over, I told him I would do what I could for his plan, and then wrote a letter to Mr. Roosevelt, explaining my motives.

Mr. Harriman made his proposals immediately, but the Japanese did not understand his blunt method of attack. While waiting for them to make up their minds, he decided he would like to be the first civilian to visit Port Arthur. He chartered a thousand-ton steamer and then, as though it were quite a matter of course, asked me to get permission for his trip from the Government. Judging from my experience of the past two years, I believed I had little chance of obtaining it, but I had underestimated his importance in Japanese eyes. It was granted.

Seeing no reason why I should not accept Mr. Harriman's invitation to go along with his party, I cabled for leave, my first such request in two-and-a-half years. A curt answer instructed me to stay at my post. I could just hear the President growling, "What's Griscom doing out there in Japan playing around with that malefactor of great wealth?"

On Mr. Harriman's departure I devoted my efforts to hurrying up the Japanese. Again I was surprised to meet no deep-lying objections. Count Katsura, never an easy person to convince, admitted he was favorably disposed. So did Vice Minister of Finance Saketani, and finally Count Inouye himself said, "We would be very foolish to let such a chance slip."

By the time Mr. Harriman reappeared in the middle of October, an agreement had been drawn up: his syndicate was to provide capital, the Japanese were to have nominal control in peace and entire charge in war of trackage in their areas, the profits were to be divided equally. Mr. Harriman went home with the signed document in his pocket.

Baron Komura arrived in Tokio a few days later, and on learning what had been perpetrated in his absence he sent for me. "I'm sorry, Mr. Griscom, Mr. Harriman's plan will have to be postponed indefinitely. We don't know yet what our rights are in Korea and Manchuria. It will take long negotiations before they are clearly enough defined to permit us to reopen the discussion."

Although completely taken aback, I rehearsed my former arguments, but I made no impression whatsoever. I could not discover whether he genuinely disapproved or whether he was piqued at not having been consulted. However, realizing he would not change his mind, I cabled Mr. Harriman that his Napoleonic plan had been blown back into the aerial regions from which it had first come.

In only a few weeks we were to depart on our long delayed vacation. Because the President had already announced he was giving me a new post, we knew we should not be returning to Japan, a prospect which we contemplated with mixed feelings. In spite of the length of our absence we were leaving a country where America was very popular and where we had made many friends. Close and continued association with our staff had drawn us together as though we were members of a family. Elsa and I had for them the deepest feelings of affection and gratitude.

Most of all, we regretted having to say good-by to the Iwasakis. They invited us to a farewell dinner, and afterwards my host took us into one of the rooms in his Western house to show us a new invention which recorded voices on a wax disk. Starting it, he asked me to speak into it. I did not find it easy to think of appropriate remarks while the machinery was buzzing away, but I made the attempt. "Iwasaki," I began, "you old rascal, I'm sure as soon as we've gone you'll revert to your Japanese ways and probably have nothing to do with any more foreigners. All the good we've done will be lost. I'm saying this so that every time you grind out my voice you'll be reminded not to retire too far into that shell of yours."

He laughed, and his parting words were, "Although you may have left Japan, whenever we wish to bring you back to us, we shall only have to play this record."

As before, Iwasaki never answered my letters. Years later, however, I sent a friend to him with an introduction, and the first thing he did was to put on this record of my voice.

On a bright clear morning in late November we steamed out of Yokohama Harbor, accompanied by a tug carrying the staff, missionaries, businessmen and others of the American colony. Cannon boomed a fifteen-gun salute; as each shell exploded high overhead, it released a paper balloon from which streamed an enormous American flag. Our last picture of Japan was of stars and stripes drifting gradually down, and then the scallop of mountains sinking into the sea.

CHAPTER XXII

ROLLING DOWN TO RIO

Once more I found myself in Washington in midwinter, walking from the cold gray streets into the old-fashioned, high-ceilinged rooms of the State Department, unhurried, quiet, remote from the world. Seven years had been long enough to convince me that change was the one certainty in diplomatic life; this was brought home to me by the repetition of the routine of reporting, and the realization that now I should not be greeted by a humorous quip from Mr. Hay. I was rather dreading the approaching interview with Mr. Root; he must have known my disappointment at not becoming Assistant Secretary, and I had no inkling of where I was to be sent.

At Mr. Hay's familiar desk was sitting a tall spare man, stiffly upright. With the slightest of gestures he motioned me to a seat, and calmly continued signing papers. At last, having finished, as though turning his mind from one file to another, he settled back in his chair and, still without a word, gazed at me fixedly. For a moment I wondered whether he were trying to stare me out of countenance. Then his severe mouth relaxed in a charming smile as he asked in his soft, high-pitched voice, "Mr. Griscom, what would you think of going as our first Ambassador to Brazil? The President wants to show the South Americans that we are their friends as well as their neighbors. As you probably have heard, a Pan-American Conference is to be held this summer at Rio de Janeiro, and the plan is for me to make it the first stop in a good-will tour of South America. Everything depends on a successful start. Will you go down and pave the way?"

While the Secretary of State was laying these facts before me in his precise legal manner, various thoughts were passing through my head — surprise and pleasure at the offer of an Ambassadorship, regret at being stationed so far from home for the fourth time, a question as to whether, after such long association with the Oriental mind, I could adjust myself quickly enough to the Latin temperament. Nevertheless, my answer was never in doubt. The instant he had concluded, I said, "Of course I'll go."

Mr. Root's demeanor at once changed. Apparently he had been needlessly afraid that coming from the center of world affairs, I might decline such a quiet post. He grew more cordial as he enlarged on his project for promoting Pan-American unity and building up trade. The countries of South America were selling to us but spending in Europe. In his estimation, the chief reason was fear of American imperialism, or at least our desire to dominate. Again and again President Roosevelt had assured them that we had no such intention, but they consistently refused to believe him, citing the Monroe Doctrine and saying, "We have not asked for protection and we don't like being patronized."

Certain that more than words were needed to combat these prejudices, Mr. Root had determined to make a personal plea, and had selected Brazil as his point of departure, because he hoped the Brazilians would be most receptive. They were exporting to us huge quantities of coffee and rubber, they had always been comparatively well disposed, and, since they were the only South Americans of Portuguese extraction, they would be flattered by the compliment of being visited ahead of their Spanish neighbors.

As Mr. Root talked, I could not help admiring how, by simply focusing his mind on the main issue and disregarding the personal element, he had conducted our conversation without a trace of awkwardness. His temperate method of expression was most effective in setting forth his argument. Half an hour earlier I, like most others, would have regarded Brazil as a post of minor importance to be especially avoided on account of yellow fever. By the time I left the State Department and started towards the White House, I had a very clear idea of the latent opportunities in this mission. In Japan I had been obliged to sit by in strict neutrality and suppress every sign of amity and good feeling. Now I should be free to use every power I had to make friends for the United States.

When I saw Mr. Roosevelt a few minutes later, I found Mr. Root had not told me all of what Brazil might lead to. "Lloyd," the President began genially, "you can either be Minister to Norway or Ambassador to Brazil."

I interrupted to say Mr. Root already had my acceptance of Brazil.

"That's bully," exclaimed the President, and slapped me on the shoulder. "Lots of people would have chosen Norway because it's in Europe, but it wouldn't lead to anything." He gritted his teeth. "If you'd taken Norway it would have been your finish as far as I'm concerned. You go down to Brazil and make Root's visit a success and you won't be there long."

I was relieved that the interview ended without any mention of the Harriman episode. As a matter of fact, I had in my pocket an urgent note from Mr. Harriman asking me to call on him. Accordingly, on arriving in New York, I stopped at his house. After a quick handshake, as though everything were settled, he announced, "Lloyd, I've a job for you."

"I've just accepted the ambassadorship to Brazil."

"Brazil! What's Brazil?" he exploded. "I'm making you manager of my New York office — creating the position for you. You'll be in charge here and work directly under me."

Such easy roads to wealth and power are offered but rarely, if they are offered at all. Nevertheless, I explained that for me to become an ambassador was the same as for a soldier to rise from the ranks to become a general. I did not believe I ought to abandon my career at the very moment I was about to reach the top, and it seemed to me that I would be of far more value to him as an ex-ambassador than as an ex-minister.

Mr. Harriman, annoyed and puzzled, shook his head. "The time to go into the business world is when somebody wants you."

The days of our vacation raced by, and, before I realized it, I was back in Washington. My instruction period was somewhat of a joke; our diplomatic disputes with Brazil were insignificant. The chief value to me of those weeks in Washington was my association with Mr. Root, not an easy person to know. One might have a dozen interviews with him without getting under his impersonal exterior. He was totally lacking in the ordinary little vanities which most of us possess; he never said disagreeable things, never allowed his private likes or dislikes to influence his judgment.

I had my first glimpse below the surface one evening when I dined with Mr. Root and his intimate friend, Charles McKim, the senior member of the leading architectural firm of McKim, Mead, and White, who was then serving on a board for the beautification of Washington. He had just come from a meeting with the President, in which the topic under discussion had been a plan for an avenue from the Capitol to the Washington Monument. The President had disapprovingly scanned the Commission's sketch of a broad straight thoroughfare in accordance with L'Enfant's original conception. Then, seizing a pencil, he had exclaimed, "Oh, no, that won't do. Let's make it wind. See here," and he had proceeded to cover the neat blueprint with a series of spirals — his idea was an avenue which would meander between pools and canebrakes. The Board was at its wits' end, and McKim was very much upset.

Mr. Root laughed. "Don't worry. The President's only thinking in terms of an African jungle where lions and tigers will feel at home. You hold your own, and he'll get tired in time."

Eventually the straight road was laid out.

Bronson Winthrop, who was Mr. Root's junior partner, had many anecdotes of his chief's triple distilled wit. The Secretary was once consulted by the Postmaster General in regard to criminal charges which had been preferred against a postmaster in a large city. The evidence was serious. The single factor which deterred the Postmaster General from removing the accused from office was a letter from the latter's wife which read, "I am better acquainted than anyone else with the whole story of my husband's conduct, but I have been denied access to you. If I could look directly into your fine brown eyes, I know I could convince you of his innocence."

Mr. Root returned the papers with just this line: "My dear colleague, if I were you, I'd risk one eye."

The Postmaster General followed his advice; the charges were dismissed.

Since Mr. Root was to arrive in Rio de Janeiro the end of July, I had no time to lose. On investigating ways and means of getting to Brazil, we found there was so little call for passenger service that the quickest and most comfortable route was via Portugal. There we first heard the Portuguese language. Diplomats had always been reluctant to study it, because they would probably never use it again and the peculiar accent was supposed to impair their Italian and Spanish. Under such circumstances, to learn it would be a particular compliment to the Brazilians. Elsa and I believed that if we could commit a thousand words to memory during the voyage, we should have enough vocabulary to serve as a start. We boarded the *Orita* at Lisbon the middle of May, well fortified with grammars and school readers.

Over smooth sunny seas we sailed on an even keel, and after two weeks entered the incomparable mountain-rimmed harbor of Rio de Janeiro. As we dropped anchor, the nineteen-gun ambassadorial salute re-echoed from the hills, and in traditional frock coat and top hat I took up my position on deck, ready for the expected reception committee.

The Government launch drew alongside, but, instead of the formal delegation I had anticipated, there were only the United States Chargé d'Affaires and a handful of Brazilian officials, all of them dressed in business clothes. Would I forgo the customary ceremonies? A fortnight before, a terrific tidal wave had struck the city and done such damage to the water front that it was still clogged with wreckage. In fact, so many wharves had been destroyed that our launch had to tie up to another boat, and we scrambled ashore over a makeshift gangplank.

I looked about for a carriage, but none was in sight. Since luncheon was waiting for us at the hotel, there was nothing for it but to open our umbrellas against the sun, tuck jackets and coats under our arms, and plod single file up the torrid street. In spite of the discomfort, we could not help being amused; it was so much like our ridiculous arrival in Persia, and so little like the arrival of Mr. Bayard as first Ambassador to England.

At lunch we were dismayed on being told that yellow fever was prevalent. The British, Japanese and Italian Ministers had died within a few months. For fear of infection not one of my colleagues would have spent a night in Rio at any price. In panic they huddled at Petropolis, high in the hills, and there a house had been engaged for us.

That afternoon we took the Petropolis boat, and for two hours chugged across the harbor to a point from which a funicular scaled the cliff three thousand feet. The seats were arranged so that we sat backward, watching the panorama that gradually unrolled beneath us. The quick tropic sunset flared up, and, as it died, long shadows stretched out over the water, turning to purple the green islands which dotted the bay. Close to us giant ferns rose eighteen to twenty feet tall, and on every tree were clusters of orchids.

Our reception at Rio had been rather discouraging as the beginning of a good-will mission, but at the Petropolis station we had unusual evidence of Brazil's appreciation of our friendly advances. The Minister of Foreign Affairs met us in person. Baron José Maria de Silva Paranhos de Rio Branco was the Elder Statesman of Brazil. He had been among the founders of the Republic, still less than twenty years old. Three times by diplomatic methods he had enlarged its territory, so that even by his enemies he was conceded to be one of the greatest living experts on boundary questions.

As we drove through the streets, the darkness on either side seemed alive with an army of tiny flashlights; I had never seen such fireflies. I caught one, as big as my thumbnail, and setting it on my newspaper, I could distinguish words by its glow. Natives used to put handfuls of them in glass jars, which they carried when they went out at night, and shook every now and then to light up the way.

We liked our house, solid, comfortable, dignified. Next morning the sun was streaming in our windows, and the garden underneath was aflame with poinsettia, bougainvillea, hibiscus, and strange tropical flowers. The servant brought coffee, steaming and fragrant. The delicious flavor was due to the Brazilian method of roasting the beans until they were practically pure charcoal, so black you could write your name or draw pictures with them.

The town resembled a German Spa. Mountain streams ran down the middle of the trim, well-kept streets; in the afternoon the band played in the plaza near our house. It was warm during the day but cool at night, and the air was always filled with the soft moist greenhouse smell of growing things.

Almost immediately I had to make a return trip to the capital to present my credentials to President Rodrigues Alves, and afterwards call on as many other officials as I could. Everybody expressed pleasure that Mr. Root was visiting Brazil first, and told me what was being done for his reception. A thirty-million-dollar civic improvement program was being rushed through, and the new building being erected for the Conference was to be christened the Monroe Palace — one of the few times any South American country had done honor to the President of the United States whose name was connected with the doctrine anathema to them. I could see that the Brazilians welcomed this visit as a wonderful opportunity for a fiesta, as well as a chance to get ahead of Argentina. They were intensely proud because their huge Empire had hung together for centuries, whereas the Spanish sections of the continent, stronger, more vigorous, and more industrially successful, had fought and split up.

When I arrived at Petropolis that evening, I was appalled to discover the round trip with lunch at the hotel had cost me forty dollars. Elsa capped this with the information that the charges for bringing our boxes from Rio were more than the freight all the way from New York. In the course of my prescribed round of the Diplomatic Corps I heard bitter complaints of the high cost of living.

Most of my colleagues made no pretense of liking their posts and held themselves aloof from the Brazilians, claiming they were unreliable, made promises without fulfilling them, constantly put things off, and all in all were impossible to deal with. It was not surprising that the sensitive Brazilians returned this disdain with interest; they ran the affairs of their country in Rio with the least possible regard for the diplomats who sat idly at Petropolis.

My time was well taken up studying Portuguese with the aid of a teacher, and preparing a schedule of engagements for the two weeks Mr. Root was to be in Brazil. This brought me in almost daily contact with Baron Rio Branco. Of the small conservative clique which dominated Brazilian politics he seemed the most progressive, and most fully aware of the profits to be gained by a rapprochement with the United States. I found another ally in one of his assistants, Domicio da Gama, writer, poet, member of the Academy of Brazil, and a leader of the young intellectual group in which many of the more cultivated Brazilians trusted for guidance. Together we discussed the vital question of trade. United States manufacturers were at a disadvantage on account of prohibitive freight rates; they could not even afford to send samples because Portugal held the parcel post monopoly and everything had to go that way.

Da Gama said one of the chief obstacles the United States would have to overcome was the close cultural tie which united the Brazilians to Europe. They might look North for their form of government, but for pleasure, luxuries, education, they went to Paris. Most of the aristocracy spoke French, and in every club and private house you saw French papers, usually *Le Figaro* and always *La Vie Parisienne*. News from the United States was of such little moment that it appeared in obscure places among the telegrams from Paraguay or Tierra del Fuego.

In the past any Brazilian politician who wanted to get a following would begin a violent press campaign, charging the United States with imperialistic ambitions. I gathered that Da Gama and his group were now ready to spread the belief that the Anglo-Saxon, however naturally vulgar and inferior to the Latin, yet could confer material benefits which made his friendship worth cultivating.

About a week before Mr. Root's arrival, Joachim Nabuco, the Ambassador to Washington, returned, to be present at the welcome, and this was the occasion for a huge banquet with some two thousand guests and a number of speakers, of whom I was to be one. I decided that here was the moment to try out my Portuguese. I wrote a speech, my teacher translated it, and we worked in a few local allusions and jokes. Then I learned it by heart.

When I was introduced late in the evening, I was greeted by a perfunctory round of applause, after which everybody settled back to be bored; no one is interested in listening to a language he does not understand. *"Meos Senhores,"* at these words I noticed heads raised to give me a second look. *"Sendo eu o unico estrangero que figuro en esta banquete, si os senhores permittem, me vou fallar em lingua portugueza . . ."* ("I am the only foreigner present at this banquet and, if you gentlemen will allow, I am going to speak to you in the Portuguese language.")

At this point the Brazilians realized what I was doing, and to a man stood up, cheering and yelling. They could hardly be calmed down so that I could continue. I ended with the fervent hope that Brazil and the United States would be found where they belonged — *"en la proha de la barca de la civilicao."* However, it would not have mattered what I had said. The audience was already won.

The next day every paper printed florid praise of the United States, and I felt well repaid for the hours spent in learning Portuguese. In a sense my speech was a trick, but a very successful one.

Not an adverse comment disturbed the good feeling during the few days to July 27th. Early that morning Elsa and I set off for Rio de Janeiro. There was an air of expectancy in the city, American and Brazilian flags everywhere were draped together, people were all hurrying towards the shore. The official welcoming party was to go out on the royal galley of King John the Sixth of Portugal, who had fled to Brazil when Napoleon's armies had conquered his country. It was now almost a hundred years old, but it had been completely refurbished — its cabin was hung with silks and cushioned with satin, and it was propelled by sixty oarsmen dressed in white.

As the *Charleston,* gleaming in the sun, came steaming up the harbor, we glided towards her across the glassy water. The cannon from the German, English, and Argentine warships roared a welcome. Mr. Root, Mrs. Root, and their daughter Edith were piped over the side, and we turned back to the wharf, lined by cheering crowds. Carriages were ready, a detachment of lancers wheeled into position, and off we trotted up the ancient Rue Ouvidor, under showers of flowers from the overhanging balconies. At the end of the ride the Secretary's only remark was, "Well, I never saw so many flies in one carriage as there were in mine."

Mr. Root's eight days at Rio de Janeiro were a constant succession of luncheons and dinners, each of which entailed a speech. He did not have the vocal equipment of an orator. Often he spoke so low it was difficult to hear him, and if he lifted his voice to create an effect, it frequently broke into a falsetto which he could not control. Repeatedly he amazed me with his mental capacity and versatility. He never failed to say something new and striking, but always on the same theme of Brazilian-American friendship.

The high point of Mr. Root's visit was the keynote address before a special evening meeting of the Pan-American Conference. We found the Monroe Palace surrounded by enthusiastic students, some playing musical instruments, some setting off fireworks, all making a terrific noise. Even from the platform within, the muffled roar was plainly audible; the clamor of the rabble at the gates of Versailles must have sounded the same in the ears of Louis XVI.

Fortunately Mr. Root's interpreter was a brilliant orator, so that the audience received the full force of each telling sentence. At the same time the speech was being relayed to the crowd outside. The

excitement rose as he continued to his peroration. "We wish for no
victories except those of peace. We wish for no territory except our
own and no sovereignty except over ourselves. We neither claim
nor desire any rights or privileges of power that we do not freely
concede to every American republic."

As Mr. Root finished, everybody sprang up and stamped and
shouted *"Viva Root-e! Viva Root-e!"* We went out to the balcony
and looked down on the courtyard, jammed and seething with
students waving torches. Mingled with the calls for Root we began to distinguish calls for the Ambassador, which grew more and
more insistent. Finally Nabuco nudged me, "You'll have to say something."

I was totally unprepared, and all I could do was repeat a few
portions of my speech in Portuguese of the week before. It was
greeted with howls and yowls of delight. Mr. Root gave a dry
smile: "Griscom, I didn't know you'd lived in Portugal for years."

The last four days of the Root party's visit were spent in the
Southern state of São Paulo. The *Charleston* landed us at Santos,
the greatest coffee-shipping port in the world. Stone docks and warehouses were heaped high with thousands and thousands of bags
ready for export. Over one shed was a sign reading "Pure Arabian
Mocha" — a term then almost synonymous with coffee. Stevedores
were loading the sacks on a British freighter bound for Port Said,
where the cargo would be transshipped, marked in Arabian characters, and arrive at Hamburg and New York, the chief coffee
markets, with every indication of being a true product of Arabia.

The wealth of the Brazilian coffee barons was proverbial, and at
the provincial capital of São Paulo, two hours away by rail, we experienced a taste of how they had lived in the days when coffee had
yielded a profit of fifty per cent. In our rooms at the Campos Elyseos
Palace, which was turned over to us, we washed our hands in water
poured from silver pitchers into silver basins, and dried them on
lace-edged towels. I was shaved by a barber attached to the house.
Before dinner every lady had a corsage of orchids delivered to her
room; more orchids were heaped on the dining-room table and
festoons of them hung on the walls. Edith Root and Elsa agreed it
was a wonderful feeling to crush orchids and not care. Afterwards
a private orchestra played to us in the illuminated gardens, and, on

retiring for the night, we stepped up on daises to lie down in carved and gilded beds.

The next morning Mr. Root was the last to appear for breakfast. His head was liberally patched with court plaster, and he looked as though he had been through the wars. At our chorus of "What's happened to you?" he eyed us solemnly. "Never let it get abroad that I was not brought up to sleep on a royal dais. I forgot to allow for the step and fell flat on my face."

Three days later, we said good-by to the Roots at Santos. The success of the Secretary's visit had been unbelievable. As I watched the applauding thousands speed him on his way, I wondered how this unemotional intellectual could have so won over the poetic, sentimental Brazilians.

For the moment the United States was at the peak of high favor, and I could get things done while European Ministers twiddled their thumbs. The tariff regulations were changed so that any country which imported four million sacks of coffee annually was granted a twenty per cent preferential reduction; the United States alone filled this requirement. The parcel post monopoly was altered so that parcels could go directly to and from the United States.

However, the prejudices of generations could not be removed in a few days. Less than a month after Mr. Root's departure, the important anti-American newspaper in the capital once more began running articles against us. From that time on my popularity veered back and forth; one minute I would be greeted with open arms and the next given a cold shoulder, because some fancied slight had offended Brazilian sensibilities.

As summer came on, all of us felt the enervating effects of the constant heat and rain. The prospect of the birth of our first child made it necessary for Elsa to leave, and I found life very lonely. There was little entertaining or diversion, since the diplomats were occupied almost entirely with preserving their health. The death of the Dutch Minister of yellow fever, the fourth fatality among the heads of mission, caused them to redouble their efforts.

The German Minister, Baron von Treutler, asked me to join him in a cure. He had imported some genuine Carlsbad water, and we carried out the routine to the letter — the first glass at seven, a walk, another glass at seven-thirty, another walk, and then another glass.

Getting up and looking out at the rain-drenched street, putting on rubbers and hoisting an umbrella, earnestly sloshing fifteen minutes away from the house, fifteen minutes back, was a cheerless start for the day.

These precautions did not save me. One morning I awoke with a high fever and violent dysentery, much the symptoms you would expect from yellow fever. As soon as other members of the Corps heard about me, they were terror-stricken and cabled to beg their Governments to move them quickly before they too were attacked.

Everyone expected me to die, including myself. Although I was sure my ailment could not be yellow fever, no doctor was able to diagnose it. Only years later did Dr. Arthur F. Chace of New York discover I had the rare but not contagious intestinal parasite, *cercomonas hominis,* and I enjoyed the doubtful distinction of being lectured about in the medical world.

I was just able to drag myself around, and was wondering how I could get through the rest of the summer, when out of the blue came a note from Secretary Root: Harry White was being transferred from Rome to Paris; how would I like to be Ambassador to Italy?

It was as though manna had fallen from Heaven. My health improved immediately. Next to London, of all places in Europe, Italy was the one I would have chosen. I wasted little time in packing up and preparing to leave. My last appearance — as Dean of the Corps — was at the New Year's reception at the Palace, when I delivered our greetings to the new President, Affonso Penna, to wish unlimited prosperity to Brazil, and unlimited happiness to its people.

Elsa was eagerly awaiting me in Paris, where we decided to spend our sixty days' vacation. I had never been there long enough to do justice to the art galleries and museums; and Elsa, with her detailed knowledge of them, was an incomparable guide, conducting me through the Louvre, the Luxembourg, the Musée Carnavalet, and many others.

One day near the Sorbonne we ran into Archibald Coolidge, who was on leave from teaching history at Harvard. In the course of his researches he had become intimate with a group of French politicians and deputies, who formed the following of a former Minister of Colonies, and used to lunch almost daily at Foyot's Hotel on the Left Bank. Several times Coolidge asked me to join them.

As I walked to their table, my first impression was of a ring of bald pates and an unequaled assortment of whiskers. The head man, who had a beard and other oddments of hair, started off the conversation, and in thirty seconds all were going *clack-clack-clack,* at an incredible pace, reviling their political opponents as villains, scoundrels, demagogues, and overwhelming their leader with advice. Coolidge could keep up but I was left far behind; diplomats took their French more slowly.

Just before I was to depart for Italy one of them remarked to me, "Have you the Legion of Honor?"

"No," I answered.

"Well, I'll see that you get it." Then, turning to his secretary, "Just make a note to have the Legion of Honor sent to Mr. Griscom."

I discouraged him as politely as I could. I did not want to have a decoration mailed to me like a Christmas card.

As the winter passed we began to anticipate more and more our approaching life in Rome. Edith Wharton, one of Elsa's oldest friends, had an apartment in Paris, and gave us the benefit of her years of experience in Italy — lists of out-of-the-way shops where we could find bargains in Italian treasures; villas and gardens we must not miss; walks and excursions we must take. Two of her greatest friends, Paul Bourget and Henry James, were also Italian enthusiasts. I often came in to find them seated on either side of her fireplace, discussing problems of art and politics.

Harry White wrote to suggest I assume his lease of the Palazzo del Drago, which had once been the home of Queen Maria Christina of Spain. It was located on the Quattro Fontane, one of the centers of Rome, diagonally opposite the Quirinal, the King of Italy's Palace. Fifteen thousand dollars a year rent seemed a great deal of money when my salary was only seventeen thousand five hundred. Nevertheless, we realized that Italy would probably be the culmination of my diplomatic career, because I could not afterwards occupy a lower post, and there was little chance of my being appointed to St. Petersburg, Berlin, Paris, or London. Accordingly, I accepted White's proposal.

One late afternoon in early March we arrived in Rome. The

usual ceremonies — the red carpet, the mayor and officials to greet us, the special door opened to let us out of the station — had the dignity of long custom. Reynolds Hitt and Robert Winthrop, the secretaries of the Embassy, were there with the Naval and Military Attachés. Then Elsa and I drove through the ancient streets in the spring twilight, and finally wheeled under a huge arched gateway. Beside the entrance stood a giant *portiero,* fully six feet four, wearing a black tricorne with red, white, and blue cockade. In his hand he carried a tall staff crowned with a brass sphere on which was engraved the arms of the United States; he clashed it on the stones as we passed.

We stepped from the carriage into a garden court, sheltered by the wings of the palace. A major domo led us by the twin marble lions through the majestic portal. Disregarding the electric lift, we mounted the magnificent stone stairway which swept up to the *piano nobile,* approximately the third floor; ordinarily this would have been occupied by the old Prince Filippo del Drago, but he had become so impoverished that he had had to retire to quarters on the street level.

From the hall we entered the White Gallery, a hundred and fifty feet long, lighted by crystal chandeliers and crystal appliqués. It opened into Queen Christina's reception room; beyond that we traversed in succession the art gallery, a formal reception room for Elsa, her boudoir where she could have tea with her friends, then, rounding the corner, we reached my smoking room, and finally our private apartments.

For once we were coming into a house fully furnished and equipped, even to servants. Everything was quiet and in order. Dinner was announced. As we looked at each other across the spotless napery and shining silver, we agreed that nothing had ever seemed so much like arriving home.

CHAPTER XXIII

NO PLACE LIKE ROME

Across the Quattro Fontane moved three royal carriages behind gold-caparisoned bays — outriders in white wigs ahead, lackeys with short powdered hair behind, coachmen in scarlet livery on the boxes. At the Quirinal door my staff and I alighted, a guard of honor saluted, and the Prefect of the Palace conducted us up a long staircase into a large reception hall, then introduced me alone into a smaller room. "His Excellency, the American Ambassador," he announced.

I was just straightening up from my low bow when a little man, hardly more than five feet four or five inches in height, with cropped sandy hair, walked briskly towards me, shook my hand vigorously, and in excellent English remarked, "You've brought a letter, haven't you?"

Without waiting for me to give him the big envelope containing my credentials, the King reached out and whisked it away. I drew a deep breath for my carefully prepared speech about international amity and good will, but before I could utter a word he took my arm and directed me towards the window where two stools faced each other. Motioning me to one, he seated himself on the second, and immediately started off, "Well, you're very young, aren't you? We've never seen anything like this here. How old are you?"

"Thirty-four, Sir."

"Good gracious. We sent a man to Turkey once who was forty-seven and it made a sensation. That was nothing compared to this. You must have begun very young."

"Twenty, Sir."

He changed the subject abruptly. "What are you when you're at home?"

"A lawyer."

"You can't practise much. You can't be much of a lawyer."

"In fact, I'm not. I had to give up the law on account of my health."

"What? You haven't bad health, have you?"

"No. I'm very strong."

"I thought so. Thin men always are." He paused to look me up and down. "You are thin, aren't you?"

"Yes, Sir. I've been living in a bad climate."

"You've been living in Brazil, haven't you? How did you like it?"

When I repeated that the tropics did not agree with me the King continued: "Oh, yes, it is a wretched place and I don't like the people. I suppose I ought not to say that. It's very undiplomatic, but then I'm not a diplomat. I once had to deal with some of those Brazilians over the boundary between their country and British Guiana, which was referred to me for arbitration. There were five volumes of evidence, and I read every word of them. The Brazilians published lots of maps which were absolutely false, and then they put in a lot of pictures of Indians in different costumes to make it interesting. Well, it was interesting, but it was a very poor argument. I might have given the whole disputed territory to England, but I gave the Brazilians half, and then I heard they abused me outrageously. Ugh!"

I murmured something pleasant about Brazil's immense potentialities, mentioning particularly the million Italians in Sao Paulo; he did not seem to want to hear any good of the Brazilians. When I told him that the State of Paraná boasted of fourteen feet of arable soil producing three crops a year, he retorted that near Naples there was land with seven meters of soil — "That's twenty-three feet," he explained. I replied we had nothing like that in any quantity in all the United States, at which he admitted, "Of course, we haven't much of it in Italy either, but we do have it in spots."

"You know," he went on, "I'm leaving April 5th with four battleships to visit Greece. No. No political significance beyond promoting good will — the usual thing that we have to do."

Without warning, the King shifted to the Cretan question. "We cannot withdraw completely from Crete and leave it to Russia and Austria and England and the rest to settle. We have to play our part. I ask our Parliament to vote a million francs a year for it, which is only two hundred thousand of your dollars. You wouldn't think much of that in your country, would you? For anything with political glory in it our Parliament will give the shirts off their backs, as we say in Italian, but for something that happens to be a short way off we have to fight to get a little money."

"Does Parliament make trouble for you?" I asked.

"Oh, no, they don't make any for *me*, but they do for the Government. This country, you know, is really ruled entirely by tradition; there never was a country that followed traditions more. You wouldn't believe the things I could tell you. You know that in Southern Italy, where they've been used to having kings since the Twelfth Century, they still look upon me as their final protector, owing to this position which I hold." (Several times he referred to "this position which I hold" but never mentioned himself as "king.")

I put in, "I suppose, Sir, one cannot think of Northern and Southern Italy in the same way at all."

"True," he agreed, "they're quite different, and here in Rome the character has altogether changed, because we've brought in about forty-five per cent of Italians from other parts of Italy. Rome was once the center of Italian tradition; it is not any more. It is a great cosmopolitan meeting place."

Suddenly reverting to his Grecian trip, the King said, "Yes, I'll not be back here for some time. I've been invited to visit a certain town in Greece which is very unconstitutional." (By "unconstitutional" I found he meant republican and against the King.) "They do not want me to go there," — by "they" he referred to his royal relatives, — "but I'm going. I never go where I'm not invited, but when I'm asked to visit a certain place I always go."

"I suppose they're anxious about your safety."

"Oh, it's no more dangerous there than in other places. If one is going to be shot, one will get shot. I cannot always be thinking about that. Naturally," he added quickly, "one would prefer not to be shot."

I said I could understand the Government, being responsible, might be concerned; we both had in mind the assassination of his father, King Humbert. He grinned. "Well, I'll take the mayor of that town in my carriage with me."

For no apparent reason he went on to give me his itinerary. I commented, "That will be interesting, won't it?"

"No, it will not be a bit interesting. However, Venice is very Red, and when I go to places like that it seems it does some good. Sicily is very Red too."

Again he changed the subject. "Do you like riding? I never liked it very much." Before I could answer he continued: "I hope you're going to stay longer than White and Meyer did." (He did not use Mister in speaking of them.) "Since I've been in this position I've seen — how many is it? — four or five American Ambassadors. How long do you think you'll stay?"

The King kept up his machine-gun questioning for at least an hour, and then terminated the interview by uncrossing his legs with the remark, "You've brought your staff with you, haven't you?" After I had presented them, I rode back to the del Drago, a trifle bewildered; I had never seen such a ruler.

If Court conventions meant little to the King, they meant still less to Queen Elena, daughter of Prince Nicholas of Montenegro. A royal marriage was rarely based solely on inclination, but the King, feeling his own short legs were directly due to the dynastic system by which cousin married cousin, had determined that he must put eugenics ahead of politics. He had made his choice against strenuous opposition, and to his satisfaction found his wife shared his domestic interests and his taste for simple living.

When I returned to the Quirinal for my audience with the Queen, a single servant piloted me to an electric lift. In her private apartments, a lone lady in waiting announced me at the door of a small drawing room. The Queen came forward, nearly six feet tall, dark-haired, regular-featured. Immediately she inquired about Elsa's forthcoming child, and went on to describe how her own mother had given birth to eleven children without the assistance of a doctor. She had wanted to do the same, but much to her annoyance the Italian Court officials had insisted she have medical attendance until an heir to the throne was provided. For centuries it had been a convention that a royal child should not be born without witnesses; there was always the possibility that a male might be substituted for a female infant, a live for a dead baby. Her first two children had been girls, then had come a boy, and now again she was *enceinte*. "This time," she asserted, "they have promised me I can have my own way."

The state maintained by Victor Emmanuel III seemed all the less regal in contrast to that of his father King Humbert, who had presided over one of the gayest courts in Europe. His widow, the dowager Queen Margherita, on whom I next called, was completely out of sympathy as well as out of favor with her son. He had resented bitterly her efforts, in collusion with Emperor William of Germany, to marry him to a German Princess, and thus cement more closely the Triple Alliance.

The constant shifts in the Balance of Power made Rome a center of diplomatic activity. I was the youngest member of a sophisticated Corps, trained by years of experience at home and abroad in concealing their own minds and confusing those of others. Our chief, Signor Tommaso Tittoni, the Foreign Minister, urbane and polished, looked as though he had a secret treaty tucked in every pocket. On the surface the nine Ambassadors and almost thirty Ministers remained on very cordial terms, but underneath went on an everlasting pull and haul. Count Anton de Monts of Germany and Count Heinrich von Lützow of Austria were there to keep the Triple Alliance firm; Sir Edwin Egerton of England, MM. Camille Barrère of France and Nikolai Muraviev of Russia were supposed to do what they could to wean Italy away.

Theoretically, the United States was outside the plot and counterplot. Under ordinary circumstances our influence would not have been great. However, Harry White had built up a personal position which had been much increased by his mission to the Algeciras Conference, called to settle the status of Morocco. During his tenure our Embassy had also gained prestige, because he had made it a social center. Altogether, he had set a high standard for us to live up to.

White could not have picked a more appropriate setting than the del Drago Palace, although at first we were somewhat alarmed by its size and inconveniences. We found we could not get on without a staff of nineteen men; each had his own little job and no amount of persuasion could induce him to do anything else. The kitchen was three flights below us in the cellar, so that at every meal there had to be a steady coming and going of servants up and down a narrow stone stairway, each carrying a dish with a metal cover and a hot-water arrangement underneath to keep the food warm.

The kitchen itself was vast, damp, dark, and infested by droves of huge voracious rats; in spite of our protests, the lazy kitchen cooks and scullery boys threw the garbage in piles, and there it remained for days until the stench caused somebody to order it removed.

Nevertheless, it was hard to be angry with any of these Italians, because they were so like children — simple, good-natured, and incredibly superstitious. The Thursday before Easter my major domo, Giuseppe, announced two clerics had arrived with incense burners and apparatus; for a fee they were ready to set about exorcising the evil spirits, and would guarantee the Palace against reinfestation for a year. Suspecting they might be taking advantage of a newcomer, and reluctant to be imposed on, I sent back the message: "I shall have to refer the matter to the *avvocato* who advises the Embassy in legal affairs. If he says it's necessary, I'll let them know."

Giuseppe grew pale. "*Eccelenza,* it is advisable that this be done at once, or some disaster may occur."

"Don't worry," I reassured him. "Everything will be all right. Tell them to return next week."

I was not at all concerned about evil spirits, but the visit suggested to me that my insurance did not begin until the following Monday, and I should perhaps make some provision for protecting the Prince's valuable belongings during the interim. I consulted the *avvocato,* who put it off by saying no business could be done in Holy Week; since the Palace had already stood for hundreds of years, it hardly seemed likely anything would happen in the next few days. I dismissed the affair from my mind.

Easter Sunday dawned bright and clear, and Elsa and I decided to attend the English church in the Piazza San Bernardo, only a short distance from the del Drago Palace up the Via Venti Settembre. We were peacefully strolling home, telling each other how fortunate we were to be in Rome, when she exclaimed, "What does thee suppose that smoke means?"

We watched the gray column curiously and then, as we drew nearer, I was horrified to realize it was pouring out of the middle of our own roof. Throwing to the winds my dignity as a new envoy, I grasped my top hat in one hand, and, coattails flying, tore full speed down the street and into our gate. "*Fuoco!*" I yelled to the drowsing *portiero,* bounded up the staircase, three steps at a time, tore into our apartment and along the gallery, still shouting "*Fuoco!*" and dashed up the stairway to the servants' floor.

I could hear the roar and crackle of flames, and while I struggled with the bolts of the attic door, I could see pink light between the cracks. The minute I opened it a sheet of fire leaped out at me, singeing my eyebrows, lashes, and forehead. As I slammed it shut, I had a glimpse of a red-hot inferno which had once been White's excelsior-filled packing cases.

Since the fire was directly over the ballroom, I rushed back and organized the servants into squads, one to remove the Prince's pictures, and the other to spread mattresses or any coverings they could find over the parquet floor. By the time the fire engines arrived, the ceiling was already crumbling and fragments of charred wood and great flaming lumps were dropping.

The firemen's ridiculous hand pump would not give enough pressure to reach the roof; they focused their stream, about as big as that from a garden hose, on the mattresses, and soon the floor was a sea of water into which the blazing debris splashed and was extinguished in a sizzle and cloud of steam. The magnificent central chandelier fell and smashed to smithereens. I watched with dismay as smoke and soot stained the red satin wall coverings.

Luckily for us, the fire could not spread downwards through the stone walls. In the end it was put out, and the fire brigade went away, leaving behind an indescribable chaos of sodden plaster, broken glass, charred and blackened wood. Our water tanks in the attic were a molten mass; every drop would have to be carried up from the cellar.

It was hours before we had our house to ourselves. Carabinieri, policemen, reporters, fire insurance agents, pestered us with questions and demanded to be taken on tours of inspection. Finally, they agreed on the theory that a spark from the chimney had flown through an open window to land on one of the inflammable packing cases. My failure to insure cost me five thousand dollars, and at that I considered myself well out of it.

After everyone had gone, Giuseppe, shaking his head in a manner which expressed as plainly as words "I told you so," said, "*Eccelenza*, this is a great pity. You should not have turned the clerics away." Without exception the servants believed the fire was directly due to my refusal to permit the ceremony, and their conviction was strengthened when that night it chose to rain for the first time since our arrival.

I let no grass grow under my feet; as early as possible Monday morning, I sent for the clerics and watched with interest their solemn procession through each room, swinging incense burners, mumbling chants, and doing a thorough exorcising job. Then and there I resolved to respect every custom and superstition in Italy.

As a matter of fact, if we had to have a conflagration, it could not have caused less inconvenience. The living quarters were not touched, Elsa would not be able to entertain for some months anyhow, and the business of the Embassy was not interfered with because the Chancery was a few hundred yards away in the Palazzo Amici on the Piazza San Bernardo. There I spent much of my time familiarizing myself with the questions on hand, almost entirely of a routine nature.

The United States was trying to get through a naturalization treaty to settle the status of citizenship of Italian emigrants who had gone to the United States without having performed their military service and later returned to Italy after having taken out first papers or even become American citizens. The Italian Government would promptly pop them into the Army and then there would be loud protests. I myself signed an extradition treaty with the representative of San Marino, the oldest Republic in the world — which now became, as he said, linked with the greatest Republic in the world.

Among my duties as American Ambassador was serving on the Board of Wardens of the American Church. The rector, the Reverend Walter Lowrie, had a curious collection of advisers. I, who presided, was a Quaker, another was a noted spiritualist, still another was a militant atheist. In fact, as I recall, there were only two devout churchmen in the group. However, we never had a quarrel, and always voted anything the rector recommended. He said no church in the world was ever blessed with a better board.

Lowrie himself was one of the characters of Rome. His sermons were often filled with accounts of treasures he had found in his archeological forays. On Christmas Day he had horrified the congregation by referring to the "very charming myths of the Bible."

His crowning sensation was caused by a parochial letter in which he alluded jocosely to the Pope as "My friend, Joseph Tailor, across the Tiber." The Vatican objected fiercely to having Giuseppe Sarto translated in this flippant fashion.

Our son Bronson was born June 2nd, 1907. He was small and delicate, and, since Elsa could not nurse him, we were desperate to know how we were going to save him. The Roman milk was not fit for use: Dr. Pestalozzi, the royal *accoucheur,* estimated that in one year the milk sold in the city contained enough manure to form a pyramid a hundred feet high and a hundred feet broad at its base. He procured for us a wet nurse, or *balia,* and told us to get Bronson out of Rome before the *scirocco,* the hot, dry, dust-laden wind from the Libyan desert, made the climate unendurable.

We selected Varese, a little town north of Milan, as a suitable place for the summer. It was so near the Alps that I thought it would be pleasant to have an automobile, and the Isotta Fraschini Company of Milan was anxious, for publicity purposes, to sell me one of its cars. As an inducement, they offered me a really master chauffeur, a rarity in those days. Luigi Gaddoni had won the Targa Floria, the greatest race in Europe, and having been to Paris for a special course in automobile mechanics, could effect miraculous repairs with the minimum of tools. Accordingly, I bought the car for the journey to Varese.

Our first trip in our own motor was an adventure. Each town and city apparently had its own traffic rules, and we had to keep shifting over from one side of the road to the other, depending on how vehicles seemed to be coming at us. At one point the surface had been mended with sharp broken stones left for passing carts to wear down. While we crunched over them, I held my breath as though I myself were crossing them barefooted and, sure enough, in a few moments there was an ominous report. Luigi pulled onto the grass, and set to work. He had the record for tire changing, but at his best speed he could not do it in less than forty-five minutes. Four times he removed and put back tires, and we had had quite enough motoring when at length we reached our hotel.

We liked Varese with its view of the lake and of Monte Rosa, loveliest of Alpine peaks; but as the days went by, to our deep concern Bronson failed to thrive. Almost the only way in which he could be lulled to sleep was for me to walk up and down with him; one of the sights of Varese was to watch the American Ambassador pacing back and forth on the terrace with his son in the palm of his hand.

On investigation the local doctor found that our *balia* used to get in such rages against the other servants that her milk was being affected. He warned us we must find another at once. Since no wet nurse was available at Varese, I summoned Luigi instantly, and the doctor and I set off in my Isotta on an extraordinary tour.

At Novara, the nearest large town, we secured a list of candidates and called on them in order. The doctor first inquired as to the health of the family, particularly whether any member of it had ever had tuberculosis or been insane. If the woman passed this test the next demand was "Show us your milk!" Immediately she would rip open the front of her dress and illustrate the plenitude of the supply. The doctor accepted this as a matter of professional routine, but all I could think of was Benjamin Franklin's remark after visiting the Court of Versailles: "I have not seen such sights since I was weaned."

One woman, with but a slight action of two fingers, shot a jet across the room which splashed against the wall. On the doctor's approval I engaged her; we quickly packed her into the car and dashed home. However, our trouble was all to no purpose. In a day or two our prize began to pine for her husband and her own baby, and demanded to be sent back. As a last resort, I telegraphed to Reynolds Hitt in Rome: although it was not among the customary duties of a First Secretary, would he please locate us a *balia* and ship her to Varese at once?

After a two-day tour of the Apennines he discovered one he thought would do, although he had to promise her wages out of all proportion before she would agree to come. In the nick of time she arrived, a stalwart mountain woman, whose great beaked nose made her look like my idea of a Saracen chieftain.

At once Bronson began to gain, but now we had new problems. It was characteristic of all wet nurses that as soon as they were established they exerted their power. First ours announced her dresses were utterly unfit and Elsa had to buy her a wardrobe. Then she brought a letter from her husband ordering her return; we sent him more money. Things reached a point where almost daily she extracted a brooch, a bangle, a silk handkerchief; we abandoned picnics and dinners at the last moment when she raised some difficulty. We felt Bronson's life depended entirely on her even temper.

In midsummer we moved deeper into the mountains, to St. Moritz in Switzerland; but we had been there only a few weeks when an Italian duke whom we had met at Rome called to inform us he had learned something he thought we should know. His valet was spending almost every night with our *balia*. He was not concerned with the morals of the matter; he merely wondered whether the *balia's* milk might be harmed. In order to remove her from temptation, we were forced to return to Rome before we had intended.

Bronson's arrival had consolidated my position there more than anything I could have done myself. One of the King's remarks summarized the reason: "Ambassadresses should not have children; they should have grandchildren." When I saw Queen Elena, who meanwhile had had her own fourth child, the Princess Giovanna, she began the interview by leaning over confidentially: "Mr. Ambassador, I did it all myself. There wasn't a doctor or anybody."

Since the King and Queen were totally uninterested in entertaining — in fact, they considered money spent in keeping up a court so much money wasted — social leadership devolved on the Diplomatic Corps. We found ourselves launched on a round of receptions and dinners. Each ambassadress had an afternoon At Home, and from three-thirty to six-thirty every Wednesday streams of callers poured in and out of the del Drago, ushered about by our eight footmen, all ex-guardsmen picked for height and appearance; they looked especially impressive in their dark tail coats, red plush breeches, black silk stockings, and patent leather pumps with buckles.

Elsa had to become accustomed to having her hand kissed by two hundred men in the course of three hours, but I had to learn how to have my hand shaken repeatedly and still be able to use it the following day. If I allowed my guests to seize it, they usually squeezed it so hard that by the end of an hour it was swollen and painful. I had to grab first. The nonogenarian Count Greppi, deploring the laxness which had crept into modern social life, said in his day an ambassador was protected by strict etiquette. He gave no more than one finger by way of greeting to a Third Secretary or anyone of similar degree, two to a Second Secretary, three to a First, and a full handshake to nobody but a fellow Ambassador or Minister.

The old Roman nobility, as a rule, was inaccessible to foreigners. They rarely went into society; the only place you saw them was at their clubs where they gathered to play cards with intimate friends. Many of them were, like the Prince del Drago, so poor that they had to rent their Roman palaces; others opened them only when a daughter had to be presented to society. Even then the form of entertainment was on the lowest possible scale — an evening reception with sickly lemonade or feeble punch and a few cakes.

Due to various circumstances we made some friends among these aristocratic families. Two of Elsa's cousins had married Italians — one was the Princess Rucellai, the other, Princess Giambattista Rospigliosi. Moreover, the sister of my English friend, Lady Crawford, was the Duchess of Sermoneta, and I used to spend week ends at Cisterna in the Apennines and go shooting in the Pontine lagoons with their youngest son, Don Gelasio Caetani, who had made a success as a mining engineer in America.

Association with Italians was always complicated by the factional split caused by the still active quarrel between Quirinal and Vatican. Many countries sent their own envoys to the Papal Court; these formed a corps of their own entirely distinct from ours. Blacks and Whites could never be asked to dine together, and often did not speak to each other. For a Black dinner the Vatican, which had its own titles and seniorities, supplied the order of precedence; for a White dinner we had to consult the Quirinal.

Classed as a Court function was the *ricevimento* which I, like every Ambassador, had to give so that official and social Rome might be presented to me. Palace chamberlains made up my list of Italian guests, and the Palace staff handled every detail; all I had to do was add the names of English and Americans I wished invited, and pay the bills.

The night of January 28th, 1908, Elsa and I felt as though we were strangers in our own house. We stood like royalty at the end of Queen Christina's reception room, as a line of unfamiliar chamberlains began calling out a list of unfamiliar names. Fourteen hundred men and women were soon milling around. I had been warned a mad scramble would follow the announcement of refreshments, but I could hardly believe my eyes when the doors of the great White Gallery were opened. Along the loaded tables, extending the length of the room, Government officials were massed three, four, five deep, reaching over each other's shoulders, grabbing food, passing it back to wives and daughters. I saw one after the other stuffing his pockets full of rolls, sandwiches, and fruit. One woman was insisting vehemently that her husband carry home some chocolate éclairs. Three times the table was swept clean and three times completely replenished. Apparently none of our guests had eaten anything that day.

Hoping for a quiet smoke, I went to my own study, where cigars and cigarettes had been laid out. Three men were there, one distributing Coronas by the handful to the others; the pockets of all were bulging. I did not mind their taking a few as souvenirs, but I did object to this wholesale plundering. Restraining my irritation, I requested rather mildly, "Gentlemen, would you mind restoring those to their boxes?"

"Who are you?" one of them asked unconcernedly.

"It seems to me you ought to know. I'm your host."

I waited patiently while these latecomers, who had not passed through the reception line, finished disgorging, then remarked, "Gentlemen, you are each welcome to one cigar to smoke as you go home." Three more humiliated individuals would be hard to imagine.

As soon as the last scrap of food had vanished, the guests melted away, most of them without attempting to say good-by or to thank us for the rivers of champagne which had flowed down their throats; four hundred bottles had been consumed. When the rooms were once more empty, even the flowers had disappeared. Nothing remained but the plates and the silver.

Surveying the devastation, I could not help thinking of the French play, *Le Roi*, where the King attended a party and afterwards stayed for a chat with the hostess. Neither of them had had an opportunity to eat, and on his suggesting a little supper, she directed a servant to bring something left over.

"Madame," he replied, "where the bureaucracy has passed there are no leftovers."

CHAPTER XXIV

A REGULAR ROYAL KING

"Will you get into this house with me?"

The King, quite unconscious of his incongruous shooting costume of yachting cap, nondescript blue coat, knee breeches, and rubber boots, waved his hand towards an enormous limousine waiting at the Quirinal door. It was eight o'clock on a crisp winter's morning as we roared away from the Palace, bound for the royal estate of Castel Porziano, twenty-five miles distant on the Tyrrhenian Sea.

In high good humor at the prospect of a day's sport, the King settled back and started to sing and whistle; abruptly he interrupted himself to begin his usual bombardment of questions — "What's the population of the City of Washington?" "How many territories have you left?" "What's the percentage of deaths from typhoid fever in the City of New York?" and a dozen others, most of which I could not answer. An ambassador was supposed to be able to supply any information requested about his own country, but I made it a rule not to pretend. When the King suddenly recited the very facts he had asked for, I realized what a narrow escape I had had.

Outside the city a policeman was stationed at every crossroad to hold up traffic, so that we never had to slacken our pace until we arrived at a gate in the wall of Castel Porziano. Going along through forest and park we came to a section fenced in by pieces of white canvas about six feet high, extending unbroken for several kilometers. Into this game had been driven the previous day.

We left the car near a little clearing and walked towards two stands in the middle, about fourteen feet high, so close as to be almost touching. At the foot I turned to take my own repeating rifle, which I had used in Persia; instead, the King reached out and seized it, saying "You'll shoot this gun," and thereat I was presented with a double-barreled rifle of a type totally unfamiliar to me.

As soon as we were both in position, almost elbow to elbow, a large and remarkable pack of dogs was loosed — fox terriers, mastiffs, assorted hounds and spaniels, mongrels and pure-breds, anything canine that had the instinct to chase game. Unlike any pack that I had ever seen, these did not give tongue but, barking and yipping, raced off towards a neighboring swamp.

The dogs, in spite of their appearance, were fast workers. In no time a wild boar, shaking his tusks and grunting fiercely, dashed by on the King's side of the clearing, a hundred yards distant; he bowled it over with a perfect shot. A deer flashed into view in my sector. I aimed and fired twice, and twice missed it clean. Before I could reload and try again, the King finished off my deer, and with his repeater continued banging away at a great rate. He made some amazing shots, picking off bounding hares with no difficulty whatsoever. To hit with a rifle so small a target, speeding so rapidly in and out of the trees, was a supreme test of marksmanship.

The stock of my gun was much too short for my long arm, and furthermore I had to face into the sun and wind. Only after a considerable number of wild shots did I grow sufficiently accustomed to my weapon to make a creditable showing. Almost no two deer seemed of the same species — they ranged in size from a goat to a cow, in color from black to beige; some were spotted and some brindled, one buck even had a short horn on one side and a long horn on the other. The King smiled at my surprise and explained he had had many types of deer brought from many parts of the world and turned loose here to see what would happen. I would have challenged any naturalist to classify the results.

When the King had had enough shooting, a hunting horn was blown, and the attendants immediately scattered to bring in the trophies, laying them in a line on the grass — a hundred and five in all, of which more than half were boar. The King promptly took his camera and photographed them, next photographed me, and then handed me the camera so that I could photograph him.

Afterwards we drove to a pavilion overlooking the beach, where the Queen and the ladies in waiting joined us for lunch, a very stiff affair. The Court expected royalty to remain exclusive and live up to the accepted principle that they were in a class above and by themselves. In consequence the King and Queen could never relax, and always had to regulate their conduct to avoid shocking their own staff. It was hard on them, since by nature they hated formality and constraint.

The Queen congratulated us upon our success, adding that she was worried because the three-year-old Crown Prince could not yet handle a rifle. An expert sportswoman herself, she could break twenty-five out of twenty-five clay pigeons. She was also a great fisherwoman, and told me how on her first trip to Piedmont she had taken her rod to try for the trout darting back and forth in the streams. "No use, Your Majesty, they will not rise to a fly," she was assured. For hours she sat on the bank watching them, and finally noticed they darted to the surface each time a particular moth brushed the water. She caught one and with colored silks and feathers made an exact copy. With this bait she filled her creel in short order.

Directly the meal was over, we three sauntered towards the beach while the entourage disappeared in the other direction. Once they were out of sight, the most remarkable transformation came over the King and Queen. They began romping up and down on the sand, throwing shells, laughing and shouting, paying no attention to me. They both had cameras and now and then stopped long enough to snap pictures of each other.

At last, out of breath, they threw themselves beside me on the beach, and the Queen busied herself changing the film in her camera, remarking that one of her hobbies was developing and making prints herself. Unexpectedly she inquired, "Mr. Griscom, what do you plan to do when you're through being an ambassador?"

"Well, I really haven't decided. I suppose I'll go back to the law. On the other hand I've always had a suppressed desire to manage a newspaper."

The Queen leaned over and whispered to the King. What she said apparently amused them both, but it required considerable urging on my part before she confessed that they wanted to ask me, if I ever did get a paper, to hold positions open for them "in case we should be turned out of here."

"That doesn't seem very probable," I replied.

"I mean it. We should both like to feel we could retire to a place where we could earn our living. The King could write editorials and perhaps handle European news. I might run a woman's department."

After the World War, when other crowns were falling, I often thought of this curious presentiment.

As our car drew up once more at the Quirinal, the King remarked, "I hear lots of unusual Americans pass through Rome, but I don't meet them. Why don't you send some along to me?"

It was quite true that more of my countrymen visited Rome to see the Pope than to see the King. I took him at his word, and among others dispatched for a royal audience the President's brother-in-law, Douglas Robinson, bursting out of my frock coat, with my top hat sitting on top of his large head. William Dean Howells, who had in his youth been consul in Venice, said he was too old and shy, but I surmounted his remonstrances. Edward D. Berwind arrived seeking coal contracts with the Italian railways, and I thought the King would like to talk with an American industrial magnate. Next to appear was a well-known Hellenist from Harvard, who returned from his interview dumbfounded, saying he and the King had spent their time discussing an abstruse point in Homer; only a handful of scholars in the world knew or cared anything about it, and all were in disagreement.

I always believed the King himself would have made a success as a university professor. He read everything that came his way — he was even wading through each fat volume of the *Cambridge Modern History* as it was published. What was more important, he had a prodigious memory. His fund of information was constantly impressing and embarrassing his Ministers. Having the inestimable advantage of permanency, he was familiar with every incident which had concerned Italy for years. He seemed to be able to pull diplomatic and legal precedents from his hat to show them when they were on the point of making errors. Several of them confessed to me that in his presence they felt like schoolboys before a headmaster.

In addition to being the single really learned monarch in Europe, the King had the good of his people genuinely at heart, and was untiring in carrying out his duties — in forty-eight hours he might launch a battleship at Genoa, inspect fortifications in the North, condole with the victims of some minor disaster on the Adriatic. The King and Queen were often charged with parsimony by the old nobility, because they gave only one Court Ball a year and that a dull one; on the other hand, they contributed unstintingly to charities. For these reasons they were greatly beloved by their subjects.

Among the King's favorite projects was the International Institute of Agriculture, in which he had been interested by an American visionary from California. On account of the rather prominent mark on his high forehead, David Lubin had been brought up in the belief that he was a Messiah, and his dream was to become one of the world's benefactors by reducing the price of bread. He had evolved a plan which sounded feasible; each country should report its crop surpluses and deficiencies to a central organization, and on the basis of these statistics the "haves" should supply the "have nots." No people should ever again starve.

England and France had been unresponsive to Lubin's idea, but in Italy he had secured the ear of former Minister of the Treasury Luzzati, who presented his case and him to the King. Lubin had not the slightest notion of Court etiquette. "King," he began. "I want to tell you something. I've not come to ask anything of you. I'm here to do you a favor. If you'll listen to me, King, I can alter your whole position. Everybody knows you're a second-class ruler. Now, I have a proposition which, if you'll back it with all your strength, will make you a first-class one."

Instead of having Lubin thrown out of the Palace, the King, delighted by this original approach, requested him to stay and explain himself. The result was a personal friendship, and the Institute was actually formed. Unfortunately, his conception of bringing the world together on the basis of bread proved too idealistic for complete success in an age of competition.

The King liked Americans; he had made a companion of Meyer and White, and he did the same with me. It was unwise for him to admit European diplomats to intimacy because too much jealousy would have been aroused. However, he could invite me to go shooting or for a picnic with him, and not be charged with favoring some nation which had an ax to grind. Our close relationship with the

King and Queen helped make Italy a post which we would not have exchanged for any other.

In early March, 1908, a telegram arrived from the retiring American Ambassador to Germany, Charlemagne Tower, asking Elsa and me to come to Berlin, March 13th, for a farewell dinner he was giving the Emperor and Empress; he also expected the Whites from Paris. We accepted.

I was intensely curious to see the Emperor. Father had often described how he, P. A. B. Widener, and J. Pierpont Morgan had once gone for a day's racing on the imperial sailing yacht *Meteor.* It was a rough trip for the old boys, who had done no physical labor since they could remember; the Emperor had set them to work immediately hauling ropes. At the end of the day, they were totally exhausted and, having transferred to the palatial *Hohenzollern,* enjoyed a dinner of many courses to the utmost, looking forward to a restful evening over cigars and brandy. They rose from their places; but to their dismay the Emperor, who clung to his habits of self-discipline, made no move towards a chair. Fifteen minutes passed and then fifteen more. He still stood bolt upright and the Messrs. Morgan, Widener, and Griscom were ready to drop with fatigue. As unobtrusively as possible, they tried to rest some little corner of themselves on the edge of a table or back of a chair. When the Emperor had finished his self-imposed discipline of remaining erect for an hour after meals, they fairly collapsed.

Full of holiday spirit, Elsa and I took the train for Berlin. In the Towers' drawing room before dinner a distinguished group of guests was lined up, awaiting the Emperor and Empress; among them were Count Friedrich von Holstein, the head of the Political Bureau of the Foreign Office, the fork-bearded Admiral von Tirpitz, the head of the Navy, several generals, and many officials.

The Emperor strode in, wearing an admiral's uniform, his left hand resting on his sword so that its helplessness was not conspicuous. At close quarters he seemed shorter than his photographs made him out. His first words to me were, "How is your Papa? He is an old friend of mine. He helped me sail my boats. Albert Ballin of the North German Lloyd says Mr. Griscom taught him all he knows about steamships."

At table Elsa, with her fluent German, immediately struck up a lively conversation with the Emperor. I was not faring so well with the Empress; my ordinary efforts at small talk were answered by monosyllables. At length, her conventional inquiry about the health of the Italian royal family gave me an opening; I decided to make a bolder attempt to break the ice with a story of a misfortune which had befallen the King of Italy when, as Prince of Naples, he had visited England in 1891. He was suddenly told he was to be invested with the Garter, but had no outfit with him including the knee breeches customarily worn for this rite. At a few hours' notice a tailor had to sew together hurriedly a cavalry uniform, which was delivered just in time for him to put on.

Like everybody else, the Prince was in awe of the old Queen, and in some trepidation approached the throne. Just as he was bowing to kiss her hand, he felt a rush of cold air, and in horror realized that the main seam of the seat of his trousers had ripped apart. Reaching round, he clutched at the two little tails of his riding tunic, only some six inches long. The rest of the ceremony he spent in complete misery, vainly endeavoring to face everybody at once, particularly the Queen.

The Empress appeared to be following the story with interest, and at the dénouement she leaned back in her chair and shook so with laughter that I thought her tiara would fall off.

The Emperor looked across at her in astonishment. "*Mein Gott,* the Empress is laughing," he said to Elsa. "Impossible! This has never happened before at a diplomatic dinner." Then, addressing me, "Griscom, you must tell me what it was that made the Empress laugh."

Much against my inclination, I had to repeat the story so that the whole party could hear.

After dinner the Emperor turned the conversation to Mr. Tower's successor, David Jayne Hill, then Minister to the Hague and formerly a professor of Greek and Latin. I was amazed to hear the Emperor express unconcealed disapproval, even referring to Mr. Hill disparagingly as "*ein ganz kleiner Mann.*" His remarks seemed particularly uncalled-for, since I knew the German Foreign Office had already approved Mr. Hill.

The next evening we went to a gala performance of the opera, which the Kaiser himself was to attend. Berlin had always been a bourgeois city until he had directed his attention to raising the social tone, and one of his innovations had been to insist that the good burghers should don evening dress on such occasions. It was his custom to hold a reception in the foyer during the intermission. Therefore, when the curtain fell on the first act, Mr. Tower, Mrs. Tower, Elsa and I went out to join the other diplomats present.

The Emperor, quickly passing down the line, reached us, and drew me out of earshot of the rest. "I am going to ask you to do me a great favor. I want you to bring to the knowledge of your President in the most tactful way possible the following circumstances. For the last few years I have devoted every effort to build up the most friendly relations between Germany and the United States. In this Mr. Tower has co-operated most skillfully, and has created for your Embassy a position never before equaled. I myself am the first Hohenzollern who ever dined there. Now, I don't mind telling you frankly that I've had great difficulty in making my people accept the idea that American friendship is worth working for. They used to think Europe was the world. Now they are clamoring to be received at your Embassy. You cannot imagine what a change this is.

"What I desire most of all is that it should be an Anglo-Saxon Embassy which has the ruling position in Berlin. The present English Ambassador is old and never does anything; the whole situation, therefore, depends on your Embassy. I was asked about Mr. Hill informally, and indicated somewhat hastily that the appointment was acceptable. Since then I have obtained other information. Mr. Hill accompanied my brother about America; my brother says he is utterly unsuited.

"We have now a little rosebush of friendship which is sprouting, but which requires the most careful nursing. It would really be a most serious thing for me, and I believe for the United States, if we should allow it to die. I am convinced it will wither if a man of the type of Mr. Hill is sent here. Let your President choose some distinguished citizen who has a national position and influence in his own country; Mr. Meyer would do splendidly. I had not seen you and Mrs. Griscom for two minutes before I realized you were the kind of people we would like for the post. But in any event, the President should know what a great position your Embassy has here in Berlin. I am determined it shall not be lost if I can help it."

As the minutes ticked by, I was becoming acutely conscious of the general scrutiny. It was nearly an hour before he dismissed me, telling Tower to bring me to the Palace on Monday and we would continue the conversation.

I went back to my place, stunned and puzzled as to what to do. The President, already committed to Mr. Hill, was certain to stand by him, especially since the German Government could not give any valid reason for turning him down. For the Emperor to object that Mr. Hill did not entertain well would seem to our State Department about as pertinent as taking exception to the color of his eyes or hair. I had high respect for Mr. Hill and knew the Emperor's criticisms were unjustified.

My chief worry was the possible harm to my own career. The Emperor having made a direct request, I had to write Mr. Roosevelt, and it was going to be very difficult to persuade him I had not gone to Berlin expressly to intrigue for the German post, which to the average American seemed far more important than that of Italy.

I squirmed in my seat until the end of the performance. The instant we were back at the hotel, I sat down to write out everything the Kaiser had said. When I read it over my heart sank at the danger of my position. I would have returned to Italy the next morning if it had not been for the appointment with the Emperor. Elsa was as troubled as I, and we spent a miserable Sunday.

The Monday interview was worse than I had anticipated. The Emperor asked me outright to be the next Ambassador to Germany. I tried to convince him what a mistake it would be to insist on rejecting Mr. Hill, who was a very able man, and assured him I could not under any circumstances leave Italy. All he would reply was, "If you cannot come, you must send somebody else." Taking just long enough to record this conversation, and without completing our visit, we departed for Rome.

What was my consternation to open a paper at Munich and find the story on the front page! Here was a pretty kettle of fish. The Italians were certain to suspect that I was trying to have myself transferred from Rome. Sure enough, a bevy of reporters was waiting at the station, demanding, "Are you going to Berlin?" I gave out a brief statement that I was proud of my present post, preferred it to any other, and had no thought of changing.

From the Embassy I sent duplicate reports immediately to the President and Mr. Root. Days before they could be received, the story appeared in the American newspapers. The evidence against me had now become far more damaging, and I could guess how furious the President must be.

Nearly two weeks passed; and then, on March 29th, I heard of the German Foreign Office's request that the Emperor's suggestion might be treated as never having been made, and the following day Tower announced that Mr. Hill would be welcomed in Berlin. Not until April did I receive from the President the curtest of notes, acknowledging my report and absolving me from all responsibility. It was the narrowest escape I ever had. Mr. Root told me later that when Mr. Roosevelt saw the newspapers, he had gritted his teeth and exclaimed, "If Griscom can't explain this I'll have him out of the service so quick he won't know what's hit him."

Some time afterwards I learned how the leak had occurred. The adroit von Holstein, aware of what was in the wind, had seized this opportunity to teach the Emperor that, if he mixed in foreign relations, as he had done in the Kruger telegram episode, he would only burn his fingers. Accordingly, von Holstein had summoned Elmer Roberts, chief of the Associated Press Bureau in Berlin, and told him to release the story.

This incident was an excellent example of how a diplomat might have his career permanently blasted by a chain of events of which he was a perfectly innocent victim.

Life gradually returned to an even keel, and seemed all the more enjoyable for the worry of the preceding weeks. One of my pleasantest associations began when one morning an oldish person with a gray beard brought me a note addressed in the unforgettable bold scrawl which at a glance I recognized as the President's. "It is ridiculous for me to introduce Sir George Trevelyan to an American. You cannot possibly do too much for him. T. R." I told Sir George immediately how much I liked his son's books on Garibaldi, and he was more pleased by this compliment than if I had praised his own *History of the American Revolution*.

As a matter of fact Sir George did more for me than I for him.

One day I was playing golf at the club in the Campagna, and near the great arched viaduct which still, as in ancient days, supplied Rome with water, I came across Lady Trevelyan painting under a fixed parasol and Sir George reading to her out loud. During the ensuing conversation, he described how his uncle Thomas Babington Macaulay, who had known Rome inside out, had said to him, "George, I intend to do something for you I've never done for anybody. I've made a list of what I consider the finest pictures, statues, churches, palaces, and gardens in Rome, and I'm going to show them to you."

Sir George proposed to repeat the tour with me, and I jumped at the chance. Of three hundred and sixty-five churches, innumerable art galleries, museums, and ancient ruins, you could not see more than a fraction without making a business of it. As Sir George and I checked off the items, one by one, I was surprised to find that in many instances I honestly could not understand Macaulay's reasons for selecting this or that specimen as the most perfect of its kind. Here was an illustration of how in two generations standards of taste and criticism had almost entirely changed. Even were I an expert, I should not care to give my list today, for fear that my tastes would be considered those of an era already past.

At the arrival of young George Trevelyan, the field of sight-seeing was enlarged. He conducted me over every inch of the ground where Garibaldi had campaigned against Rome. I had always been a good walker; but Trevelyan tired me out, and I was somewhat chagrined until I discovered he belonged to an English pedestrian club, the members of which prided themselves on their ability to cover phenomenal distances on foot. Once after he had been absent for several days, I asked where he had been. He named a village on the farther side of the Apennines.

"Did you go by motor or train?"

"Neither, I walked."

"Hold on." I produced a map. "It's a hundred and sixty-one miles. You've only been gone three days. That's a daily average of some fifty-three miles."

"That's right, I did two days at sixty, and then had a shorter one over the mountains."

With some annoyance at my skepticism, he described his method

— to sleep in the middle of the day, and then walk all night when the roads were cool and most free of traffic and dust.

Everyone in those days dreamed of spending a winter in Rome, Americans and foreigners alike. At one of Elsa's At Homes, there appeared with his American wife another Englishman. Although he was inconspicuous to look at — small, graying slightly, with a drooping mustache, wearing horn-rimmed glasses, and dressed without regard to fashion — at the name of Rudyard Kipling everybody put down his or her teacup to stare. He hated being lionized, and we asked the Kiplings to have tea with us a few days later alone. He returned again and again, always amusing, jumping around from subject to subject, quoting poetry, and telling stories.

Rome was by no means dependent for interest on people who came from outside. It was one of the archeological centers of the world. The head of the American School of Archeology was Dr. Jesse Benedict Carter, a plump, well-tailored man with white spats, whose classes at Princeton had been known affectionately among the students as "Carter's Little Latin Lectures." He persuaded us to make a motor pilgrimage in search of Vergil's farm.

We progressed by way of country lanes alongside the Po, followed the Mincio towards Mantua, picnicked by the river. When some curious farmhands from the adjoining fields gathered around, Professor Carter in rapid Italian began to fire questions at them as to where Vergil had lived.

The first man, puzzled, shook his head, "I cannot tell you." The others shook theirs in agreement. "We have never heard of Vergil." Finally a graybeard volunteered, "Oh, yes, I think I know. The farm of the man named Vergil is just over there, but you will not find him. It is too bad. He is dead."

"How long since?"

"Some years. I have heard my grandfather speak to me about him. I think he knew him."

As our summer passed peacefully, a series of events was leading Europe to the verge of war. The political web which Abdul Hamid had been spinning so industriously for more than thirty years was punctured by the Young Turk rebellion; I wondered what Constantinople would be like with a constitution and without censorship or spies. Turkey's acute symptoms, particularly in Crete and

Bulgaria, brought her doctors almost to blows over the course of treatment.

Suddenly in September attention shifted to Morocco, where at Casablanca the French arrested five deserters from their Foreign Legion, two of them German, after the German Consul had granted them safe conduct. While no one knew from day to day whether France and Germany would fight, Austria took advantage of the crisis by declaring Bosnia and Herzegovina annexed.

This shelving of the Treaty of Berlin let loose pent-up national jealousies and hatreds. In Italy the years of effort to make the Triple Alliance popular were swept away by an upsurge of anti-Austrian feeling. Press and public vainly demanded compensation, but words were not effective weapons, and Italy was in no position to fight for what she wanted; her army was being reorganized, and she had no adequate supply of modern artillery. Similarly, no other nation in Europe was prepared to precipitate a general war by trying to compel Austria to restore the status quo. Instead, all of them fell to building up armaments, so that when some new "incident" occurred, force could be met with force.

Of more immediate concern to me than the troubles of Europe was the election in November, 1908, of William Howard Taft to succeed Mr. Roosevelt. An incoming President always had his own candidates for high diplomatic posts, and I had no reason to suppose an exception would be made in my case. I realized that in a few months my diplomatic career would be over.

Seldom is a man's life so marked off that he can look back upon a certain portion of it, and weigh it objectively. I had entered the service expecting to find romance and glamour, and I had not been disappointed, but I had also found that for what I gained there was a corresponding loss. At the beginning I had discounted the fact that my salary would not cover my expenses, or that some diplomatic upheaval at home might cut short my career. Elsa and I amused ourselves one evening by tabulating our further conclusions after years in our Government's service.

Pro: Both Elsa and I enjoyed travel, and had grown familiar with strange parts of the world under the most pleasant circumstances. *Contra:* No sooner did we make friends and become at home at one post than we were transferred to another; we never could live in the United States, which we agreed we liked best of all the countries we had seen.

Pro: Diplomatic rank gave an entrée anywhere. We had met statesmen, artists, literary figures, the eminent in every field; even an American brought up in a small town and exposed to this milieu for a few years emerged a completely changed person. *Contra:* Since we had to entertain the people we ought to have, rather than the people we wanted, much of our entertaining became a duty rather than a pleasure.

Pro: I could arrange my working hours to suit my convenience and tastes, and had leisure to explore the country to which I was accredited. *Contra:* Our lives were constantly subject to regulation, just as in the Army or Navy. We were the slaves of protocol, the code of conduct which dictated exactly what we should do under each set of conditions.

Pro: In times of crisis I had the exhilaration of playing for tremendously high stakes. In those days, when Washington could not call you up on the transatlantic telephone, your responsibility was far greater, and you could make many more decisions on your own initiative. *Contra:* You never lost the enjoyment of the sense of power in official position, and it was a temptation to think you were personally important.

Up to this point in our lives the *pros* had far outweighed the *contras.* However, the birth of Bronson had altered the balance. A diplomat's lot was not a happy one for his children. Frequently, you were in a country which did not afford facilities for their proper care, education, or companionship. Inevitably they seemed to be spoiled; a general phrase for describing objectionable children was *"Oh, ce sont de petits enfants d'embassade."*

Luck had played a tremendous part in my reaching top rank so young, and perhaps the luckiest thing of all was that I could leave diplomacy before my family life was affected to any great extent. I had still many active years ahead of me during which I could start anew in my own country.

I had always remembered a bit of advice which Mr. Root had let drop when he was in Brazil. "Don't wait too long before going home. If you uproot a tree once, it recovers; if you uproot it twice, it may recover; but if you uproot it three times, it loses its ability to take permanent hold anywhere."

CHAPTER XXV

EARTHQUAKE AT MESSINA

In spite of the rumors of war, 1908 seemed destined to be rung out with no black marks against it. Only three days of the old year were left when, at breakfast on the 29th, I noticed in my newspaper a headline that communications with Sicily and Calabria had been cut, probably due to earthquake. While I was reading the meager account, I was summoned to the telephone. Earl Dodge, my secretary, was calling from the Chancery to say he had heard the earthquake was far more serious than had been first reported. What did I think we ought to do about Americans in Sicily? I told him I would stop at the Foreign Office to see whether they had more complete information.

I stepped into the street, shivering in the icy damp *tramontana* blowing down from the mountains; it was not the sort of weather in which anyone would choose to be outdoors. The Government officials were distinctly worried. Although they had no direct confirmation, they feared the disaster might be the worst in years. The King and Queen were going to Naples at once.

Wild stories began to circulate — the Lipari Islands swallowed up in the sea, the Calabrian Coast devastated by a tidal wave forty feet high, Messina leveled and its population exterminated. All the next day cables from the State Department piled in, demanding news of Americans in Taormina and elsewhere in Sicily.

With the arrival of refugees from Messina there could no longer be any doubt that an overwhelming catastrophe had taken place. Though still too dazed to speak coherently, they managed to convey a tale of destruction that was the more horrible because of the unexpectedness with which it had burst upon them.

The Messinese had retired to bed the night of the 27th, secure in the peace of the Christmas season, fires burning cheerfully to keep out the unprecedented cold. In the blackness of early morning the sleepers were hurled back to consciousness to find themselves in a world gone mad. Their ears were deafened by shrieks of agony, the wrench of beams torn asunder, the thunder of toppling masonry. They tried to struggle to their feet. The floors rose and rocked, the roofs over their heads gave way, the walls folded in about them. Husbands or wives, parents or children, were crushed beside them. Without stopping to put on their clothes, they flung themselves into the streets.

Outside there were only added terrors for the panic-stricken fugitives. The low-hanging clouds glowed an angry red, reflecting hundreds of fires; where kerosene stoves had been overturned the flames flared up like giant matches. Great cracks yawned in front of them as the earth continued to shake. They could see others, fleeing like themselves towards the open country, engulfed in crevices or buried under wreckage. Screams for aid rent the air; no one dared stop. Of those who reached the fields and orange groves few were unscathed. Bruised, cut, and maimed, they huddled together for warmth while the chill earthquake rain pierced to the marrow of their bones.

At the same time across the straits in Calabria a tidal wave had swept a half-mile inland, leaving nothing but stone floors and stubs of trees to show where whole villages had been whipped away. There again, those who remained alive were without clothes, shelter, or food.

No disaster in recorded history matched this one — a hundred and fifty thousand dead, a half-million homeless, unknown thousands wounded and in need of help.

Who was to help them? Apparently the Italians were too bewildered to know how to deal with this misfortune, and furthermore Italy was a poor nation. No organized international relief then existed, but American response was immediate. Dozens of my countrymen in Rome came to the Embassy repeating, "Can't we do something?" and I was certain that their feeling would be reflected at home.

Although I had no precedents to guide me, I went to Signor Tittoni and asked whether he would like to have the assistance of the American Red Cross. His diplomatic reserve vanished completely, and I thought he was going to kiss me on both cheeks. He warned me, however, that transportation would be a problem; the single-track railway to Naples was already clogged with the military. If I could find a ship anywhere, she could load at Civita Vecchia, and he would furnish a special train to deliver our supplies there.

The difficulties of organizing relief in a foreign country, without knowing what co-operation I would get from the United States or what would develop at Messina, might have caused me to hesitate if I had stopped to consider. I had no time for that. I hurried to the Chancery and messages began to go out — one to the Red Cross requesting a million dollars, others to consuls inquiring the whereabouts of American vessels. When none proved available, I was stumped for a minute — then wired Albert Ballin. Had he a ship near by which we could charter? Having heard the Consulate was destroyed, I dispatched Major Landis, my military attaché, to recover the bodies of the consul and his wife.

Meanwhile, all the Americans who had volunteered their services were notified that, if they still wanted to help, they should be at the del Drago Palace that evening, January 3rd. Every single one turned up, and most of them early. In true American style we formed ourselves into a committee and elected officers — round, bald, jocular William Hooper of Boston was treasurer, Nelson Gay, writer and historian, was secretary, the lawyer Samuel Parrish was delegated to keep the accounts. My aides-de-camp were to be my naval attaché Commander Reginald Belknap, Winthrop (known as Winty) Chanler, who came regularly for hunting on the Campagna, and the artists John Elliott and Robert Hale.

We made a list of the food, tools, clothes, and medicines we thought would be most needed, and every member of the committee was assigned a single category, such as shoes, canned goods, macaroni with tomato sauce (I was warned the Italians would not eat it without some relish). Each was to set forth the first thing in the morning, ascertain how much of his commodity could be procured in Rome at what cost, and report that evening.

Promptly I had had a wire from Herr Ballin offering the use of the *Bayern,* laid up for the winter at Genoa; all we would have to pay were the expenses of her operation. Shortly after, I received one from the Red Cross — the organization had no standing fund for relief, but an executive meeting was being called, and they would start raising money at once. However, they could not authorize me to spend any sum until they had it in their hands. Under the leadership of Mabel Boardman, ably assisted by Robert Bacon and many others, the Red Cross was girding itself for the greatest effort it had hitherto made.

Now, if ever, was a case where giving quickly meant giving twice. I remembered what an old regular army quartermaster had said to me back in the Spanish-American War, when he saw me one evening struggling with tables of figures: "Don't worry. A quartermaster's accounts never come out right in time of war. Whatever you do, though, don't show small losses. If you're several hundred or even a thousand shy you'll have to foot the deficit from your own pocket. But make it a million dollars and Congress will be sure to pass a bill to relieve you of liability."

A million lire was more than I had in the world; nevertheless, at the committee's session that evening I explained that, since the Red Cross funds were delayed, I would guarantee two hundred thousand dollars. Parrish and Hooper instantly spoke up, insisting on sharing the responsibility.

As one by one the members reported on their assignments, it became clear that we could not possibly fill our ship from the supplies to be had in Rome. I telegraphed to our consul at Genoa, which was a commercial city, to spare no expense, buy everything in sight, and load it on the *Bayern;* in twenty-four hours she was to sail.

I needed a temporary consul at Messina, and was wondering where I should find one, when Elsa's cousin, Bayard Cutting, arrived at the Embassy, asking to be sent there. He had settled in Italy some years before in the vain hope of being cured of tuberculosis. The most pathetic feature of such an illness was that it deprived the sufferer of all end or object in life, and to give him some occupation I had had him appointed vice consul at Milan. However, I was unwilling to grant this request because the strain might easily be fatal. He maintained that he wanted to spend his remaining few months in doing something worth while, even though his life was thereby shortened. Since his wife agreed with his decision, I did not feel justified in refusing, and he departed at once with Chanler to pave the way for the *Bayern.*

We ourselves had less than two days for preparations, and never was work done more swiftly or effectively. A committee member walked into a shop, laid down a list, signed a receipt, hurried the goods into a van, and walked out, leaving the owner gaping. Some went to the heads of the medical profession and inquired, "What do we need for a complete medical outfit?" and then proceeded to organize a hospital unit with doctors, nurses, operating tables, medicines, and first aid equipment. Such efficiency was unprecedented in Rome; Mayor Nathan said, "You Americans are an extraordinary people"; and he meant it.

By noon of January 6th our special train was waiting for the signal to pull out. I was ready to go with the rest, leaving the Embassy in the capable hands of John Garrett, who had replaced Hitt as First Secretary. All Rome was at the station to speed us on our way — the Mayor, a band, the ladies' committee with Elsa at its head, citizens waving American and Italian flags.

At Civita Vecchia the *Bayern* had just docked, and we had to take off our hats to the consul at Genoa for his accomplishment. Stevedores began loading on our part of the cargo, but a few minutes of watching convinced us we were not going to get away that afternoon unless we turned to and helped. We threw aside our coats and, spurred by our example, the Italians worked harder than they had ever worked before in their lives. By four o'clock the last case was trundled up the gangplank, and that very second the *Bayern* cast off and headed south.

We did not have much rest during the night. The cargo had been rushed on board in such a hurry that it was in complete disorder. Each member of the Committee started assembling the category for which he was responsible, and the hold soon re-echoed with "Where are my shoes?" "Whoever owns these cheeses come and get 'em." "Anybody seen my case of iodine?" If some tired fellow sat down for a second to catch his breath, there was a chorus of banter and jeers. Poor old Hooper, in charge of the lowest hold, must have lost ten pounds.

The next day we were still at it, stopping only long enough to take a good look at the cone of Stromboli — which, in spite of the rumors of its disappearance, was in its usual place. Hooper, gazing at the terraced vineyards, remarked wistfully, "I wish we had a butt of Stromboli Malmsey right now."

The afternoon was nearly gone as we entered the Straits of Messina, and in rain and gathering dusk dropped anchor off the quai. In front of us lay blackness, punctured here and there by bobbing lanterns. Suddenly a searchlight from one of the warships in the harbor brushed rapidly across the water front, illuminating what seemed to be a long line of buildings. For a moment we had the illusion that the city was not destroyed at all, only deserted. Then the beam passed, and a flash of lightning, or the glow of a fire shining from behind, showed we had glimpsed nothing but ghosts of consulates, palaces, government buildings, and business offices.

Our launch was lowered, and we made for a group of lanterns on a near-by quai; the wet air was rank with the smell of decay. Landis, Cutting, Chanler, and the prefect of the city were there to lend us a hand. As my head came over the top, I saw the first signs of tragedy — dead bodies laid out in rows and Italian soldiers piling up more.

It was too late to inspect anything that night except the ruins of the consulate. Sailors from the American gunboat *Yankton* had already cleared a path there. Chanler led the way, warning me to watch for the crevices, which even on the stone quai had opened five feet wide. We skirted heap after heap of solid lumps of stone tangled with twisted and bent steel girders. Presently Landis pointed to one of these, "That's it," he said. "The sailors have been working for hours and have reached no farther than the attic." Some days afterwards they found the consul and his wife crushed in their bed.

Suddenly I stepped back hurriedly. In the darkness I had almost stumbled over a body; all efforts had been directed towards saving the living, and there had been no time to take away the dead. I was glad to reach the little room where Cutting had established his headquarters. No sooner were we seated than the floor seemed to lift and shake, and in a few seconds I heard ominous rumblings. Such tremors recurred every few hours, and they doubled the danger of rescue work because loosened masonry was constantly being dislodged.

It was obvious already that the *Bayern* had not brought nearly enough supplies to clothe and feed the destitute. Unwilling to assume the responsibility of deciding how the cargo should be apportioned, I told the prefect he must manage the distribution;

my only stipulation was that pregnant women and families with numerous children should be provided for first. After agreeing to meet early the next morning for a survey of the city, I went back to the ship.

When we assembled on the quai, Cutting handed me a handkerchief soaked with medication, and advised me to tie it over my nose; otherwise I would not be able to stand the nauseating stench of rotting and roasted flesh. Immediately we began to pass naked bodies — fifty in a hundred yards. Many were half buried in the debris, many badly mangled; in some cases fingers were missing, cut off for their rings by looters who had been set free by the destruction of the jails. One young girl was hanging by a foot from two third-floor girders. What made the corpses especially repulsive was the universal nakedness; Southern Italians believed it unwholesome to wear clothes of any kind in bed.

Advancing along the streets was like mountain climbing in the Alps. In some places crevices were still gaping ten to thirty feet deep. In others the wreckage was piled to the second story, and from the summit we could look into the ruins. Here and there, in the midst of the desolation, my eye was caught by a remnant of wall on which by some curious freak an uncracked mirror hung, still decorated with a palm from last year's Palm Sunday, or a shelf holding a clock the hand of which pointed to five-twenty; at this hour every timepiece in the city had stopped. Out of the rubbish I kicked several books and various household utensils. I put in my pocket what appeared to be a dirty tin can of an unusual shape, and promptly forgot about it. Years later I cleaned it and it proved to be a solid silver cup.

Buildings were constantly falling without warning; now and again we heard crashes and saw clouds rising slowly into the air where the military were blowing up the most dangerous ones. Every few feet we had to halt to decide whether it was safe to go on; a great bulge in a wall above our heads gave us a distinctly uncomfortable feeling.

Calls for help incessantly sounded in our ears, sometimes muffled and far away, sometimes seemingly at our elbows. It was heartbreaking to be so near and yet be utterly powerless to aid. We met a party of excavators and paused to talk to the lieutenant in charge, who explained some of the obstacles. Messina was a stone city; there were not many wooden buildings. Removing the wreckage was like a game of jackstraws, the straws being steel beams. If you pulled the wrong one the whole mass would collapse. Repeatedly they had almost freed a victim only to see him crushed before their eyes.

A little farther along a group of Russian sailors were gathered around a hole from which a baby's plaintive cries came filtering up. One of them, red-faced and gasping for breath, was handing a trowel and a rag, soaked with condensed milk, to a second. As we stepped closer, they lowered him head first down the hole, and the baby's cries ceased. The infant was trapped in a sort of box, so that the rescuer could just reach to stuff the rag in its mouth with one hand, while with the other he scraped away to make the opening bigger.

The next day when I passed this same spot the sailors were still there, brokenhearted; the baby was dead.

The enthusiasm of the Russian and English sailors was untiring; they had literally to be hauled back to their ships at the end of the day, promising those whom they were trying to release that they would return the first thing in the morning. Tragedies were frequent, because there were no landmarks in the expanse of ruins. We used to encounter parties disconsolately toiling up and down one street after another, unable to find the place where they had been working the night before.

Curiously enough, the Messinese themselves were the only rescuers who required urging. The Italian soldiers, mostly natives of Piedmont and Lombardy in the North, were constantly assuring us that the Messinese were lazy and shiftless and not worth saving. One young fellow had begged the Americans for help in digging his parents out of the ruins. Landis had promised, adding "But you must work too."

"How much will you pay me?"

"What? Pay you to look for your own father and mother?"

"Well, I have to earn something, don't I?"

He had reported the next day, but he came empty-handed. "Go get your shovel!" Landis had directed.

"Will you buy me one?"

"Of course not. Use your own."

"Then you must pay me for its use."

A pitiful crowd had gathered at the quai when we returned —
dirty, ragged men, hollow-cheeked women with children clutched
under their shawls. They closed in around us, holding out their
hands, pleading "*Aiutateci! Aiutateci!*" With difficulty we escaped
and pushed off in the launch. For fear of a riot we did not dare try
to land our goods without a guard, and borrowed escort squads from
the English ship *Scorpion*.

I realized the food, clothing, and medicines we had brought were
only palliatives. These people had no homes, no means of livelihood;
everything they possessed had been swept away. What they would
need most were houses in which they could settle down and resume
their jobs of earning a living. It seemed to me reconstructing
the city was the best use to which American money could be put.

The prefect, Belknap, and I went to look at possible sites among
the orange and lemon groves to the south. After making tentative
estimates of costs, I promised we would construct three thousand
wooden dwellings, each large enough to hold one family. Belknap
and I made a rough sketch of a great central piazza on which were
to be the public buildings, and then distributed the houses along
streets running at right angles. We were both surprised to see what
a metropolis we were going to have.

Just at this moment when I was most eager to get back to Rome,
Admiral Sperry with four American war vessels put into port. Since
the *Bayern* was to continue her relief cruise to Calabria, I welcomed his offer to take me to Naples in his flagship, the *Connecticut*.
There I dispatched a long cable to Mabel Boardman, setting forth
my plan and the amount of money it would require.

On reaching the del Drago Palace, I found Elsa and her committee had converted it into a sewing establishment. Bales and
packing cases obstructed the hall, the floor of the White Gallery was
covered with lint, and tables had been piled up with the most extraordinary collection of garments donated by the inhabitants of Rome.
Every hour of the day or night some of the workers were there,
cutting down, and making over, ripping, measuring, stitching, hem-
ming. The bereaved refugees were begging for black garments, and
the colored ones all went for underwear.

Waiting for me was a reply from Miss Boardman that the Red

Cross was sending as soon as possible shiploads of lumber, portable houses, about two hundred carpenters, and funds for immediate use. In the meanwhile, I arranged for a few skilled workmen to be rushed from Switzerland and Germany with what materials were available to allow Belknap to make a start.

With the prospect of relief money pouring in, I had to decide how it should be divided. The Queen convinced me part of the funds should be employed for a large hospital she wanted built at Messina; we built it, and when it was presented to her she named it the Ospedale Elizabeth Griscom. The *Bayern* returned from Calabria with more accounts of the indescribable devastation there. I organized a relief program with headquarters at Reggio; Winty Chanler volunteered to take charge there, and gallantly remained at his post even after his fellow members of the Committee had left Messina. We had heard that the inhabitants of many mountain villages, cut off from the outside world, were in great need, and Earl Dodge headed a relief train to circle the coast. At the foot of each valley he unloaded his automobile, filled it with food and medicines, and with his helpers drove it as far as he could up the ruined road; then they packed in the supplies on their backs over the rough trails.

I thought I had been working hard, but Belknap must have been working harder; long before I expected it, he sent me word that one block of houses was almost ready and would be allocated as soon as I could get there. The prefect, who again was managing the distribution, had announced that pregnant women would be given priority over the others. The day of the assigning, a big crowd gathered outside the stout railings with which Belknap had surrounded his project. Our appearance was the signal for women in all stages of pregnancy to begin shoving to the front, waving brooms, mops, kitchen utensils, calling shrill abuse at each other.

The prefect beckoned forward as his first candidate a woman who was obviously near her time. Instantly howls and shrieks and curses broke from the throats of the others. An Amazon armed with a broom flung herself at the successful applicant, hit her a terrific blow on the abdomen, then seized her and started ripping a mass of stuffing out of her clothing. Even we could not help joining in the laughter which greeted the exposure of this hoax.

In a few hours the families had moved in, and the carpenters had moved on to the next block. However, by morning they were being summoned back for repairs. These women had never been accustomed to the luxury of a fireplace. If they had wanted heat, they had heaped up the kindling in the middle of the earth floor and lit it. When they resumed their former habits, the new wooden floors promptly burst into flames. Considerable damage was done before they could be taught how to make the smoke rise safely and peacefully from the neat brick chimneys.

The prefect now put in a special plea. More than houses were necessary to restore the prosperity and happiness of Messina. The businessmen wanted a hotel so that traveling salesmen and merchants would have a place to stay; otherwise they would not come. The women were miserable without a church. Finally, the whole town needed diversion; would we build them a moving picture theater? These could not be strictly classed as essential for relief, but since they were essential for reconstructing the life of the city, I thought I could properly use part of the funds to comply with the prefect's request.

Belknap continued turning out houses, but in the following weeks we began to learn how impossible it was to administer charity without treading on somebody's toes. The Messinese clamored for our houses in preference to those being erected by the Italians to the north of the old city, and jealousy inevitably arose. Our fireplaces, for example, cost us forty dollars each; the Italians were paying a hundred and twenty for theirs, which were not so good. I made up my mind we ought to finish quickly and get out.

In the course of the winter news came that President Roosevelt was departing, directly after Mr. Taft's inauguration, to shoot big game in Africa. The King, hearing that "the most unusual American of all" was passing so near Italy, declared, "He must stop and shoot with me." I transmitted this informal invitation with an urgent one of my own that Mr. Roosevelt also inspect what we had done at Messina. He replied it was not his intention to make a round of visits to foreign potentates, "most of whom would be as profoundly uninterested in me as I would be in them." He did agree, however, to spend a few hours at Messina. I told the King that if he really wanted to meet Mr. Roosevelt he might happen to be viewing his project at the same time I was showing the ex-President ours.

Just before Mr. Roosevelt was due to arrive, all Rome was up in the air over a forthcoming demonstration flight by the Wright brothers. It is practically impossible now to adjust your mind to an era in which nobody believed man could fly. I felt as though I were talking to people who had been to Mars, when Wilbur and Orville Wright, with their sister, called at the Embassy to ask me to arrange for the use of the artillery field. After five minutes' conversation I was possessed by the desire to experience this new sensation of soaring through the air.

The idea of rising off the earth meant one thing to me — the story of the Ata Beg and the Frenchman's balloon. I told it to them, adding, "The King will be out to watch you. I'm sure he'll be more impressed with your machine if you take me up."

At first they refused flatly. It was far too dangerous; they could not run the risk. I invited them to lunch, and kept at them until finally, still under protest, they agreed. Elsa was away; she would never have allowed it. Rod, who was visiting me, continued his attempts at dissuasion even on the drive out to the field.

I had a few qualms myself as I looked over the machine. It resembled a big crate made of slats without so much as a solid floor upon which to rest your feet. In some places struts and supports had been reinforced and repaired with ordinary household twine of every size and description; in others they had been wrapped around and around with wire. Wilbur Wright, who was the pilot, sat on one side so that his weight exactly balanced that of the engine on the other side. My position was in the dead center where I would not upset the equilibrium.

The King arrived, all curiosity, and immediately climbed into one of the seats. While Wilbur Wright explained levers, controls, steering gear, the King bombarded him with questions, "How does it feel to fly?" "How far did you go up the first time?" "Have you ever fallen?" Then he hopped out and began to take pictures.

I got in. Wilbur Wright did the same, and pointed to a piece of twine stretched between a lever on the engine and a strut near his hand, dangling within an inch of my neck. "Watch out for that string. It's the only way I have to stop the engine. If it's pulled at the wrong time we'll both probably be killed. Don't raise your hands even if your cap blows off."

First Rod and then the King reached up and shook hands with me, saying "good-by" as though it were forever. The last thing I saw was the King getting out his camera and focusing it on me.

The engine caught, a deafening roar filled my ears, and the whole machine shook and trembled. To give the plane a start, it was set at the top of an inclined track, and a rope was attached to its nose, which ran to the end of the track, round a pulley, then back, and to the top of a tower behind us where it was fastened to a heavy weight. The trigger was pulled that released us, and, shooting forward, we went bump, bump, bump along the ground. I sat stiff upright, not daring to move, feeling as though a pebble in our path would tip us over. Suddenly the bumping ceased, and I realized the ground was dropping away. I lifted my eyes and almost stopped breathing. We were headed straight towards a line of telegraph wires bordering a patch of woods on the far edge of the field. I did not see how we could clear them. We grazed the tops of the trees; my feet were practically in the leaves.

The wind was now causing the throttle string to flap hard against my throat; I could scarcely resist the instinctive impulse to push it back. Next my nose itched unbearably, and my cap needed settling more firmly on my head. It was all I could do to make my hand stay by my side.

When I looked down once more, I found we were coming around in a curve and straightening out directly over the wires. I thought how unpleasant it would be to fall on them and be sliced to pieces, "Why doesn't he go somewhere else?" I kept saying to myself.

It seemed an hour before the cord yanked against my neck, and I welcomed the thud as the skids struck the ground. The crowd cheered; Rod and the King shook hands with me all over again. We had been up ten minutes, and had ascended to the dizzy height of two hundred feet.

On April 10th I was at Naples as the *Hamburg* steamed into the harbor. The ex-President was on deck with Kermit, and was bubbling over with high spirits, which cooled somewhat at my suggestion that he come ashore long enough to call on the Duchess d'Aosta. This daughter of the Comte de Paris, pretender to the French throne, had hunted big game in many countries, and did not want Mr. Roosevelt to escape without her comparing notes with him.

After considerable urging he finally consented, and we set off towards the Palazzo Capodimonte, Mr. Roosevelt grumbling, "It's very hard for me to live up to the idea these foreigners have of me from the comic papers. I suppose they would be satisfied if I hit the Duke."

The Duchess took one look at Mr. Roosevelt's wrinkled old silk topper, and asked, "Where in the world did you get that hat? Did you borrow it especially for this call on me?"

At this unexpected opening the ex-President brightened up, and the next thing I knew the Duchess disappeared with him, leaving me to struggle with the Duke, who was famous for never relaxing his royal dignity. Our meager supply of chit-chat was quickly exhausted, and we sat for the most part in silence until he decided it was time to find out what had become of his guest. As we approached the Duchess' reception room, we could hear a lively interchange of question and answer, Mr. Roosevelt's voice booming exclamations of admiration. We were greeted by the sight of the tall slender Duchess and the chunky ex-President, perched on the back of a sofa, examining the stuffed heads and photographs of lions, tigers, and elephants which lined the wall; both were so absorbed they never noticed us. I had difficulty dragging him away.

The *Hamburg* delivered us to Messina the following morning. Belknap and his staff conducted us on an all-inclusive tour. At the center of the new city, where the Piazza Roosevelt was bisected by the Via Griscom, so named by the Italian Government, the ex-President poked me in the ribs with the comment, "There's at least one place in the world where our names will go down to posterity."

Suddenly rounding a corner, we came face to face with the King. Without any words from me he and Mr. Roosevelt marched forward and shook hands; both began talking at once, each constantly interrupting the other. Mr. Roosevelt declared it was a shame nobody had ever done justice to the magnificent charge of the Piedmontese cavalry at Montebello, which he considered a far finer performance than Balaklava.

"That's true," agreed the King, "but unfortunately no poet happened to take a fancy to it."

Then they turned to the War of the Spanish Succession, and cited chapter and verse to prove the respective merits of Marshal Vendôme, and the King's ancestor Prince Eugene of Savoy. Long before they had finished, the *Hamburg's* whistle started impatiently blowing, and in a few seconds, with a wave of his hand and a flash of teeth, the ex-President was off for Africa.

By June the last nails had been hammered, the last bricks laid at Messina, and the American work was done. This disaster had shown clearly who were the givers of the world. Italians had contributed to the limit, but after all this was to be expected — it was their earthquake. The Lord Mayor of London had raised a sizable fund, but it was not available for use until the day we dissolved our committee. Germany had supplied a small amount, France a sum hardly worth mentioning, and the other countries little beyond sympathy. The United States had donated more than all the rest put together.

In token of their gratitude, the King and Queen themselves attended the presentation to the Italian Government. We walked towards the piazza along the streets planted with mulberry trees. If you pretended they were elms, you could look at the white houses with green shutters, each separate with its little garden, and imagine you were in a New England village. The sun shining on happy faces, the sense of life going on again, combined to make a scene all the brighter in contrast to that black afternoon when the *Bayern* had first steamed up to ruined Messina. The reconstructed community was also a monument to the untiring efforts of the committee, and particularly of Bayard Cutting, who had made the greatest sacrifice of all; he died shortly afterwards. I was glad to think that in leaving Italy I could leave behind this permanent record of American friendship.

Our departure from Rome had been delayed because Mr. Taft had written me to remain in Rome until the relief work was finished. Now that this moment had arrived, Elsa and I began our farewells. The King said in his abrupt way, "The Queen and I are very sorry. No use talking about it. The disagreeable part of our position is that, just as we make friends, which always requires some time, their Governments take them away from us. If you wish, I'll give you the customary formal farewell banquet, but the Queen and I have talked it over and decided to let you choose between that and a quiet dinner with us."

I said the dinner by all means. The King appeared pleased and added, "By the way, come over tomorrow afternoon with Mrs. Griscom. We'll show you our gardens."

Accordingly, about four Elsa and I were conducted down a cypress-bordered path and found the King and Queen with their children inspecting the children's turtles. "Have you ever tried racing them?" I asked.

"No. Tell us how," the children chorused enthusiastically.

This was a new idea to me also, but together we formulated rules. The path, some six feet broad, was to be the race course. Pushing was forbidden, but we provided ourselves with switches which we could use to tickle. We four adults and the two little princesses each selected a champion, the King shouted "One, two, three, go!" and we released them. Some started backwards, some sideways, but none straight ahead. The children, who were on their stomachs, seemed to be doing so much better at directing than we, that first the Queen, and then the rest of us, flopped down in a row, waving our twigs, calling encouragement. Finally, one of the children's turtles crossed the line, to the intense delight of its owner.

After the race the King and Queen led us to a small flagged circle. The Queen left us in the center, saying, "Wait there!" Suddenly, with a whistle and a swish, jets of water spurted up around us twenty feet high, shutting us within a circular wall of white spray. We jumped instinctively; but, so carefully were the spouts arranged to slant outwards, that not a drop touched us. Shrieks of laughter came from our audience. Presently we were set free, and the King, whose disappearance we had not noticed, returned with a broad grin. "These gardens were made by the Popes and priests," he remarked, "and this was one of their amusements. Silly, isn't it, but it gives us a lot of fun."

Such an afternoon with the King and Queen did not occur often in the beaten paths of diplomacy, and the farewell dinner had the same charm of informality. We talked of the pleasant times we had had together — shoots, picnics, walks on the shore — and on rising from table the King asked, "Would you care to see some of my coins?" Knowing he owned one of the greatest collections in the world, I answered, "Of course I would."

I followed him through his bedroom, through his bathroom where my eye lit enviously on a sponge nearly two feet across, and into a hallway, from which a small iron staircase circled to the floor above. Our trip ended in an enormous room fitted from baseboard to ceiling with thin drawers, each labeled in the King's own copperplate hand.

The King specialized in coins of the House of Savoy, and as he pulled out tray after tray, each with its row of carefully marked specimens on velvet, he told me why certain ones had been struck, perhaps for a wedding, for a victory, or for the accession of some ancestor. He was his own curator, and the cataloguing and labeling must have been almost a lifework.

At the end of the evening, as we were taking our leave, the King turned to me, "I hear you have no wild boar in your country. How would you like me to ship you some?" Without thinking what in the world I would do with them, I accepted with thanks.

Next day Elsa and I boarded the train for Paris, private citizens once more. We anticipated a sense of letdown, but as a matter of fact we felt nothing but relief, as though we were children being let out of school for the summer. Fall and the new career seemed a long way off.

Mr. Harriman was staying in Paris after a cure in Austria. I had not seen him lately, and, when I called, was shocked to observe how feebly he walked and how ill he appeared. Nevertheless, his mental vigor was undiminished. With his usual forthrightness he attacked me: "So you're finally going home. You're through with diplomacy. Now what do you want to do?"

Talking with Mr. Harriman was almost certain to give you ideas you never would have had in conversation with an ordinary person. My submerged desire to enter journalism expressed itself. Without thinking of the almost certain humiliation I should be storing up for myself, I replied: "Direct a New York City newspaper."

Mr. Harriman, not at all bothered by my complete lack of experience or qualifications, came immediately back at me: "Which newspaper?"

"Well, the Mills-Reid interest seems tied up to the *Tribune* and Mr. Ochs would never part with the *Times*. I don't just know. I'll have to go home and look into it."

"Very well, look into it, and then tell me what you find out. I don't see why I shouldn't buy you a paper."

Mr. Harriman promised to send me word as soon as he returned to America, and Elsa and I set sail on the first boat for home.

Mr. J. P. Morgan, Sr., had offered us the loan of Camp Uncas on Raquette Lake in the Adirondacks, and we settled down for a summer of tennis, canoeing, all the outdoor sports we enjoyed so much. I completely forgot about the King's wild boar until one day I received a telegram from a frantic shipping agent, saying they were at the New York docks. Would I have them removed at once?

I had made no provision whatsoever for boarding or housing these beasts. My initial solution was for Father to have them on his big plantation near Tallahassee, Florida, where he went to shoot quail each winter. I sent a wire to Dolobran, and promptly he wired back a categorical refusal — he would let loose no such menace on the peaceful countryside.

Then I made the same offer to Mr. Morgan for Camp Uncas. After some persuasion he agreed to harbor the boars temporarily, but as soon as the inhabitants learned that they might be released, they petitioned Mr. Morgan *en masse* not to allow it. Tourists or hunters would be frightened away from the boar-infested woods, and what would then become of the guides of Raquette Lake? In the end, Mr. Morgan found sanctuary for the beasts on Jekyll Island off the coast of Georgia. There they have thriven and increased, and there their progeny may still be hunted through the tangle of cat briar and jasmine.

In early September I had a letter from Mr. Harriman, saying he had returned, and inviting me to Arden to discuss buying that newspaper. From his note I would not have guessed that he had only a short time to live. A few days later came the news of his death.

Attractive as Mr. Harriman's proposal had seemed, I had never been enough of a gambler to count on stepping into a ready-made position. I knew I should always have regretted letting my legal training go by the board. I was glad, therefore, when that fall I found an opening in the New York law firm of Philbin, Beekman, and Menken, where I could start immediately to try to build up a position for myself as a specialist in international law.

CHAPTER XXVI

INTO POLITICS

After ten years of pomp and circumstance I was a plain American citizen, going back and forth to my office. From our house at Seventy-second Street it was pleasant to stroll across the Park to the spur line terminus of the Sixth Avenue Elevated at Fifty-ninth Street. Each morning banker and broker and lawyer exchanged greetings as they puffed up the stairs, took their accustomed places on the eight-thirty train, shook out their newspapers, and settled themselves to read. Anyone who disturbed their routine was the target for frowns and irritated glances.

At the very front of the front car, entrenched behind the outspread wings of the *Tribune,* was invariably to be seen Joseph Choate. Once a garrulous fellow traveler plumped himself down by the leader of the Bar, and began in the most chatty manner, "Mr. Choate, will you tell me why you always choose this end seat?"

Mr. Choate, lowering a corner of his paper, eyed the intruder sternly. "I sit here, Sir, so that I can be bored only from one side."

I had had but a few days to become accustomed to my new role, when one afternoon I reached home to find Elsa entertaining a fairly tall, clean-shaven, rather ascetic-looking individual. It was Herbert Parsons, the New York Congressman and chairman of the New York County Republican Committee, who had been to Japan with the Taft party. He greeted me, "Griscom, we've been talking about your future and we think that you ought to go into politics. There's a city election in a few weeks and a state campaign next fall — fine opportunities for everyone interested in decent government."

Heartily as I sympathized with Parsons' revolution against the Platt-Odell machine in New York City, I was uncertain whether it would be wise to spare time from brushing up on the law. Without committing myself, I told Parsons I would think over his suggestion.

The next day, happening to meet Mr. Root, now Senator from New York, I put the question to him; his response was immediate. "The best thing you can do. You want people to know you're back and not still living in Italy. Ten thousand lawyers are trying to make a start in this city, and, if any one of them can get as much as a sheet of tissue paper under his feet, he'll be ahead of the others."

That decided it. As a first step, I determined to join my local Republican Club; in each of the thirty-five districts of New York County, which then included the Bronx, the club was the focus for all Party workers. Here they chose captains for the various precincts, who in turn elected a leader, and sent delegates to the County Committee which directed Party activities.

When I presented myself at the headquarters of the Twenty-ninth, the so-called "Silk Stocking" District, the suite of rooms was filled with groups discussing the city convention, only a few days off. Although the citizens were aroused by the crimes of Tammany, Parsons did not believe enough Republican strength could be mustered to win the election; his strategy was to nominate fusion candidates around whom would rally all honest-minded citizens, regardless of party. The captains were making plans to get out a record vote, and I asked them to let me know if there was anything I could do to help. Arriving home later in the evening, I was handed a message; one of the delegates to the convention could not be present and perhaps I would care to take his place.

According to my instructions, on the afternoon of September 22nd I appeared at Carnegie Hall. Friends were greeting each other loudly, slapping each other on the back, hailing each other as "Jim" and "Joe" and "Jack." Through clouds of tobacco smoke I made my way to the New York County section, and sat down with my own group from the Twenty-ninth. We had a huge delegation, because the number allotted a district was determined by the number of Republican votes cast in the last election, and ours was the banner Republican district.

Just before we were called to order, the district leaders came bustling in, and the whisper circulated, "Parsons says Otto Bannard for Mayor." I heard some murmurs of disapproval and doubt as to whether the President of the New York Trust Company and such an out-and-out Republican as the Treasurer of our County

Committee could get sufficient votes to win as head of a fusion ticket. However, Parsons' choice was the convention's choice, and Bannard was quickly nominated. Two young reformers, Charles Whitman and John Purroy Mitchell, were picked for District Attorney and President of the Board of Aldermen respectively.

In the excitement of selecting the rest of the candidates, apparently the four coroners had been completely overlooked. Parsons hurried from one leader to another asking, "Don't you know anybody who wants to be a coroner?" After several consultations four names were produced. As one speaker pointed out, it was, by pure accident, a perfect coroners' ticket — two doctors to tend the citizens until they died, an undertaker to bury them, and a marble cutter to carve their tombstones.

The following morning I went to the Headquarters of the County Committee in the Metropolitan Life Insurance Company building at Twenty-third Street and Fourth Avenue, and told Parsons I was volunteering for the campaign. "You're just the person we're looking for," he returned. "I've always remembered the way you organized the Taft party visit. How would you like to form a Business Man's Municipal Association to put out banners, hold rallies, and raise money?"

Accepting his proposal, I selected John Claflin, the drygoods king, to be President; his name would be a magnet to draw support which I, as Chairman, could turn to good account. At the first meeting of our committee, I suggested that we choose a group of leaders in each business or profession, and have them canvass their own ranks — doctors among doctors, jewelers among jewelers, engineers among engineers. The arrangement was so successful that from the start contributions rolled in to us as fast as they did to the County Committee.

Parsons had brought in a group of young men who were working without thought of reward, a rare phenomenon in a democracy. Some of them were old friends — Bronson Winthrop, William Chadbourne whom I had met in Japan, Gordon Knox Bell, and John Henry Hammond; among my new acquaintances were B. W. B. Brown, Frederick Tanner, and Linford Bates.

The Democrats, thoroughly scared, nominated a reform candidate, William J. Gaynor, who, in his long service as judge, had become popular for defending citizens against bullyragging by the Tammany police. Spurred to redoubled activity, we held rallies every noon and meetings every night, with sixty speakers traveling around in carts. In the Italian districts I made addresses in Italian, and was greeted with wild applause by those with relatives at Messina.

We ended up in a blaze of enthusiasm. As I crossed Central Park on election eve, I saw lines of torchbearers converging from four directions on Durland's Riding Academy, singing for reform and shouting "Down with Tammany!" Parsons had passed the word for a full turnout, and six thousand people crowded the arena, yelling and howling when the speakers declaimed: "The horsecars must go!" "Clean up the pay rolls!" "Government is an institution to live under — not on!"

The next day New York's citizens went to the polls and voted our ticket in — everybody but our leader, Bannard.

The jubilation was not diminished by the fact that, following a long period of scanty pickings, a lot of offices would now be available for distribution. This spoils system has universally been criticized as the root of all evil in our Government. However, it seemed to me those who labored to get out the vote month after month and year after year deserved the rewards — if they were honest. Unfortunately, the line was very hard to draw between a reward for service in the past and the price of a block of votes in the future. Once in office, the Party organization was tempted to support candidates who would maintain the status quo, regardless of whether the Government was being run for the good of the people.

Some of the more obnoxious aspects of the spoils system were evident in state politics, on which the Republican Old Guard had a strangle hold. Big business wanted this bill passed or that bill tabled; the politicians needed money for themselves and their cohorts. One of the results of this alliance between business and politics was a very co-operative group of Senators and assemblymen at Albany, known as the Black Horse Cavalry.

Governor Charles Evans Hughes had been elected to clean up the state on his record of cleaning up the insurance companies. His remedy was a direct primary bill, according to which candidates for office would be nominated by the people instead of by conventions. Naturally the Old Guard, left to their own devices, were not going to vote themselves out of power, and opposed it tooth and nail. Hitherto proofs of corruption had been so successfully suppressed that it had been impossible to stir up public indignation.

Suddenly, in January, Republican Senator Ben Conger charged Senator Jotham P. Allds, his party leader, with having taken a thousand-dollar bribe back in 1901. The agent for the bribers proved to be a Sunday school superintendent named Hiram G. Moe; he had made frequent trips to Albany, armed with a little black bag from which he doled out, not religious tracts, but persuasive documents in the form of thousand-dollar bills. Although in the face of the damning evidence the Senators had to vote an investigation of the Allds charges, they were determined not to allow the general investigation demanded by Governor Hughes. The Republican party seemed headed for a first-class split. The Democrats, who had been snowed under for many years, began to pop up their heads — as one Democratic Senator remarked to another, "Well, I've been here for twenty years and nobody with a little black bag has come around to see me."

Once the city campaign was over, political activity had died down as far as I was concerned, and I was rather surprised when, January 30th, Otto Bannard called up and asked me to lunch. No sooner had we unfolded our napkins than he announced, "Parsons is resigning as County Chairman. As head of the Nominating Committee I asked him yesterday whom he would recommend for a successor and the only person he could suggest was you. The election is tomorrow. It's short notice, but we hope you'll accept."

My jaw dropped. I rather suspected that an ex-diplomat among experienced politicians would find rough sledding. Nevertheless, no matter what trouble I might get into, I was not going to miss this opportunity. "All right," I answered, "I'll do my best."

Abandoning any thought of returning to the office that afternoon I set off for home. Elsa agreed it was a rare chance and canceled our dinner arrangements for that night, so that I might compose my acceptance speech undisturbed.

The next evening I arrived early at the auditorium on Murray Hill where the meeting was to take place. Parsons and Bannard introduced me to the other officers of the Committee: Tom Whittle, the secretary; Collin H. Woodward, the first vice president; and

Samuel S. Koenig, the second vice president, who had performed the remarkable feat of turning the Tammany Sixth District into a Republican citadel.

The astonishment caused by springing Bannard on the convention a few months before was nothing to that now caused by springing me on the Committee. Sitting on the platform, I felt six hundred pairs of eyes scanning me up and down, but whatever opposition there was had been ironed out in the Executive Committee of district leaders, and the ayes had it without difficulty. I delivered my address, including an unqualified endorsement of Governor Hughes, acutely conscious all the time that at least a third of my audience was mistrustful if not actually hostile.

The instant I had finished, a crowd of reporters, district leaders, and captains surrounded me, and I was overwhelmed by more names than I could possibly attach to faces. The newspapers, although opening their eyes in mild surprise, on the whole were friendly. The *Sun,* commenting a little skeptically on my nine languages, asked, "What we would like to know is whether Mr. Griscom can speak and understand the language of the politicians of the East and West Sides of New York City."

My initial test came a few days later at my first meeting with the leaders. Realizing my prestige would depend in great measure on how much patronage I could get for them, I promised them I would work as hard as I could to see that they were well provided for, but in return I would insist that they be most particular about their recommendations for offices. If any of them landed me with a bad candidate I would be suspicious of him ever after.

When B. W. B. Brown, leader of the Twenty-seventh, resigned in my favor from the State Committee, I had to take a stand at once on Party affairs in the state. Like other good Republicans I had been wondering whether there might not be some way of patching up the impending rift, and believed I might have the answer in a letter from President Taft: "Whenever you wish to call on me for any aid that I can give you I shall be delighted to make the effort."

If the President, who had hitherto taken no stand, would give us some sort of endorsement, the threat of losing the all-important Federal patronage might persuade the Old Guard to compromise. Both the President and Governor Hughes were to attend the New

York City Lincoln Day dinner, a great Party event. I sent invitations to them as well as to a selected group from both factions to come to a reception at my house the afternoon before the dinner to meet my leaders.

Most of the prominent political figures, including the Governor, were still only names to me, and on finding I had a number of appointments which had to be approved personally by Mr. Hughes, I decided to go to Albany to look over the terrain. Although Parsons, almost single-handed, had secured the nomination of Governor Hughes for his first term, a coolness had grown up between them concerning state patronage; Governor Hughes claimed Parsons had recommended candidates who did not measure up to his own lofty standards.

Not quite certain what welcome Parsons' heir would receive, I drove up the hill to the Capitol and was ushered into the Governor's office. Nothing was revealed by Mr. Hughes's countenance — keen eyes that gazed searchingly at me, and all other expression hidden behind a bushy beard. I was not convinced that the Governor's direct primary bill was the best way to quash corruption in the state; people would be likely to vote for the man who could rouse them with the sound and fury of his words rather than the man who presented them with cold abstractions, no matter how just and right. Nevertheless, I sympathized so entirely with Mr. Hughes's purpose that I began by assuring him he could count on the full support of New York County, and I would do everything I could to range our assemblymen and senators at Albany on his side. He returned a polite "Thank you," but I could see he was reserving judgment.

We sat down to go over my list. The Governor questioned me minutely on the fitness of each applicant, and I passed on the information given me by the district leaders. In due course, we came to the four Wardens of the Port of New York, offices regarded as highly desirable plums, because they paid some twenty-five hundred dollars a year and, as far as I knew, entailed little else than wearing uniforms and wandering around the harbor to make sure that ships were not loaded above the Plimsoll line. The Governor pointed to the name of Morris Levy. "Tell me, Mr. Griscom," he asked in his deep resonant voice, "what naval experience entitles Mr. Levy to be selected as Port Warden?"

Realizing that the Governor was only seeking some excuse to approve my list, I cast about for an answer and recollected that Levy had gained considerable popularity in his Twenty-fourth District by hiring a small excursion steamer every summer, packing as many of his followers in as he could, and sailing up Long Island Sound for an all-day clambake.

"Mr. Levy," I pronounced solemnly, "is an authority on the overcrowding of steamers in New York Harbor."

Mr. Hughes, with a twinkle, nodded assent, and I left the Capitol with every one of my appointments approved. So far, my language was clearly understandable to the "boys."

That evening Senator George Agnew from my own district took me to the Fort Orange Club, the rendezvous for all the politicians. Legislators and bosses crowded round our table to view for themselves the singular type of chairman that New York County had projected into their midst — William Barnes of Albany, big, burly, frank-spoken; Chairman Timothy L. Woodruff of the State Committee, ingratiating, smooth, wearing a waistcoat you could not keep your eyes from; George W. Aldridge of Monroe County (Rochester), plump and rosy-cheeked and affable, exactly my idea of what a boss should look like; Francis Hendricks of Onondaga (Syracuse), wizened, shrewd but kindly; William Ward of Westchester, New York's representative on the Republican National Committee, a veteran of many fights, deaf enough never to hear you if he did not want to. Finally, among the strange faces, I glimpsed one that I recognized: James Wadsworth, the Speaker of the Assembly — who had married Alice Hay — was just the agreeable, talented sort of person I liked to see in politics. However, he was a dyed-in-the-wool Old Guarder, and I did not need long to conclude that it would be difficult for his faction and mine to find common ground.

Whichever way the conversation turned, it invariably reverted to a denunciation of Governor Hughes. I was surprised at the personal animus expressed against him by most of these legislators; many would not go near him. Naturally the Allds scandal was discussed and the Old Guarders, not at all ashamed, seemed to consider the exposure as a piece of bad luck. Barnes said to me over and over again, "You fellows down there don't know how *we Republicans* feel about this," and then recollecting, attempted to explain. The Old Guard were Republicans first and all the time; they regarded us as of another breed — fusionists first and Republicans afterwards.

Two of the county leaders shared my own convictions. Frederick Greiner of Erie, Postmaster of Buffalo, controlled the next biggest county to my own, and Frederick J. H. Kracke, Naval Officer of the Port of New York, led a large faction in Brooklyn. Their readiness to stand firmly for a clean-up was particularly courageous, since both held Federal offices, which they might lose if Mr. Taft should approve the Old Guard. Few of those I met in Albany were so altruistic, and I came away appreciating more than ever that the President's support might be the one thing which could hold the Republican ranks together.

The afternoon of February 12th, Seventy-second Street between Park and Lexington Avenues was filled with secret service men, detectives, reporters, and photographers. A red carpet and canopy were out in front of my house to welcome the President, the Governor, the Senior Senator from New York, Chauncey Depew, Wadsworth, Woodruff, and Bannard; I had asked them to arrive early, hoping a little private conference would have beneficial results. Everybody greeted everybody else, but that was the limit of cordiality. After the first few moments I knew we were not going to make much headway, because whenever anyone mentioned Allds the President hastily changed the subject.

Downstairs where all the city leaders were waiting, the atmosphere improved at once. Here Mr. Taft was the soul of geniality, shaking hands with one leader and then another, often making some personal comment. "How are you, Mr. Koenig, and how are all your good people on the East Side? I remember well the fine reception they gave me during the campaign." I could see my stock with the Committee shooting up, and this was some consolation for the failure of the main purpose.

My first two weeks as County Chairman had been so occupied with the state business that work had piled up for me. Since both Whittle and Bannard had decided to resign I had to arrange for a new treasurer and a new secretary. According to a rule put through by Parsons, the treasurer could cast thirty-five votes in the Committee which, together with my fifty, in a close issue might prove decisive.

I finally selected Ogden L. Mills, a young lawyer anxious for political experience, on whom I could count absolutely.

The secretary was equally important, because he kept the list of offices to be filled, and looked up the records of applicants. Tristram B. Johnson of the Twenty-fifth suggested John Boyle, another young lawyer. As long as I was in office I had only to say to John, "How about this fellow?" to get a completely trustworthy report.

Distributing the patronage was far more of a responsibility than I had ever imagined; in one year I calculated I was a clearing house for appointments from which the salaries totaled at least a million dollars. Every afternoon about four-thirty I would arrive at the committee rooms to find a waiting group, each with a list of favors. One day a district leader proposed the name of an important member of his organization for an office involving the handling of large sums of money. As usual, I requested his assurance of the man's honesty. He hesitated, squirmed, at last said, "I wish you wouldn't ask me that question."

"I'm sorry, but if you won't guarantee him, how can I have him appointed?"

"You don't understand, Mr. Griscom, what this means to me. If I don't get him the job it will be my political finish."

I was sorry for this man — faced with the alternative of compromising with his conscience or of risking his future. I realized how hard it was for a person to be honest in politics even though he wanted to be. However, on such a question I had to be firm. The leader eventually left in despair, saying, "I hope you can see some way of changing your mind."

A few days later one of our ex-representatives in Congress, who hoped to return to office, called on me, and after some hedging, urged me to recommend this same individual. To him also I put the question, "Will you give me your personal assurance that this man is honest?"

Instead of answering, he told me that, if I granted this favor, I could be County Chairman for life. When I still refused, he burst into tears, declaring he would lose his position, never be elected to office again, and in short would be ruined. It was a very painful interview. Neither of the special pleaders ever forgave me, although actually neither lost his job; without my knowledge a place was found elsewhere for the object of their affections.

I soon discovered I could not confine my political activities to the Committee rooms; they followed me right into the home. Often Elsa and I had a large dinner party at eight, and having been delayed at the office I would turn up at nine in day clothes, tired and unwashed; Elsa was a grand ally, and never complained. Often I brought home a district leader or out-of-town visitor; Elsa entertained and made friends with all of them.

Three or four times a week I had to go out to attend some political gathering or party in my honor, and everywhere I had to deliver a speech — sixty of them in ninety days from the Battery to the Westchester line, one of the greatest physical strains and mental ordeals I ever went through. Almost every district gave a ball, and no court affair demanded more complete regalia; Elsa put on her jewels, and it was white tie, kid gloves, and top hat for me. The first event was the grand march, which I led off with the wife of the leader, and in our wake paraded the local Congressman, the office-holders, the captains, and the prominent Republican guests.

As long as women were present, the entertainment was highly respectable, but sometimes at stag gatherings the joy was somewhat unconfined. During the Bohemian Club vaudeville, the lady comedian began telling more and more suggestive stories, each greeted with louder and louder applause. After a particularly rough anecdote, District Attorney Whitman, who was sitting beside me, leaned over muttering, "My God, I ought to be raiding this place."

Hatchets were buried at these gatherings, and everybody was a jolly good fellow; even Abraham Gruber, leader of my loyal opposition, a criminal lawyer and partner of my old chief, District Attorney W. M. K. Olcott, was my firm friend for one evening. Yet neither he nor the rest ever seemed able to forget I came from a more formal atmosphere. I called all of them by their first names, but very few of them ever called me by mine. It was said I could not be a success as County Chairman because of this, and indeed it was a handicap.

No serious trouble threatened until one of the most important Federal offices, the surveyorship of the Port of New York, suddenly fell open. I had a candidate in General Nelson H. Henry, a man of high standing, who, in my opinion, deserved the eight-thousand-dollar salary. Having secured the approval of Senator Root, who always supported me loyally, I went to Washington to present General Henry's name to the President.

Mr. Taft invited me to lunch, took me for a spin in his White Steamer, and assured me General Henry was already as good as appointed. As we said good-by on the steps of the White House, I repeated, "It's all settled about that surveyorship, isn't it, Mr. President?"

"Yes, Griscom. Here, shake hands on it," and we did.

I thought no more of the matter, except to spread the cheering news to the Committee that we were going to secure our share of the Federal patronage. Some two weeks later a friend, just returned from Washington, entered my office, very much excited. "Do you know what I've heard? The President's decided to appoint as surveyor that Ohio man, Frederick H. Bugher, our acting Police Commissioner."

"I can't believe it. The President promised me."

"I haven't a doubt that when you left he had every intention of appointing your man, but, as you know, with him it's a good deal a question of the last person who sees him."

If the President were really intending to withdraw the Federal patronage, I might as well give up my position as County Chairman. I would have jumped on the first train to Washington if I had not learned the President was on his way to New York. I picked up the telephone and arranged an interview.

The moment I walked in Mr. Taft looked at me sheepishly, "Griscom, don't tell me you've come about that surveyorship."

"Yes, Mr. President, I have."

"Before you say a word, let me explain. Ohio's my home state. My old friend and backer, John R. McLean, owns the *Cincinnati Inquirer,* and is making an absolute issue of getting this office for his nephew. I can't afford to antagonize him."

"Mr. President, of course, if you insist, I'll have to withdraw my suggestion. But the Chairman of New York County should be a man whom you feel you can support. If you have anyone in mind who would suit you I should be glad to use my influence to ensure his election."

"You don't mean you're going to resign?"

"I'll have to. If Bugher is made surveyor the district leaders will take it as a demonstration of your lack of confidence in me."

"You can't do that. Wait till I call up Washington. Bugher's nomination is on my desk, ready to be sent to the Senate tomorrow."

The new instructions were received in time, and eventually General Henry was sworn into office. This incident showed me that the Chief Executive's problems of patronage were more difficult to handle than my own.

Meanwhile public indignation over the Allds scandal was running at high pitch. I was constantly receiving communications from perfect strangers, men active in public life, offering their adherence to any group that would clean things up. The first real test of the anti-Old Guard movement was approaching, the election of the Senate leader in place of Allds. Governor Hughes threw his influence to Harvey L. Hinman, author of the direct primary bill; the Old Guard was for Senator George Henry Cobb.

I went up to Albany to be on hand for the meeting of the Caucus, March 8th. Our little New York group, reinforced by those from Greiner's and Kracke's districts, were prepared to put up a stiff fight, and we hoped enough would join them to elect Hinman. The first ballot showed the Hinmanites had nowhere near enough votes to win; on the other hand the Old Guard did not possess a two-thirds majority. When after five hours of balloting it was apparent the Old Guard had no intention of surrendering, we finally submitted to Cobb's election.

The victors held a celebration that night while Greiner, Kracke, and I sat down to plan our next move. Although the Old Guard had the legislature gripped tight, we felt certain that the voters would turn out and elect Hughes again in the fall. That would be a checkmate more than sufficient to offset this defeat.

Six weeks later I was summoned to Albany by the Governor. He went straight to the point. "The President has offered me Justice Brewer's place on the Supreme Court. I have accepted it."

I was stunned. All the hopes of our group were pinned on Governor Hughes, and now he was deserting us. My dismay must have been evident, for he explained apologetically that he was tired, his health would not stand the strain, the Supreme Court was in the line of his profession which he loved. "I'm very sorry, and I'm very grateful to you and your friends. I'm going to stay on here until October, and I'll do what I can for you."

My political future had been staked in supporting Governor Hughes to the limit, and here I was left high and dry. I broke the news to Greiner and Kracke, who were thoroughly discouraged — we were unorganized and leaderless, with but a few months before the State Convention in August.

The Old Guard was justified in believing we were beaten all along the line, but I still had the firm conviction we were on the right side and the public would back us. I gathered our group for a council of war. It so happened that the Twenty-ninth District was holding a monster banquet of fourteen hundred guests in my honor May 2nd. We transformed it into a declaration of war. Parsons came up from Washington, Hinman came down from Albany, Bannard, Mr. Choate, and Attorney General George Wickersham also appeared, and one and all we warned the Old Guard that there was no man so great that he could not be replaced, and served notice that we had just begun to fight.

For the moment our chief hope was that Governor Hughes would succeed in getting his direct primary bill passed. All sorts of conferences were called in the effort to formulate amendments which would please everybody, and throughout the spring Governor Hughes kept the legislature in session. The more they argued the question the more they disagreed.

Towards the end of May, with no sign yet of a break in the deadlock, I decided on another attempt to persuade the President to commit himself. He replied to my letter at length, the sum and substance being that, like Sir Roger de Coverley, who would not give his judgment rashly, he thought "much might be said on both sides." However, he was willing to discuss it further, and Greiner and Kracke went to Washington to present our point of view; Bill Ward and Vice President James Sherman, an Old Guard stalwart from Utica, upheld the opposition.

While the outcome was still in doubt, the eyes of the politicians were drawn Eastward where, looming closer and closer on the horizon, was the return of the ex-President. Everyone was speculating as to what he would do, and particularly what his relations would be with Mr. Taft. Many of us believed he should retire to

Oyster Bay and, as the Sage of Sagamore Hill, exert his influence in public affairs rarely, and only on matters of great import. Above all things he should avoid mingling in party politics, which might possibly lead to humiliation and a diminution in his world-wide reputation.

The politicians were uneasy, but the people of the country from one end to the other rejoiced; they loved Theodore Roosevelt as they have loved no other American in our time. Headlines in every paper in the United States swelled the chorus of welcome. "Teddy's Coming Home! Teddy's Coming Home! Teddy's Coming Home!"

CHAPTER XXVII

THE OLD GUARD NEVER SURRENDERS

Flags and bunting decorated Fifth Avenue and Broadway the morning of June 18th, 1910. Bandsmen were assembling here and there, crowds were already gathering, policemen were putting up ropes. The harbor was alive with every kind of craft that could float as the city tender, carrying the party to welcome Mr. Roosevelt, steamed out to meet the *Kaiserin Augusta Victoria*. Before we drew alongside the German liner, we could see the ex-President leaning over the rail, beaming and waving.

Among the members of the Committee I had found Nick Longworth, now Alice Roosevelt's husband, who had agreed with me it would be unfortunate for the Colonel to make any political pronouncement. Thanks to his family position, we led the rush on board, and closed in on Mr. Roosevelt, each of us whispering, "Don't, for heaven's sake, say anything about politics."

He laughed heartily, "You needn't worry. I'll be good," and immediately he was inundated by a flood of reporters, snapping photographs and firing questions.

In a few moments the Colonel extricated himself from the mob, and preceded us to the deck of the revenue cutter *Androscoggin*. A lane was opened between two lines of ships, which dipped their colors at our passage, and followed in our wake. Cheers rent the air as the Colonel stepped ashore at the Battery, cheers as he spoke briefly from the platform, cheers as he sprang into an automobile and started up Broadway behind a company of Rough Riders in their old uniforms.

It was growing hotter and hotter, but the Colonel did not seem to mind; he was smiling and bowing and tipping his hat. Every hundred feet or so a band blared above the tumult at his approach; some had come all the way from Houston and Los Angeles. A million people had shouted themselves hoarse by the time he reached Fifty-ninth Street. In the Plaza the Rough Riders wheeled about, Colonel Alexander Brodie in front. Mr. Roosevelt leaped to the ground and hurried over to them, "Oh, this is great. This is what I like. These are my boys. Brodie, how are you? How's everybody?"

At the end of the demonstration the ex-President departed for Oyster Bay, apparently ready to settle down to a peaceful life. Nevertheless, I was still afraid he would be deflected from this goal, as Atalanta was from hers, by tempting apples constantly being strewn in his path. The first was going to be dropped in front of him in only a few days; as President of the Alumni Association of Harvard University he was to attend Commencement, June 29th, at which Mr. Hughes was to be given an honorary degree. This would offer an unparalleled opportunity for the Governor to enlist Mr. Roosevelt's support for his direct primary bill, shortly to be voted on. Since I had received a letter from Mr. Taft, announcing his decision not to take any part in New York state politics, I decided another word of warning to the ex-President was indicated. If he were in the fight and the President out of it, people might begin to query, "Who is the head of the Republican Party?"

To reach Sagamore Hill was a simple matter for me, because Elsa and I were spending the summer at Verna, her old home at Fairfield, Connecticut, not far from the Stamford ferry across Long Island Sound to Oyster Bay. From the Roosevelts' entrance the drive wound a half mile between trees and shrubbery up to a plain shingled frame house, with a large porch around two sides. I found the Colonel in an enormous living room, in which each inch of space was occupied by the spoils of his active life: lion- and bearskins on the floor, heads on the wall, hideous porcelains presented by the German Emperor in a corner, and everywhere else the most extraordinary assortment of other gifts.

"Quite a change from the last time I saw you, Lloyd," he greeted me. "How about taking your mind off politics with a little tennis?"

Knowing Mr. Roosevelt's attachment to the game, I had come prepared, and in a few moments the balls were whizzing back and forth. The Colonel had never learned a real stroke; charging the ball fiercely with teeth gritted, he slammed it at me and we were soon wringing wet. After a hard second set, he laid down his racket, shouted for candidates to go swimming, and the whole family flocked to the beach; they were all water rats.

Sagamore Hill furnished a perfect outlet for the ex-President's unbounded energy; he could chop and dig and bustle to his heart's content. During these activities he was constantly getting injured. Mrs. Cowles told me that once, while she was sitting with her sister-in-law on the veranda, her brother suddenly rounded the corner, blood streaming over his face. She gave an exclamation and jumped to her feet, but all Mrs. Roosevelt did was to admonish calmly, "Theodore, do go somewhere else and stop dripping on the porch." Then, quite undisturbed, she went to fetch bandages and antiseptics. The Colonel, entirely indifferent to pain, was still grinning and displaying his teeth; like a small boy, he wanted to show off what a good wound he had. Climbing to the top of the windmill to see the view, he had inadvertently started the machinery and a vane of the fan had caught him on the side of the head.

If Mrs. Roosevelt had been at all excitable, she could never have survived life with Theodore more than a month, especially when the fancy seized him to go lion hunting or discovering Rivers of Doubt in South America.

Mr. Roosevelt's enemies were always setting stories in circulation to prove that he used his physical prowess and love of outdoors to build up his own popularity. On one week end he was to confer with a delegation of politicians at a certain hour. They were directed to the barn, but apparently arrived before they were expected, because they claimed to have found the Colonel standing in the middle of the barn floor, fork in hand, calling to the farm hands in the mow: "I think you've thrown down enough hay for me to pitch up today." He used to be much amused by these apocryphal tales.

During lunch I introduced the subject of politics, and the Colonel again pooh-poohed any idea of his becoming involved. Purposely, therefore, I avoided elaborating on our direct primary fight. However, I did take the precaution of telling Chadbourne, who was also going to Cambridge, to keep a weather eye cocked and warn me if anything happened.

The next thing I knew came a telegram from Cambridge, June 29th, signed "Theodore Roosevelt": —

During the last week great numbers of Republicans and of independent voters from all over the state have written me urging the passage of direct primary legislation. I have seen Governor Hughes and have learned your views from your representative. It seems to me that the Cobb Bill with the amendments proposed by you meets the needs of the situation. I believe the people demand it. I most earnestly hope that it will be enacted into law.

My worst fears were realized. If I did not publish this telegram, I knew the Colonel would rush it into print himself with big-stick words. I summoned the newspapermen, and without comment handed them copies of the telegram. The ex-President had stayed in retirement only ten days.

Directly after Commencement Governor Hughes, having brought off his coup, returned to Albany for the vote on the direct primary bill, and I went up from New York to bolster our forces. On entering the capacious Speaker's room back of the platform of the Assembly, I was greeted by a cheery "Hello!" from Jim Wadsworth, who was busily lining up his adherents and was well aware of my errand. Pointing to some chairs across from him under a window, he remarked genially, "You'll need headquarters. Why not stay here?" There, on opposite sides of the same room, we each interviewed our supporters, and occasionally he would stroll over to ask good-naturedly how I was getting on; our difference in political opinion never made any difference in our personal friendship.

Even with the Roosevelt sanction, we did not have the ghost of a show. When the vote was taken in the Senate, we lost, twenty-five to nineteen. Barnes, who had a score to settle, announced gleefully, "Teddy is licked to a frazzle. We no longer worship the gods, we laugh at them."

With the coming of summer, all attention was focused on the fall election. If the liberal element were to gain control of the State Convention, which was to meet at Saratoga at the end of September, we must in some way rescue the temporary chairmanship for one of our own members. This office was more important than it sounded, because the holder named the Committee on Credentials, which could seat and unseat delegates, and gave the keynote address outlining Party policy. Ordinarily, the Convention accepted as a matter of course the candidate selected by the State Committee.

Since Mr. Roosevelt was evidently not going to be the Sage of Oyster Bay, and was actually one of the Nassau County delegates to the Convention, I decided he was the man to be temporary chairman. He consented to let me put up his name, and in the course of our ensuing discussion, I had another idea which I submitted to him. "Of course, nobody really wants to split the Party. If you could get together with some of the Old Guard, you might work out a compromise." To this also he agreed.

Three days before the next meeting of the State Committee, I arrived at Beverly on the North Shore of Massachusetts, where Mr. Taft was spending the summer. A word from him might go far towards securing the co-operation of the "boys." Mr. Taft, who was for Party unity at any price, heartily approved the suggestion I had made to the Colonel, and the evening of August 13th he drafted a telegram to Vice President Sherman, urging him to save the situation in New York State by persuading Ward and Woodruff to have a conference with Mr. Roosevelt.

After the Harvard Commencement, Senator Lodge had taken Mr. Roosevelt to Beverly, in the vain hope that the coolness between President and ex-President might be dispelled by an informal chat. Now, Mr. Taft seemed so friendly towards "Theodore," and so pained that "Theodore" felt slighted — that had never been his intent — that I proposed a second meeting. He said that as President he could not make the first move; if I could bring it about in a natural way, he would like nothing better.

I reached home Monday, the night of the 14th, to be greeted with the startling news that the Old Guard had just held a powwow at Sherry's. Somehow they had got wind of my plan to put forward Mr. Roosevelt. To turn the tables on me, they had determined to nominate a temporary chairman the very next day, and their candidate was no less a person than Vice President Sherman. Not only were they disregarding the President's recommendation for a conference with Mr. Roosevelt, but they also aimed to head off any chance of his taking an active part in the campaign. In a few minutes I had the Colonel on the other end of the telephone, and the receiver almost jumped from my hand at his burst of rage. "Lloyd, what are you going to do?"

"Get up tomorrow and nominate you, and say if you're not chosen,

I'll carry the fight to the floor of the Convention and let the delegates do the deciding."

"Bully for you. Go ahead. I'm with you."

The next afternoon I ran into Jim Wadsworth outside the State Committee rooms near the Public Library. "Hello, Jim, I hear the temporary chairmanship's on the carpet today."

"Yes, Lloyd, and it's all settled. Sherman's the man."

When I entered, there was a shuffling of feet and a nodding of heads. Soon I noticed old Ward whispering to one member and then another; and presently someone whispered to me, "Ward's telling everyone he's just talked on the telephone to the President, and the President says he wants Sherman chosen."

At this moment the meeting was called to order, and Barnes immediately sprang up. "I nominate James S. Sherman for temporary chairman."

Before the words were out of his mouth, I was on my feet. "I move to substitute the name of Theodore Roosevelt."

Although outraged by the chicanery of the Old Guard, I was helpless. Having had no time to organize a counterattack, I could only sit and hope that the Colonel's name would be more powerful than the fear of losing Federal patronage. Ward's whisper had done its work. We were beaten twenty to fifteen. The press played up the incident as if President Taft had deliberately attempted to deprive Mr. Roosevelt of the temporary chairmanship.

In as strong language as I could use to the Chief Executive, I telegraphed the President, stating what had happened, and urging him to make clear at once where he stood in this conflict for clean government in New York State. In reply, he repudiated any conversation with Ward, and asserted he had had no idea that Sherman's name was to be presented until he had read it in the newspapers.

The Old Guard did not care what anybody said. We had been put in our place, and they went home to their districts and forgot about us. Nevertheless, we had not yet been beaten in a fair fight; to discuss our future strategy I journeyed once more to Sagamore Hill. The Colonel was on the eve of leaving for a Western trip during which he intended to deliver several speeches, and, like everybody else, I had been wondering whether there was anything behind all the talk of a third term now beginning to circulate. If he had in the back of his head any notion of running in 1912, or even in 1916, I wanted to resign my chairmanship immediately so that I could be on his side. As long as I continued to receive favors from Mr. Taft, I would be bound to support him for renomination.

I opened the conversation with Mr. Roosevelt by asking directly, "What about this third term?"

"Lloyd," he announced categorically, "I haven't the slightest intention of being a candidate again. Dismiss it from your mind."

"In that case," I said, "for the sake of Republican unity, would you object to my arranging a meeting between you and Mr. Taft on your return? He's more than willing."

The Colonel assented rather skeptically, adding, "If I do this, I'm pretty sure he'll use it somehow to convince the public I'm going out of my way to try to make friends with him."

With the convention about six weeks away, we buckled down in earnest. For some time I had been on the lookout for a gubernatorial candidate who would have a strong public appeal, and yet not be in the Old Guard's bad graces. One day I was lunching with Parsons at the Downtown Association, and seated only two tables distant was Henry L. Stimson, then United States Attorney for the Southern District of New York, and a law partner of Elihu Root. He had recently secured a conviction against the sugar trust, and had helped send Charles W. Morse to prison for misusing the funds of the National Bank of North America.

On the spur of the moment I asked Parsons, "How about Harry Stimson for Governor?" Parsons put his napkin on the table, pushed back his chair, and said, "That's your job, not mine." However, he warned me: "No matter whom you pick, be ready to take charge from the instant you arrive at Saratoga. Most of the delegates don't know whom they're going to vote for. The fellow who comes with his guns loaded is the fellow who's likely to win."

I consulted both Mr. Root and the ex-President; both refused to decide for me, asserting it was my responsibility. The more I thought about it, the more I thought Stimson would fill the bill. When I broached the subject to him, he said he was willing to make a try.

Next I set to work to raise money, build an organization, compose literature urging citizens to help clean up the state by having their delegates vote for Roosevelt. In order to leave no time for the Old

Guard to get its steamroller in motion, we waited until August 30th to launch our campaign. Then groups of young men went out with our pamphlets on a' house-to-house canvass of the state. One thoroughgoing enthusiast rang Sherman's own doorbell in Utica, and handed in a complete assortment of denunciations.

We wanted especially to reach the small towns, and someone suggested the local newspapers, which were read from cover to cover by every inhabitant. We persuaded a firm that supplied them with boiler plate to accept well-written articles on the need for good government, if we paid the expense. Our boiler-plate articles were successful beyond our anticipations. A number of editors shifted to our side — valuable conversions, because editors were nearly always delegates to the conventions.

Every resolution had to be planned and given a mover and a seconder. Honors had to be divided so that not a single friendly county should be omitted, and no religious or racial groups go unrepresented. We made out typewritten slips, "Mr. X of Erie County will move so and so," "Mr. Y of Dutchess County will second," "Mr. M of Otsego County will head the committee to bring Mr. Roosevelt to the chair." There were dozens of these; even a motion to adjourn had to have a mover and a seconder.

I had not forgotten that I was to arrange for a Taft-Roosevelt meeting. Learning that the President was to pass through New Haven September 19th, soon after the ex-President was expected back from the West, I had Bannard, Mr. Taft's old friend and classmate at Yale, ask President Hadley to give a luncheon. Earl Dodge, my secretary in Italy, who owned one of the fastest speed boats on the Sound, agreed to transport the Colonel from Oyster Bay to the Black Rock Club near Bridgeport, where I would pick him up and take him in my car to New Haven.

The wind was blowing a gale when I reached the Club, and the Sound, usually so placid, was standing on end with no boat in sight. I had my watch in my hand, counting the minutes; it looked as though we would never make it. Just as I had almost abandoned hope, I caught sight of a tiny speck bobbing up and down, breaking through the spray, and soon Dodge and Mr. Roosevelt, a soaked and bedraggled pair, scrambled on to the pier. The Colonel shook himself. "Well, we almost didn't get here, but here we are. Never saw the

Sound rougher in my life." I hustled him into my car, the police sirens shrieked, and we tore up the Post Road as rapidly as we could travel.

The President had already arrived. Greeting each other in the friendliest manner, the two went into a huddle alone in the corner of the room, while Bannard, President Hadley and I sat with our fingers crossed. At lunch the conversation became general, and there was no way of guessing how much ice had been melted. I was on tenterhooks until the President's train had to leave, and the instant the Colonel and I started back, I asked, "How did it go?"

"I did my best. We'll have to wait and see."

To my horror, on opening my paper the next morning, I found the official report of the meeting given out from Mr. Taft's car implied the very thing against which Mr. Roosevelt had warned me — that it was he who had gone out of his way to make up with Mr. Taft and solicit the President's aid in the New York State fight. "What did I tell you?" boomed the Colonel over the telephone.

The President denied he had ever authorized any such statement, but the damage had been done. Mr. Roosevelt had been publicly snubbed, and I felt it was my fault.

A few days later I registered at the vast wooden barn of a hotel which served as Convention headquarters in Saratoga. It was so crowded that no sitting room was to be had, and my room was adopted as the gathering place for our supporters. My bed was behind a sort of glass partition in one corner, but I had little opportunity to sleep, because towards midnight, when I thought I could no longer keep my eyes open, leaders and delegates piled in ready to go to work.

We all turned out for a great victory parade to welcome the Nassau County delegation. Flourishing his Western sombrero, Mr. Roosevelt bounded to the platform, the band struck up, the crowd cheered, and down the street we marched with the Colonel at our head, waving his hand right and left.

The next morning the Convention Hall was perfect bedlam. Hundreds were milling outside, the aisles were flooded, and every seat filled. In addition to the thousand or so delegates, there was room for five thousand spectators, but it looked to me as though twice that number were trying to get in.

The ex-President's appearance was the signal for an ovation —

people on their feet, standing on chairs, stamping, yelling, clapping, whistling. At noon Woodruff, who was attempting to preside, began pounding away with his gavel, but no one paid the least attention. In desperation he commanded the lone member of Saratoga's police force to oust every spectator who was in a delegate's seat. The efficient officer at once spotted the center of commotion, stalked down the aisle to where Mr. Roosevelt was sitting, and inquired whether he was a delegate. "Tell Roosevelt to use his Big Stick," howled the crowd.

Half an hour passed before enough order could be obtained to allow the Chaplain to invoke a blessing on "this assembly which is gathered to take sweet counsel together." Even the bitterest partisans had to smile.

Woodruff announced "The next order of business is the election of the temporary chairman." While he and the seconder were stating the reasons for nominating Vice President Sherman, it was as though a muffler had been clapped on the multitude. The second they finished, Congressman Hicks, the venerable Quaker from Nassau County, put in nomination the name of Theodore Roosevelt; his voice was drowned in a furore of enthusiasm from the crowd, and a triumphal fanfare from the band. The tumult and shouting went on and on.

Speakers clamored to be recognized, and Woodruff selected Abe Gruber, famous for his oratory, to do his bit for the Old Guard. Looking like a fat robin in the tight frock coat he always wore, he rose, only to be greeted with hisses, and interrupted constantly by cries of "Cut it out! Get the hook!" Mr. Roosevelt sprang up, "I bespeak a fair hearing for Colonel Gruber." But poor little Gruber eventually had to sit down; nobody had any idea of what he had said.

At two o'clock the rollcall was finally announced, and all over the hall leaders were polling their delegations. "Albany County." Barnes's big voice resounded: "Albany County casts —— votes for Sherman." Every delegate knew how many were necessary to win, and had his pencil out totting up the score as county after county put itself on record. Whenever a doubtful one was added to the Roosevelt column, our partisans roared their approval. "Schenectady County," "Schoharie," and now "Schuyler." You could have heard a pin drop, because, if it went for us, we had won. The second its leader pronounced the name "Roosevelt," the lid was off, and no attempt was made to put it back. The final tally was 567–443.

Escorted by our Committee, the Colonel swung up the aisle, mounted the platform, accepted the gavel from Woodruff, banged for order, and his voice pealed through the hall: —

"The men who by trickery keep control of the State Committee, and who now come here in an effort to dominate the Convention, are the very men who were responsible for the corruption which produced Allds, and for all that has been discreditable in the Party management."

Victory was very sweet. That night the hotel re-echoed with our rejoicings. In the general jubilee, the only discordant note was the remark of an upstate leader to me: "The boys have washed their hands of this Convention. They don't care a hoot who you nominate. They're sitting back and waiting for election day to get even."

"You mean they'll cut the ticket?"

"Exactly."

As far as the Convention was concerned, this was true. The fireworks were over, and the next day we made Senator Root permanent chairman, and wrote direct primaries into the platform. That night my room seethed with county leaders and their henchmen who had candidates they wanted on the ticket. I kept retiring behind my glass partition for a cat nap, but each time somebody hauled me out. Not until four in the morning was the last fight settled from sheer weariness, and everyone stumbled off for a few hours' rest.

At the closing session speeches were delivered by the candidates' friends, the platform adopted, and we all went home. The defeat of the Old Guard seemed clinched at the deposition of Woodruff from his chairmanship of the State Committee in favor of Ezra Prentice.

We felt no doubt about winning the election, especially after the Democrats put up a weak candidate, John A. Dix. Confidently we proceeded with plans for Stimson's speaking tour; even if the Old Guard did cut the ticket, we expected his great charm would more than counteract their defection. His first words from the platform sent my heart to the bottom of my boots. He was neither an experienced stump speaker nor a handshaker; without intending to, he produced a chilling effect on the Party workers who got up his meetings. I realized that he was a perfect example of the intellectual type who would make a fine governor, but would be most difficult to elect.

We were losing ground every day, and I believed only one person could reverse the trend — Mr. Roosevelt. I asked whether he would help. "You bet I will," he answered.

The Colonel's whirlwind tour of the state was to end by his speaking nine times in New York City on election eve. I arranged the meetings, procured a motor cycle escort, and, holding in my hand a schedule made out to the minute, took aboard Mr. Roosevelt, and the marathon was on. Tooting police horns cleared the streets for us, brakes screeched as we pulled up in front of a hall. We dashed through a side door on to the platform; at sight of the Colonel the crowd yelled madly, and the speaker stopped in the middle of a sentence to give him the floor.

The Colonel raised his hand for silence; in a few seconds, with a joke or anecdote, he had the audience with him. He declaimed, gesticulated, pounded his fist, hammered in his points, apparently so wound up that he would go on for hours. Sitting beside him, I kept my eye on my watch, and in ten minutes began pulling his coat-tail. He looked around, "Just one word more I must say . . ." but after the one word had expanded into dozens and hundreds, I literally had to drag him off the stage backwards, shouting and waving his arms as he disappeared in the wings amid cheers. He never showed fatigue, never repeated the same speech twice, and at the end of the evening was ready for more.

This grand finale bolstered our hopes throughout election day. We still thought we had a chance while we waited for returns that evening at the State Committee rooms. At first Stimson and Dix seemed to be running neck and neck, and then gradually the latter edged ahead. Glumly we tried to console ourselves with the thought that, if the campaign had lasted a few more days, we should have won. As it was, we lost by only fifty thousand votes.

I had learned a lesson. Granted that the moral tone of politics was improving, the voters would never raise a hand merely for the principle of pure politics; they needed an issue which affected their daily lives if they were to be lifted out of themselves. A leader with ideals and principles might arise, who for a time carried everything before him; yet inevitably a day came when he stepped from the

picture, or the fickle populace turned away. The only permanent factor
was the organization; a member here and there might drop out, but
the machine went on forever. If you wanted to reform politics,
you had to reform the organization.

The Old Guard took up the reins again. January 23rd at the
State Committee meeting they moved to make Barnes chairman.
There was no question of our preventing his election; the issue was
whether, for Party unity, it should be unanimous. I realized we had
fought and lost, and now we ought to support the winner. I made
the motion, and the Old Guard gave us a spontaneous cheer.

Our efforts had not been in vain. The Liberal Republican movement had received a tremendous fillip. It attracted many clean and
hard-working young men, and after the Allds scandal the Black
Horse Cavalry never again closed its ranks.

All fall I had been struggling against splitting headaches and
other after-effects of my Brazilian *cercomonas*. When Dr. Chace
ordered an operation which would remove me from active life for
many months, I decided it would be best to resign the chairmanship,
so that New York County might have a leader who could make a
fresh start. I advised the Nominating Committee to choose Sam
Koenig, a fighter with political ability and few enemies, and always
a loyal supporter of Parsons and our group.

During the spring and summer of 1911 I recuperated at Verna,
seeing Mr. Roosevelt occasionally, and watching with interest the
events leading towards the great schism. I did not think he intended
to come out for a third term until the seven Progressive governors
appealed to him in February, 1912, saying: "You got us into politics,
and those men who stand for everything we're struggling against
have the President's ear. You must not desert us." That was the
kind of cry Mr. Roosevelt could not leave unheeded. He never let
his following down. "All right," he said, "my hat's in the ring."

Almost as a matter of course, a recently retired County Chairman
was made a delegate to a National Convention, and I accompanied
our enormous contingent under Barnes and Parsons to that cheerless
affair of 1912 at Chicago. Although all my personal loyalty and
admiration was for Mr. Roosevelt, I still had my debt to pay to the
President. It was our delegation which stood firm and prevented a
Roosevelt stampede. Then the Convention did its duty and nominated

Mr. Taft; the Republican Party had to choose him as their candidate, or else admit publicly that he had been a failure. After all was over, I went to find Elihu Root, the temporary chairman, who, having decided he could not wreck the Party, had been responsible for unseating the Roosevelt delegations. He was alone in his room. Neither of us had anything to say, and we just sat there in dismal silence.

Most discouraging was the fear that I might have lost Mr. Roosevelt's friendship, and it was a relief to hear him declare at our next meeting: "It's quite all right. I understand why you had to do it. But as for Elihu Root, I feel very differently."

I could not follow the Colonel in the Bull Moose crusade; on the other hand I could not fight against him, and withdrew from politics completely. Bronson Winthrop put into words what we were all thinking: "The bad part of politics is that it hurts too much when you are beaten."

The next two years were the quietest I had ever spent in my life — winters in New York, summers at Verna. In the fall of 1912, Father died. He had always been the head of the family and his going seemed a milestone causing us to realize more than ever that we wanted to build a house of our own and settle permanently among our friends. Beautiful as Fairfield was, I did not relish the five hours a day spent in commuting, and the mosquitoes were beyond description — Bronson was fairly eaten to pieces.

In Syosset, Long Island, Bronson Winthrop helped us find a site on a rise of land looking along the hills of the North Shore, and there, during the winter of 1913–1914, William Delano built us a house. Little Bronson clamored to go with me each day to view progress; he knew every workman, and kept track of every nail. As soon as the frame was up, he would climb to the top, perch there, and carry on an animated conversation with the carpenters.

Elsa was not well enough to come with us; our son Lloyd was born February 5th, 1914. In the spring we moved to Huntover, but she had only a few weeks there before being operated on for a serious illness. The following eight months were tragic and hopeless; in November she died.

I felt completely bereft. Elsa and I had shared so many unusual adventures in so many parts of the globe; she had always been ready to laugh when things had gone wrong or back me up when I needed support. Tributes and sympathy flooded in from all over the world.

For the rest of the winter I took the children to stay with my mother at Horseshoe Plantation in Florida. Augustus met us at Thomasville, Georgia, and we set out towards Tallahassee along a narrow red dirt lane, arched over by spreading live oaks, heavy with Spanish moss. At every hollow we had to ford a slue, almost impassable after a rain; there were no bridges. It seemed a long twenty miles between woods and fields and lakes before we arrived at the horseshoe-shaped house which stood above Lake Iamonia.

In those days the shooting was fabulous. Pansy and I would get up early in the morning and be on the water at daybreak for the first flight of ducks; fifty thousand used to winter there — canvasbacks, mallards, and vast flocks of the little black ringnecks from the Mississippi Delta. Later in the day in the warm sun we went after quail in the shooting wagon, high-wheeled so as to clear the brush. Over the fields and through the woods we jounced, setters and pointers whimpering in the cage behind, eager to be with the two others ranging ahead. Giles, who knew where every covey ought to be, rode in front, calling "Close Lad!" "Get on, Mike!" — and then at the word "Point!" we scrambled out. The birds burst from the broom-straw like an exploding bomb; it was a test of skill to bring one down as they dipped and swerved in their whirring flight. Sometimes we put up as many as thirty coveys; now, fifteen is very good.

In the spring I returned North to find that the European War overshadowed every other topic of conversation. From the first there had been no doubt as to where my sympathies lay. I continued with the law, hoping the moment would come soon when America would join the Allies.

CHAPTER XXVIII

NO PROBABLE POSSIBLE SHADOW OF DOUBT

One fall day of 1915 I had a message from Paul Cravath, the head of a leading New York law firm, requesting me to meet him at the Piping Rock Club. Wondering whether this were to be business or pleasure, I drove over from Syosset to Locust Valley through the narrow lanes, brightened with autumn red and yellow. I found Cravath already there, a dominating figure, huge in build, who looked not only important but wise.

"How would you like to go to England?" he asked.

"What do you mean?"

"I've a very ticklish case just in your line — international law and diplomacy."

"That sounds interesting."

"Well, it is. One of my clients, the Chicago packing house company of Sulzberger and Sons, is trying to settle its claim against the British Government for seizure of its products on the high seas. But there are a lot of complications." And he went on to describe them.

Since the preceding November, about fifty cargoes containing packers' products had been condemned by British prize courts on the ground that, although consigned to neutral countries, they were really destined to feed Germany, and were therefore contraband. The total sum involved amounted to some twenty million dollars, the largest case in international law with the exception of the *Alabama* claims paid by England after the Civil War.

The packers had promptly appealed to the British Privy Council. The four law lords, who comprised the judicial branch of this body, were high-minded and impartial, comparable to our Supreme Court justices; they might easily set aside the decisions of the prize court, admittedly partisan, and decree that the meat products must be paid for. This would set a precedent most awkward for the British Government, because it might invalidate other seizures and force them to pay out millions of pounds for similar claims. To preclude such a possibility they could interpose so many delays before the case was tried that the parties concerned might be dead or the companies in bankruptcy; the *Alabama* claims had taken eight years to arbitrate.

Compromise was infinitely better than a remedy that came too late, and some months previously the Sulzbergers had joined with Armour, Swift, Hammond, and Morris in seeking a settlement out of court. The attempt had failed, and the other packers put the blame on the inclusion of the Sulzberger claims; the nominal head of that company was known as an ardent pro-German. They now had decided to act on their own, and had engaged as counsel Chandler P. Anderson, an experienced international lawyer, who had formerly been legal adviser to the State Department, and also to the Embassy in London. The Sulzbergers, left out in the cold, had hastened to retain Cravath.

"You won't find it easy to represent a house with a German name in England, but no one is available in our firm. Will you go?"

I went home to think it over — the mission might be not only difficult but even disagreeable. The British were certain to regard the Sulzbergers as Germans, and anybody who tried to make them pay money to their enemy was likely to be considered an enemy himself. Paradoxically enough, however, by paying an enemy, they would be gaining us as a friend. Their high-handed seizures of our cargoes had created almost as much enmity as the sinking of our ships by Germany. The beef case had been the main cause of a series of bitter diplomatic notes addressed by the United States to England. Settling the case would really contribute to more cordial Anglo-American relations. I accepted Cravath's offer.

When I arrived to collect the data at the Sulzberger offices on First Avenue, I realized I was right in the slaughterhouse; the first whiff of my case almost knocked me down. I could hardly pay attention while the officials, totally unaware that anything was wrong with the atmosphere, routed out boxes and boxes of documents, bound in huge files, classified according to items, destinations, prices, dates. As soon as possible I beat a hasty retreat, wondering how anyone could work in such a nauseating stench.

I knew I was not going to win my case simply by brushing the dust off this truckload of documents. If I tried to present my small claim separately, I should have little hope of attention. Somehow or other I had to get my clients readmitted to the fold.

Essentially, all the packers' cases were identical. The Sulzbergers, whatever their origin or sympathies, were American citizens operating an American company under the neutral American flag. If the State Department would declare that the question of principle would not be decided until the claims of every single packer were satisfied, then my clients could not be disregarded.

The affairs of the packers were under the watchful eye of Frank L. Polk, counselor for the Department of State, whom I had known when he was a young lawyer in New York. Once more I walked up the steps of the State Department, sought him out, and told him what I was about to do. "Can you see any reason for distinguishing between these cases?"

"No," he replied. "Only the settlement of all will remove the bone of contention."

Since the other packers could now gain nothing by acting alone, I went to see Anderson, who was also in Washington. He agreed we should present a united front, and we began discussing ways and means. It occurred to me that we should have difficulty securing favorable terms as long as British officials could go through all our papers and read all our communications. Supposing negotiations reached a point where we could cable, "We're offered twelve million dollars. Shall we accept?" If the answer came back, "Take it if you have to, but try for fourteen," clearly the British Government would be bright enough not to give us the fourteen.

Polk volunteered to help us out of our dilemma. We might store our confidential documents in the safes of the London Embassy. Also messages to our clients could be transmitted in code to the State Department, which would deliver them after censorship. A cable was immediately drafted to Ambassador Page, ending with the request that he extend "every unofficial assistance."

Thus having prepared the ground when we reached England, I thought it would save time and trouble in getting my papers past the port authorities if the British Ambassador, Sir Cecil Spring Rice, would drop them a word. Accordingly, I called on him. At the first mention of Sulzberger, he seemed to shudder. I had expected at least the courtesy of our profession, but to my astonishment met a wall of impenetrable frigidity. Facilities for me were out of the question. My errand was equivalent to aiding the enemy. He could not understand why Americans were not at that very moment in the trenches, shoulder to shoulder with his countrymen — not realizing how much it might help to get them there if the Sulzberger thorn were extracted from the side of Anglo-American relations. Spring Rice appeared to be a very tired and exhausted old man, quite changed from the warm-hearted, quick-witted young secretary I had known years before.

Having pulled all the strings I could in Washington, I went back to New York to put my case in order. The Sulzbergers sent from Chicago as my assistant a serious-minded young lawyer named Brown, a specialist in international law, who was familiar with the material. He called my attention to sheaves and sheaves of invoices. "These cover shipments of casings. What possible good can they do the enemy?"

"What are casings?" I asked curiously.

"Sheep or pig gut used for sausage skins, violin strings, and medical purposes. You can't digest them, and I don't see how they can be utilized for anything connected with war."

I consulted a chemist, who confirmed Brown's statement that casings were utterly without food value; obviously, therefore, here was one item which the British could not claim as contraband and object to paying for.

After the loss of the *Lusitania* and the *Arabic,* everybody had been nervous about crossing the Atlantic. Even though Germany had promised not to sink any more passenger ships without warning, Anderson and I equipped ourselves with Gieve's waistcoats, made of rubber with cloth outside. The instant you were torpedoed, you pulled out a little pipe, and blew and blew until you had blown a life preserver around yourself, quite safe and warm — unless you had a puncture.

I spent Christmas with Bronson and Lloyd, and three days later met Anderson and Brown at the Holland-Amerika Line pier. *Rotterdam* was splashed in great red letters along the side of our vessel; they were lit up at night by bright lights so that no mistake might be made. Photographers and reporters were all over the place:

Colonel Edward M. House was also sailing on some sort of mission; as the President's *alter ego* whatever he did was news. Cameras were flashing until the moment we backed into the river.

On the voyage I saw a good deal of Colonel House, a thin wisp of a man, so fragile that you would think he would blow away. He spoke in a voice that was scarcely audible, yet you could not help listening to him. In all my experience no one ever gave me more the impression of being what you might call in simple terms a "wise man." One of his friends told me that in early days the word had gradually spread in Houston that whoever wanted advice should consult Colonel House. His home each morning had been like a doctor's reception room, filled with "patients" waiting to ask guidance on every kind of subject. Soon city, state, and even national politicians had begun to confer with him; now he was an international figure.

In the course of his projected tour of the belligerent capitals, Colonel House was planning in England to talk with Sir Edward Grey, the Foreign Secretary, and Lord Reading, the Chief Justice, two people who would have profound influence in my case. He grasped instantly how important the settlement of this quarrel was, and promised to speak a word for me if I needed it.

Outside Falmouth a navy patrol boat met us, and guided us zigzagging through the mines into the harbor. British intelligence officers clambered on board; we alien goats were separated from the British sheep and stood waiting for officials to make up their minds about us.

Only after a thorough investigation were we released.

Arriving in London, even in the gloom of January, had always had something of the cheerful excitement of arriving home. This time I was struck by the air of depression. Somber-faced, set-jawed soldiers were drilling in every vacant square. They were even tramping to and fro in Green Park, right under my window at the Ritz. Warnings were posted in the room to draw curtains tight after dark that not a flicker of light could escape; anyone who left his shade up as much as a slit would be fined a pound.

While I was unpacking, I heard a knock on my door, and who should walk in but Gerald Fitzmaurice. Just as though thirteen years had not passed since we had said good-by at the gates of

Isfahan, he remarked with that queer cynical smile of his, "Well, here we meet again. It's a long way from Persia, isn't it?"

"Where the devil did you come from, and how did you know I was here?"

He threw back his head and laughed. "That's the business of the Intelligence Service, to keep track of suspicious strangers like you."

Fitzmaurice and I went on to talk about old days in Turkey. Naturally he had had to leave at the beginning of the war, but a well-organized secret service had remained. Some months afterwards a King's Messenger had been traveling to England with reports from Constantinople, when an Austrian submarine had blown up his ship. He had failed to attach the usual weight to his pouch, and it had been fished out of the ocean. Within two weeks every British spy in Turkey had been "liquidated," and a whole new system had had to be set up.

"Better watch your step, Griscom," Fitzmaurice said grinning as he rose to go. "We have our eyes on you."

As I emerged from the hotel on my way to dinner, I plunged into murky darkness. Along the streets only a few lamps with shades painted black or green emitted a faint glow. More people were said to have been killed by the automobiles which dashed about without headlights than by the Zeppelins. That evening everybody was discussing which part of a building was safest in case of a raid. If a falling bomb hit the roof, it would penetrate a floor or so; if it exploded in the street, it would wreck the lower stories. Space in the middle was at a premium because London buildings were not very high.

I had arrived during a bad winter for England. The attack at Festubert and Loos had failed with terrific casualties. The Dardanelles venture had proved disastrous, and the troops had been withdrawn. Sir John French had just been replaced as commander in France by Sir Douglas Haig. Feeling was running strongly against Prime Minister Asquith and Lord Haldane, the Minister for War. I thought, as I drove home, that I had never seen such an atmosphere of restlessness and uncertainty in England.

The point of Fitzmaurice's jocular parting remark was evident when, back at the Ritz, I discovered my baggage had been thoroughly ransacked. In order not to lose a minute in getting our documents in sanctuary, Anderson and I hurried early the next morning to call on Mr. Page. In addition to keeping our papers and messages, the only favor we asked was that he or some member of his staff should arrange our first interview at the Foreign Office, and intimate to them an "unofficial interest." To my amazement, he announced freezingly: "Your case is a private one, and you must handle it without any assistance from me. I am the official representative of the United States in England, and therefore every act of mine is official."

This was an extraordinary statement. Almost the first thing you learn in diplomacy is that the real achievements often come as the result of informal actions. All he had to do was say to Sir Edward Grey, "I'm not here officially, and I don't know anything about this case myself, but I do know that my Government would like very much to see it out of the way." Apparently he considered we were trying to put him in a position where he would be making trouble for the British by helping to extract money from them.

Mr. Page was an excellent example of a man who had set out to be *persona gratissima,* and had accomplished his end; no Ambassador of ours was ever more liked. But from the point of view of the State Department, he could hardly be regarded as successful. When he was charged with delivering a formal and disagreeable note to Downing Street, he had been known to soften it verbally so that it lost its effect.

Since I was unable to get any aid from the Ambassador, I went to the Counselor, Irwin Laughlin, who had been with me in Japan, and asked him to make the introduction. He too flatly refused. Certain that the Embassy must have received the State Department's cable, I could not understand their attitude. However, with the Embassy hostile, there was no advantage in opening negotiations. Anderson and I decided to notify Polk what had happened, and then sit tight and wait for developments.

At first I was glad of a little leisure so that I could renew former friendships and associations. Throughout the years I had kept my membership in the Bachelors' Club. As I had always done in London, I dropped in at the earliest opportunity and ordered some tea. All about me groups were conversing, and I could not avoid overhearing their remarks. A young Guardsman mentioned there was going to be a big push in a particular sector, an official from the Foreign Office told some inside news, finally an old gentleman declared it was a shame the Americans did not lend a hand, and the others chimed in with derogatory remarks. I gulped down my tea and left hastily. I did not want to eavesdrop on their secrets. It was their club and their war and no place for me.

On the street a woman, seeing me in mufti, tried to pin on a white feather. "I'm an American," I protested.

"Oh, one of those who're too proud to fight," she retorted, and threw the feather at me.

Everywhere I was asked, "Why doesn't America come in?" One old lady in the presence of a company embarrassed me by observing she hoped we were not so mean and cowardly a race as she had been led to believe. There was no arguing the point; neither she nor her friends were in the mood to listen. I could not get used to being treated as an alien by the same people with whom I had had so many good times.

The meetings with my own friends were often sad ones. Charley Crichton's only son Hubert and his nephew, Viscount Crichton, were dead, together with others whom I had known well years earlier. The English were bearing their casualties with a fortitude that was beyond praise. I called up Lady Yarborough to say how sorry I was to hear that her eldest son had recently been killed. Under the circumstances she probably would not care to dine and go to the theater with me.

"On the contrary, I'd be delighted," she answered. "No matter what our personal feelings, we have to keep our chins up in war-time."

I was relieved when, after two weeks, Anderson and I were summoned to the Embassy. The State Department must have sent a sizzling cable, because Laughlin was now only too ready to co-operate. We should bring our papers over, and he would arrange an interview at once with the permanent undersecretary of the Foreign Office.

Sir Eyre Crowe was very courteous. The British Government would appoint a body of twelve men with whom we could negotiate, including himself, the legal adviser of the Foreign Office, representatives of the Admiralty and Board of Trade, the Procurator

General, the Solicitor General, and, as chairman, Commander Leverton Harris, the head of the Blockade Bureau.

Before the first meeting of the Committee, Brown and I set about lining up our cases. In the process I discovered my clients were about to receive a severe financial setback, because the British Government was planning to bar their products from being sold in England. I was sure the English could not know that the control of the Sulzberger Company belonged to American banks, mainly the Guaranty Trust Company, from which England had to borrow. In hitting the Sulzbergers, she was really hitting her best friends. Furthermore, the bankers had thoroughly cleaned house, and every trace of German affiliation had been eliminated. I cabled Cravath that he should have the New York banks protest to the Midland Bank in England, which in turn should protest to the English Government. The ban never was put into effect.

Realizing, however, that the English could not become enthusiastic over products labeled "Sulzberger," I urged my clients to lose no time in carrying out their intent to change the company's name. Soon "Wilson" hams were on display in British butcher shops.

On some points I had to get a barrister's opinion, a momentous undertaking. He could only be approached through a solicitor, a humble fellow who prepared your brief, marked it in the corner with the price you would pay — four pounds, a hundred pounds, a thousand pounds — then sent it on to a barrister. If he turned it down, it went to a second, and even a third or fourth, until at last one deigned to accept it.

No American would understand the unique divinity which hedged about an English barrister. The story was current of a judge who, in the midst of a trial, looked up, glared, thundered, "Proceedings in this court will cease. There is a stranger within the bar." Every eye was focused instantly on an unfortunate solicitor. In whispering something to a barrister, he had inadvertently stepped into the sacred enclosure.

After what seemed to us an inordinately long delay, we were notified that the barrister would deliver his opinion at four o'clock the next day. Our solicitor saw to it that Brown and I were ten minutes early. As we passed the window, we glimpsed a man reading and smoking, his feet on the sill, and his chair tilted back comfortably. We entered the outer office. The clerk, recognizing the solicitor, asked rather curtly, "What do you want?"

"We've an appointment for four o'clock," the solicitor answered meekly. The clerk glanced at the clock. "Well, you may wait," he said as though doing us a favor.

We waited. Not a second before the hour were we ushered in. The barrister spoke to the solicitor, but treated Brown and me as though we were not in the room. He pocketed our fee, rendered a very clear opinion, and then dismissed us without even an attempt at the ordinary courtesies. He had accepted the Sulzberger Company as a client much as a criminal lawyer would take the case of some villain he knew to be guilty.

When the Board finally met, it was an imposing array of talent, containing some of the sharpest brains in England. As Anderson and I had agreed, he debated the legal aspects of the case. Thus we avoided the prejudice that would have been inevitably aroused by introducing the name of Sulzberger. Since settling for one meant settling for all, every argument that he advanced applied also to my case.

By merciful providence Commander Harris and I took to each other from the start. I described to him the tremendous volume of accounts, affidavits, bills of lading involved in my case alone. "We'll never read all this stuff. Let's try to find some way to decide it in principle, and then we'll hire chartered accountants to go through the mess and set up fair valuations."

"Yes," he assented. "I haven't any time either. Let's stick to that."

I had constant informal meetings with the Committee, at one of which I suggested the elimination of casings from discussion. "They are," I pointed out, "inedible and indigestible — in exactly the same category as the tins which hold sardines. You can claim the sardines themselves are food products, but it would be difficult to do the same with the tins."

The Committee, which had begun by being rather stiff, laughed and agreed to exclude the casings.

Shortly Commander Harris asked me for a week end to Camilla Lacey, his house at Leatherhead where Fanny Burney had once lived. He knew everything about her, had collected everything of hers he could lay his hands upon, had jammed every room with Burney memorabilia. When he drew from me the confession that I had never read *Evelina,* he brought out a copy, and at his insistence I read it and was delighted; it formed a bond between us.

The Commander had also invited other members of the Committee. We were served a dinner prepared by his famous chef, and afterwards, over our port, they started chaffing me about my German clients, an excellent sign.

"You think your case is complicated," said Commander Harris. "Well, listen to this one: You Americans apparently wanted your canary birds, war or no war, and clamored so loudly for them that a group of neutral bankers decided it would pay to make up a big cargo to fill this demand. From the Hartz Mountains in Germany thousands of birds, worth several hundred thousand dollars, were shipped to a Dutch port, and lay there for two or three months before being loaded on a Swedish ship. On putting out to sea, she was promptly hauled in by our blockading squadron, and the cargo confiscated on the excuse that it was of German origin. The bankers employed a clever counsel, and soon we found we had stirred up a hornets' nest. He divided the birds into five categories, and tried to argue that four of them, each worth thousands of dollars, could not possibly be considered of German origin.

"Look here," Commander Harris finished, and shoved over a memorandum : —

1. Birds born in Germany and shipped out — indisputably German.
2. Fledgelings hatched while awaiting shipment in the Netherlands from eggs laid in Germany — German or Dutch?
3. Eggs laid in the Netherlands but conceived in Germany — German or Dutch?
4. Fledgelings hatched on Swedish boat, a floating bit of Swedish territory, from eggs laid in the Netherlands — Swedish or Dutch?
5. Eggs laid on Swedish boat — Swedish.

One of the interested parties went to a member of Parliament and urged him to ask questions about the case of the intercepted canaries. It happened to hit the House of Commons' sense of humor, and was greeted with roars of laughter. The members began speculating as to when a canary bird acquired a nationality — at the moment of fertilization, as an egg, at the time of hatching, or when it was mature enough to feed itself.

I spent several pleasant week ends with members of the Committee, and on the surface our business seemed to be progressing smoothly. Actually, we were getting nowhere. Colonel House arrived at the Ritz from Germany, February 9th, and I saw him daily during his fortnight's stay. We agreed he should now put in a word.

Nevertheless, the business still hung on. The Government, loath to pay out so much money unless absolutely necessary, interposed an endless series of delays, and I could see that years might elapse before the finer points of international law could be exhausted. Not the least of our troubles were the barristers, who were constantly going off shooting. The solicitors accepted this as a matter of course, and could not understand our impatience.

We had to remain in London all week, and for exercise I used to drag Brown off on long walks about the town. He was efficient, hard-working, and knew his job, but to my mind was obtaining little benefit from his first trip abroad. I did my best to stir up his curiosity. "There," I said, "is Buckingham Palace. The roof is covered with sandbags to protect the royal family from falling steel and iron." He glanced up casually and grunted.

I thought I would try him on something modern. "Over on that great arch at Hyde Park Corner is a searchlight and an anti-aircraft battery." Another grunt.

Next I showed him Stafford House, now a museum, but in my youth the home of the Dukes of Sutherland, where I had often been. I indicated the ever-lovely view over St. James's Park — the bit of water and the stately Foreign Office as a background. Brown sighed deeply, "Heavens, I wish I could be back in my office in the stockyards of Chicago."

Brown had formed a deep-seated disapproval of monarchies and aristocrats. He even looked askance at me because of my British associations. I told the Committee about him, and they were delighted, making me repeat again and again his remarks about "arrogant aristocrats."

Finally, one day in March, Lord Reading sent for Anderson and me, and tentatively inquired our lowest figure for settlement. We set it fairly high; nothing was to be gained by concession. To my surprise we met no opposition at all. Suddenly the Government capitulated. I always believed Colonel House's recommendation might well have turned the scales in our favor. The chief credit, however, was due to Polk's persistence; he left no doubt in English minds that the United States was determined to press for a settlement in which Sulzberger must be included.

The packers' case was historic because it established a vital principle of international law: that if a belligerent seized goods he could not clearly prove were contraband, then he would have to pay for them. The one great cause of friction between the British and American Governments was thus removed. The State Department could now stop bombarding England with disagreeable notes, and the way was paved for our ultimate entrance into the war on the side of the Allies.

The negotiations ended, as do few such long drawn out controversies, with amity on both sides; each thought it had driven a good bargain. Our Committee told me they had known all along they were going to pay eventually, but they had to put up a fight.

Before our departure Anderson and I decided to celebrate the conclusion of our efforts with a good-will dinner to the Committee, and include our unbelievably large array of counsel; not only did each packer have his own barrister, but we had retained others to help prepare the legal briefs we were planning to submit to the Privy Council. The solicitors said they could not possibly attend unless, as one rather naïvely suggested, the permission of the barristers could be secured. This we did without difficulty.

The one person who refused to attend was Brown. The Committee really wanted him produced, but he still felt that the dastardly British had behaved so badly to us in the Revolution that he ought not to consort with them. Anyhow, he did not approve of their monarchical form of government.

About halfway through dinner Commander Harris pulled out of his pocket a small piece of material, some six inches long and four wide, which he handed to me.

"Can you tell me what that is?"

I examined it carefully. One side was like fine cotton drill; the other was a shiny smooth substance, semitransparent. The two were glued together. "I give up," I said.

"Did you hear that we had shot down a Zeppelin at the mouth of the Thames?"

"Yes."

"The report was true. This is a piece of the bag."

"Yes," I said, still wondering.

"Do you see that shiny side? Do you know what that is?"

"No."

"Well, those are your damn casings, your sardine tins. If I had learned about this forty-eight hours sooner you'd never have been paid for those. The Germans weren't importing them for sausages, but for Zeppelins."

CHAPTER XXIX

THE DISTANT DRUM

I was walking down the long corridor of the War Department one mid-May morning of 1917, when a door in front of me suddenly opened. A tall, stiffly erect officer, whose uniform bore the stars of a general, almost collided with me, and I found myself looking into the keen blue eyes of John J. Pershing, newly appointed commander of the American Expeditionary Force. We had not seen each other since Tokio, and the meeting was so unexpected that, following the first greetings, all I could think of to say was, "I wish you'd take me to France with you."

"Sorry. I'd like to, and I certainly would if you were a trained officer."

Although I was determined somehow to get in the Army, I had not intended my remark seriously. A brief handshake, an exchange of "good lucks," and I continued my search for the Adjutant General's department — I had been told that at my age and state of health an adjutant was all I could be.

The Army was apparently the place to meet my friends; I reached my destination, and there behind a desk I caught sight of George Read, my companion of Cuban days, now a colonel after years in the West and the Philippines. The result of this happy reunion was that the next day my library at home was littered with a mass of literature, including the Articles of War, the Army Regulations, and the rules for court martial. I set to work preparing for my examination which was to come in a few weeks.

Promptly on our declaration of war against Germany, April 7th, the inhabitants of Syosset, East Norwich, and Jericho, like other communities all over the country, had formed a Home Guard to protect our reservoirs and generating plants from possible sabotage by German spies. Regularly each evening we gathered on Bronson Winthrop's lawn — the rheumatic, asthmatic, dyspeptic, and overweight, along with the young and able-bodied, all intent on doing our bit to "save the country." When we were able to "Shoulder Arms!" and "Squads Right!" to the satisfaction of our Plattsburg instructor, Francis R. Appleton, Jr., we removed to the fields of the Meadowbrook Club, where we were reinforced by a cavalry detachment of crack polo players, among them Devereux Milburn, Charles Cary (Pad) Rumsey, and the Waterbury brothers.

As a test of our prowess, one sweltering June afternoon we divided up into Red and Blue forces and, feeling much like Boy Scouts in our brand new khaki breeches and tunics from Abercrombie and Fitch, marched off to fight the battle of Syosset. The grass had recently been burned off in many of the pastures and in a few minutes we were black and grubby. Sweating and panting, we had to work our way up and down little gullies and ravines, and batter through the woods interlaced with briars and poison ivy, foul ground for foot soldiers. I gazed enviously at our polo-player cavalry who from time to time dashed by, brandishing sabers and despising the lowly infantry.

Finally word was delivered that the enemy was at hand. Flat on my belly I flopped obediently, wondering how in the world I would identify an enemy, since we had no distinguishing marks. Soon everybody had disappeared in the underbrush, and, after I had crawled around for what seemed hours, I dragged myself out of the woods into the Kennedy garden. There I found Billy Delano, who had recently been ill, stretched on the lawn in a state of utter exhaustion. The battle raged until sunset, but he was the only casualty; who was victor or who vanquished the opposing forces could never agree.

On the day of my examination I took the train again for Washington. On seeing me, Read turned to Colonel William M. Wright at the next desk and they put their heads together. "I don't suppose," said Wright, "that we ought to make an ex-ambassador answer a set of questions like a schoolboy." Leading me down the corridor he told me to stroll around the neighborhood for half an hour, and on my return he announced in a loud voice that I had qualified. To help me with the Medical Board, which could have refused me on a dozen counts, he gave me a note stating I was applying for staff duty, and mentioning my former association with General Pershing.

In spite of this introduction, I was directed to strip and join several hundred other applicants who were wandering about, also quite naked. I stood and I stood, until an officer hauled me over to a basket of colored wool and had me pick out strands of green, blue, or yellow. An hour later another called, "Come over here!" I had hardly gone ten steps before he ordered, "Stop there!" and began whispering at me. Another looked at my fallen arches, sniffed disparagingly, "Oh, after all, you'll be on the staff and you won't have to march." I felt like a steer being pushed around in the Chicago stockyards.

Finally, at the end of the day I was informed I had passed; apparently the note had had some efficacy. Back at the Adjutant General's office I was sworn in, commissioned a major, and instructed to go home and wait. A few days later I received an order to report for duty June 26th at Governor's Island in New York harbor, the headquarters of the Eastern Department.

My first taste of military discipline after so many years was distinctly uncomfortable. The boots of my new uniform were too stiff, my breeches too tight. All I could slip into the pockets of my close-fitting tunic was a flat cigarette case. My neck was held as though in splints by a stand-up collar of the same type as that devised by the British generations ago to conceal the dirt on a soldier's shirt — if he happened to be wearing one; we went through the whole war suffering from this preposterous fashion which the British themselves had long abandoned.

A little ferry transported me from the Battery to Governor's Island, and I presented myself at the headquarters of General James Franklin Bell, former Chief of Staff, and now a senior major general. He introduced me to his chief aide, Major William N. Haskell, who assigned me for instruction to none other than Willard Straight, only a major like myself, but with the inestimable advantage of a week's longer experience.

As much was happening now in seven days as in seven months before the war. Day after day I sat at a desk learning how to handle operations orders, how to fill in forms, everything which had to do with the business end of running an army. Shortly I had several adjutants under me, whom I was supposed to instruct. Officers were constantly being fed out here and there to meet the demands caused

by creating a new army and, at the end of two months, I was one
of the senior members of the Adjutant's Department.

One day in August Major Haskell announced to me that General
Bell had been ordered to Yaphank, Long Island, to organize the
New York City draftees into the Seventy-seventh Division. "He's
selected me for his Divisional Adjutant, and I'd like to have you
for my assistant."

This was far better luck than I had hoped for; to be assigned to
duty with one of the first divisions to be trained seemed a long step
towards active service at the front. However, my first view of my
new surroundings was not prepossessing. Camp Upton was in the
most bare and desolate central portion of the island, approached by
a narrow, deep-rutted road through a rough expanse of scrub oak and
pine. As I drove into the clearing hammers were banging, saws were
rasping, trucks noisily unloading, gangs of laborers putting up
barracks — unpainted structures hardly better than barns. On a
roll of land stood the Headquarters office building, not very much
more attractive than the rest, and around it clustered huts for the
staff.

Immediately Haskell, now a Lieutenant Colonel, assigned me
an office and, as my chief assistant, delegated Lieutenant Louis
Gerow who had risen from the ranks of the regular army, knew
every detail of adjutant's work from A to Z, and was a lifesaver to
a newcomer like me. Only a few draftees had yet arrived, but already
we had business enough to swamp us. At its full strength an American division numbered over twenty-eight thousand men, and the
tremendous detail of organizing — assigning recruits, adjusting
complaints, supervising discipline, issuing staff orders — came in
our department. I had to have more assistants at once. Harry
Cushing, III, was a young second lieutenant distinguished by a
full-blooded Elizabethan sense of humor and the ownership of
the most beautiful boots in his artillery unit. Fred Krenson was a
gay little Southerner from Georgia, and Earl Boothe, who had
managed everything from theaters to motor racing, took charge
of the records.

Haskell had a remarkably well-ordered mind and had worked out
a comprehensive plan for running the business of the division —
including a Personnel Bureau, to take care of the draftees who be-

gan pouring in, five thousand on a single day. Each recruit went through a sort of receiving pen. His whole history was recorded on a card with a tab, which indicated by its color his occupation — chauffeur, carpenter, plumber, or whatever he might be.

The new recruits were not only of every occupation, but represented every race. I used to watch new arrivals being herded through the Personnel Bureau — little Jews in derby hats from the East Side, Italians from Grand Street in pinched-up greenish suits and yellow shoes, swarthy Spanish, Cubans, Puerto Ricans from the upper end of Central Park, Hungarians from the East Seventies, Germans from Yorkville, Armenians, Turks, Rumanians from Brooklyn Bridge, Orientals from Mott Street, Negroes from Harlem, artistic extremes from Greenwich Village. Many were hollow-chested, round-shouldered, flat-footed, undernourished, pasty-complexioned. Hundreds had venereal disease and had to be sent for cure to a hospital. Dozens were found to be addicts of various drugs, chiefly heroin.

To determine what religions were represented, Washington ordered a census which should include all sects with central churches and at least two branches. I supposed I would find at most about twenty-five, but actually we listed over three times that number; we had all the ordinary ones and a lot more you would never suspect — Buddhist, Shintoist, Confucian, Baha, and various cults of special enlightenment and redemption. The heading "Mazdaznian" caught my eye, because *Mazda* was the Persian word for light. I was so surprised to see the lone member had an English name that I sent for him; he turned out to be a real fire-worshipping Zoroastrian — from Brooklyn.

Every trainload brought a small percentage of slackers. Now and again one of my old district leaders journeyed down to put in a word on behalf of a loyal follower. I always retorted, "You're a good Republican, aren't you? You should be proud your club is so well represented." If they could not come themselves, they bombarded me with letters. Happening to meet a particularly persistent correspondent, I remonstrated, "For God's sake stop pestering me; you know I can't get these men released."

"Oh, I don't expect you to, but if I write you and then show my man the copy, that lets me out."

Even the war had not made the politicians lose their touch.

Any dragnet which swept through the slums of New York was bound to catch many strange characters. We had our full share of gunmen, thugs, and burglars. The English used to offer freedom to ex-convicts who would enlist, whereas we Americans had the idea that they would convey some sort of contamination. One great bullet-headed burglar with pimples, a most repulsive creature, laid down on my desk his certificate of conviction. "You can't hold me," he said triumphantly. It was useless to argue the point, but out of curiosity I asked him a few questions. "What do you do now for a living? You've given up burgling, I suppose."

"I'm chauffeur for a rich guy over in Brooklyn."

He admitted his employer was ignorant of his record, but the man looked so unreformed that I wondered whether I should be morally responsible if there were a robbery in his district. I finally decided to give him the benefit of the doubt.

Conscientious objectors were our knottiest problem. If a man were a member of a religious sect, such as the Quakers, which honestly disapproved of war, he was immediately excused from military duty. One extraordinarily handsome young Jew, whose spiritual and ascetic face an artist might have used as a model for a classic Jesus, stated almost apologetically that he belonged to a family of hereditary priests. "It probably will sound very odd to you," he said, "but I'm absolutely limited in what I may eat. I cannot break the rule, but I'm perfectly willing to fight and go to France if my special food can be provided."

The idea of a private taking his own cook to war was ridiculous, yet this man, a skilled accountant, would be extremely valuable. I had him assigned to the permanent Quartermaster Department of the camp where he could make his own food arrangements. He was sincerely delighted.

When conscientious objectors first arrived, they were, like all the others, enrolled in companies. Some refused to obey orders, actually cutting the buttons off their uniforms and rejecting what they called "the degrading insignia of slavery." One particularly violent protester announced to his captain, "My conscience will not permit me to do any military duty."

The captain countered, "Well then, my conscience will not permit me to let an honest, upstanding soldier spend his time cooking for such a fellow as you."

The objector at once telegraphed a protest to the Assistant Secretary of War, and in no time the rumor spread that at Upton conscientious objectors were now being fed raw meat to make them savage.

Washington ordered an investigation. If the accusation were true, the offender should be court-martialed. The captain frankly admitted to me the facts, but added, "The man doesn't have to eat his meat raw. He has a perfectly good stove he can use if he wants to, but he won't."

When the matter came before General Bell, that old campaigner thundered, "Only over my dead body will that officer be court-martialed."

The War Department had sent strict orders to handle conscientious objectors with the utmost care. Accordingly persistent cases were segregated in one barrack, fed well, and required to do no drilling or work. We acquired eight, twelve, sixteen, and then the number halted at eighteen. Cushing reported that they were occupying their time with the card game "casino." Unfortunately, since it required four players, two always had to be left out. "Why should we have to keep drawing lots?" they asked. In the hour allowed them for their daily walk they set forth with a will to uncover two more tender consciences. The next day, five full games were going.

In a way our kind treatment was a wise policy, because most of these slackers were undoubtedly looking for martyrdom, of which they were thus deprived. However, it made us boil to have to assign soldiers to cook for them and to use a valuable building for housing them. After we had sixty I took the matter up with an Army doctor, a member of our mess, pointing out that the medical reports indicated most of them were addicted to some form of sexual perversion. "Normally healthy young men enjoy a fight. What about giving them a mental examination?" I suggested.

"Fine. Send them over. I'll have a special board to deal with them."

The next troublemaker had long hair which he refused to have cut, and was good-looking in an unpleasant sort of way. At the end of the routine questions I ordered him to report for medical examination.

"I'm perfectly well. Why should I?"

"All conscientious objectors must appear before the Medical Board."

He was duly pronounced mentally unsound and shipped to an asylum. From that time forth the epidemic subsided.

The winter of 1917–1918 was one of record cold. The cracks in our huts grew larger and larger, so that finally we could stick our fingers through. The men suffered terribly from wind and exposure; for days on end it was impossible for them to drill outdoors. Yet, in spite of these hardships, the efficiency of the division was steadily increasing. These outpourings of the city were now being well fed, made to live under strict discipline, compelled to exercise from morning to night. After only a few months it was amazing to see them transformed into stalwart husky fellows plodding through mud and snow.

With the virtual withdrawal of the Russians from the War, and the terrific disaster to the Italians at Caporetto, the outlook for the Allies was growing blacker. One by one the regular Army divisions and some of the National Guard were going over to France. Everyone in camp began asking, "When are we leaving?"

General Bell seemed to have the idea our training was to continue forever. One notable evening he summoned some four hundred field officers to headquarters, and for an hour and a half we listened to an interminable address on beautifying the camp. He even proposed prizes for the companies which should have the neatest barracks and best-kept grounds, the finest blooming flower beds, the most luxuriant display of growing shade trees, so that in years to come Upton would not only be less drab but even a thing of beauty. At the conclusion of that lecture, it would have been hard to find a more thoroughly disgruntled lot of men. At this rate we would never get overseas.

Foreign officers were now being detailed direct from the battlefield to show us how to use machine guns and trench mortars, and teach us gas technique. The English bayonet instructor was a big handsome major of the Guards, who had been promoted from the ranks; in his uniform he looked every inch the perfect officer and gentleman, although he spoke with a marked Cockney accent.

When Mr. and Mrs. Charles Alexander asked me to bring to their ball in New York as many officers as I could, I invited the English major. His eye went wavering over the array of beautiful girls as I was introducing him to his host, a charming old gentleman with pointed side whiskers and the manners of a bygone era. "I'm so glad to have this opportunity to talk to you about the war," said Mr. Alexander earnestly. "We're frightfully shocked over here. It's a terrible war, isn't it?"

"I don't think it's much of a war," answered the major automatically, his eye still focused on the girls.

"Oh, yes, it's a terrible war, a terrible war," insisted Mr. Alexander.

"Well, it's a great deal better than no war at all," casually replied the Britisher, who without it would still have been a sergeant major.

In late winter the War Department, realizing that commanding officers needed training on the battle front, decided to send them to France for instruction periods. In February, General Bell was ordered abroad and Lieutenant Colonel Haskell with him. Our senior brigadier, General Evan M. Johnson, succeeded temporarily to the command. I was wondering who my next chief would be when, to my own astonishment, for no civilian officer had yet held that post, General Bell, on Haskell's recommendation, appointed me Divisional Adjutant.

Among my new responsibilities was dealing with the requisitions which the War Department was constantly making for men in special categories. "Send immediately one hundred best chauffeurs to Port of New York to join overseas forces." "Send fifty experienced telegraph operators." "Send a hundred expert motorcycle riders." The outflow never ended. We had to take men out of the units where they were being trained and knew their captains. It was disheartening for the whole division to have to keep filling the gaps with raw recruits.

On the morning of March 21st, only about a month after I had become Adjutant, we suddenly heard that the Germans, following the greatest artillery bombardment in history, had fallen upon the British in Picardy, had broken through the Fifth Army, and might even reach Paris. The German Crown Prince was boasting that Easter would see Germany victorious. Frantic appeals for help came from the Allies. "Send us men. Never mind further training. What we want is men."

American response was immediate. Everywhere in the United States schedules were speeded up. Months before we had expected it, we received embarkation orders for the Seventy-seventh, the first draft division to be sent overseas.

Our arrangements were being made quickly and quietly. Then, at the last moment, came peremptory commands to cast out everyone suspect of sympathy with the enemy. We had so large a percentage of recruits whose names ended in *-stein, -burg, -mann,* that we knew we could not possibly eliminate them all. We instructed the captains to hand in lists of the most doubtful, and to our consternation the numbers totaled nearly three thousand. These we had to replace on the spot with raw recruits whom we bundled into the ranks only a few hours before leaving.

I had no time to go home; Mother, Rod, and Bronson Winthrop brought Bronson and Lloyd to say good-by. Because of the absolute secrecy imposed on every department there was none of the excitement usually associated with going off to war. We had little packing to do — hardly more than our uniforms; the Allies were to equip us with everything — rifles, guns, motor transport, horses, mules.

At 5 A.M. of March 28th, only a week after the German drive had started, the train carrying General Johnson and his staff pulled out of Camp Upton for an unknown destination. All that day it stopped and started, rattled and swung from side to side. At night we slept fitfully to the monotonous clicking over the rails, waking when the lights of some city flashed in our eyes. After twenty-three hours we drew up on the dock at Portland, Maine, alongside the White Star liner *Megantic.*

I was frantically busy all morning, organizing the distribution of rooms and appointing military guards for our contingent of seventeen hundred. We set sail at three in the afternoon; it was one of those clear sparkling days peculiar to Maine. The soldiers, in fine spirits, gathered at the rail, waving good-by to a handful of stevedores, who speeded our departure with one faint cheer.

CHAPTER XXX

THE PERILOUS ROAD TO WAR

Two mornings later five ships, splashed and daubed, checked and barred, like apparitions from some nightmare, formed convoy off Halifax harbor. The *Megantic* steamed up along one side of the antiquated British cruiser *Prince Edward;* the *Carmania,* which carried more of the Seventy-seventh, fell in on the other. Outside us was the freighter *Ceramic* loaded with Chinese coolies, and outside the *Carmania* was the *Cassandra* with a cargo of lumber. The warship, acting as pivot, began wirelessing constant orders for us to turn this way and that.

To watch the land sink away gave us an eerie feeling. Every time I looked down I saw my life preserver either hanging over my arm or ready by my chair, a reminder that a troop ship was fair game for any submarine. There were not enough lifeboats to go round, and my assistants were assigned to a square raft with nothing to prevent them from being washed overboard but lines of rope loops. Deck space was so limited that the men could only be allowed up in relays for exercise; I was sorry for them, but they remained remarkably cheerful, singing and joking, quite unconcerned by the thought they might be torpedoed at any minute.

Day after day our convoy plodded ahead through smooth seas at ten knots an hour, which was as fast as the poor old *Cassandra* could go. We knew we had reached the danger zone when, several hundred miles off the Irish coast, we were joined by six English destroyers. They kept dashing here and there while we zigzagged back and forth more sharply, patterning the ocean with our wakes. We scanned every patch and every shadow to be sure it was not a periscope, and peered over at the spot where our own Captain Bradwell had lost the *Cymric*. After dinner, as we were playing bridge, the ship lurched viciously and we heard an ominous rumble.

Automatically we clutched our life preservers, even though we had been warned practice depth charges were to be exploded.

That night we went to bed in our clothes. For a long time I lay counting mechanically as the *Megantic* swung around on each new tack. I dozed off only to start awake again apprehensively — it was nothing but the creaking of the ship; our engines were pounding regularly on.

Morning finally came, calm and peaceful. I looked out to see the *Prince Edward* plowing steadily through the glassy Atlantic in her usual position a few hundred yards away, and beyond her were the familiar folds of the Irish coast. Much relieved that we would be safely ashore in a few hours, I lathered my face and set to shaving.

One side was still smothered in soap when a terrific *Boo-oo-m* reverberated through the silence. The sea seemed to hiccup and I was banged against the wall. "They've got us," I thought. Then I saw through the porthole a broad column of water shooting a hundred feet into the air from under the stern of the *Prince Edward*. I pulled on my boots and my coat and grabbed my life preserver, but on my way to the door I caught a glimpse of my half-lathered face. I decided the Adjutant could not make an appearance in that ridiculous condition, and stopped to give a few quick slashes at my unshaven cheek and smudge it clean before hurrying on deck.

Close beside us the ocean was seething. Like terriers after a rat, the destroyers were circling around the cruiser, dropping one depth bomb after another. The *Megantic* shook repeatedly from stem to stern. The unfortunate soldiers below decks might well have imagined that any one of these explosions was a torpedo blowing the hull apart. I myself could hardly believe we were not being hit.

From the sinking stern of the *Prince Edward* men poured forth like ants, carrying the captain's furniture and everything movable out of reach of the rising water. Calm still hovered in the background — the Giants' Causeway astern, the lighthouse on the Mull of Cantyre marking the tip of Scotland, the dim faint outline of Islay in the blue distance.

The convoy never slackened speed, and at first the *Prince Edward* kept up with us, but as gradually she sank lower and lower she fell behind little by little, and a guardian destroyer drew in on each side. Somehow she dragged along with us around the northeast corner of Ireland, and opposite Belfast, plainly in sight, she veered towards shore. The last we saw of her she was still struggling gamely with her stern awash and bow high in the air. We heard later she was safely beached, and that the torpedo which had struck her had missed the *Carmania* by only thirty feet.

This section of the Irish Sea near the Isle of Man was a happy hunting ground for submarines. When a mist settled down, pairs of officers were assigned to watch for periscopes. Suddenly what appeared to be a great conning tower loomed off our bow. A look-out called the alarm, and simultaneously a destroyer rushed full speed at it, ramming it so hard that she practically turned over on her side before running into the mud. Nerves were so keyed-up by the morning's experience that a simple can buoy with a spar, which marked the submarine nets, had been mistaken for a submarine.

General John Biddle, who was in command of all American troops in England, met us with our orders and the latest news. Three days earlier the Germans had shifted from Picardy to Flanders, and were hammering and hammering along a narrow front around Mont Kemmel. The British desperately needed support behind them, and were offering the short Dover-Calais route, hitherto reserved exclusively for their own wounded because it was the quickest way home. Instead of having the customary five days at a rest camp the division entrained immediately for Dover.

Our transports, regular Channel packets, were waiting, and a lot of the British military were on hand to take their first look at the Americans. Ahead of me up the long narrow gangway trudged a porter, precariously balancing my treasured dress suitcase on his shoulder. Halfway across the open water I was consternated to see it topple, fall with a splash, and disappear with all the precious personal belongings that mean so much to a soldier away from home. The list of its contents flashed through my mind — the photographs of the two boys, my medicine box full of simple remedies, my favorite big cigars, and a thousand Knickerbocker Club cigarettes.

By what seemed a miracle, the bag rose to the surface, and began bobbing tantalizingly up and down. Along came a sailor with a great boathook who, amid much excitement, jeers, and laughter, fished for it. On the fourth attempt he hooked the handle and hauled in the dripping suitcase. Hastening to my cabin, I opened it with dread, then sighed with immense relief. Not a drop of water had penetrated; my private war equipment was still intact.

Our boat was so packed with soldiers that few of us could find a seat, but we were all too excited to care. The whole Channel was alive with trawlers, mine sweepers, miniature armed vessels of every description. Little destroyers joined us for a moment or two and then hopped off. Airplanes on the watch for submarines circled above us, or wheeled away to investigate any gathering of gulls; flocks of birds congregated whenever an undersea boat had to put out refuse.

Abruptly, due perhaps to some shift of wind, the rumble of guns reached us, sometimes low like distant thunder, then louder and fading again. The buzz of conversation among the noisy doughboys ceased while they listened to these first sounds of battle. On the long sea wall protecting Calais, a crowd of German prisoners were unloading coal. As we slowly steamed by, they all stopped work to stare stolidly at us. We stared back, wondering what impression they had from this glimpse of America coming into the war.

Calais was decked out in welcome and, to the strains of "The Star-Spangled Banner," our men paraded down the broad quai, making a fine showing. At the same time train after train was pulling in with wounded en route for England.

At the Grand Hotel we talked to many British officers who were on their way to or from the front. The wave of depression everywhere was intense. All the British reserves had been used up — Armentières fallen, Passchendaele taken, Calais itself threatened. Twenty-four hours before General Sir Douglas Haig, the British Commander in Chief, had issued his unforgettable "backs to the wall" order of the day. "There is no other course open to us but to fight it out. There must be no retirement."

That night our ears were deafened by bombs from German planes and the tremendous fire of the aerial defense guns, the "archies." The sky was rent with prodigious fireworks from exploding ammunition dumps.

After three days at Calais we were assigned divisional headquarters at the Château de Cocove, fifteen miles out of the city, in the area of General Plumer's Second Army. When we arrived, we found it scarcely more than a second-rate country house in shocking disrepair. Four of us were given a servants' room upstairs, a bare, gloomy place with one tiny window. However, we were well ventilated; through a great gap in the ceiling where the plaster had dropped, I had a full view into the attic. The bedding on our cots was damp and ice cold, and we had to move repeatedly to find dry spots out of reach of the rain leaking through the roof. In the middle of the night, with only one candle burning, I glanced up to see a ring of gimlet eyes fringing the hole above: resentful rats were reconnoitering.

The British themselves must have been conscious they had not done well for us, because they informed us we would soon have much better headquarters at the Château d'Éperlecques. I rode over to make the arrangements for our transfer. Almost from the moment of our landing it had rained in the daytime, snowed and frozen at night. In spite of the continuous strings of prisoners and coolies who were busy repairing the road, it was heavily worn and rutted, and in many places had softened into a pudding, from which every passing truck splashed mud and water far to the side.

I was bespattered from head to foot when I reined up once more at Cocove. Cushing and Krenson were on the steps, fairly jumping up and down with excitement. "Major, you're in for it. Pershing and Harbord have sprung a surprise visit on us. General Johnson's mad as hell because you're late. They all went in to lunch a half hour ago. You'd better hurry."

This visit of the Commander in Chief was the most dramatic and thrilling event so far in the brief annals of the Seventy-seventh. We all knew he had come to size us up, and the fate of the division commander might well hang in the balance. Cushing and Krenson dragged me into my room; one seized a sleeve of my tunic while the other began wiping the clay off my boots. The second the last button was buttoned they rushed me to the dining room door. I walked in and tried to close it behind me, but Cushing had inserted his foot in a kindly endeavor to hear in what particular manner I was going to be annihilated.

General Johnson, answering my salute, said sharply, "Major

Griscom, I'm not accustomed to having the officers of my mess late for meals."

At this reprimand General Pershing looked towards me, then grinned broadly, jumped from his chair, came round the table and shook my hand: "For heaven's sake, Griscom, how did you get here?"

"I'm Adjutant of this division."

"Well, I never expected to see you today. Sit down and eat your lunch."

I took the only vacant seat next General James G. Harbord and a plate of food was thrust in front of me. Not even the presence of the Commander in Chief and his chief of staff could prevent me from gobbling it and calling for more. General Johnson was in the midst of describing the prime condition of his division when General Pershing glanced across the table and exclaimed, "Why Griscom, you never used to eat like that in Japan. You're a changed man."

General Johnson raised his eyebrows, and the rest of the staff looked bewildered. I had not mentioned my diplomatic career to any of them.

At the end of lunch General Johnson announced one of our brigades was paraded for inspection. "One minute," replied General Pershing, and, putting his arm through mine, drew me into a corner out of hearing. He began talking about the old days in Japan; his wife too had died since then. "Anything I can do for you?" he concluded.

"Not a thing. I think I'm very lucky to be here."

"All right. I shan't disturb you." We shook hands again, and he rejoined General Johnson.

The next day we moved to Éperlecques, better built and roomier than Cocove. Being seven miles nearer the battle line made a great difference; it was a severe test for green troops who had never been in the trenches. We were actually within range of the biggest German guns. The thunder of cannon was constant, sometimes so loud as to shake the windows. At night the sky in the east was streaked with flames and flashes where the furious assault on Mont Kemmel continued. Each morning we woke up, went out, listened, and said, "It's much closer today." We all had the curious illusion that the sound was getting louder and that the Germans must be breaking through.

Every clear night German planes came over Éperlecques and we quickly learned to distinguish their curious interrupted zzmm — zzmm — zzmm from the steady zmzmzmzmzmzmz of the English. They were raiding the vast supply dumps of Calais and we were on the direct line of flight.

The control of the air in this sector frequently depended on the presence of an outstanding ace, such as the German Richthofen, who could bring down lesser flyers without danger to himself. If an allied ace of equal ability were sent against him, he was immediately shifted miles away to another area where he could continue his deadly work unmolested. Although the British had many able aviators who were only too willing to face Richthofen, rather than sacrifice their precious lives the British commander often requested the aid of one of the three French stars who alone could confront him successfully.

In response to one such appeal, the French returned word that an ace was already on the way; suitable accommodations must be provided for him. At the appointed hour a motor drew up before the pleasant inn close to the aviation field. A valet emerged, stalked in, demanded in a lordly manner, "Where are the rooms for *le Capitaine?*"

The landlord led the valet upstairs. He took one look. "Pff! This will never do. Show me something better. On the sunny side, too."

"But the English General is already occupying that suite."

"Show it to me."

The landlord shrugged his shoulders and obeyed. The valet nodded approval, "These will do."

"But I've told you they are already occupied by the General."

"If my captain does not have these rooms, he will go back to Paris."

Under this threat British opposition evaporated, and the General agreed to evacuate. Then the valet asked, "Now, where are the rooms for Mademoiselle?"

"What mademoiselle?"

"Why, my captain never travels anywhere without his *amie*. She must have rooms next him."

More British officers had to be turned out. About this time another motor appeared, and the captain's mechanics also had to be satisfactorily accommodated. Finally, up glided a shiny military car, and from it descended, amid bowing and scraping from the hotel staff and acclaim from all present, the brave captain and his beautiful companion.

The position of an ace was something new in warfare; he was as privileged and popular as an operatic prima donna.

Only a few nights after our arrival at Éperlecques I was working in my office about nine-thirty, when without warning the lights went off. Knowing this signaled an *alerte,* officers, clerks, and stenographers trooped out into the park and, with no particular apprehension, gazed into the heavens. Since there was an unwritten agreement that neither side would bomb the other's Headquarters, no one hurried to obey the order to seek cover which would prevent their enjoying the display.

Over the military center of St. Omer, about five miles away, the bursting shells from the "archies" sparkled in the sky. Searchlights were playing frantically, their long pencils of white swinging in every direction. All at once I saw one catch a plane in its beam, and I said to Major Cooper, the divisional inspector, "It looks to me as though that one were heading straight for us."

"I think you're right. We'd better go inside."

Leisurely we mounted the few steps to the first floor, where we found a window in the brick wall, just wide enough for us to get our heads and shoulders through. We could now see the plane easily, almost overhead. Suddenly a shrill whistle pierced our ears, followed instantaneously by a deafening crash.

Both of us were blinded by the flash and knocked backward into the room by the force of the concussion. Shrieks and screams of pain came from outside.

I was the first to jump up and thrust my head again out the window. Below me bodies were squirming on the ground. My eye immediately picked out the distinctive red head of Earl C. Bates, my gentle little stenographer whom I had had since the first days at Camp Upton. I rushed down to help carry him into the hall. The ends of the tendon cords of his knee were uncovered, his belly was riddled through and through, his intestines protruding. I did what I could with my emergency kit. He did not realize he was mortally wounded, saying only that he felt numb.

Bates was the first casualty of the Seventy-seventh. Ironically the lottery of war had selected the one person who supposedly occupied the safest position in the whole division.

The next morning I went to the scene of the explosion, inspected the hole in the ground, then gazed up at the window from which Cooper and I had been leaning. Every inch of the wall around it was gashed and pitted and spattered where the flying fragments had hit. Only that one small space, as though a shield had been held in front of it, had not been touched.

Other detachments of the Seventy-seventh followed in our wake, and quickly our billeting area, some ten miles across, was filled. Part of my job was to visit the tiny villages or outlying farms in which they were quartered, adjust complaints, and take up any other question that needed attention. Just as at Upton, everyone had his hands full and it quickly was obvious that no thought had been given to distributing the vast mail which came to twenty-seven thousand men. Great sacks of it began to be dumped in our office. The pile rose higher and higher.

I knew the soldiers would be waiting more and more eagerly for news from home, and I was sure no regular officer had time to be postmaster. "What about the chaplains?" I asked myself. They had as yet little to occupy their attention and I could not see how, in this emergency, letter carrying would interfere with Sunday services. Moreover, it ought to help them to make friends with the men. I offered the Salvation Army chaplain the position of temporary postmaster, with a staff to do the sorting, if he would get the other chaplains to handle the deliveries. He agreed, and soon our spiritual advisers were distributing happiness with the mail.

Unfortunately, word somehow reached the Chaplain General, Bishop Charles H. Brent of the Philippines, whom I had known in Rome, that the Adjutant of the Seventy-seventh had taken the chaplains away from their duties and turned them into postmen. Rising up in his wrath, he ordered the dangerous precedent to be abandoned forthwith. He made me feel as though I were a sinner beyond redemption.

We were steadily building up our organization with British aid and they acted as our mentors. One of our visitors from General Plumer's headquarters was the chief intelligence officer, a very efficient and agreeable man, who came to find out about our counter-espionage. I said of course we had issued instructions to the captain of every company to be watchful and report immediately anything out of the ordinary.

"Well, if you don't mind, I'd like a list of any men whom you suspect. We're certain German spies have been placed in your American divisions."

"What's your idea of a suspect?"

"First, every soldier with a German name or anyone known to be of German or Austrian origin. We'll put one of our men on each of these just to make sure. Then perhaps we should pay attention to those with Irish names. How many men, do you think, would come under these headings?"

I made a rough guess. "Well, we threw out about three thousand before we sailed and probably we still have about three thousand left."

His expression was one of incredulous amazement. "For God's sake, you don't mean that seriously?"

"I certainly do."

"Why, we haven't as many men as that in our entire counter-espionage service."

It is hard to describe what a pill the Seventy-seventh New York City division was for the British to swallow. Everybody in England with a German name was suspect. Now here were thousands of possible enemy sympathizers moving about freely in the sacred British area. This seemed to be the first realization the British had that we and they were not all of the same racial stock.

In spite of the well-known lack of cordiality between the English and their own colonials, they had expected our men and theirs to fall on each other's necks, play games, and follow out the old idea that blood was thicker than water. Since so much of our blood was Polish, Austrian, German, Irish, and even Chinese, it was not surprising this did not happen. Our troops mixed readily with Canadians and Australians, but would not associate with English. In an *estaminet* groups of doughboys would be seen drinking their beer at one section of tables, groups of Tommies at another. Moreover, our interests and sports were different. The British played cricket, we played baseball; they drank tea, we drank coffee. Much of the slang of one was unintelligible to the other. Many individual friendships were made, but there was no general fraternization.

British and American officers, however, usually hit it off well. The great privilege for the staff was to go to St. Omer, a fair-sized city, uninjured except by air raids. Its only good restaurant was always filled with British officers. We would sit down and join a group of them who were having a gay time, drinking champagne, telling jokes, perhaps passing around one of the curious acrostics which were then in circulation, such as: —

Who was the individual most responsible for the war?	K A I	S E R
What small country was the immediate cause of war?	S E R	B I A
Who was the first French commander?	J O F	F R E
Who was the first British commander?	F R E	N C H

My business often took me to various British headquarters in the neighborhood. I noticed that everywhere they made a particular point of trying to provide entertainment to keep up their spirits. In this way I saw some of the best talent the London music-hall stage could offer. The story which brought down the house one evening concerned an English Tommy just arrived in Blighty on leave. During the long railway journey to his home in the North, he had to wait at a junction and entered the station restaurant.

"Please, Miss, might I have a cup of tea?"

The girl behind the counter, taking her time, turned round, filled a cup, and shoved it across to him.

"Please, Miss, might I have some sugar?"

More crossly even than before she pushed the sugarbowl at him.

"Please, Miss, might I have some milk?"

Sharply she retorted, "There'll be no milk until the boy comes."

The patient Tommy lost his temper. "And how do you know it's going to be a boy, Miss?"

I went on one errand to the British G.H.Q. (General Headquarters) in the medieval town of Montreuil-sur-Mer; its ramparts and bastions crowned the top of a hill rising suddenly out of the plain to the south of Boulogne. I made my way through narrow, time-darkened streets crowded with officers, orderlies, messengers.

When I had finished my business, I dropped in to see Robert H. Bacon, our ex-Ambassador to France, who was General Pershing's liaison officer with General Haig. He had been tremendously successful. Whenever the British disagreed with our point of view, he would go to them and with his pleasant smile explain everything so disarmingly that they would say, "Oh, all right," and that would be the end of it. His young assistant, Major John G. Quekemeyer, was an efficient and adroit soldier, and between them they got what they wanted.

Part of General Pershing's plan to whip an army into shape as soon as possible was to send around shrewd officers to inspect each division — to be sure that it was adequately equipped, and that its training was going forward at full speed. Every day or two a new pair would pop in from Chaumont to look us over. We did not realize at first that these nice quiet visitors, so pleasant and polite, who dined with us and poked around in each department, were actually making out reports which might cause a complete shake-up in the division; on occasion even the commanding general was removed.

The Seventy-seventh had been about three weeks in France when we were assigned a permanent commander straight from the fighting line. Major General George B. Duncan, as Brigadier of the First Division, had been the first to take American troops into the front trenches. We had heard of his reputation as a firm disciplinarian, but nevertheless were a bit disconcerted by his initial order: Every staff officer must be at his desk on the stroke of nine under penalty of court martial.

At exactly two minutes past nine General Duncan walked in my door. I rose and saluted; he sat down and systematically began going through my papers, asking as he picked one up, "What action do you propose to take on this?"

I told him. He indicated another. "You seem to have had this for several days. Why haven't you sent it on?"

"It concerns a company which is moving from one billet to another. I'm waiting until the captain gets his men settled."

"You're quite right," he agreed.

General Duncan repeated his visit for three mornings, and then the whole atmosphere changed. "I've made up my mind about you," he said. "I won't bother you again, and when we really get into action we're going to leave behind all these cases and chests you have around here."

We never knew from day to day whether the British could hold the Channel ports or keep a wedge from being driven between themselves and the French. After Mont Kemmel, so long and bitterly contested, finally fell on April 26th before the German onslaught, we thought the call for us might come at any minute. In case of a German break through, the Seventy-seventh was to occupy a position ten miles nearer the front and directly on the line by which the enemy would advance. As a preliminary test the division was ordered to march there and back again, each man carrying his full sixty pounds of equipment. This was a lot to ask of those last thousands who had been so hastily thrust into our ranks on the eve of sailing.

The General delegated me to act as an observer. The staff work went off without a hitch, and most of the men reached their destinations in fair shape. As I returned, however, I saw the roadside littered with our casualties. They were sitting in clumps every few yards, with shoes off, hats off, coats off. Some of them for very weariness had dozed off on their packs. At least two thousand had to be ignominiously carted home in lorries and ambulances.

From the instant of our arrival we were never allowed to forget we were soldiers who were being made ready to join a fighting army. Our senses were keyed up to a point where the mere routine of living had a keenness about it unknown to the occupations of peace. In contrast, my own diplomatic and legal career seemed humdrum.

At the end of only five weeks came the moment we had been anticipating — half of our division was ordered into the frontline trenches.

Everyone was excited, the wires were humming, officers were packing their kits. Colonels Harold B. Fiske and Hugh A. Drum were up from Chaumont, the former to correct any defects in training, the latter to go over our operations orders. In the height of the rush came another telegram — an order for Major Griscom to report for duty at once to General McAndrew, Chief of Staff at Chaumont.

CHAPTER XXXI

THE MEASURE OF A LEADER

The tree-shaded château of Éperlecques was just taking shape in the gray dawn of May 26th as I set out with Colonels Fiske and Drum in their staff car for Paris. I looked back with a pang of regret. After almost a year of the closest association I was intensely disappointed to leave the division at the moment it was about to go in the line, and I had not the slightest idea why, at this last moment, I was being summoned away.

All that day we moved in and out among endless lines of supply trucks, guns, munitions, food. Darkness had fallen before we reached the environs of Paris. The city was blacked out, and for hours we blundered from street to street; it was nearly dawn again as we entered the Place de la Concorde. We walked into the Hotel Crillon to the shrill sound of an *alerte*. On the stairway I brushed past a scurrying, ghostly procession of men and women in nightshirts, nightgowns, pajamas, kimonos — all cellar bound. Some were barefoot, some were in curlpapers, some were hardly clad within the bounds of decency. They paid no attention to me, and I was too tired to turn and follow them. I found my bed and fell into it. No reveille for me that morning. I intended to sleep the clock round.

It seemed only a few moments later when the persistent ringing of the telephone by my ear pulled me back to semiconsciousness. "Damn!" I muttered, and lifted the receiver, at the same time glancing at my watch; it was 9 A.M.

"Is that you, Lloyd?"

"Yes," I answered, trying to identify the voice, and wondering how in the world anybody could know where I was.

"This is Peter Bowditch." Drum had mentioned that the ex-secretary of former Governor Cameron Forbes of the Philippines was among General Pershing's aides. He continued: "General Pershing wants to talk with you. We're at Ogden Mills's house in the Rue de Varennes but he's leaving at once. Don't be more than a quarter of an hour."

"Hold on, Peter, I'm still in bed. I can never make it."

"Good Lord, can't you? Wait a minute."

I waited. Presently he came back. "It's all right. The General will stop at the Crillon in twenty minutes to see you."

Between gulps of black coffee I hurried into my clothes. Still buttoning my tunic and straightening my Sam Browne belt, I reached the bottom of the stairs, just as the large doors into the square were thrown open in front of me. General Pershing strode in, and we found a vacant writing room. "I realize you want to stay in the fighting line," he began rapidly, "but here's my problem. I must have a trained diplomat to represent me in London. We disagree with the English on many vital points. I've learned already that it's difficult to get on with Lloyd George. But the Secretary for War, Lord Milner, is a straightforward fellow. I can deal with him. We've talked things over, and we think we can smooth out our troubles if only we have direct communication with each other. After my association with you in Japan I'll never give you an order, but as a favor to me, will you act as my personal representative at the War Office and with the English Government?"

I answered immediately, "Of course I'll do my best."

"That's settled then. I've already spoken to General McAndrew. He'll arrange with each department of the General Staff to give you all the information we have, how many men are in France, where they are, what they're doing — everything. I want you to stay at my château and I'll go into this with you further when I get back there."

As the General made his concluding remarks he started towards the door. In the street a crowd had gathered around the big olive-drab motor with its four stars; the sight of any one of the Army commanders was an event. They made way for us; a quick handshake and the General was gone — the whole thing seemed to be over in a minute.

I returned to my room to ponder this sudden revolution in my affairs in a leisurely bath, my first in a real tub since I had left the *Megantic*. At peace with the world I sauntered downstairs, anticipating a pleasant day in town. Instead, I was met in the lobby by the news that the Germans, abandoning the Northern attack, had made a surprise thrust between Soissons and Rheims, apparently catching the French totally off guard. Already they had swept over the Chemin des Dames and were crashing ahead unchecked.

By next morning Paris was in a panic. The Germans were driving straight for the city. Could they be stopped? Was the population to be evacuated? The wildest rumors were in circulation.

Nevertheless, as I drove eastward, the French countryside, ablaze with roses of many colors, appeared as placid as ever. When I reached Chaumont towards evening, it was as though I were back in America — American faces, American cars, and American military police with American accents directing me to an office in one of the vast stone barracks which housed the personnel. There I found General McAndrew.

Word had just come through that our First Division, going over the top for the first time, had taken the stronghold of Cantigny in Picardy, blotted out a German salient, and was holding off all counterattacks. This slightly offset the sobering news of further German victory. The French had apparently lost all power to resist, and were falling back steadily towards the Marne. General McAndrew gave me what details he had as we drove together to the Val des Écoliers, General Pershing's château, about five miles away in a little valley by a charming river.

In the morning from my room I looked down upon the quiet garden, quite apart from war except that I could barely see a sentry's head and the point of his bayonet. Later at General McAndrew's office I was surprised again by the calm and orderliness. He pulled up a chair for me at the opposite side of his desk, spread out papers and maps. "These'll show you the position of every division now in France or arriving at base ports."

Forty-eight hours before I had had almost no idea of what was going on; even at divisional Headquarters it had been the hardest thing in the world to get definite information. Now I was poring over the most intimate secrets of the war while General McAndrew was interviewing one officer after another. Occasionally he would turn to explain something to me. Finally he said, "You ought to see how troop movements are being conducted. I'll take you over and introduce you to General Fox Conner in the Operations Section."

As we opened the door, telephones were ringing in bewildering succession. Nothing seemed to disturb General Conner. Unhurriedly he dealt with every call, and in a quiet interlude remarked to me, "The French are bothering the life out of us trying to persuade us to put our half-trained divisions into the front line. They say it's the greatest emergency of the war. I don't know when to believe 'em. One minute they're on the crest of the wave and the next at the bottom of the lowest trough."

Suddenly, without even a knock, in rushed two French officers: "*Oh, mon général, mon général. C'est terrible! C'est affreux! Les Boches sont arrivés au Marne. Au secours!*"

These gentlemen were General Ragueneau of the French Military Mission and his assistant. They went on and on to paint their desperate need. "We'll send buses, we'll send lorries, we'll send trains. Only give us men!"

General Conner calmed his excited visitors as though they had been children. "Don't you worry too much. We'll help you out. That's what we're here for. We'll send you our Second Division."

"Fine! Fine!" said General Ragueneau. "But it's not nearly enough. We must have more."

General Conner took up his map; "Well, General, we hate to put an untrained division into the battle line, but if it really is a crisis we'll go ahead."

"Oh, it couldn't be worse," the Frenchman insisted. He actually had tears in his eyes.

General Conner lifted the receiver. "Get me the Headquarters of the Third Division," he said to the operator. His call came through quickly. "Hello, Bob, that you? Can you have your division ready tomorrow morning to go into the line? . . . Yes, I know you haven't had any trench training . . . Yes, it's an emergency — the French will get you there — How about it?"

Evidently the staff officer was gasping at the other end of the wire; but in a few moments he apparently said "O.K.," because General Conner announced: "Everything is arranged."

"I'm going to call up our G.H.Q. and tell them," exclaimed the French General; "it will give them extraordinary courage," and he and his companion hurried off in the seventh heaven of joy.

General Pershing approved the orders. Instantly, without regard for food or sleep, the Americans were rushed to the critical point — the Third Division to Château Thierry, the Second to Belleau Wood. They began firing practically the moment they tumbled out of camions, buses, and trains. An appalling number of them died where they stood; the rest held firm with a spirit that had not been seen in France for many a day. Not the wisest could tell, however, how long they could bear up under the incessant pounding and find new strength for counterattack.

When General Pershing returned in a few days and stepped out of his car, his face looked tired, but he walked with his usual firm, brisk tread; his endless endurance, mental and physical, was the talk of the staff. The three strong young men who followed him in — Bowditch, Quekemeyer, and Carl Boyd — appeared completely worn out.

Dinner started quietly; we all felt the strain, yet we combined to divert the General and make him relax. He thoroughly enjoyed a good joke, even sometimes poking fun at himself. Few except those who lived at the Val des Écoliers saw him in this lighter mood and knew him as a person as well as a general. Clearly his staff had not only an affectionate regard for him, but also a genuine admiration; there is no greater tribute than to be wholeheartedly admired by those who know you best.

After dinner General Pershing had an opportunity to explain exactly what he wanted of me in London. I discovered that his phrase "disagreeing with the British on several vital problems" was decidedly an understatement. General Pershing had insisted from the outset, and was still insisting, that our soldiers should be formed into an army of our own, fighting under our own flag and officers; the British, and the French, too, were equally determined that our arriving divisions should be fed into their depleted ranks.

Again and again General Pershing urged the Allies: "Let us organize our divisions and put them into an easy sector until they are ready. The quicker we get together an American Army, the quicker you will win the war."

Nevertheless, General Pershing had been willing, in case of an emergency, to make concessions. In the March crisis he had hurried immediately to Foch's headquarters, and with an eloquence unusual in him, said: —

"At this moment there are no other questions but of fighting. Infantry, artillery, aviation, all that we have is yours; use them as you will. . . . I have come especially to tell you that the American people will be proud to take part in the greatest battle of all history."

On other occasions also General Pershing had met the Allies halfway. At the Abbéville meeting of the Supreme War Council of Prime Ministers and Generals, May 2nd, he had agreed that only infantry and machine gun units should be brought over that month and that these should be put temporarily in British areas. Now he had just come from another meeting of the Council. Although the thunder of the American guns at Château Thierry was plainly audible, the Allies, in the face of our achievements, had persisted in trying to dictate to us how we should fight.

"You can see what I'm up against," went on General Pershing. "Since we disagree on this main principle, practically every move either of us makes may cause friction. Whenever any such point arises with the French I can talk directly with Foch, or Clemenceau, or Pétain. But if I want to discuss anything with Lord Milner, my message has to go across the Atlantic and back — from me to our War Department, to our State Department, to the British Ambassador at Washington, to the Foreign Office at London, finally to him at the War Office. We can't reach an understanding with the British unless I have someone in London like yourself who knows my mind and can give a first-hand account of our army. I'll accredit you also to the French so that you can get in touch with them if necessary."

It seemed to me that never in all my career had a greater responsibility been given me. I was going back into diplomacy with a vengeance, and my instruction period was much too short for all I had to learn. Every evening I returned to the château, my head fairly buzzing. I could hardly have chosen a better moment for being initiated into an army's activities. Day by day we waited breathlessly for news from the Marne, where each side was trying to blow the other to pieces. Important decisions had to be made every few hours.

Even in those days of stress and strain, the same cheerful atmosphere continued at the Val des Écoliers. In the fresh early mornings we used to take the most glorious rides up or down the valley of the Marne and across the hills; this was the only way any of us could snatch at exercise. Sometimes we were joined by the head of the French Mission de Liaison: Count Adalbert de Chambrun and his friend Captain Charles de Marenches, the personal representative of General Pétain, the French Commander in Chief.

De Chambrun was an old hand at peace-keeping. He confided to me his recipe for maintaining harmony between his two chiefs. "Every time I see General Pershing I tell him what a great man General Pétain is; every time I see General Pétain I tell him what a great man General Pershing is. In time, they both come to believe it."

After nine days of concentrated effort, I thought that I had grasped at least the principles on which our staff was operating, and was ready to leave Chaumont. General Pershing gave me an order directing the commanding officer of every unit in the army to furnish me any information I desired. On my way to London I was to familiarize myself with the military positions held by our troops in the vital spots — Château Thierry, Belleau Wood, and Montdidier — so that I could speak with authority from first-hand knowledge. His parting words were, "Remember you can act for me whenever anything comes up. Of course, if there's a misunderstanding, and you commit me to something with which I do not agree, I'll tell you privately I consider it a mistake, but no one else will ever know about it. I'll protect you absolutely. Good-by, and good luck."

Paris seemed almost deserted the evening of June 9th; a million people were said to have fled. The rest were anxiously awaiting the result of the fresh German thrust delivered that morning towards Compiègne. The hotel manager at the Ritz told me I could go upstairs and pick my own rooms. He said some liked them fronting the Place Vendôme, but this he did not recommend because a bomb had just broken all the windows on that side. On the other hand, neither could he recommend the side overlooking the garden because, a few days before, another bomb had made a direct hit there. Broken glass was shoveled into piles three and four feet high.

I had a comfortable feeling the lightning would not strike a third time in the same place. As an officer the hotel could charge me no more than seventeen francs a day, no matter where I slept.

I spread out in a suite normally reserved for visiting sovereigns or multi-millionaires.

On my way out to dinner I passed a group of very pretty young women standing on the steps. "Who are those?" I asked the hall porter.

"They're waiting for the Saturday leave train."

At that moment up drew a great Paris bus from the Gare du Nord, and out of it filed a long line of smartly turned-out British officers. As each stepped to the pavement, a girl threw her arms about his neck, and the couple disappeared into the hotel. When the bus drove away, the porter and I were left standing alone again at the entrance.

"They won't bother us until Monday morning," remarked the porter.

I wondered who was responsible for such beautiful staff work.

According to General Pershing's suggestion, I called at the French War Office across the river. My general impression was of the utmost despondency. As though I were an intimate friend instead of a perfect stranger, the Chief of Staff, obviously one of the busiest men in the world, started pouring out his troubles. "France is on the brink of catastrophe. She is exhausted. Every bayonet is in the front line, we've drained our factories of their best workmen, we've crippled our service of supply, our railroads can hardly operate."

He must have continued in this vein for an hour before he paused and looked at me questioningly. "If you will, you can render us a great service. You see, the British take the war differently than we do. Their able-bodied men by the thousand are mining coal to sell at a profit all over the world. In their munition factories they have far more healthy sound men than they need. It is well known the number who can go on their fighting fleet is limited, yet their navy is crowded. Now is the moment for forcing the *embusqués* into the battle lines of France. But we cannot make them comprehend our desperate straits."

Here the Chief of Staff picked up a thick typewritten report. "We've made a comparative study showing how the man power of France and Great Britain is occupied at the present moment. I'm going to ask you to read this and then present it to the British War

Office. Do, I beg you, bring home to them the urgency of putting more men into the fighting line."

The document was, in essence, a most damning indictment of the British Government. If the figures were correct, then the French were thoroughly justified in protesting.

When I arrived at the French G.H.Q. at Chantilly, the atmosphere of gloom was far deeper. General Pétain was away, and General Anthoine, his chief of staff, took me in charge. With wild gesticulations he declared, "All is lost! Nothing can save Paris! Nothing!"

I tried to slip in the remark that General Pershing's feeling was quite the reverse, and even his own chief at the War Office did not see things so darkly.

"What do they know about it? It is we who are fighting the war who know. You as a stranger can have no idea of what losing Paris means. Paris is not only our capital, but also our greatest manufacturing city. Without it we are lost. All our arrangements are made to fall back to the South, but with Paris gone, France is gone. Every Frenchman realizes that."

Clearly General Anthoine was exhausted, his nerves on edge, his nature unusually volatile and I was inclined to discount much of what he said. Furthermore, I suspected that he was putting on a little song and dance for me to report to General Pershing. I spent an hour trying to reassure him, all the time aware of the absurdity of an American major, just two months over from the United States, consoling a French veteran who had headed armies in the field. When I left, he shook my hand warmly. "You Americans are giving us *du courage!*" were his parting words.

Outside his office I ran into a friend of mine, Rex Benson, attached to the British Military Mission. Liaison officers formed a sort of fraternity, and he invited me to lunch. I expressed my astonishment at General Anthoine's outburst before a complete stranger, but the British only laughed. "Oh, that's nothing. We spend most of our time trying to buck up the French. It's our principal function."

After lunch I set out for our Third Division at Château Thierry under General Joseph T. Dickman. My order worked like a charm. He sent a young major from his staff to take me to the front line. We set off towards Crezancy. When a sunken road blocked our way, we continued on foot to the edge of a large open field, beyond which we could see the fringe of woods marking the river's bank. The major waved his hand at a lot of planes overhead. "We'll have to look sharp. Lucky for us most of those are only enemy photographers mapping our lines."

It was a horrid feeling to have no defense aviation of our own, and the Germans absolutely in control without even a gun being shot at them. As we stepped into the open, I cocked a leery eye upwards, and kept careful measure of the distance to cover. We were in the middle of the field when two planes headed straight for us. The major grabbed my arm, "There's a tree. If you want to get out of here alive, run for it."

We spurted as fast as we could and plastered ourselves to the trunk. It was hardly more than a foot in diameter, but it was a good deal better than no shelter at all. The planes circled just above us. We dodged from one side to the other, trying to keep that miserable trunk between us. Bang went a bomb into the ground a hundred feet away, splashing us with dirt. After a few more swoops, however, they gave up and flew away. We took a deep breath and did not stop running until we were safe in the woods.

From an observation post camouflaged with branches I looked down on the Marne, about seventy yards wide, winding through a flat grassy meadow, carpeted with wild flowers. We were in the crook of an elbow made by the river. The major pointed to the opposite high cliffs which curved around us. "Simply packed with German troops over there," he commented. Not a sound broke the calm, but at any second the Germans, who enfiladed us, could let loose a barrage from the front and side which could change the peaceful river bank instantaneously into a death trap.

Although the battle had died down momentarily at Château Thierry, a few miles west the Second Division, commanded by General Omar Bundy, was still in the thick of it. The next day I set out to find General Harbord's Marine Brigade, which was fighting at Belleau Wood. Almost as soon as we turned off the main road, our car was blocked by a disorderly rabble of exhausted French soldiers pelting back from the front, chucking their rifles to right and left.

Approaching from the opposite direction was a neat and trim

column of our troops. "Where do you think you're going?" a French soldier called derisively.

"Oh, up to see the war," came the prompt reply.

"Too late. The Germans have broken through. You'll be wiped out."

Imperturbably good-natured, our men passed by, stepping over or kicking aside the abandoned French equipment. When the road was clear again we went on.

I arrived at La Loge Farm, General Harbord's headquarters, in time for lunch. He looked a fit commander for the hard-bitten Marines — steel-trap mouth, powerful jaw, eyes that nothing escaped, features weatherbeaten by many a campaign in the Philippines and Cuba. He was the type of man who inspired confidence in all who surrounded him. When I had last seen him at Éperlecques, his expression had been genial and charming. Now he looked drawn and tired as did everybody else. The struggle for Belleau Wood had already been going on for more than a week, a few yards gained here, and a few yards there, the Germans contesting every inch. As we ate, the thunder of artillery was constantly audible.

The General delegated his young aide, Lieutenant R. Norris Williams, II, the amateur tennis champion of the United States, to show me the battle. We had to try several roads before we could find one free enough of shrapnel to allow our passage. Our objective had been the little village of Lucy-le-Bocage, but as we approached, it went up in clouds of red brick dust under the German artillery fire. We crawled beneath a hedge until we reached the southern edge of the wood, captured from the Germans just a few days earlier. I did not see how our troops had ever got over such ground — covered with second growth, dense with underbrush through which strands of barbed wire had been run, strewn with giant boulders which made perfect protection for machine guns.

Finally we dropped into a hollow. Outside the door of a farm building stood a colonel, watch in hand, his eyes on the wood which began again a hundred yards or so ahead — his men were about to go over the top. His voice tense with anxiety, he announced in the uncanny silence, "Sixty seconds — Forty-five — Thirty — Fifteen — "

From all sides poured in the sputter of machine guns, the deeper

growl of artillery, both nearly drowned in the answering bellow of
the German bombardment. Almost simultaneously a ribbon of
stretcher-bearers unrolled out of the wood. Blood dripped from the
litters, leaving a trail of red close beside us. Some of the wounded
were howling and screaming and writhing in all stages of suffering.
Others, unconscious, jolted limply with the motion of the stretcher.

The colonel stood unmoving, his eyes still strained toward the
wood. It was fifteen minutes before a runner broke through the
brush — the attack had been successful, all objectives had been
obtained.

Williams and I scarcely spoke on our way back to headquarters.
Nothing I had hitherto experienced had brought home so deeply
the horror implicit in war. That night at the Ritz I felt ashamed
to be in safety and comfort.

My last visit to the front was to the victors of Cantigny, the First
Division, still at the end of six weeks holding its sector near Montdidier. Here again I was taken over ground in dispute between
Germans and Americans, led crouching through woods where great
trees splintered like matches around us, and entire limbs showered
down on our heads. The only comment made by my guide was
"After Cantigny the Germans moved in some of their best divisions
to teach us a lesson and they've been at it ever since."

As soon as we were back at headquarters, I started across France
for Montreuil, and arrived at Bacon's château to find him preparing
to dine with Sir Douglas Haig. "You must come along," he said.
In the Commander in Chief's drawing room were assembled some
twenty officers, among them the Quartermaster-general from the
War Office, Sir John Cowans, a good six foot three, very heavy,
genial, and full of humor; he was the only member of the High
Command to serve in the same capacity throughout the War. Bacon
introduced me to General Lawrence, Chief of Staff. His first remark
was, "Maybe you can put in a word for us in London."

"What do you mean?" I asked.

"Well, you'll discover at the War Office that they don't see eye to
eye with us in the field. To be sure, they can call us by telephone and
we can reach them in the same way, but in reality we are as far apart
as though we belonged to another nation. They supply us with arms
and ammunition, and yet we feel their lack of confidence. We're

doing the best we humanly can; they aren't satisfied, but they can't show us how we can do any better."

Before I could make any reply, Sir Douglas Haig walked in stiffly, said, "Good evening, gentlemen," and came over to Bacon, who presented me. The General personified the smart, perfectly turned-out English cavalry officer — determined face, penetrating eye, healthy skin of a man who led a wholesome outdoor life. Taking my arm, he led the way in to dinner and seated me beside him. He spoke in the most complimentary way of our arriving divisions, of the excellent training of the men, of the intelligence of the officers. "You have no idea what a sense of comfort it gives to have these fresh troops here and feel they are our allies."

I seized this opportunity to sound out General Haig's opinion on the moot question of a separate American Army. All he would say was "The P.M. (Prime Minister) feels very strongly on this subject."

I went back with Bacon to his château, where he gave me a sketch of the strained relations between General Haig and the High Command in London. Quite naturally, his own sympathies were against the political cabal which wanted to remove General Haig, and was solely prevented by the fact the British Army would not stand for it. Such a situation offered the gravest danger to the successful conduct of the war.

Before the dinner had broken up, General Cowans had invited me to lunch with him on the "leave" boat from Boulogne the next day. On board not a chair was available; the deck was jammed with tired officers, jubilant at their prospective holiday. I made a pile of my equipment, and sat down on it to wait. At nearly one o'clock a magnificent Rolls Royce drew up on a platform alongside. General Cowans and his staff got out, a crane reached over and swung car and platform aboard, and we promptly put to sea. I was wondering whether my invitation still stood when General Cowan's A.D.C., Fitzgerald, hailed me. "Come along. Lunch is ready."

On one side of the pleasant saloon, way up above the top deck, was an enormous pile of leather dispatch cases. Orderlies kept bringing in more and more, until there were so many of them that I thought the British must be removing all their confidential data to England. To each Fitzgerald solemnly tied a sinker with a rope; if we were torpedoed, they could not possibly fall into enemy hands.

Near the end of a perfect lunch, General Cowans said, "Fitzgerald, what about a little cheese?"

"Which kind, Sir?"

The General referred the matter to me. I could not imagine where it was to come from, but ventured "Camembert."

Fitzgerald walked over to the pile of dispatch cases and studied them reflectively, "Hmm, I think it's this one."

Undoing the lock, he lifted the cover, and there, instead of secret documents, were packages and packages of Camembert — compact remembrances for the General's friends.

CHAPTER XXXII

GIVE ME AN ALLIANCE TO FIGHT

As I went up to London through the trim rolling Kentish country-side, the slanting rays of the sun were turning its rich green to gold. I sat looking out of the window wondering what the next few days had in store. For the third time in my life I was embarking on a mission in England. On this occasion I was like an ambassador arriving in a country in which he had no official standing, no high rank, no imposing staff, and no definite instructions to guide his actions. Yet at least I was not arriving in London as in 1915, a suspected alien with a German client. I was in uniform and an ally.

Before I went to the War Office the next morning, I paid my respects to General Biddle, who was still in command of the American troops in England. I could see that to have an officer in London not under his command might be awkward for him, but he went out of his way to offer assistance. "I'll be glad to give you any help you need — office, stenographers, car. Have you any idea where you're going to live?"

"No."

"I'm only in temporary quarters myself. Why shouldn't we take a house together? It would cost us less and we'd be more comfortable."

I realized at once how essential it would be in my diplomatic capacity to entertain, and, since General Biddle's interests coincided with mine, he would be an ideal person with whom to share a house. Therefore I readily agreed.

At the War Office I asked for Herbert Creedy, the permanent secretary, who led the way to the Minister's private office. Lord Milner, former High Commissioner of the Cape Colony during the Boer War, an elderly, quiet, and self-possessed man, stood up to greet me, and said he was glad I had come. Then, wasting no more time in preliminaries, he put a series of questions, and listened attentively to my answers. No one else had yet brought him direct news of the Americans in battle. I gathered he was apprehensive as to what General Pershing intended to do with our five divisions now in training with the British, and was afraid we were going to form them into a corps and move them away. When he seemed to have nothing more to ask, I handed him the French indictment, explaining how it happened to be in my possession.

Lord Milner turned over a few pages, glanced at the conclusion, smiled. "This is the same sort of thing we've had to deal with before. We can never make the French understand how many calls we have on our man power. We have to mine the coal to keep industry going and we have to have crews for the fleet that brings food, war supplies and troops. They probably gave you this for the impression it might make on you rather than any effect it might have on us."

From the very start I liked Lord Milner, and, just as General Pershing had been, was struck with his straightforward manner. Finally, in his unhurried way, he got up and opened a door behind him into a smaller room where two officers were seated at desks. "I say, I want Major Griscom to be a member of my personal staff. Couldn't you fellows make a place for him here?"

Although it must have been a shock to have an officer of another nationality thus thrust upon them, Colonels Bowly and Amery said it could be managed easily; and before I knew it, I was established at a desk in the War Office in a room next to the Secretary himself. Bowly, a rather small man with a humorous twinkle in his eye, was the military secretary who kept liaison with the rest of the War Office. L. C. M. S. Amery, M.P., an unusually wise and clever youngish-looking man, was the political secretary, the intellectual aide — an experienced writer, who had been with Lord Milner in South Africa.

While Colonel Bowly arranged an interview with Sir Henry Wilson, the all-powerful Chief of Staff, I wrote out a complete verbatim account of my conversation with Lord Milner, just as I had done in my diplomatic days. Then I was conducted down long corridors and presented to Sir Henry Wilson, a tall, lanky, North of Ireland Irishman with a large head and a strong face, the sharpest

imaginable contrast to Lord Milner. His first remark startled me:
"Have you any news of my cousin?"

"What cousin?"

"My cousin Woodrow. Has he retracted that statement about your
'being too proud to fight'?"

Every time I went to see Sir Henry, he started off with some
thinly disguised slur, and I could not help resenting his sarcastic
references to the Chief Executive of my country. I could understand
how his other mannerisms might irritate many people. He mis-
pronounced names, often purposely, and had nicknames for everybody and used them. Lloyd George he always addressed as "Prime
Minister," and Clemenceau he called "Tiger" to his face.

Now Sir Henry launched into a dissertation on General Pershing's
"ghastly mistake" in refusing to allow American troops to be
brigaded with the British. He could assure me the Prime Minister
was not disposed to let the matter lie. "You lack staff officers accustomed to handle large forces of troops in battle. It has taken us
four years to learn how; you can't expect to learn in four months."

I was already well acquainted with the general Allied belief that
our troops were of little value, but it seemed tactless for Sir Henry
Wilson to begin by emphasizing it so vehemently. However, I accepted his challenge — our troops were better trained and had a far
higher morale than he realized; he should not underestimate the
ability and knowledge of the American Army officer; our West
Point training was the best in the world, bar none.

He looked at me skeptically. "What difference do you think that
makes over here? This is a modern war. The only experience that
counts is what you get on the spot. Tell me, how soon do you suppose
American troops can really render us any important assistance?"

Apparently the Chief of Staff enjoyed putting me on the de-
fensive, but again I went to bat. "They're rendering it right now.
In a few months they'll be a major factor in the war."

Sir Henry smiled at me condescendingly. "I'm an old soldier, and
I tell you it will be at least a year. Some time in the summer of
1919 — if we can hold out until then — the American Army will
begin to contribute materially."

To encounter such unshakable prejudice on the part of the British
Chief of Staff almost took my breath away. Obviously, any further

effort of mine to convince him would be absolutely wasted, and I could not imperil my mission by entering into an altercation with him. I wondered what would happen should his remarks come to General Pershing's ears. Then and there, I made up my mind I was going to hear many things which, were I to maintain friendly relations, I could not repeat to General Pershing.

During my first few days I was kept busy completing the round of visits which Bowly had planned for me. I had not been in the War Office a week before I discovered that the English were receiving their impressions and basing their judgment of the American Army entirely from French accounts, a perfectly natural procedure, since our troops were fighting with French armies and Sir Henry Wilson, who had formerly been liaison officer with the French, was very close to Marshal Foch and his Chief of Staff Weygand. To my astonishment I found again and again that these reports were extraordinarily inaccurate, colored, and even biased. The result was that the whole War Office was remarkably misinformed of what our troops were doing or even what they had already done.

My interview with the Prime Minister was arranged through his secretary, Philip Kerr.[1] Scholarly, learned, serious in disposition, he was an admirable foil for his volatile chief. From the moment I had shaken hands a torrent of words began to pour forth from this fiery little Welshman on the subject I would so much have preferred to avoid. He seemed to feel a definite personal grievance at General Pershing's refusal to feed our troops into the depleted British divisions. His references and comparisons were so like Sir Henry Wilson's that there could be no doubt of the source of his information.

Deciding to be perfectly frank, I told him General Pershing regarded the matter as settled; I could not possibly bring it up again. "Perhaps you can't," he said gruffly, "but that won't stop my doing it."

Feebly I suggested it might be better to let the Americans fight together. He only grunted and the subject was changed.

The principal topic of conversation at the War Office continued to be American man power. The German Army in Italy had crossed the Piave River the day I arrived in England; they had been driven

[1] Later Marquess of Lothian and Ambassador to the United States.

back but no one was quite sure whether or not this reverse was temporary. Soon I was summoned to Sir Henry Wilson's office. He was insistent on knowing what plans General Pershing had made for sending American divisions to Italy. As though he had never even heard we wanted to fight by ourselves, he announced the British would like to have us put a contingent under their command. He was genuinely disappointed when I had to tell him General Pershing believed we should not divert any portion of our military forces from France to Italy unless Marshal Foch so ordered.

Almost immediately I had an illustration of the natural reluctance of allies, even in the direst peril, to give up military supplies to each other. General Pershing wrote me that we needed seventy thousand horses, and the French could give us no more; now it was up to the British. Lord Milner promised to discuss this with General Cowans, but nothing happened.

It is a very hard thing to get a good horse away from an Englishman, and I knew we would not be satisfied with the horses the British wished to get rid of. Therefore I went around myself to see General Cowans, and he greeted me like an old friend. However, when he heard my errand, he was noncommittal. Fortunately, I discovered in the course of the conversation that we were both spending the week end at the Duchess of Marlborough's place in the country at Crowhurst. Feeling sure that would offer a better opportunity for persuasion, I abandoned my efforts temporarily.

The week end proceeded pleasantly enough, until in the middle of the first night a fellow guest woke me, saying Sir John Cowans was very ill — could I suggest anything to do for him? I hurried to his bedroom. He was rolling about in absolute agony, the sweat pouring off him. For some reason a fat man seems to suffer more than a thin man; perhaps because there is so much more of him. Obviously, Sir John was in excruciating pain. It might have been gallstones or duodenal ulcer, but I was fairly sure it was appendicitis.

We summoned a doctor, the only one in the neighborhood who had not gone to war. He gave General Cowans a little morphine and then ordered a purgative. I was horrified. If it really were acute appendicitis then a purgative might be fatal. By this time all the other guests had gathered in the hall outside. I asked them whether they would back me up if I fought it out. They said they would.

I confronted the doctor. He declared he had made his diagnosis and prescribed treatment; he would not be responsible for Sir John's life if I persevered. I had visions of the flags on the buildings of the Quartermaster's Department flying at half mast, all on account of my interference. Yet I believed I was right, especially since I realized the doctor was a most inferior type of country practitioner.

The next morning we got General Cowans to the hospital at London. His appendix had just burst but the infection had not spread. His physician told him that had he taken a purgative, he probably would not have lived. He never forgot this incident; he used to introduce me jokingly, "You know this beggar saved my life." Thereafter he always did his best to help me out. Eventually a horse trade was concluded whereby the British furnished draft animals for three divisions, and we brought over heavy artillery.

At this moment came up a matter which, utterly ridiculous on the surface, yet threatened to disturb Anglo-American relations in certain high quarters. Paul Cravath, who was in London to deal with the problem of lending money to the Allies, was much concerned about the possible ill effects of the controversy between General Cowans and General Pershing's best friend, Charles G. Dawes.

Dawes, as General Purchasing Agent of the American Army, occupied a position far out of proportion to his nominal rank of lieutenant colonel of engineers. When he had been a bank clerk in Lincoln, Nebraska, General Pershing had been military instructor at the college there. Now the commander, needing someone upon whom he could rely absolutely, had dragged Dawes into the Army. But there was no hope of turning him into a military man. General Pershing used to say, "Charley, while I'm in front of the men, don't come up with your cigar in your mouth and say, 'Good morning, Jack.' I don't give a damn what you call me if we're alone, but after all I'm the official head of the A.E.F., and you're one of my officers."

Before the great conference at Abbéville, General Pershing was giving a last minute inspection to his staff, drawn up to await the arrival of Marshal Foch. To his horror his eye lit on Dawes, standing comfortably at ease with a big cigar in his mouth, tunic bulging, two buttons undone, showing his shirt underneath.

"For heaven's sake, Charley, can I never teach you how to be a soldier?"

With his own hands the Commander in Chief pulled down the tunic and buttoned the buttons.

Although Dawes was a character if there ever was one, he was also an outstanding banker, and in that role was trying to form a unified Allied purchasing commission. He had found that Great Britain and France were actually bidding against each other for mules, horses, onions from Spain, optical goods, watches, field glasses from Switzerland, copper and all sorts of much needed supplies in other parts of the world.

A meeting was arranged in which he could submit his plan for co-ordinating the purchases of supplies to Sir John Cowans and various British officials. Sir John listened without enthusiasm, said stiffly and coldly, "Oh — ah — ouah — you know, we've so many important things to attend to already we'll have to put this matter over for a month."

Then Dawes rose from his chair, banged the table with his fist, delivered himself of a speech that would never be forgotten by those present. "No, by God, you won't put this over for a month. You've been fighting this war for three years. Where have you got? Now we're here and we're going to tell you how to run this war. It's time for you British to learn that, if you're going to win, you've got to give up the methods of an effete monarchy."

"Effete monarchy" was too much for General Cowans. Furious, he jumped to his feet. "I can't stand this," he ejaculated and walked out of the room; the conference broke up in confusion.

The Cowans–Dawes affair had produced an open breach; you could not afford to have such misunderstandings between allies. I hoped that some occasion might present itself for bringing about a reconciliation.

Everything else was driven from my mind, however, when one morning, on arrival at the War Office, I was told I was to be included in the group leaving July 1st for a meeting of the Supreme War Council at Versailles. A distinguished party stepped aboard the special train at Victoria Station — Mr. Lloyd George, Lord Milner, Foreign Secretary Balfour, Premiers Borden of Canada, Hughes of Australia, Lloyd of Newfoundland, and assorted secretaries and aides. We had the Channel boat to ourselves, and as

usual zigzagged frantically back and forth, the radio aerials crack-
ling with messages.

At teatime Mr. Lloyd George asked me to sit by him, and burst
forth again on "General Pershing's great mistake"; he was even
sharper and more severe in his criticism than at our first interview.
There was nothing for me to do but preserve discreet silence until
he ran down and shifted to his troubles with Clemenceau. He admired and respected the French Premier, but found it very hard to
get on with him. "When we're together the sparks are apt to fly,
but it always ends happily. I think we really have discovered a
method of working together."

I started to express my great pleasure, but he went right on to
discuss the British Army in the field, supplying statistics and details of the horrors of Ypres and Passchendaele, stressing the seven
hundred thousand men lost in the 1917 offensive. "It was a terrible
blunder on Haig's part and I'll never forgive him. It bled England
white."

One of Mr. Lloyd George's weaknesses was his blind and bitter
dislike of the military. Remembering General Lawrence's request
that I should put in a good word for the High Command in the
field, I pointed out to the Prime Minister that American divisional
officers had been given Haig's battle orders as a model to study in
the course of their training. He did not mind my talking back to
him. Nevertheless, I thought it unbelievable that he should pick
upon an American officer close to Pershing as his confidant for
scathing criticism of the head of his own armies.

On the quai at Dieppe French military cars were waiting, and we
set out on one of the wildest drives of my experience. With sirens
going full blast we tore over the country, flying up into the air as
we hit a bump, shooting to one side as we slued around corners.
The chauffeurs never slackened their terrific speed even when we
ripped along narrow, winding village streets. Donkeys and carts
were snatched out of the way, women and children plastered themselves against the walls. Tired and nerve-racked, we ground to
a standstill at the doors of the Villa Romagne at Versailles, the
headquarters for British officials attending the conference.

The only one I found up and around the next morning was the

energetic Prime Minister, who had the normal English love for a good hearty breakfast. The storm and stress of the preceding day had vanished; he was very cheerful. He said he would like to make some sort of public statement in praise of American aid, and asked my opinion as to the best time and place.

"What would you think of addressing an American division in the field day after tomorrow? It's our national holiday."

"Splendid. But I'm busy the Fourth; would the fifth do just as well?"

"I don't see why not," I answered.

Bowly ran me into Paris where, with some difficulty, I reached General Pershing by telephone. He approved the idea. "Part of the Thirty-third is with General Rawlinson's Fourth Army near Amiens. Get in touch with General Bell and say you have my authority to make all arrangements."

To ensure proper publicity I rounded up a group of English and American newspapermen who promised to be present. Then I hurried back to Versailles, and reported the program to Mr. Lloyd George.

The next morning I met General Pershing at the Rue de Varennes, and on our way out to Versailles asked his advice on the Dawes–Cowans imbroglio. "Dawes is here at the Ritz," he said. "Why not see him yourself?"

The Hotel Trianon had been taken over for the meeting, and for blocks around *gendarmerie* were stationed so that nobody without the proper credentials could approach. I joined Bowly and Kerr, who were sitting outside the long gallery which ran across the front. All we had to do was to wait there until the conference was over. One by one the leaders arrived — Lord Balfour and Lord Milner, Marshal Foch with General Weygand close behind, General Pershing followed by General Conner, M. Clemenceau, who occupied the place at the head of the table.

The glass doors were closed; M. Clemenceau rose to deliver a harangue, his walrus mustaches wagging. Soon he began banging with his fist, waving his arms, raising his voice so that we could even catch a word or two. It was perfectly patent that wigs were on the green. Mr. Lloyd George leaned over to Lord Milner and then grew equally excited, shaking his fist also, giving tit for tat.

M. Clemenceau consulted General Weygand and broke out again. Generals Pershing and Conner were going through papers and discussing something earnestly. After a while, however, they all calmed down enough to continue with their business.

It was a protracted meeting. To my astonishment the minute the doors were opened M. Clemenceau grabbed Mr. Lloyd George by the arm and the two marched out and by us into the restaurant room at the end of the gallery, where they sat down for a cup of tea. In a few moments both were laughing merrily.

The English always said some of the best business of bringing the Allies together and coming to important agreements was done over the Versailles teacups. Everybody gathered at little tables, nibbled sandwiches and cakes, sipped tea amid a buzz of conversation. I enjoyed it particularly since it furnished me an opportunity to meet the leaders and find out what had caused the excitement.

M. Clemenceau had sounded the old French theme that the Allies were very badly off. They had a certain number of divisions in either the line or reserve; the Germans had many more. Desperate measures had to be taken, there must be no holding back of men or the war might easily be lost. Unceremoniously Mr. Lloyd George interrupted, "M. Clemenceau, Lord Milner advises me our figures do not tally with yours."

"Marshal Foch himself gave me these. Who should know better?"

The two Englishmen again conferred. "We're sorry, M. Clemenceau, but we can't make our figures coincide with yours. We show twenty divisions more."

At this point M. Clemenceau's rage became monumental, he shouted that it was intolerable for Mr. Lloyd George or anybody else to attempt to inform him how many divisions the Allies had. His figures must be accepted without question. He had the most absolute confidence in his military advisers.

Mr. Lloyd George shouted back he too had the utmost confidence in his military advisers. He could not permit anybody to tell him he was wrong. The British information was as good as the French.

You could imagine the Allies in this grave crisis quarreling about principles of strategy, but not about a matter of simple mathematics. A more ridiculous situation would be hard to conceive; it had an absurdity equaled only by Alice's tea party.

After fully fifteen minutes of tension, it occurred to these gentlemen simultaneously to look at each other's lists. All was at once plain. M. Clemenceau had entirely omitted to include in his calculations the Belgian divisions which the English had counted in.

Everybody at the Villa Romagne that evening was in excellent spirits at having caught the French in an egregious error. Both Prime Minister and War Secretary were in a much happier frame of mind and saying nice things about the American Army and General Pershing; they even joked about the Dawes–Cowans controversy.

The next day, the Fourth, I took the opportunity of a few hours' leisure to look up Dawes. As I walked into the Ritz, I happened to run into Mrs. Leeds, widow of the great tin magnate. She said she would like to give a real celebration dinner. I could have carte blanche to order whatever I wanted — champagne of the rarest vintage, caviar, anything. If I would invite other American officers, she would invite ladies. Of course I accepted.

I then went to Dawes's office. He rose from his chair as I entered, lifting his arm as though to ward off a blow. "All right, Griscom, I know what you're going to say, but go easy."

Dawes was tall, thin, with a whimsical sort of face, a man obviously full of good humor, certainly not the sort to prolong a quarrel. I began my little speech about the folly of antagonizing the British Army and particularly its Quartermaster-general, who was so vital to Dawes's own plan.

"Wait, now," he interrupted. "I want you to hear my side. Years ago I found in business that if you were talking to a fellow and he took a condescending attitude, there was no better way to negotiate than to haul off and hit him a crack in the belly. Then he began to notice who you were and to think you might be somebody. I don't actually hit anybody with my fist, but I do with my tongue. If ever a person behaved poisonously, it was Sir John Cowans. I knew I would get nowhere if I didn't hit him. Crack! I did it, knowing exactly what I was doing, and I think you'll find it will work in the long run."

Dawes was a natural actor and had a method of approach which for sheer audacity I never saw equaled. I could not help laughing — his explanation was so plausible. "If I can interpret your peculiar technique to Sir John, and in some way bring about a re-opening of relations, will you meet him halfway?"

"I'll promise to be as meek as a lamb."

"Fine. Come to dinner tonight and we'll have a glass of champagne on it."

Dawes occupied the seat of honor between Mrs. Leeds and Lady Sarah Wilson, aunt of the Duke of Marlborough, a most dignified white-haired *grande dame,* who had been a figure in London society for a generation. I could not help overhearing the conversation. As soon as soup was served, the waiter started to fill Dawes's glass with champagne. "Here, waiter, you take that away. You go get me a big cup of coffee and some cream."

Lady Sarah viewed him with surprise. "Colonel Dawes, if you are dining as a lady's guest and want something different, don't give the order to the waiter but ask your hostess. I'm sure she would be glad to order it for you."

"I'm a plain American, and I don't pretend to understand these fancy European customs. We plain Americans like a big cup of coffee with our suppers — Say, I didn't catch your name. Who are you?"

"Lady Sarah Wilson."

"Lady Sarah Wilson? I can never get these titles over here straight. I'll give you a choice. I'll call you either Mrs. Wilson or just plain Sarah."

You could have knocked her down with a feather, but she was equal to the occasion. "Of the two I think I prefer to have you call me Sarah."

"Then you call me Charley," said the unabashed Dawes.

By the end of dinner, they were having a wonderful time, and she asked him to come to see her in London. It is certain she never forgot that evening.

Early next morning the Prime Minister, Lord Milner, Premier Hughes, and I drove to the headquarters of General Rawlinson near Amiens. We found him somewhat worried. The previous day without General Pershing's authority, he had put a regiment of the American Thirty-third Division into the line at Hamel with the Australians. At the last moment before the action, General Pershing had ordered the troops out, but it was too late. The men had fought fiercely and well and had just come out of the lines.

It was a perfect day, warm and sunny. Far off we could hear the thunder-rumbling of the battle. We watched the Thirty-third review with their music, a fine display, and then the men were massed in a bowl in the hills. Above them the Prime Minister stood up in the back of his car to speak. He took Anglo-American solidarity as his theme, and then expressed approval of President Wilson's Fourth of July declaration of war aims. "If the Kaiser and his advisers are prepared to accept the conditions stated by your President, he can have peace not only with America but also with Great Britain and France."

It was as impressive a speech as I had ever listened to. He was not restrained by the dignified tone required in the House of Commons and the little hollow was filled by his penetrating voice. Vigorous gestures intensified his words; his long graying hair floated out as he shook his head for emphasis.

When his voice died away, and the distant mutterings of the cannon once more became audible, the densely packed Americans cheered his speech to the echo, and, thanks to the newspapermen, it was heard round the world.

CHAPTER XXXIII

ALL IN GOOD LIAISON

When once again, after five days, I found myself back in the large comfortable house which General Biddle and I had rented at 41 Upper Grosvenor Street, the only tangible evidence that I had been away were my dispatch boxes filled with cheeses. However, my trip had impressed on me anew the well-known fact that the greatest weaknesses of an alliance were the points at which two nationalities touched, and had also shown me how much the Allies would gain if misunderstanding and mistrust among its leaders could be avoided.

The Dawes–Cowans controversy was still uppermost in my mind, and, in the hope of effecting a *rapprochement,* I traveled down to Sussex to see the General, who was recuperating at his cottage by the sea. Sir John loved golf and, in spite of being temporarily deprived of his favorite sport, on sunny mornings he used to choose a spot on the near-by links, close to the rough, where the gorse flourished in bristly, dense, impenetrable thickets. There he sat, puffing away on his pipe, his retriever by his side. Soon a ball bounded into view and disappeared into the thorniest part of the underbrush. Players approached, and a caddy said discouragingly, "You'll never find anything in there." The moment they were out of sight General Cowans spoke to his dog which darted off, and shortly its master was the richer by another golf ball.

The General's pockets were bulging when I arrived, and he seemed in such good fettle that I made bold to mention I had met Colonel Dawes in Paris. Although my host was at once very much on his dignity, I went on to describe the interview as humorously as I could. To my gratification General Cowans began to laugh, and continued, "After all, Colonel Dawes is General Pershing's most intimate friend; he has a serious scheme that both the General and the French War Office believe in. You may have thought he behaved in an extraordinary fashion, but he is an extraordinary American."

Sir John's antagonism evaporated. "I suppose it's time I learned something about Americans if we're going to fight a war together. Probably I was never more insulted in my life, but you tell Dawes to come back, and I'll try to get on with him."

A remarkable friendship resulted. The two men, so entirely different, grew to respect each other greatly, and at the end of their association parted on terms of unusual affection.

I settled down again at the War Office, where every moment was occupied in handling a steady stream of inquiries from our G.H.Q. Soon I realized to my regret I could not hope to do justice to my English duties and synchronously maintain liaison with the French. After forwarding the English reply to the French indictment, I devoted my attention exclusively to London.

To answer even the most elementary requests often involved me in unexpected difficulty. For example, I was asked to report exactly how many men Great Britain had in France. That will be easy, I said to myself, and set forth confidently. To my surprise, although every department could give me figures for its own activities, nowhere could I obtain complete statistics. If Lloyd George had demanded them, he would undoubtedly have had them, but I was not the Prime Minister.

On Paul Cravath's advice I went to consult Maynard Keynes at the Treasury, who was supposed to have all such information at his finger tips. I threaded my way through a perfect warren of paneled hallways and winding, twisting stairs, up three steps here and down four steps there, until finally I tracked my quarry to his desk in a small ancient room. He admitted the Treasury paid the salaries of all the soldiers, yet even from him I could not learn how many there were or where they were.

I expressed my amazement to Dwight Morrow, of the Allied Maritime Transport Council, that no one could give me these simple facts. "Wait a minute," he broke in, and pulling out a little black notebook, read me off the list I wanted.

"Where in heaven's name did you get that?"

"Why, a few days ago I had some business with the Quartermaster at Montreuil, and during our conversation I asked him whether he had the figures of the total British man power in France. 'Of course,' he said, 'I have to feed and clothe them.'"

Morrow's little black notebook was famous. If he heard anything that interested him particularly, out it would come; and in his meticulous handwriting he would make notes; in time, it was a thesaurus of information.

Frequently I had to obtain details of what the British considered military secrets. The head of our Ordnance Department, having heard of a new British gun, wanted to know how many there were, and whether we could get any. When I broached the subject to the official in charge, he immediately grew indignant. For fifteen minutes he elaborated on the colossal cheek of the Americans, and at length demanded, "Why the devil should we give you fellows these guns that we've worked so hard to develop?"

That was my cue. With a smile I replied, "In April, 1917, our President declared war on Germany and we found ourselves engaged in hostilities with the German Army. During these months we've learned the British are also engaged in similar hostilities. Since our interests seem to be the same, we're venturing to ask you to tell us about this weapon."

"Oh, confound you! Come around in a couple of days, and we'll have a memorandum ready for you."

Nobody could have been received with greater frankness and trust than that which I encountered everywhere. The top of my desk was often the repository for papers of the most confidential nature, such as notes made by Lord Milner after a cabinet meeting. I used to threaten Bowly and Amery jokingly that someday I would read them. "Well, that might do the politicians a lot of good," dryly observed Bowly.

The cheerful spirit which prevailed at the War Office made the atmosphere particularly pleasant. Every new joke or anecdote was quickly repeated there. Perhaps someone would drop in and inquire, in all seriousness, "I say, you fellows, if you had to have a wound, what kind would you choose?"

We fell into profound deliberation until, unable to hold in longer, our visitor interrupted, "Well, how'd you like to have a WAAC on the knee?"

The Women's Army Auxiliary Corps was always the subject of good-natured chaffing.

Only once did I experience anything that approached want of

co-operation. In order to obtain for Colonel Dennis Nolan, the head of our Intelligence Department at Chaumont, an accurate picture of what was going on in Russia, I went to the British Intelligence, where most elaborate reports were on file. Unchallenged, I walked by the barrier, and then suddenly an office functionary in an unpleasant way told me to get back. I was somewhat hurt by this rebuff and remarked to Bowly, "I'll have to let Colonel Nolan know of this lack of sympathy." I meant to imply that we, on our part, might have to retaliate. I was sorry afterwards. Naturally Intelligence services were reluctant to explain their methods, and both British and French guarded their secrets from one another for fear of imperiling their agents.

Several days later I received a courteous invitation from General Sir George MacDonogh, the head of Army Intelligence, to lunch at the Carlton Hotel. I arrived to find he had arranged it as a demonstration to make up for any ill feeling I might cherish. Almost every member of his staff was there, including the Duke of Northumberland and others in the inner circle whom I had never met before. General MacDonogh went out of his way to stress the necessity of close relations between their Intelligence and ours, and thereafter I was able to send to Chaumont whatever material Colonel Nolan requested.

Since I had become a fixture at the War Office, I soon had my share of what was called "paper work." The British had an elaborate system of passing on documents from one department to another. The legal department, on perusing a brief account of a court martial, might append a few remarks with the concluding comment, "This department can advise about law, but the case in point includes subjects which are respectfully submitted to the Director of Military Operations." That official would heavily underline: "The time of this department is amply taken up directing military operations. Respectfully submitted to the Assistant Chief of Staff." He in turn would suggest the matter was more for the police than for the military. It should have "the attention of the Chief of Staff to whom it is respectfully submitted." The Chief of Staff might add politely that he had no intention of being saddled with this question, which involved politics, and was likely to be brought up in the House of Commons. The person who should really decide it was the Secretary of State for War, to whom he "respectfully submitted it."

Anything touching America was shoved on to me, and one morning I started to wade through a bulky document referred to "Major Griscom for his kindly comment." It seemed one of our army sergeants on the Siberian expedition had been ordered home in disgrace from Murmansk. He had written to the Philadelphia *Public Ledger,* complaining of the outrageous conduct of the British, who sat back in the taverns and played with the town girls, while the Americans were being marched out in the ice and cold to do all the fighting. The British Ambassador had sent the clipping to the Foreign Office with the notation that it might have unfortunate repercussions in America.

As these "papers" moved around, they increased so in volume that departmental officers grew more and more loath to read them through. Buried among the many endorsements was one by a high War Office official: "Everybody knows the Americans are an ignorant and vulgar people. This is just what might be expected of them. Why bother with such trash?"

Often comments were facetious, but obviously this was not meant to be funny. I perused it again, becoming more and more angry, although I realized those who had referred it to me could never have seen it. I could not possibly initial this paper myself. If I forwarded a copy to General Pershing, it would raise a terrific stir, and I was put in London to preserve peace. I went home to sleep on it.

During the night I had an idea, and in the morning I took the paper into Creedy's office. "I never seem to get used to your system of endorsements. Here's one that I think I could comment on, but I'm not quite sure what I ought to say."

"I'll help you. Let's see it."

One glance was enough. Creedy's expression was a study. He hemmed and hawed and coughed. I continued, "If I were to draw up my comment alone, it might be rather emphatic. Perhaps we should do it together. I won't bother you any more now. We can discuss it tomorrow."

Normally at the end of the day I cleared off my desk, but this time I carefully left the folder conspicuously displayed on the top with the endorsement face up. The next day it was gone. I slyly remarked to Bowly that there must be thieves in the War Office, because certain papers of mine had disappeared. He never smiled. "We'll have to look into that," was all he said.

Not long after, Creedy explained he had carried the paper to Lord Milner. "The chief will never mention this question to you. It's not supposed to exist. I merely wanted you to know he had written your endorsement for you and the responsible official has been on the carpet. We're much obliged to you for not letting it go further."

The scope of my activities was by no means confined to the War Office. One day an Irishman of national prominence came to me, bubbling over with a plan for General Pershing's consideration. He admitted his countrymen had given no more assistance to the English than they could avoid, and that Irish girls had refused to be English WAACs. But he thought he had found a way to alter the whole anti-Ally feeling in Ireland. Now that so many American soldiers were arriving in France, he proposed to collect five thousand young Irish girls, and send them over to carry on those services of the rear for which women were so admirably adapted — such as driving motor cars, or acting as telephone operators, secretaries, and stenographers. Over in Ireland, he said, they liked the idea very much, and in England he had talked with the Archbishop of Canterbury and many others, who approved wholeheartedly.

It was not hard to imagine what would happen if five thousand British-hating Irish colleens were dumped down in the midst of the Americans, but I did not wish to offend my well-meaning visitor. It seemed to me that the Archbishop was the logical person to quash the plan. Rather to my surprise his number was listed in the telephone book like that of any other subscriber. When I heard a voice, I asked for an appointment with the Archbishop. "This is the Archbishop speaking. I'd be glad to see you any time." It was as though I had called the Vatican and the Pope himself had answered the telephone.

We had an amicable interview, and he agreed the Irish girl proposition should be dropped.

A case which offered more serious potentialities for causing friction was presented one day by Sir Matthew Wilson, Lord Beaverbrook's principal assistant in the Ministry for Propaganda in

Friendly Countries, who rushed in to my office in great excitement. Mr. Edward Bok, the editor of the *Ladies' Home Journal* and son-in-law of Cyrus H. K. Curtis, was threatening to rouse American mothers to join a moral crusade to protect their sons.

Mr. Bok, who had come to England as one of a delegation of distinguished American publishers and editors, had been exploring around London to see how the many American soldiers on leave there were being treated. The preceding evening, on the way to visit a Y.M.C.A. hut near the far end of the Strand, he had been confronted by the amazing sight which those who beheld it will never forget. To the casual observer it seemed as though all the English young women of the oldest profession in the world were concentrated in that short street, milling on the sidewalk and swarming over the pavement, in crowds so dense that a passer-by had to push his way through.

Mr. Bok was horrified. At the hut he asked a number of Americans whether they had ever been approached by women.

"Of course," was the unanimous answer.

One boy proudly boasted that within two hundred yards of the hut he had been accosted by seventeen. Mr. Bok, even more scandalized, returned at once to his hotel and drafted a lengthy and sensational exposé of this feature of the war, so familiar in Europe but so new to him; his remedy was to ban London for soldiers on leave, and instead establish camps in the country for them.

Mr. Bok presented his article to Lord Beaverbrook, saying, "I want you to print this on the front page of the *Daily Express*. Then I want you to bring pressure on your Government to do something about it. Otherwise I will reveal to two million American mothers what temptations their boys are exposed to in England."

Mr. Bok's point of view was a novel one to two such men of the world as Lord Beaverbrook and his assistant. "Are not American soldiers exposed to temptation in American ports before they sail?" Sir Matthew exclaimed in conclusion. "My God, Griscom, don't they do that sort of thing in America?"

As tactfully as I could I replied, "It's more taken for granted here after four years of war than in the United States."

Mr. Bok was one of the most high-minded men I had ever known, filled with an earnest desire to help his fellows. It is the little slights that hurt a man's pride; if the British paid no attention to his request he might go home and with his influence make a most disagreeable stir. "Publish the article," I advised.

It was published. That very morning Mr. Bok called upon me, delighted with what he had done, but at the same time anxious for approbation. Very mildly I suggested his country camp plan might work hardship on all those American soldiers who would get instruction and diversion out of visiting the historic city of London, which they might never see again.

He looked doubtful. "I should not like to do anything to make our men unhappy. Perhaps I acted too much on impulse — I was terribly shocked."

Mr. Bok, nevertheless, departed from Great Britain with his mind at rest, and a few days later the subject was forgotten.

Just as in diplomacy one of my chief duties was to gather information. I sent regular reports to General Pershing, and in addition Colonel House asked me to relay to him any items of news I might pick up in London of potential interest to President Wilson. I realized I could not serve two masters and agreed, provided each report went first to General Pershing.

In London one of the most satisfactory methods of learning what was happening behind the scenes and confirming rumors was to accept invitations. Nearly all the upper strata of English society were connected in some capacity with the Government, and traditionally it was impossible for high officials to keep from sharing secrets with their friends — So-and-so was going in or out of the Cabinet, So-and-so was a failure in such and such a position and was to be removed. However, they formed so close a corporation that it was doubtful whether much valuable information reached the wrong ears.

We on our part gave several dinners, and then General Biddle, anxious to return the many kindnesses of the Duke of Connaught, former Viceroy of Canada, proposed a party for him and his daughter, the Princess Patricia. The affair began to assume bigger and bigger proportions. When General Biddle's trio of attractive aides — Alexander Biddle, Howard Henry, and Jack Potter, all of Philadelphia — said they could get the band from the Grafton

Galleries, the most popular of the night clubs, we invited dozens of extra guests for a ball after dinner.

During the War there was no question of a season because the court frowned on any social activity; whoever wished to dance had to go to a hotel or a night club. I thought if ever there was a need for a little gaiety it was at a time of such great strain. Some forty-eight hours before the event, one of the English Guards officers confided to me that the Prince of Wales and the Duke of York had heard we were having an American dance and would like very much to be asked. We asked them.

As the result of saving up our food tickets, we dined sumptuously, and in due course we adjourned to the ballroom, already crowded. Glancing about, I noticed several little yellow-haired bits of fluff sitting around eating supper, or dancing with officers, some evidently intoxicated. Each of us had our own guests and, deciding that the others had extended some ill-advised invitations, I refrained from raising any question. At last Howard Henry came up to me, much worried: "I don't suppose you know anything about these extra people."

Since everyone was equally puzzled, I walked up to one couple, requesting of the British officer, "Would you be kind enough to tell me your name?"

"Why should I?"

"This happens to be my house, and my party."

"Do you mean this isn't a night club? Why, at the Grafton Galleries they said the band was playing at 41 Upper Grosvenor Street. A lot of us followed it over here."

In all, there must have been twenty uninvited couples. I summoned Lady Astor, and we approached the only American I saw, an ensign dancing with a girl who obviously had been picked up on the Strand. He gave me his name and then I inquired, "What's the lady's name?"

"Just a friend of mine."

Lady Astor interrupted, "Look here, you bad boy, you take this young woman back where you found her; after that come to me and I'll see that you have a good time."

The poor ensign, embarrassed, looked at the girl, looked away, and finally with great positiveness asserted, "I asked this lady out with me, and I guess I'd better stay with her."

And off they walked.

Notwithstanding this slight contretemps, the ball was a huge success. The Prince of Wales and the Duke of York arrived, the former blond and attractive, his brother shy but thoroughly enjoying himself. I presented many American officers to the old Duke, who resembled King Edward VII except that he had no beard — English army officers were not allowed to wear one unless under doctor's orders to protect their throats from chills. In the Navy, on the other hand, you had to have a beard or go clean-shaven — a mustache was never permitted.

Everyone was eager to dance with the Princess. In spite of my attempts to maintain the rules of Court etiquette, the young officers insisted on cutting in, even tapping her on the shoulder in the most friendly way — "Well, Princess, what about a little fling?" She did not mind in the least, and told me she wanted to be treated like anybody else. Certainly, the presence of royalty did not spoil that party.

I could not help observing again and again how the War was modifying the social formulae to which I had been accustomed in the England of the Nineties. Once, after a big charity ball at the Albert Hall, I left my box with ex-King Manuel of Portugal. "I wonder how I'll get my carriage," he said helplessly.

Rather sorry for the exiled monarch, I volunteered to locate it if he cared to wait. Approaching a bobby directing traffic outside I asked: "Will you have the King of Portugal's carriage called?"

"King of what?"

"King of Portugal."

"We've no arrangements for calling anybody's carriage." I tried another bobby — the same answer. By this time I felt responsible for getting the King home. Walking to the curb, I took my stand in my evening clothes under the glare of the lights, and shouted at the top of my lungs, "The King of Portugal's carriage!"

No reply. I walked on a little way. "The King of Portugal's carriage!" I bellowed louder.

Chauffeurs and passers by gazed at me curiously. At length I heard a faint response; it was the missing driver. I sent him on, not envying the position of an ex-king.

Some weeks later my courtesy to the King of Portugal was repaid by one of his former diplomats. Following a very formal dinner, where I was lowest in rank, the men went in turn to the washroom. Naturally I was last. On emerging, I found the old Marquis de Soveral, former Minister of Portugal to England.

"I hope Your Excellency is not waiting for me," I said.

"Griscom, I want to tell you that in the course of a long life, one of the standards by which I have measured a gentleman is that he will never let the last man go in alone to join the ladies."

Still another facet of my liaison work developed during the summer. In the course of building up good will between G.H.Q. and London, I expected I should have to interpret General Pershing to the English, but I had never anticipated I should have to justify him to my own countrymen.

Early in my stay I talked with Admiral Sims, the commander of the American Fleet in Europe. To my complete amazement, he was honestly convinced that the French and British criticisms of General Pershing were warranted. He pointed to the fine showing of our Thirty-third Division on July 4th, which proved the British right in thinking our troops sufficiently prepared to be turned over to them for service in the front lines.

Knowing that the Admiral was in high favor in Washington, I sat down to try to convince him he had totally misunderstood General Pershing's intent. If there were a crisis the British commanders had a free hand in using any of our troops in their area for defense. But in the case of small offensives, where their participation was quite unnecessary, General Pershing objected to their being thrown in without his express permission, especially when, as was the case with the Seventy-seventh, they had reached France with thousands of absolutely green men in them.

Before I left, I had the satisfaction of seeing the Admiral's point of view veer around entirely. However, this interview brought home to me the importance of having accurate information circulated among Americans about General Pershing and our Army. Every few days distinguished fellow citizens of mine would arrive in London, nearly all of them on some sort of official mission. I did my best to make sure that none who might have influence or power at home should depart with erroneous ideas.

One of the evident places where misrepresentation of General Pershing and our Army could occur was in the English newspapers; many of their articles were regularly reprinted in America. A simple method of getting him a good press was to arrange for leading writers and journalists, such as James Barrie and Lord Milner's friend, Geoffrey Dawson, editor of the London *Times,* to meet him when they went to France.

One week end, while I was staying with the Pagets at Coombe, I found a fellow guest was Colonel Charles aCourt Repington of the *Morning Post,* perhaps the foremost military critic in England, and among the few who dared write what he thought. His caustic pen, pointed by a sardonic sense of humor, often made the War Office writhe. Between tennis and charades we struck up a bargain — I would keep him informed about our Army and he would show me what he was going to print. I would have done the same thing for any other writer, but nobody else wanted it.

One of General Pershing's most marked characteristics, which I had noticed from the day he had walked into my office in Tokio, was his unwillingness to talk of himself; he was incapable of any effort to gain credit no matter how much he deserved it. For that reason he was a peculiarly easy mark for criticism. Anyone who knew the inside story of the war that summer could not fail to realize how unfair these criticisms were.

General Pershing was a man of action and determination. In May, at the very moment the French were in headlong retreat towards the Marne, he had begun to urge on Marshal Foch a forward movement. The Marshal at first had held back, saying our divisions were untried; if they took the offensive they would have to be supported by his own priceless shock troops. Furthermore, it was too great a gamble; in the event of defeat he had not enough reserves to block the way to Paris.

General Pershing retorted in effect, "We've come here to fight the Germans. If you won't let us make an attack in this sector, let us form a corps somewhere else. But we want to fight, and we've proved we're ready."

Marshal Foch finally agreed to a plan. Our First and Second Divisions were to assume positions south of Soissons at the root of the salient, and between them would be put the shock Moroccan

Division, including the Foreign Legion. The attack was set for July 18th.

Our troops were actually en route when the Germans made their fourth drive for Paris, and this time beat their way across the Marne. Thinking of those threatening heights which I had seen only a few weeks before, I was not surprised to hear that the Third Division had been driven back. Yet although some of the units lost as many as fifty per cent of their men, they refused to be defeated.

The First Division, under General Charles P. Summerall, and the Second, now commanded by General Harbord, attacked on schedule, taking the Germans unaware, and pushing ahead so irresistibly that the Germans were forced to evacuate the Marne salient. This was one of the smashing victories of the War, and also proved General Pershing's point — our troops would and could go forward against the best defense the Germans could oppose.

Our counterattack was followed August 8th by a British thrust at the Amiens salient. From Bacon I learned that Haig, having formulated his plans, had discussed them with Foch; at first flatly refusing consent, the Marshal had given in only after great argument. Haig's success was immediate, and in its way as decisive as General Pershing's.

The world's praise for these two victories was heaped high on Foch, and little mention was made of Pershing and Haig. On my next visit to British and American Headquarters, indignation among the staffs was running high, but the American and British commanders were too good soldiers to protest.

"Don't ever forget," a British general warned me, "that the history of the war that is accepted by posterity will be written by Foch and his entourage. When all's said and done, he's the supreme commander."

No one would want to detract from Marshal Foch's accomplishments. He was adroit, shrewd, a masterly strategist, and undoubtedly inspired the Allies with confidence. He threw in the French reserves to Haig's aid although he could easily have withheld them. It was an inestimable advantage to have one person make the ultimate decisions, instead of three such dominant personalities as Pershing, Haig, and Pétain, each urging his own plan as the one to be adopted.

Even after the repeated American successes, the old friction over the separate American Army, which I supposed had been totally forgotten, again flared up. I arrived one August morning to find the War Office in unusual agitation. Lord Milner had discovered privately from General Rawlinson that American divisions were being removed from English areas. I had heard nothing about it, but came in for a full share of displeasure. Sir Henry Wilson was so angry he could hardly speak civilly, and Lord Milner icily informed me he thought the removal premature, and the manner of removal without consulting him showed want of consideration. He deeply regretted our good relations should receive this blow, and feared to tell the Prime Minister, knowing how furious he would be.

Here was a danger signal. I hurried to telegraph General Pershing. His prompt reply did not mince words. He too had believed the matter settled, and had assumed he and Haig had full authority to make whatever arrangements were necessary.

I took the answer to Sir Henry Wilson who, barely glancing at it, said bluntly that a separate American Army, formed too soon, was a menace to the Allies. General Alexander Godley, who commanded a British division near our troops, had reported to him that our terrific casualties were unnecessary and caused by defective staff work. "We've had experience, and we know how to move our armies forward. You don't. If you have an army of your own and make an attack, I can tell you what will happen. If you meet the Germans in force, you'll lose half your men. If you find them unprepared, you'll go forward a little way and then be bogged down — your staff won't function, and your service of supplies won't be able to keep up."

For some days after this outburst there was an underground current of unrest throughout the War Office. Constant rumors were coming to my ears of the Prime Minister's wrath — he was merely waiting for the impending arrival of Secretary of War Newton D. Baker before demanding General Pershing's removal.

I had no idea what effect a diatribe from the hot-headed Welshman might have on Mr. Baker, who was entirely unknown to me. While I was wondering what would be my best course, Lord Milner announced we were going to France again. Since Mr. Baker was already there, this was my opportunity to warn him of what was in the wind.

We crossed the Channel September 11th on a tiny little craft called a "P." boat, even smaller than a destroyer; it was a rough trip in a gale of wind. As soon as we landed, I hurried to Montreuil to compare notes with Bacon. The British had just finished pushing the Germans out of the Somme salient. Under the circumstances, I would have expected General Haig to have shown a little jubilation. However, the only change in his normal serious demeanor was his admission that there might be a faint possibility of ultimate success.

The next day came the news of a great American triumph at St. Mihiel. The whole salient, which had defied the French for four years, was now in our possession, and Secretary Baker was viewing the victory at first hand. Hearing he was bound to Paris, I too headed for the capital and located him at the Rue de Varennes. He reminded me of E. H. Harriman — small in stature, but with that same impression of latent intellectual power, and the same soft, gentle voice; it was hard to believe the reports of his oratorical talents.

Not until we were on the train to Boulogne the following evening, en route for England, was there an interlude of calm in which I could tell him he should be prepared for the most bitter criticism of General Pershing by the Prime Minister, and in fact for a direct request for the Commander in Chief's removal. Mr. Baker listened attentively, and then replied noncommittally: "Thank you. Your information may be very useful." As to what he really thought I could get no inkling.

Mr. Baker was to be my guest at Upper Grosvenor Street, and we arrived to find a message from the Prime Minister to the effect that he would disobey his doctors and come to London if Mr. Baker would not drive down to the country to see him. He had something he felt he must say.

I was convinced General Pershing's fate might well lie in the balance, and awaited with anxiety the result of the meeting. Mr. Baker returned at nightfall, as usual calm and unmoved. I naturally asked him how things had gone. "I am entirely satisfied," was his only comment. We had a dinner for him, one of our best — Lord Milner, General Cowans, Sir Henry Wilson, and many others were there. Afterwards he went to bed, still leaving me completely in the air.

In the morning, however, at the War Office, my ears were filled with the doings of the day before. Admiration for Mr. Baker was unbounded. Everyone was exclaiming, "There's a great man," "A real statesman," "What an orator!"

I managed to piece together what had happened. At the end of lunch, Lloyd George, with obvious premeditation, had half turned his chair at the table so that he faced Mr. Baker, and then began to speak with vehement emphasis. He complained that Great Britain had stripped necessary Empire services of ships in order to carry American troops to France. These had scarcely reached British areas before General Pershing had pulled them away and taken them into his own custody on another part of the line. He continued in this vein for fifteen minutes, getting more and more wrought up, concluding with the categorical statement that, as far as Great Britain was concerned, the American Army was perfectly useless, and the shipping devoted to bringing it over utterly wasted.

Mr. Baker now displayed in full measure his extraordinary gift for employing the English language. He expressed profound astonishment at Mr. Lloyd George's accusations. He had just been in France. On General Pershing's war maps he had observed the number of German divisions stationed opposite the Americans, and had been persuaded that at least our soldiers were detaining troops which might otherwise be added to the concentration against the French and British. He recognized the duty of the Prime Minister to utilize the resources of Great Britain in any way that seemed most advantageous. Quite clearly, if carrying American soldiers to France was not the best use which could be made of British ships, Mr. Lloyd George ought to withdraw that service at once and devote them to whatever would be helpful.

"If you decide to withdraw your shipping, I shall cable immediately to Washington to cease sending troops on British ships, which may then be released at once. I have been led to suppose the thing most desired in France is man power, and America is the largest available reservoir from which man power can be brought. But if this is an error, it is my plain duty to transport only such troops as we can find passage for on American ships, and send sustenance for in American cargo steamers."

Gradually this little man lifted his voice, and banged on the dinner table. "Mr. Prime Minister, we are not in need of advice from any foreign nation as to who should lead our armies. General Pershing possesses the fullest confidence of President Wilson and myself, and except for the most unusual and sudden emergency, American troops must fight as American units and be commanded by American officers."

Mr. Lloyd George retreated precipitously from the attack, never voicing his demand that General Pershing be removed. With a few scattered remarks on the value of British training to our soldiers, he said he had to fight the war with Turkey, and retired to his room.

Years later Mr. Baker himself finished the story. He had set off for London with Lord Reading and about halfway the Lord Chief Justice had said with diplomatic casualness, "Oh, by the way, Mr. Secretary, the Prime Minister sent for me before we started and asked me to excuse his not saying good-by. Incidentally, he also asked me to say to you that you should think no more about the matter which he raised for discussion after lunch."

CHAPTER XXXIV

THE LAST GUNS

Mr. Baker left immediately, having by his forthrightness buried another bone of contention. Yet we at the War Office could not settle down to our normal routine. We all knew that the Allied armies were gathering themselves together for their most ambitious effort — a knockout blow to push the Germans out of France and Flanders.

September 2nd General Pershing had proposed to Marshal Foch and General Pétain at Bombon a plan to cut the lifeline of the German forces in the West, the Metz-Mezières-Maubeuge Railroad. Secretly by night he would move into position a half million American soldiers, fully supplied, and make a surprise attack where it was least expected.

To the left of Verdun the heights of the Meuse and Argonne formed a narrow V, the mouth of which, twenty miles wide, faced the Allied lines. Commanding the entrance was the fortress rock of Montfaucon, and behind it stretched an unending succession of sharp ravines, jagged hills, treacherous marshes, and thick forests. The Germans, supplementing nature's defenses, in four years of leisure had constructed four systems of fortifications, several miles apart, firmly welded to the heights on either hand, each an inextricable tangle of barbed wire, concrete shelters, trenches, machine gun pits. Anywhere a handful of men could hold back a regiment. There the Germans, confident of security, had set up camps for their tired divisions, complete with *Bierhalle,* grape arbors, bowling alleys.

Again, as before the Marne attack, the argument was long and heated, although ultimately Marshal Foch agreed to General Pershing's plan and promised to co-ordinate the American endeavor with a synchronous attack by the British and French. At the British War Office I heard no words of cheer — it was six weeks to the fall rains, hardly time for any decisive break-through. How could our staff transfer a half-million men unbeknownst to the Germans? Sir Henry Wilson remarked to me, "Why, the French have been in front of the Argonne for four years without making an impression. How do you think you Americans can do anything?"

On the afternoon of September 26th the Chief of Staff sent for me. Shaking his head, he announced that the Americans had launched their attack; black reports had just come from Foch's headquarters. Our losses were staggering, our untried divisions of the National Guard and National Army could not hold our advances. Of the three roads which led forward, two were under flanking fire and useless, the third was a narrow dirt country lane shot to pieces again and again. Artillery, supplies, and fresh troops could not be brought up. Our services of the rear were in chaos, our staff work had collapsed completely.

Unable to believe this information was true, I tried to get through by telephone to General McAndrew at Chaumont. It was impossible. I rushed back to Sir Henry Wilson's office to find him even gloomier. Everything was worse than if we had never insisted on this mad attempt. Even allowing for the Chief of Staff's temperament and the inaccuracy of French accounts, I could hardly sleep that night.

The next day the tension was increased when the British attack to the north was started by General Rawlinson's Fourth British Army, which included the Thirtieth and Twenty-seventh American Divisions under George Read, now a general; Cushing, Krenson, and others of my old friends were on his staff. Between Cambrai and St. Quentin, the Americans hurled themselves against the Hindenburg Line at a point where the canal connecting the Oise and the Scheldt went underground through a tunnel, transformed by its defenders into an apparently unassailable stronghold. In their impetuous rush, our troops swept clear over it and advanced several miles. Then the Germans, pouring out of shafts, fell on them from the rear, and they were being severely mauled until an Australian division arrived to do the mopping-up.

Everybody in the War Office congratulated me on the American achievement at St. Quentin, but still I could obtain no direct news from the Argonne. In my anxiety I scarcely noticed my promotion to lieutenant colonel, which reached me one morning in the mail. I would have gone to France myself, if, at the end of the third day, I had not finally got Chaumont on the telephone.

It was quite another story I now heard. Everywhere we had smashed the front line defenses. The Bois de Cheppy, Dannevoux, Montfaucon itself had fallen. True, we had been held up on the wings, and the Germans from the heights on either side were raking us on the flanks. But there was no rout, no panic. The attack was being steadily pushed, and my own Seventy-seventh Division was in the thick of it.

Sir Henry Wilson professed pleasure, although adding pessimistically, "You fellows don't know what you're getting into. The farther you go, the worse off you're going to be."

Every day further discouraging reports were received from the French: We had been halted just where they had said we would be; everything was in confusion, exactly according to their forecasts. Marshal Foch went so far as to suggest the command in the Argonne should be taken over by the same French general who had been encamped there so long, regarding the job as hopeless. General Pershing refused. Later de Chambrun told me the inaccuracy of the French dispatches had been due to the jealousy of the French reserve officers in that sector. When Marshal Foch finally discovered the truth, he was furious that he had been deceived and led into a foolish position.

After the first delay I was able to obtain regular American reports, which were in sharp contrast to the French. As a matter of fact, one of the principal reasons for our being held up was the failure of General Gouraud's forty divisions on our left to capture the group of hills called Les Monts and keep pace with our advance. Finally at Gouraud's request General Pershing sent him the Second and the Thirty-sixth Divisions; they stormed Blanc Mont, following which the French moved forward, and the Germans on the western heights of the Argonne, being thus outflanked, began to retire.

By the 10th of October the Americans had straightened their lines and could resume the frontal attack against the Germans' second system of defenses. For a time daily progress was so small — from bush to bush, from tree to tree, from farm to farm — that often it was hard to tell on the map that there had been any accomplishment. But our troops pressed ahead, little by little, cleaning out a machine gun nest here, taking a hill there, pushing through a patch of woods somewhere else.

Simultaneously, in other parts of the world, Germany's allies were weakening. The Bulgarians threw down their arms and left the road to Constantinople unguarded. Allenby's Army was in Damascus, and Turkish resistance in the East was crumbling. Prince Max of Baden became German Chancellor — it seemed the German Government itself was unsure. October 8th, Austria and Germany addressed a joint plea to President Wilson for an armistice.

In spite of the signs of German collapse, few at the War Office appeared able to grasp the idea that the end of the war might be at hand. Sir Henry Wilson gave me three reasons why imminent overwhelming German defeat was doubtful. First, the English Army was very tired; second the French Army was even more tired; third the American Army was incapable of using its great force to the best advantage. We had only a few more weeks during which the weather would permit fighting. The war would run on at least until the next spring.

Nevertheless, events moved so fast in the last half of October that talk of peace ceased to be academic. The Germans were abandoning the Flemish coast, the Italians were across the Piave, Ludendorff himself resigned. Suddenly a meeting of the Supreme War Council was called for October 31st to draw up armistice terms; with scarcely a moment's notice I was on my way to Paris with the Prime Minister and the heads of the War Office.

Generals, statesmen, members of the press, representatives of racial groups were pouring into Paris. Sunday, October 27th, Colonel House, who had arrived to speak for President Wilson, invited me to breakfast with him at 78, Rue de l'Université. He wanted to know immediately General Pershing's private opinion of the military terms for an armistice agreed on the previous day by the allied commanders at Senlis for submittal to the Council. Unfortunately, General Pershing was confined to his house with a severe attack of influenza; Colonel House, faced with critical responsibilities, was reluctant to risk his own delicate health in a personal interview. Would I act as intermediary?

When I reached the Rue de Varennes, General Pershing was going through papers in front of the fire, wrapped in his dressing gown, a blanket draped over his knees; he looked so ill that I told him he ought to be in bed. Although he admitted he had a temperature of one hundred and two, he brushed aside the suggestion, insisting he had far too much work to do. Then I explained my errand, and added that I had the impression Colonel House was inclined towards mild armistice terms.

At these words, the General's habitual imperturbability disappeared; he sprang to his feet and began pacing up and down. "Mild terms!" he burst forth. "That's what General Haig wants." With an emotional vehemence I did not know he possessed, he described how General Haig had argued that, should the Germans in desperation strike back, the British had no divisions left in reserve. In the heated discussion that followed, the British commander had let drop a remark to the effect that one reason for his disquiet was the inability of the American staff to function adequately.

"What right has anyone to make such a statement?" exclaimed General Pershing. "I'll guarantee that our soldiers in the Argonne will go through to the Meuse and beyond by winter, and our second army is ready and waiting to march on Metz. We have the whip hand, and there's no reason why the terms shouldn't be stiff enough to prevent a war such as this ever having to be fought again."

Never in my experience had General Pershing been so completely upset. Something had to be done at once. As soon as I had repeated his emphatic stand to Colonel House, I hurried to enlist Bacon's cooperation. He agreed with me it was far too late for the two commanders to fall out over such a misunderstanding, and we were both certain General Haig could not have intended his remark as derogatory to our armies. While Bacon took his chief for a walk in the Bois, I told Lord Milner what had happened, described General Pershing's just resentment, and declared I would have to resign if such criticism were to continue.

"It's most unfortunate," concurred Lord Milner. "I'll talk to Haig myself."

That very night, the British commander wrote an apology to General Pershing and had the official minutes of the meeting changed. As a further mark of good will, Lord Derby, the British Ambassador, gave a special lunch at the Embassy for the two Generals, and Bacon and I had the satisfaction of seeing them in friendly accord.

Meanwhile soundings were being taken in preparation for the official sessions of the Supreme War Council. Every morning I reported to the Rue de l'Université, where the Prime Ministers, Generals and Admirals met for preliminary discussions of what they were going to say at the afternoon meetings at the Quai d'Orsay. The 29th I started my rounds as usual. Colonel House was lying on a couch under a blanket, white and frail, suffering from indigestion. Our talk was interrupted by Joseph Grew, then his secretary and later Ambassador to Japan, who rushed in with a telegram announcing Austria's unconditional surrender. The Colonel, forgetting his aches and pains, sat up, full of fire and excitement. "That ends it; the war's over!"

Wherever I went that day everybody was recommending terms for Austria. At the Villa Romagne, Lloyd George, Milner, Bonar Law, Wilson, Kerr, Bowly, Amery, all were offering suggestions. I even found myself being consulted, and made some emendations which, to my amazement, Lord Milner promptly embodied in the text.

Austria had not been disposed of completely before someone brought in the news of the capitulation of Turkey. More excitement and new difficulties. The great problem was now "To whom should Turkey surrender?" Lord Milner dispatched me posthaste to ascertain what Colonel House thought.

Later the Colonel told me the Prime Ministers had wasted nearly the whole afternoon at the Quai d'Orsay disputing as to whether the Turks should surrender to the British or to the French Admiral, who was the senior. The debate was terminated by Mr. Lloyd George's turning with some asperity to M. Clemenceau, "Well, all this seems absurd when the facts are we fought a campaign in Mesopotamia by ourselves, we captured the Turkish Army by ourselves, and the only help we ever had from you was one battalion of black troops which you sent to guard the Holy Sepulcher."

At three o'clock on the afternoon of October 31st I joined Bowly in the gallery of the Hotel Trianon to watch the Supreme War Council at work. They listened to Marshal Foch's demand for severe terms for Germany, and most of the session discussed what to do about the Hapsburg Empire. At tea the atmosphere was joyous and happy.

The next day came the news that the Americans had broken

through the second line of defense in the Argonne and were driving ahead, unchecked; Haig too had nothing but open country in front of him. In the afternoon, as soon as it was evident the Supreme War Council was setting to with a will, Kerr suggested we might have time to run upstairs and look at the intelligence maps. A staff officer showed us how almost the entire German Army was massed against the Americans in the Argonne and against the British to the north. Nothing but exhausted and reserve divisions were opposite the French, whose only offensive power lay now in a very few fine shock divisions; clearly any major attack was up to us and the British.

The armistice terms were formally agreed on at the final meeting, November 4th — evacuation of the invaded territory and Alsace-Lorraine; surrender of practically all German fighting equipment, including the fleet; occupation of a specified zone in Germany along the left bank of the Rhine; and other provisos intended to make Germany helpless.

One of the first to emerge from the meeting was Lord Balfour, apparently in a state of tremendous anxiety. Walking straight up to me he said: "Griscom, the terms are much too severe. It's the height of folly. The Germans will never consent."

We had tea together and Sir Henry Wilson and Bowly joined us. They were all convinced Germany could not accept the terms and would make a counteroffer. To me it seemed extraordinary how the prestige of Germany still struck consternation into Allied hearts.

Early next morning Colonel House gave me a copy of the terms to take to General Pershing, who was directing operations from his train at railhead in the Argonne. The sense of the futility in war was overpowering as I crossed the Marne and went north and east. Every village was shot to pieces. The city of Rheims was a single great ruin. Around the shell of the cathedral were piles of broken stone and heaps of stained glass, scintillating and sparkling purple, blue, and red in the sun. Nobody was at work clearing up the debris; it was just lying there.

I reached the Headquarters train at nine o'clock to find the General and his staff at dinner. His natural elation at the thought of victory so near was tempered by the cruel responsibility with which he was now faced. No one wanted to be killed or even wounded on the concluding days of any war, yet he could not stop the attack, however certain he might be that an armistice was coming. A victorious commander must keep his enemies on the run and not allow them breathing space to reform and make another stand. Any other course might mean infinitely more dead and wounded. Although all the General's advisers agreed his course was the only possible one, there was intense bitterness over the casualties of those last few days. This was felt by the soldiers; it was felt immeasurably more by parents who lost their sons.

All day long General Pershing had been sitting in his car, issuing orders and receiving reports. The Germans were retiring everywhere, and the Americans were close to Sedan and the railroad. To obtain eyewitness accounts he sent his aides in all directions. The next morning I was lucky to be able to accompany Bowditch and de Marenches towards Sedan. Negro regiments were shoveling dirt in the potholes of our road, often stopping work to lean on pick or shovel and watch our fresh units pass towards the front. Good old American chaff was going on all along the line. "Hey, Sam! Hey, George! Drop that shovel and come on up with us and see the war."

"No, thank you. Ah's jest about as near dis war as Ah aims to git."

We kept working our way north. The Germans had left only a few hours before. There was every evidence of a rout — dead horses, munitions, rifles, clothing. Everywhere were hastily and freshly dug graves, although many Germans were as yet unburied. Ahead I saw the body of a German boy, lying by the road, very young, blond-haired, handsome. A truck lunged through a puddle and specked his white face with mud. Another followed and another, each spraying more. I looked back. His face was entirely veiled. All our hostility against him as a German vanished. You merely thought that here was a boy, as nice as any American or English boy, dragged into this war without knowing what it was all about.

As we drove over the top of a ridge a mighty roar of battle rose from the valley of the Meuse. No more trenches were visible anywhere; it was open warfare at last. Since we had to report at the train by nightfall, we turned around at this point, and by patience and persistence we arrived at seven to hear our troops were within five miles of Sedan.

November 7th, the next day, I went with Colonel Boyd to Verdun; it seemed unbelievable to find France's greatest fortress, the secrets of which had once been so carefully guarded, now swarming with American soldiers. From there we proceeded north by Fort Douaumont up the east bank of the Meuse, with heavy artillery shells flying in both directions over our heads.

Beyond Consenvoye the Germans had barely left. We were the first motor to follow our troops. Far off to the right we could see them advancing across fields, nobody in front, and no enemy planes overhead. The Germans had run away by the main road; it was too arduous and slow trudging across lots and over fences.

There had been no time for looting. As we passed by the farmhouses, the inhabitants were emerging from their cellars and gathering in the yards, amazed that no damage had been done; even the little villages were intact. Many of the houses had been used as billets and bore the names of commanding officers on them. I pulled down a few of the German signs to bring back as souvenirs for my boys.

"Those fellows must have been in a hurry not to have mined this road," we kept saying to ourselves. But Boyd was a hard soldier and plowed straight ahead. Perhaps we would have been wiser had we not risked driving so near the front. That same day, on another part of the battle line, Quekemeyer's car was blown up and he was deafened for life.

We decided to cross the Meuse and return via Montfaucon. As we stood on the hill, we could see all the way to Verdun and an immense distance to the south. It seemed impossible that our troops had taken it — the plain was so very far below, the rock slanted so steeply up, the enormous battery emplacements were so solid.

From the reports brought back by the staff it was obvious the Germans must soon make peace. We watched eagerly the course of negotiations. November 8th, the German delegation was whisked to the Forest of Compiègne and its members given seventy-two hours to make up their minds; they found the terms so severe that, before signing, they sent a courier for further instructions. While the plenipotentiaries sat behind their drawn and closed blinds, imperial Germany was ending — the Kaiser abdicated, the Socialist Ebert became Chancellor, revolution broke out in Berlin.

General Pershing ordered his car from the Argonne to Paris, and on November 9th we woke up there. Still no news. That night we started for Chaumont, and all that next day, too, we waited. The night of the 10th we were still waiting. The deadline was nearer each minute.

Nobody at the Val des Écoliers wanted to go to bed. We discussed what we would do if the Germans signed, what we would do if they did not sign. But they must sign; they had no other recourse. Then the round began once more. Every time the telephone rang we listened. Occasionally I got up and walked about. I peered out of the window, but it was pitch-dark and I could see nothing.

Not until six o'clock was a jubilant telephone message received from Colonel Bentley Mott at Foch's Headquarters. The Armistice had been signed; the war would be over at eleven that morning.

We looked at each other's faces, expecting to see the reflection of some change — they seemed the same. We felt we ought to do something special, yet we kept on doing the same things. Breakfast was served as usual to the accompaniment of the same sort of conversation. There was still no certainty of what the future would bring forth. An armistice was not a definite peace.

We all drove in to Chaumont. Everybody was sitting around, talking and glancing at his watch. I went into General Pershing's private office. He was alone. Never in his career had there been a moment that could equal this. All that he and the Army had come to France to accomplish had been accomplished. At Cantigny an American division had first shown it could make a serious advance against veteran troops; at Château Thierry and Belleau Wood we had been largely responsible for blocking the June thrust towards Paris; below Soissons we had driven the wedge which had hurled the enemy back across the Marne in July; at St. Mihiel more French territory had been taken from the Germans than in any other action since the start of the war; finally, in this last offensive, the Americans had done the impossible — two divisions in the center of the British attack had penetrated the Hindenburg Line along the St. Quentin Canal, two more had broken ground for Gouraud's army by a frontal assault on Les Monts in Champagne, two more had piloted Degoutte's divisions over the Scarpe River in Flanders; a whole army had forged through the impenetrable Argonne to cut the enemy's artery of supplies.

General Pershing must have experienced some sense of exultation, but not a gesture, not a word, betrayed any hint. A solitary, impressive figure, he walked to the big map on the wall and began describing in detail the exact plan to take Metz. "I suppose our campaigns are ended," he concluded; "but what an enormous difference a few days more would have made!"

Time had never passed so slowly. Five minutes to eleven . . . Boyd came in. It was like the finish of a great football match when the score hangs on seconds to go. Nobody spoke. My mind went back to the American colonel I had watched standing at the edge of Belleau Wood, checking off the intervals to the zero hour. Four minutes left for us . . . Three . . . Two . . . One . . . And then, shattering the silence, a tremendous salvo of cannon.

The war was over.

CHAPTER XXXV

SO PEACE RETURNED

In a second the whole office came to life. We shook hands, clapped each other on the back, and then shook hands again, laughing, congratulating each other, talking all at once — "Well, it's over, it's over! Wonderful! Can you believe it?" People kept pouring in and out from other departments. The French General commanding the district arrived to thank General Pershing for what the American Army had done. Tears were streaming down his cheeks, and his words flowed so fast that I, who was interpreting, was almost inundated. At one moment I thought he was going to kiss the embarrassed General Pershing on both cheeks.

This visit helped everyone forget his Anglo-Saxon reticence. Even General Pershing threw off his habitual formality. Dinner at the Val des Écoliers that evening was a merry one. Afterwards we turned on the victrola. Everybody danced, including the General. We danced with each other and we danced alone, and we packed up our troubles in our old kit bags for good and all. Then we boarded the train and sped towards Paris.

The capital was recovering from a night of unparalleled gaiety. No business was going on; the broad boulevards were teeming with milling crowds. Closets and attics had been ransacked to find clothes to make this a carnival of carnivals. Soldiers of all nationalities were forming squares and dancing on the Champs Élysées. In the Place de la Concorde the General was recognized, and men and women clambered on the running board and on top of the hood; they closed in so solid around us that American soldiers had to open a way for our car, a few feet at a time.

That evening, as though by common impulse, everybody I knew gravitated to the Ritz. Champagne corks were popping; there was more handshaking and more congratulating. Not only the guests, but even the waiters joined in the merrymaking. The band struck up and the whole room with one accord started singing — popular songs, war songs, any old songs, and we danced with a joy we had not felt for many a long day.

Next morning we were ready to look around more soberly. Like everybody else I wanted to get home, but General Pershing asked me to go back to London until the convening of the Peace Conference, when I would return to be his personal representative. He had talked with Colonel House, who would arrange my status.

It was a peaceful drive by way of Montreuil to Boulogne — no military movements on the road, no thunder of battle, no planes. The Channel crossing was equally peaceful — no escort, no zigzagging, no mention of submarines, although we still had to be guided into the harbor, because the mines had not yet been removed.

It seemed as though I had been a long time away from the War Office. In three weeks the high pitch of excitement had given way to routine. The instant history ceased to be made by what happened on the battlefield, the opinions and desires of the Army became of secondary importance. The War Office was now concerned chiefly with returning soldiers to civil life.

In December Lord Milner invited the commanders of the British and Colonial Armies to London for a celebration dinner with the heads of the War Office, a historic affair, since probably never again would all the army leaders be gathered together. The event was still a week off when Creedy remarked to me one morning: "Of course, Lord Milner expects you to be at the dinner."

"Well, I appreciate being asked, but I'd be out of place as the only American present."

The next day Creedy brought up the subject again. "Lord Milner told me to tell you all his personal staff are going. You're a member. He wants no more talk about it."

Under the circumstances, I accepted.

The dinner was at eight. I felt I should arrive on the dot, or even a minute or two earlier, especially as I was certain to be the lowliest in rank. A servant ushered me up the broad stairway to the second floor and led me around the balustrade. There, to my horror, I saw advancing towards me, like the gods going into Valhalla, a formidable procession of at least thirty beings, resplendent in ribbons and medals and gold braid. The Generals were on their way in to dinner and I was the last arrival.

Making myself as small as possible, I shrank back against the wall. When Lord Milner and Field Marshal Haig, who were leading the way, came abreast of me, the whole line had to halt while the two shook hands with me. In my American uniform I felt particularly conspicuous. As each couple passed, I could see one asking another who I was and why I was there. I fell in at the end behind Bowly and Amery, who were grinning with pleasure at my embarrassment.

"I thought I was on the minute," I whispered.

"You go in to a military dinner as the clock strikes. We were here fifteen or twenty minutes ahead."

During the banquet everyone was a little uneasy because of the well-known friction between the Chief of Staff in London and Headquarters in the field. There was a shifting of chairs as Lord Milner started his speech of welcome, paying tribute first to Sir Douglas Haig and then to his generals. The Commander in Chief rose to reply, obviously deeply touched; the credit for the victories on the field was due not only to his generals, but also in equal measure to the staff of the War Office, and especially to Sir Henry Wilson. Though he made no pretense at being a speaker, his appreciation was so gracefully phrased and sincere that you could feel the tension lessen.

Sir Henry Wilson in his reply utilized to the full the happy gift of expression which characterizes the Irishman whether of North or South. By his speech he gained wholehearted admiration, even from those who had felt most bitterly against him. This was peace in the truest sense of the word. To have been included on such an occasion was one of the greatest privileges I ever enjoyed.

The Peace Conference was to open January 18th, and a few days before I left for Paris. Rarely had I seen the city in such a state of activity. Where at the time of the Armistice there had been ten, now there were hundreds of interested peacemakers, civilian experts, financiers, journalists. The barny corridors of the Crillon were filled with delegates and their staffs. On General Pershing's behalf I hurried from him to General Tasker H. Bliss, the American representative on the Supreme War Council, Henry White, and Colonel House, who were both members of the Peace Delegation.

At the end of a few days it was evident all that General Pershing

would be asked to contribute was opinions on a few technical matters of minor importance. One of the curious phenomena of this
war was that the Generals disappeared from the public eye immediately it was over. The great figures of previous conflicts — Julius
Caesar, Frederick the Great, Cromwell, Napoleon, Wellington —
had been political leaders as well as commanders in the field. In
this one, no military hero afterwards attained political distinction.
The personality of Haig was completely overshadowed by Lloyd
George, that of Pétain by Clemenceau, and that of General Pershing
by President Wilson.

General Pershing quite agreed it was futile for me to remain
in Paris longer, and I prepared to return to England where, in my
absence, Winston Churchill had replaced Lord Milner at the War
Office.

One night, shortly before leaving, I was dining with Lord Balfour, and mentioned I was about to go back to London to meet
my new chief.

"Why, what's happened to poor old Milner?"

"He's taking the Colonies."

"He'll like that. He'll like that. Nice quiet place."

Naturally, I then congratulated him on retaining his own post
at the Foreign Office.

"Oh, what's that? Has Lloyd George put me in again?"

"Surely you've heard about it. . . . It's even announced in the
papers."

"No, as a matter of fact, I don't read them."

It would be hard for anyone who did not know Lord Balfour
to believe that I was the first to give him the news, but apparently
he had only the slightest interest in the whole thing.

When I presented myself at the War Office, Creedy announced
my arrival to Mr. Churchill. He came himself to the door — short,
stubby, red-cheeked, more American than British in the manner in
which he pulled me in, welcomed me, began discussing the problems
facing us, as though I were to remain forever.

I interposed, "But my work here is practically finished."

Mr. Churchill jumped up and paced across the room and back.
"We still have a tremendous job ahead of us. Our armies are to
occupy lines next each other in Germany. We have a joint force

in Murmansk. A lot of questions are bound to arise. Why, you'll have to stay at least another year."

He would not listen to my protests, and I had to promise to remain until September.

In the corridor outside I ran into the Assistant Chief of Staff, General Harington, with his arms piled high with papers. "Have you met the new chief?"

"I've just left his office."

"I'm just going in." He rubbed his hand across his forehead with an expression denoting extreme weariness. "Winston is certainly a terrible fellow to work for. He never seems to get tired himself, but he's nearly killed us off already one by one. He won't accept anybody's opinion; he has to go over every paper himself and form his own. Look what he's sent for this time. Probably, if we live through this shake-up, it'll do us a world of good."

I went back to my desk. To my regret, Bowly and Amery were no longer at the War Office; but the new secretary, Major Sir Archibald Sinclair of the Guards, Member of Parliament and a great landowner in the north of Scotland, proved to be remarkably congenial.

No day was ever dull in the vicinity of Mr. Churchill. Years before, on becoming First Sea Lord, he had been described as bowling over the Admirals like ninepins. Now, instead of letting the office down to the usual post-war pleasant bureaucratic leisure, he was driving the staff even harder than during the war, and he spared himself as little as he did any of his subordinates. He started the morning by sitting up in bed smoking a black cigar and working for an hour or two while most statesmen were still fast asleep. He had much of the vitality and personal charm of Theodore Roosevelt. When aroused and interested, his eyes seemed to sparkle, his ordinarily vigorous manner grew almost pugnacious. He had one of the most active and untiring minds of anyone I had ever encountered in public life. In the end, I was not sorry I had stayed.

Although my duties during the winter and early spring were mainly routine, in March they had one memorable interruption — a tour of inspection on which I conducted a selected group of English Government officials and generals, as well as our new Ambassador, John W. Davis, to see what America had done in the war.

On General Pershing's private train and under General Harbord's guidance, we began by showing them the Service of Supplies. We covered nearly the whole of France, viewing endless docks, warehouses, railways, all built by Americans from American materials: towering piles of lumber, huge munition dumps, stores of all kinds in Gargantuan quantities. One morning Sir John Cowans looked at his printed program, and exclaimed in horror: "Good Lord, Griscom, you don't intend to make us go through your delousing plant, do you?"

To round out the tour, General Pershing took our guests to Columbey-les-Belles, not far from Toul, to watch a formal review of the Twenty-eighth Division of the Pennsylvania National Guard, and the presentation of decorations. I was ushering our visitors to their places on the reviewing stand when Quekemeyer rushed up to me. "You're wanted forward at once." I was hustled on to the field and planted in the middle of a line of six men, three officers and three privates, stationed in front of the Division.

The next thing I knew General Pershing was pinning a Distinguished Service Medal on my tunic; the whole thing had been planned especially as a surprise for me on this trip with the British.

We seven were led through the mud to the stand, and the three privates were put on the right of the line to take the review in General Pershing's place. The band struck up, the flags fluttered as the color guard advanced; line by line and section by section the solid phalanx split apart and swung across the field. General William H. Hay passed the stand, saluted; we returned his salute.

The privates beside me were not at all impressed. Each looked on indifferently until his own particular unit approached. Then a gleam came into his eye. I heard one mutter, "There they come, the sons of bitches. Now let 'em salute me!" And as his company went by, in tones of even greater jubilation, "Just look at 'em down there walking in the muck!"

I had not been long back in London when I had another surprise. On my appearance at the War Office one morning Sinclair began pumping my arm up and down. At first he was mysterious, and would not divulge the reason for this unusually energetic reception; but finally I dragged out of him that I had an engagement with the King for the following day at eleven.

"What for?" I asked, still not taking him seriously.

"He's going to give you the K.C.M.G." (Knight Commander of the Order of St. Michael and St. George.)

Going to see King George V turned out to be the most casual sort of a morning call. At Buckingham Palace a gentleman in waiting led me along passageways and opened a door for me. The King was standing in the middle of the room by a table. In a conversational tone he said, "You were a friend of President Roosevelt, weren't you? We were so sorry to hear of his death. We liked him so much."

The King then described an afternoon which the late ex-President had spent with the royal family in 1910. "You should have seen him telling my children about lions and tigers and elephants in Africa. And finally he got down on the floor and played bear with them, crawling about and growling."

Abruptly the King picked up a box from the table and, without opening it, handed it to me. "I have this thing to give you," he remarked in the shy, embarrassed manner that any English gentleman uses when he presents a gift to which he does not wish too much value to be attached.

"Your Majesty — " I began my formal expression of thanks, but he never let me finish. "That's all right," he said, and changed the subject.

It was a simple ceremony that added a great deal to the value of the decoration.

As the spring passed, there were constant demands that General Pershing should pay a visit to England. Mr. Churchill and I concocted a scheme for an Anglo-American parade — a real blood-thicker-than-water celebration. A tentative date was set for May 24th, Empire Day; but General Pershing had to refuse because he felt he ought not to leave his post until the Germans had signed the treaty, and a day in July was agreed on.

In May, I acted as the General's proxy to receive an honorary degree from St. Andrew's University in Scotland. On the occasion of Marshal Haig's installation as Lord Rector this distinction was to be conferred on the three men, exclusive of British, who in his opinion had made the greatest personal contribution towards winning the war. He told me his reasons for naming his candidates.

King Albert of the Belgians had saved the Allied cause at the beginning of the War by sacrificing his troops and thus giving England and France time to rush their forces to the rescue. Foch had held the Allies together at a critical period of the war and had displayed supreme ability as a military strategist. Lastly, General Pershing, by his strength of character, had built up an effective American Army in the face of almost insuperable obstacles, and then had used it superbly to deliver the vital strokes that had ended the war. Such appreciation of General Pershing, coming as it did from the leader of the British armies, I considered the greatest personal tribute he ever received.

Out of a clear sky one day in June came a telegram with the bare announcement that General Pershing was about to arrive at my house on a brief unofficial visit to receive an honorary degree from Oxford University. He said nothing about any other engagements but I thought it would never do for him to depart without at least making an informal call on the Prime Minister and the Secretary for War. I had just enough time to make the appointments before dashing off to Dover to meet his boat. On our way to London I explained what I had arranged for him.

"Griscom, I can't do that."

"But, General, I'm afraid the English may be offended if you don't. They'll only take a minute or two."

"No. Sorry. I can't do it."

"Well, I'll have to make some sort of excuse so that they will understand."

Rather sheepishly, General Pershing replied, "The truth is, I've promised to go that day to the christening of Charley Dawes's godchild."

I gasped, but managed to ask: "Well, where do you have to go? How far is it from London?"

He mentioned a town in Kent, and little by little came out with the whole story. It seemed that Dawes, on first reaching England, had heard of a County family of his own name, who he believed might be related. Characteristically, without losing a moment, he had written to them, saying he would like to meet them. Before the visit could take place he had word from his "cousins" that a daughter of the house had given birth to a son and heir who without hesitation had been named Charles G. Dawes. Wishing to return the compliment, Dawes had enlisted General Pershing as co-godfather. "I promised Charley I'd do this," ended the General.

I did some rapid calculating — thirty miles down, a christening and a lunch, thirty miles back. "Well, General, the only way out is to explain that you committed yourself weeks ago to a private engagement of the greatest importance, but that you'll be able to reach Downing Street at five and the War Office a half-hour later."

"All right. That'll be fine."

The first thing in the morning Dawes called me up and said there was going to be a bang-up time at the christening and I had better come. In the course of carrying out the rather humiliating task of changing the hours for General Pershing's calls, I found he had broadcast invitations around the War Office, and one and all had accepted, including Sir John Cowans.

At about eleven, a cavalcade of fourteen army motors, loaded with officers, started off from Dawes's hotel. We tore through one quiet town after another, leaving the inhabitants gaping after us, and finally entered a typical Kentish village of brick houses, some thatched, some roofed in red tile. As we drove down the narrow main street we came face to face with a gaily bedecked triumphal arch bearing the words, "Welcome General Pershing." There was no doubt that we had reached our destination.

On the terrace of the manor house our host, a middle-aged squire, was waiting with his wife. In the great hall all the relatives, old and young, from near and far, had assembled to honor General Pershing and to meet the American cousin; there must have been a hundred of them. At first sight they all took to Dawes, and Dawes in his way took equally to them. He had a keen eye for the pretty young girls, and promptly kissed each one, "How are you, Cousin Mary, Cousin Imogene, Cousin Betsy?"

The christening was a huge success. Innumerable toasts were drunk, and all the English officers agreed it was one of the merriest parties they had ever been on. Back we tore to London and whirled up to number 10 Downing Street at fifteen seconds to five.

The signing of the Peace Treaty in June added significance to the General's approaching visit. I found myself again with my old job of arranging schedules. Quekemeyer wrote me to be sure that the General and his staff had good horses for the Victory Parade. The War Office assured me the Horse Guards would attend to this. When I inquired whether I might try out the one intended for General Pershing, this request was taken to imply want of confidence in their judgment, and I dropped the matter.

Only a few days before the Commander in Chief was to arrive, Mr. Churchill sent for me. I found him working away in his shirtsleeves, the only Englishman in high office I ever knew make such concessions to the weather. His face was redder than usual. "Damn it all, Griscom, do you know what's happened? The French Ambassador's just been around to Downing Street and says if there's going to be any Victory Parade Foch wants to be in on it. How can we refuse if the Supreme Commander insists on being present. But there's one thing I shall stick to," and he banged his fist on the table, "Pershing shall lead this parade."

What we should have realized before was now perfectly obvious — a Victory Parade should include all the Allies. Soon London streets were filled with foreign uniforms — the horizon blue of the French, the dark green of the Italians, the gray of the Belgians, and the olive drab of the American regiment known as "Pershing's Own," picked for height and soldierly bearing, and drilled so that its marching was said to rival that of the West Point cadets. General Pershing arrived with his staff and five Generals, including Harbord and Summerall.

We were all up early the morning of the parade and off to Rotten Row where our horses were waiting. I fully expected General Pershing would be furnished with a fine old steady charger, accustomed to the stir of crowds and the noise of military bands. Instead, he was to ride a small animal, nervously snorting, tossing its head, rolling its eyes, swishing its tail. When Quekemeyer tried it out, it pranced, cavorted, stood on its hind legs, and then, coming down on all fours, dashed up Rotten Row, pulling like mad. Quekemeyer returned in a minute or two, very angry, tested out several other horses, and luckily found one that was big enough and apparently placid. We started to mount, General Pershing arrived and took the lead. A few yards behind him followed the Generals, then another open space and the staff with myself on the left of the last row.

Directly ahead of me was Colonel George Marshall, the man responsible for the masterly movement of our troops into the Argonne and now attached to General Pershing's personal staff. His horse began to lash out dangerously with both heels; and mine, a good-sized animal with a mouth like iron, proceeded to rear violently and never stopped.

Nevertheless, we managed to get in formation and danced out of Hyde Park Gate across Knightsbridge and down Sloane Street. A drizzling rain had made the pavement like glass. The music and the jangling of our swords seemed to madden the horses. One moment I would be up in the air and the next down. It was impossible to keep a proper interval. We crossed the Thames into the South side of London, following a long route through a quiet, little-known part. My horse continued his obstinate rearing as we turned north, recrossed the river, and came to Whitehall by the Houses of Parliament and the Abbey. Trafalgar Square was a solid mass of humanity. The police with locked arms were trying to keep a way clear. The sides of the narrow open lane would surge forward like a wave until they nearly met, and then the tide would recede. I was afraid someone would be hurt before we were through.

Just as we turned safely left under the broad Admiralty Arch, the band burst forth anew, the sound reverberated in a terrific roar, and every horse was immediately again on its hind legs. Marshall's mount reared and tumbled over backwards, but he himself slid from beneath with amazing agility, and somehow or other got on again. We were glad to be out of that arch.

In front of us was the familiar but ever-magnificent sight of the Mall, with Buckingham Palace at the end, and everywhere handkerchiefs and flags were fluttering, toy trumpets blowing, rattles revolving, cheer bursting on cheer. The royal reviewing stand, gay with green and gold, had been erected by the Victoria Memorial. The King returned General Pershing's salute as the band began playing "Over There." My horse at that moment took it into his head to try a last rear, and as I actually passed the King I was bobbing up and down, one hand grasping the reins, the other painfully straining to hold my sword stiffly to my forehead.

After four strenuous hours in the saddle I dismounted at Constantine's Arch, so lame I could hardly stand. Nevertheless, I stayed to watch as one by one the detachments of the Allied armies passed.

At the head of the British rode Marshal Haig, behind him more Generals than I had ever seen. At the head of the French rode Foch, bearing in his right hand the purple baton of a Marshal of France. The massed standards of the British regiments moved by, each crowned with laurel, the colors streaming triumphantly above the dull background of the uniforms.

Here were the symbols of victory, and for a moment all of us who were in that parade or who saw it from the sidelines felt peace had really come, and that this last marching of the Allies together was a prelude to that better world which had been heralded to all of us by President Wilson.

My ears were echoing with the music of the bands and the rhythmic tread of the tramping men, but my legs would hold me up no longer. I dragged myself to the house of Lord and Lady Portarlington in Belgrave Square, only a few hundred yards away. They had not returned, but the sympathetic butler escorted me to a couch in the study. I dropped down, and the next thing I knew my hostess was waking me up for tea.

The following morning at the War Office I was really angry for the first time during my stay, and said it was inexcusable for the Horse Guards to have furnished us such unsuitable mounts. They agreed with me and reprimands were dealt out wholesale. By this time, however, everybody concerned decided to forgive and forget. The marching of our regiment was the talk of London; the Guards themselves admitted they had never seen anything finer.

The English omitted nothing in showing their esteem of General Pershing — dinner at the House of Commons, the freedom of the city of London at the ancient Guildhall, lunch at the Lord Mayor's mansion. At Cambridge, after he had received an honorary degree, the students in their enthusiasm hoisted him on their shoulders. I watched the extraordinary sight of my Commander in Chief lying out horizontally with toes and nose pointed to the sky, being wafted along in this particularly undignified position across the town. It was a new honor, but he loved it.

After I saw General Pershing off at Dover, my work in London seemed finished; even Mr. Churchill had to agree there was little more for me to do. Constantly uppermost in my mind was how soon could I return home. Then, one day in August, I received an order

I needed no urging to obey. I was to close out my duties and proceed to France to accompany General Pershing and his staff back to America.

I dined with Lord Milner for the last time. I said good-by to Mr. Churchill, Archie Sinclair, and my other friends at the War Office, to General Biddle and his three aides who were to remain until all the American troops had gone. I met General Pershing at Paris, and his special train took us to Brest, where the *Leviathan* was waiting. General Pétain and other French Generals had gathered to wish General Pershing *bon voyage*. This was his farewell to France after more than two years, the end of associations that went far deeper than friendship. The two leaders walked down the dock. Townspeople crowded in, shouting, *"Vive Pershing!" "Vive Pétain!"* A band on the pier plunged into "The Star-Spangled Banner"; faint echoes came from other bands on the war vessels in the harbor. At the gangplank the two Generals halted; they shook hands, then suddenly General Pétain leaned forward and kissed General Pershing on both cheeks.

The hawsers creaked, a vibrating blast burst from the whistle, and we moved slowly out across the sparkling water between lines of war vessels which dressed ship as we passed — a sailor on every ratline, on every yardarm, on every step. The cannon from the fort at the harbor's mouth roared a triumphal salute; it seemed everybody was firing guns as the huge *Leviathan* cleared the land. For miles out to sea the flotilla followed us, and only at dusk turned back, leaving us to head westward over the broad Atlantic.

CHAPTER XXXVI

RING IN THE NEW

We steamed into New York Harbor early one September morning as the mists were lifting. None of us will ever forget that homecoming. One after another the seventeen guns of the general's salute boomed across the water from Fort Wadsworth. From near and far we heard the sounds of welcome; whistles — bass, tenor, falsetto — bells clanging, the sharp roar of an airplane which swooped down to drop a message from Mayor Hylan. Bands played us in to the pier at Hoboken. A flourish of trumpets, a ruffle of drums, and General Pershing stepped ashore.

Guards stood at attention with fixed bayonets, and behind them were rank on rank of volunteer women's organizations in their uniforms. The pier seemed to stretch a quarter of a mile as we passed between the two solid ribbons. Halfway along a familiar voice called, "Hello, Lloyd!" and there was my sister Pansy, standing stiffly at attention. I ran over to her. I had had no idea she was in New York or in the American Women's Auxiliary Service.

On the upper deck of the pier was a dais, and there Mr. Baker made a little speech of greeting, read a message from the President, and at the end of the ceremony handed the Commander in Chief his commission as full General of the Armies of the United States — placing him with Washington, Grant, and Sherman, among those few who had received this accolade of military achievement.

The Mayor's reception boat ferried us across the harbor, every craft in sight blowing for all it was worth. From the Battery to Bowling Green there was not a vacant space. I was hardly off the gangplank when I heard screams and shrill cries, and spied my boy Bronson, his eyes shining with excitement; Lloyd was hopping up and down beside him. It was a wonderful family reunion, more important than anything else to me. Each took my hand and never left my side.

Rows of open motors were waiting. We three climbed in the one next the General's; Bronson perched by my shoulder on the rear of the back seat. Apparently everybody knew that General Pershing was meeting his young son Warren, because the minute the crowd spotted Bronson they shouted, "There's Warren Pershing." With great delight Bronson yelled and waved back.

As we progressed slowly through the financial section, the ticker tape snowed around us so thickly that the bottom of the car was covered with it inches deep. The throng kept calling, "Pershing! Pershing!" At the City Hall Governor Alfred E. Smith and Mayor Hylan were waiting. Another address of welcome and another reply, and on we went. All the way to the old Waldorf-Astoria there were people cheering.

In honor of the Victory Parade September 10th was declared a civic holiday. We assembled on Fifth Avenue opposite the upper end of Central Park. Anxiously I glanced at the horses, and it was a glorious relief to discover we had been given the mounts of the New York Police. As I swung into the saddle, I felt as though I were in a comfortable chair at home. We fell into position behind General Pershing, a tall figure on a tall horse. The band struck up and we were off, an escort of police leading, our picked regiment following, and after them the men of the First Division.

All New York was on the sidewalks, at the flag-draped windows, packed in special grandstands erected at intervals. From the buildings to our left streamers were floating down, and here and there came a shower of flowers. Now the asphalt was carpeted with green laurel, now with confetti and paper snow.

As we passed the Knickerbocker Club at 62nd Street, every window was jammed with heads of members. Clearly above the surging roar I heard a stentorian voice calling my name. I knew the military regulation that friends should not be recognized during a parade, but I decided this day all rules were off, and I turned and waved as warmly as I could. My behavior was far more undignified when a few hundred yards farther on at 711 I caught sight of Bronson and Lloyd at the window, screaming like mad and yelling "Dadda." At other windows were my mother, Rod, and Pansy. I shouted greetings to them all.

The bells of St. Patrick's Cathedral were pealing as hard as they could. In front was a stand and there I had a glimpse of the thin ascetic face of Cardinal Mercier of Belgium in his red robes. General Pershing stopped for a moment to speak to him.

To my delight my horse was utterly unmoved by such a commonplace thing as a walk along Fifth Avenue through clamoring crowds. He had a sleepy look in his eye as though very bored with it all. Once in a while he had an impulse to stop at some cross street and take up his usual position directing traffic, but the slightest word sent him on. His greatest excitement was to wag an ear or shake off a fly, or occasionally give a swish of his tail.

Below Fiftieth Street the crowds were even denser. In front of the Public Library was a swaying mass of howling, shrieking humanity, letting themselves go as rarely happens in life. I had thought the reception in London had reached the limits of enthusiasm, but this ovation from the people of New York passed all bounds. The thrill of it was indescribable.

At Twenty-third Street came a momentary hush. Under the Victory Arch the General's color bearers dipped his four-starred flag in salute to the memory of the dead, and the band behind us followed with muffled drums. We emerged once more into the noise and tumult. Fifth Avenue was a vast hallway with a blaze of color on each side, and down it we went riding amid the flutter of bunting and the mad applause.

It seemed an incredible time before we wheeled into Washington Square. There we turned and watched for a moment the flat helmets and glistening bayonets of ".Pershing's Own" pouring through the arch. As we dismounted, General Pershing asked me where I was going.

"Home," I answered.

THE END

INDEX

ABDUL HAMID, Sultan of Turkey — relations with Great Powers, 136–137; spy system, 143; methods of rule, 144–145; Selamlik, 160; audience with, 162; private opera company, 167–169; settlement of Armenian claims, 169–174; earthquake at Dolma Bagché Palace, 175; final audience, 180–181; contrast with Shah of Persia, 197; deposition, 304

Abercorn, Duchess of, 33, 101–102

Achmet, Persian servant, 195, 208, 215, 219

Adams, Henry — friendship with, 17–18, 38

Adee, Alvey Augustus, Second Assistant Secretary of State, 178

Agnew, George, New York State Senator, 332

Ahmed Bey, Admiral, 164

Aix-les-Bains, 127–128

Alabama Claims, precedent in international law, 355–356

Albert, King of the Belgians, 454

Aldridge, George W., boss of Monroe County, N. Y., 332

Alexander, Mr. and Mrs. Charles, 376

Alexandra, Princess of Wales, 20, 25, 33, 34; Queen, 217

Ali, Persian Cossack, 208–209, 212, 215

Ali Hassan Akbar, Persian muleteer, 206–207

Allds, Senator Jotham P., accused of bribery, 329; public scandal, 337, 350

Allen, Horace, Minister to Korea, 234

Alves, Rodrigues, President of Brazil, 271

Amapala, Honduras, yellow-fever port, 83–84

Ambro, M. d', Austrian Minister to Japan, 228

American Line, founded by author's father, 10; launching of *St. Louis,* 70–71

American Tobacco Company, Japanese claims, 240

American Trading Company, Japanese claims, 223, 240

Amery, L. C. M. S., political secretary to Lord Milner, 407, 421, 441, 449, 451

Anderson, Chandler P., counsel for packers, 356–357, 361–362, 367

Anderson, Larz, second secretary of London Embassy, 27, 36, 45, 51, 63–64

Andrews, Roy Chapman, 111

Anethan, Baron Albert d', Belgian Minister to Japan, 228

Anthoine, General, French chief of staff, 400

Aosta, Duchess d', visited by ex-President Roosevelt, 319–320

Appleton, Francis R., Jr., 370

Archfield, Augustus, family coachman, 6, 12, 24, 354

Arco-Valley, Count, German Minister to Japan, 228

Argonne, Pershing's plan of attack, 436; Allied disbelief in American ability, 437–438; progress of campaign, 439–446

Argyle, Duke of, 67

Arisugawa, Prince of Japan, 227, 251

Arizona Territory, 105–110

Armenian indemnity claims, history of, 134; settlement of, 161–162, 167–174

Arshak, Persian Cossack, 196, 202–203, 207–209, 212, 215

Asquith, Herbert, member of "Souls," 41; Home Secretary, 69; Prime Minister, 360

Astor, Lady, 427

Ata Beg, Grand Vizier of Persia — balloon ascension, 193–194; gift, 197; sanctuary, 203; with the Shah in London, 218; fall from power, 237

Atlanta, American warship, 87

Auguste Victoria, Empress of Germany, 298–300

BACHELORS' CLUB, London, 40, 51, 361

Bacon, Robert H., 310, 390, 403–404, 431, 440

DATE